# Doll Values

## ANTIQUE TO MODERN

**Patsy Moyer**

**COLLECTOR BOOKS**

*A Division of Schroeder Publishing Co., Inc.*

The current values in this book should be used only as a guide. They are not intended to set prices, which vary from one section of the country to another. Auction prices, as well as dealer prices, vary greatly and are affected by availability, condition, and demand. Neither the Author nor the Publisher assumes responsibility for any losses that might be incurred as a result of consulting this guide.

## Searching for a Publisher?

We are always looking for knowledgeable people considered experts within their fields. If you feel that there is a real need for a book on your collectible subject and have a large comprehensive collection, contact Collector Books.

**On the Cover:** Composition Effanbee Lovums, all original in white dress, slip, and bonnet, ca. 1930. 12½" all vinyl, $425.00. Glitter & Gold Jem by Hasbro, $50.00. Courtesy Linda Holton. 16" French fashion-type, blue glass eyes, mohair wig, gusseted leather body, with trunk and two extra outfits, $3,500.00. 27" Little Lady with gold heart hang tag, all original, in velveteen dress and bolero, human hair wig, blue sleep eyes, $500.00+. Courtesy Vickie Applegate.

Cover by Beth Summers
Book design by Holly C. Long

Printed by IMAGE GRAPHICS, INC., Paducah, Kentucky

# Credits

Victoria Applegate, Charles Backus, Elaine Beling, Ruth Brown, Cathie Clark, Hank Collins, Patsy Corrigan, Debbie Crume, Rosemary Dent, Susan Dunham, Sondra Gast, Angie Gonzales, June Goodnow, Shirley Grime, Patti Hale, Amanda Hash, Janet Hill, Linda Holton, Chantal Jeschien, Iva Mae Jones, Waneta Jost, Sue Kinkade, Karen Koch, Sharon Kolibaba, Paris Langford, Shirlee Larson, Connie Lee Martin, Matrix, Sally McVey, Diane Miller, Pidd Miller, Peggy Millhouse, Bev Mitchell, Dorisanne Osborn, Stephanie Prince, Catherine Ritter, Rosalie Whyel Museum of Doll Art, Pat Schuda, Sherryl Shirran, Tammye Smith, Virginia Smith, Billie Stevens, Linda Lee Sutton, Jean Thompson, Dorothy Vaughn, Harriet Wagner, Toni Winder, and very special thanks to Shari McMasters of McMasters Doll Auctions.

# How To Use This Book

This book is divided into two sections, *Antique* and *Modern* as a general way to separate dolls made of older materials, like bisque, wax, cloth, and wood, and dolls made of newer materials, such as composition, hard plastic, and vinyl. This immediately becomes confusing to the novice, because some of the composition modern dolls are as old as the bisque dolls in the Antique section. We do this only to help the reader who can save time looking for older dolls in the front Antique section and newer dolls in the back Modern section. A new classification is emerging that refers to dolls made in the last 30 years as "collectible." In this book, collectible dolls are grouped with modern. Many published references have been used for descriptions and marks. Every effort was made to check early advertising, where possible, but the main references are Anderton, Axe, Colemans, Cisleks, Izen, Judds, and Schoonmaker. My thanks to these respected authorities and others who have contributed so much in research to collectors. A helpful bibliography is listed at the back of the book.

**The dolls in each section, Antique and Modern, are listed alphabetically by manufacturer or type, including a brief history, marks, description and prices.** Dolls are identified by the type of material used on the head — for example if the head is hard plastic, the doll is referred to as hard plastic, even though the body may be of another material. They may be further classified as a type, such as Oriental, black, or souvenir dolls. We have tried to use the general classifications set forth in prior issues of this book, but have taken the liberty to add new categories or delete some old ones.

**Some of the things to consider in evaluating a doll are quality, condition, rarity, originality, and desirability.** These can vary considerably as any two collectors may rate one or more of these attributes differently. Two identical dolls can differ greatly with those same factors. Condition and originality are always very desirable factors to keep in mind. It is smart buyers who familiarize themselves with as much knowledge about the subject as is available. This guide is a good starting place.

**All dolls were not born equal.** Dolls from the same mold can vary because of the conditions at the time of their manufacture. Successful production techniques developed over time. Sometimes there were conditions that arose only with the passage of time. Bisque dolls could be made with different grades of porcelain giving a range of fine to poor quality. Humidity and temperature could affect the production techniques of composition made up of various formulas of glue, wood pulp, sawdust, and other ingredients causing their finish to later crack or peel. The formula used for some rubber and early plastic dolls caused them to turn darker colors or become sticky. The durability of the material did not show up immediately; only after the passage of time.

It is important for the collector to become aware of the many different factors that influence the manufacture, durability, and history of a particular doll. It takes time and effort to know the subtle differences in the exact same model of one doll, much less the endless variations and differences that can exist in a particular era, category, or type of doll. This guide will serve as the starting point in your search for knowledge in the areas you choose to pursue.

**Quality** is an important consideration when purchasing a doll. Buy the best doll you can afford. Look at enough dolls so that you can tell the difference in a poorly finished or painted doll and one that has been artistically done. The head is the most important part of the doll. Signs of quality include good coloring, original clothing, wig, and body, and a pleasing appearance to the beholder.

The **condition** of the doll is a very important factor in pricing a doll. A beautiful doll re-dressed, dirty, and missing a wig should not be priced as high as a beautiful doll with original clothing, a well-done wig, and a clean and unrepaired body. Only consider composition dolls that have cracks, peeling paint, or lifting paint if they have added incentives, such as wonderful coloring, original clothes, boxes, and tags. Try to find composition dolls without severe crazing, cracks, lifting, or peeling. Look for a smooth finish with rosy cheek color as well as bright crisp clothing.

**Originality** is also important. Original clothing is an advantage on any doll, but especially if it is in good condition. Also important is the correct body with the correct head and original wig. Patricia Schoonmaker once told me that we are only caretakers of our dolls for a while — they then are passed on to someone else to care for. As older collectors put their collections on the market, some doll heads may be found on different bodies having been acquired before the importance of originality and the knowledge to identify the correct body became known.

**Rarity** is another consideration in dolls. Many dolls were made by the thousands. Some dolls were not made in such quantity. If a doll was a quality, beautiful doll, and not many were made it may be more desirable and higher priced. Age can play a factor in pricing dolls, but not age alone. Modern dolls such as Shirley Temples or Barbies can out-price some older antique dolls.

**Desirability** is another factor in choosing a doll. Some dolls may be rare, in original clothing and still just not appeal to others. Beauty can be in the eye of the beholder, but some dolls are just not as appealing as others because they were poorly made or unattractive from the start. A well-made doll of quality is generally the one sought after, even in dirty, not original condition. A poorly-made doll of inferior quality will always be a poorly-made doll whether it is in top condition or cracked and damaged.

The **pricing** in this book is based on a number of factors including information from informed networking collectors, doll shows and sales, auctions, and doll-related publications during 1995 and 1996. These factors have led us to build a database of actual sales during the past two years, however some earlier photos reflect current pricing. This database consists of records of over 10,000 dolls and you may see what actually is happening in the auction market place. Although any one auction's prices may vary widely; tracking the results over a period of time does reveal some consistency. The rarity and desirability of the same doll will fluctuate from area to area and with time.

**This guide makes no attempt to set price standards and should not be considered the final authority.** It is simply meant to report prices realized in areas that can be tracked and reported. Every effort has been made to present an unbiased and impartial viewpoint to the collector in the results found in the areas researched. The goals are to bring together information from many sources to give the collector an additional viewpoint so that he can make his own personal choice. The collector has the final decision in buying or selling a doll; it is his decision alone.

The area of categories is immense and no one can be familiar with all of the changing and different areas. For this reason, I have consulted with a broad group of knowledgeable collectors who keep up-to-date with the sales market in their particular field. Some of these collectors have agreed to provide their name and address as references in certain areas. These can be found in the Collectors' Network section at the back of the book. If you would like to become part of this network and are willing to share your knowledge with others in your particular field, please send your name, address, field of specialty, and references to the address listed. The more collectors network and share, the more we all gain from the experience. If you have questions, you may write the individual collectors listed. It is common courtesy to send a self-addressed-stamped envelope, if you wish to receive a reply to your question. If you would like to see other categories added to this guide, please drop us a line and tell us what your interests are. If possible, we will add categories when enough interest and data is available. We would like to hear from you.

The collector needs to be well informed to make a proper judgment when spending their hard-earned money in buying a doll. The more information he accumulates, the better he will be able to make that judgment. Collectors can turn to a national organization whose goals are education, research, preservation, and enjoyment of dolls. The United Federation of Doll Clubs can tell you if a doll club in your area is accepting members or tell you how to become a member-at-large. You may write them for more information at: United Federation of Doll Club, Inc., 10920 North Ambassador Drive, Suite 130, Kansas City, MO 64153.

There are also many smaller focus groups that network on particular dolls or on some aspect of doll collecting. A list of some of those groups and their interests is located in Collectors' Network at the back of the book. You gain more knowledge, and the collecting experience is more enjoyable when you participate with others.

**Happy collecting!**

# Antique and Older Dolls

◀
*15" bisque, Kestner, baby marked 257, $650.00. Courtesy McMasters Doll Auctions.*

▶
*5" bisque, Beck & tschalck child, $275.00 Courtesy Masters Doll Auctions.*

▲ *12½" bisque socket head automaton, key wound, lifts foot, moves hoop, head moves, $1,500.00. Courtesy McMasters Doll Auctions.*

7

# Alexandre, Henri

**Henri Alexandre, Paris, 1888 to 1892.** Bisque head, paperweight eyes, closed mouth with a white space between the lips, fat cheeks, and early French bodies with straight wrists.

*Too few examples in database for reliable range.* First price indicates doll in good condition, but with flaws or nude; second price indicates doll in excellent condition, in original clothes, or appropriately dressed.

*Mark:*

H⃢A

| | | |
|---|---|---|
| 18" | $4,750.00 | $6,250.00 |
| 22" | $5,250.00 | $7,000.00 |
| 25" | $5,625.00 | $7,500.00 |

## BEBE PHENIX

Alexandre was succeeded by Tourelle in 1892. In 1895, Bebe Phenix trademark was used by Jules Steiner, who in 1899 was succeeded by Jules Mattais. Bisque head, closed mouth, paperweight eyes, pierced ears, composition body.

*Mark:*

PHÉNIX
★ 95

### Child, closed mouth
| | | | |
|---|---|---|---|
| #81 | 13" | $1,375.00 | $1,800.00 |
| #85 | 15" | $2,175.00 | $2,900.00 |
| #88 | 17" | $2,925.00 | $3,900.00 |
| #90 | 19" | $3,375.00 | $4,500.00 |
| #91 | 20" | $3,900.00 | $5,200.00 |
| #93 | 22" | $4,125.00 | $5,500.00 |
| #95 | 24" | $4,275.00 | $5,700.00 |

### Child, open mouth
| | | | |
|---|---|---|---|
| | 17" | $1,350.00 | $1,800.00 |
| | 19" | $1,575.00 | $2,100.00 |
| | 23" | $1,875.00 | $2,500.00 |
| | 25" | $2,100.00 | $2,800.00 |

## All Bisque, French

Jointed at shoulders, hips, neck, delicate body with slender arms and legs, glass eyes, molded shoes, or boots and stockings. Many all bisque thought to be of French manufacture are now believed to have been made in Germany expressly for the French market. Allow more for original clothes and tags, less for chips or repairs.

First price indicates doll in good condition, with some flaws, undressed; second price is for doll in excellent condition, with original or appropriate clothing.

**Bare feet**

| | | |
|---|---|---|
| 5" | $975.00 | $1,300.00 |
| 7" | $1,500.00 | $2,000.00 |
| 9" | $3,375.00 | $4,500.00 |

\* *Too few examples in database for reliable range.*

**Swivel neck,** glass eyes

Socket head, molded shoes or boots

| | | |
|---|---|---|
| 5" | $500.00 | $750.00 |
| 7" | $625 | $825.00 |
| 9" | $925.00 | $1,225.00 |

Five strap boots

| | | |
|---|---|---|
| 5" | $1,350.00 | $1,800.00 |

Painted eyes, blue boots, ethnic costumes

| | | |
|---|---|---|
| 2½" – 4" | $150.00 | $200.00 |

Jointed elbows

| | | |
|---|---|---|
| 5½ " | $1,800.00 | $2,400.00 |
| 8½ " | $2,475.00 | $3,300.00 |

Jointed elbows and knees

| | | |
|---|---|---|
| 6" | $2,250.00 | $3,000.00 |
| 8" | $2,850.00 | $3,800.00 |

Marked E.D., F.G., or other French makers

| | | |
|---|---|---|
| 7 – 8" | $1500.00 | $2,000.00+ |

S.F.B.J., Unis

| | | |
|---|---|---|
| 5" | $395.00 | $525.00 |

*5" all bisque, French socket head, glass eyes, closed mouth, mohair wig, jointed shoulders and hips. $500.00. Courtesy McMasters Doll Auctions.*

# All Bisque, German

Many German firms made all bisque dolls in smaller sizes from 1860 to 1930. Some made by well-known firms such as Amberg, Alt, Beck & Gottschalck, Bahr & Proschild, Hertel Schwab & Co., Kammer & Rheinhart, J.D. Kestner, Kling, Limbach, Bruno Schmidt, and Simon & Halbig may have corresponding mold marks. Some are only marked "*Made in Germany.*" Some may also have a paper label.

They were often marked inside the arms and legs with matching mold numbers.

First price indicates dolls in good condition, but with some flaws or nude; second price is for dolls in excellent condition, original clothes, or well dressed with original label.

**BABIES, CA. 1900+**

**Rigid necks** (molded to torso), painted eyes, jointed shoulders and hips only, bent limbs, painted hair

| | | |
|---|---|---|
| 3½" | $40.00 | $75.00 |
| 5" | $85.00 | $165.00 |

Glass eyes

| | | |
|---|---|---|
| 4" | $125.00 | $250.00 |
| 6" | $175.00 | $350.00 |

9

# All Bisque, German (cont.)

**Swivel Necks** (socket neck), jointed shoulders and hips, wigs or painted hair

Glass eyes

| | | |
|---|---|---|
| 4" | $125.00 | $250.00 |
| 5" | $175.00 | $350.00 |
| 7" | $225.00 | $450.00 |
| 9" | $275.00 | $550.00 |

Painted eyes

| | | |
|---|---|---|
| 3½" | $75.00 | $150.00 |
| 5" | $100.00 | $200.00 |
| 6½" | $125.00 | $250.00 |
| 8½" | $175.00 | $350.00 |

**Babies with Character Face, ca. 1910+**

Jointed shoulders and hips, molded hair

Painted eyes

| | | |
|---|---|---|
| 4" | $90.00 | $175.00 |
| 6" | $125.00 | $250.00 |

Glass eyes

| | | |
|---|---|---|
| 4" | $175.00 | $350.00 |
| 6" | $225.00 | $450.00 |

Swivel neck, glass eyes

| | | |
|---|---|---|
| 6" | $300.00 | $600.00 |
| 10" | $550.00 | $1,100.00 |

Swivel neck, painted eyes

| | | |
|---|---|---|
| 6" | $200.00 | $400.00 |
| 8" | $225.00 | $500.00 |
| 10" | $400.00 | $800.00 |

Mold #830, 833, and others

| | | |
|---|---|---|
| 8" | $300.00 | $575.00 |
| 11" | $600.00 | $1,200.00 |

**Baby Bo Kaye, #1394**

Designed by Kallus, distributed by Borgfeldt

| | | |
|---|---|---|
| 5" | $550.00 | $1,100.00 |
| 7" | $700.00 | $1,400.00 |

**Baby Bud**

Glass eyes, wig

| | | |
|---|---|---|
| 6 – 7" | $650.00 | $1,300.00 |

**Baby Darling, #497, Kestner, #178**

Swivel neck, glass eyes, more for toddler body

| | | |
|---|---|---|
| 5" | $225.00 | $500.00 |
| 9" | $450.00 | $900.00 |

One piece body, painted eyes

| | | |
|---|---|---|
| 7" | $225.00 | $450.00 |
| 9" | $350.00 | $700.00 |
| 11" | $450.00 | $900.00 |

**Baby Peggy Montgomery**

Made by Louis Amberg, paper label

| | | |
|---|---|---|
| 4" | $200.00 | $400.00 |
| 6" | $300.00 | $575.00 |

**Bonnie Babe**
    Molded on clothes, dome head, swivel neck, jointed arms and legs

| | | |
|---|---|---|
| 4" | $250.00 | $475.00 |
| 6 | $325.00 | $655.00 |

Glass eyes, swivel neck, wig, jointed arms and legs

| | | |
|---|---|---|
| 5" | $325.00 | $625.00 |
| 8" | $550.00 | $1,100.00 |

Immobiles, one piece in various poses

| | | |
|---|---|---|
| 3" | $175.00 | $350.00 |

**Mildred (The Prize Baby), #880, ca. 1914+**
    Made for Borgfeldt, molded, short painted hair, glass eyes, closed mouth, jointed at neck, shoulders, and hips, round paper label on chest, molded and painted footwear

| | | |
|---|---|---|
| 6" | $750.00 | $1,500.00 |
| 7" | $900.00 | $1,800.00 |

**Tynie Baby**
    Made for E.I. Horsman
    Glass eyes

| | | |
|---|---|---|
| 6" | $425.00 | $850.00 |
| 9" | $700.00 | $1400.00 |

Painted eyes

| | | |
|---|---|---|
| 6" | $300.00 | $565.00 |

*5½" all bisque Bonnie Babe in original swim wear, $625.00. Courtesy Connie Lee Martin.*

**Pink Bisque Candy Baby, ca. 1920+**
    May be German or Japanese, lesser quality paint finish, given away with purchase of candy.

| | | |
|---|---|---|
| 4" | $15.00 | $25.00 |
| 6" | $30.00 | $40.00 |

Toddler, swivel neck, with glass eyes
#231 (A.M.)

| | | |
|---|---|---|
| 9" | $1,025.00 | $1,400.00 |

#369, 372

| | | |
|---|---|---|
| 7" | $545.00 | $725.00 |
| 9" | $875.00 | $1,100.00 |
| 11" | $1050.00 | $1,400.00+ |

# CHILDREN
**All Bisque Child, Rigid Neck, Glass Eyes, ca. 1890+**
    Head molded to torso, sometimes legs also. Excellent bisque, open/closed mouth, sleep or set eyes, good wig, and nicely dressed. Molded one-strap shoes. Allow more for unusual footwear such as yellow, multi-strap boots

| | | |
|---|---|---|
| 3" | $115.00 | $225.00 |
| 5" | $150.00 | $275.00 |
| 7" | $200.00 | $375.00 |
| 9" | $300.00 | $575.00 |

**Bent knees**

| | | |
|---|---|---|
| 6" | $145.00 | $285.00 |

# All Bisque, German (cont.)

**Mold #100, 125, 150, 225 (preceded by 83/) (Alt Beck & Gottschalck), ca. 1911+**

*7" Prize Baby with original box, outfit, molded painted shoes and stockings, $350.00.*

Chubby body and limbs

| | | |
|---|---|---|
| 5¾" | $115.00 | $225.00 |
| 6¾" | $150.00 | $300.00 |
| 8½" | $225.00 | $450.00 |
| 10" | $350.00 | $700.00 |

**Mold #130, 150, 168, 184, 257, 602, 790 (Bonn or Kestner)**

Painted blue or pink stockings, one-strap black shoes

| | | |
|---|---|---|
| 4" | $150.00 | $295.00 |
| 6" | $200.00 | $385.00 |
| 7" | $215.00 | $425.00 |
| 8" | $250.00 | $500.00 |
| 9" | $300.00 | $675.00 |
| 10" | $375.00 | $750.00 |
| 11" | $450.00 | $900.00 |

**Mold #155, 156 (smile)**

| | | |
|---|---|---|
| 6" | $225.00 | $450.00 |

Swivel neck

| | | |
|---|---|---|
| 5½" | $300.00 | $600.00 |
| 7" | $400.00 | $775.00 |

**Mold #160, molded hair**

| | | |
|---|---|---|
| 5½" | $165.00 | $325.00 |

**All Bisque Child with Glass Eyes and Swivel Neck, ca. 1880+**

Pegged or wired joints, open or closed mouth, molded-on shoes or boots and stockings. Allow more for unusual footwear such as yellow or multi-strap boots

| | | |
|---|---|---|
| 3" | $150.00 | $275.00 |
| 4" | $165.00 | $325.00 |
| 5½" | $250.00 | $500.00 |
| 7" | $325.00 | $650.00 |
| 8" | $375.00 | $750.00 |
| 9" | $425.00 | $850.00 |
| 10" | $625.00 | $1,250.00 |

**Mold #130, 150, 160, 208, 602 (Kestner)**

| | | |
|---|---|---|
| 4" | $250.00 | $500.00 |
| 6" | $300.00 | $600.00 |
| 8" | $450.00 | $900.00 |
| 10" | $650.00 | $1,300.00 |

**Simon & Halbig or Kestner types**

Closed mouth, excellent quality

| | | |
|---|---|---|
| 5" | $400.00 | $775.00 |
| 6" | $600.00 | $1,150.00 |
| 8" | $975.00 | $1,900.00 |

Jointed knees

| | | |
|---|---|---|
| 6" | $1,500.00 | $3,000.00 |

Original factory box with clothes and accessories

| | | |
|---|---|---|
| 5" | $1,750.00 | $3,500.00 |

Bare feet

| | | |
|---|---|---|
| 5" | $800.00 | $1,600.00 |
| 7½" | $1,200.00 | $2,400.00 |

Early round face

| | | |
|---|---|---|
| 6" | $425.00 | $850.00 |
| 8" | $635.00 | $1,250.00 |

**#184, Kestner, sweet face**

| | | |
|---|---|---|
| 4 – 5" | $350.00 | $700.00 |
| 8" | $800.00 | $1,600.00 |

**Mold # 881, 886, 890 (Simon & Halbig)**
Painted high-top boots with four or five straps

| | | |
|---|---|---|
| 4½" | $400.00 | $775.00 |
| 7½" | $800.00 | $1,600.00 |
| 9¼" | $1,000.00 | $2,000.00 |

Long stockings, above knees

| | | |
|---|---|---|
| 4½" | $325.00 | $650.00 |
| 6½" | $450.00 | $900.00 |

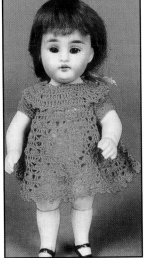

*7½" all bisque, Kestner, child marked 218, $175.00. Courtesy McMasters Doll Auction.*

**#102, Wrestler (so called)**
Fat thighs, arm bent at elbow, open mouth (can have two rows of teeth) or closed mouth. Stocky body, glass eyes, socket head, individual fingers or molded fist

| | | |
|---|---|---|
| 6" | $600.00 | $1,200.00 |
| 8" | $800.00 | $1,600.00 |
| 9" | $1100.00 | $2,100.00 |

**All Bisque Child with Molded Clothes, ca. 1890+**
Jointed at shoulders only or at shoulders and hips, painted eyes, molded hair, molded shoes or bare feet, excellent workmanship, no breaks, chips, or cracks

| | | |
|---|---|---|
| 4½" | $75.00 | $150.00 |
| 6" | $150.00 | $300.00 |

Glass eyes

| | | |
|---|---|---|
| 5" | $200.00 | $385.00 |
| 7" | $265.00 | $525.00 |

Lesser quality

| | | |
|---|---|---|
| 3" | $45.00 | $85.00 |
| 4" | $50.00 | $100.00 |
| 6" | $70.00 | $140.00 |

**Molded on hat or bonnet**
In perfect condition

| | | |
|---|---|---|
| 5 – 6½" | $190.00 | $365.00+ |
| 8 – 9" | $250.00 | $500.00+ |

Glass eyes

| | | |
|---|---|---|
| 5½" | $225.00 | $450.00 |
| 8" | $300.00 | $600.00 |

**Stone (porous) Bisque**

| | | |
|---|---|---|
| 4-5" | $70.00 | $135.00 |
| 6-7" | $85.00 | $165.00 |

**Swivel Neck, early round face**

| | | |
|---|---|---|
| 7" | $1,725.00 | $2,300.00 |

## All Bisque Child with Painted Eyes, ca. 1880+

Head molded to torso. Molded hair or wig, open or closed mouth, painted-on shoes and socks, dressed or undressed, all in good condition. Allow more for unusual footwear such as yellow boot

| | | |
|---|---|---|
| 1½ – 2" | $45.00 | $85.00 |
| 4 – 5" | $90.00 | $175.00 |
| 6½" | $115.00 | $225.00 |
| 8" | $175.00 | $350.00 |

**Black Stockings**, tan slippers

| | | |
|---|---|---|
| 6" | $200.00 | $375.00 |

Ribbed hose

| | | |
|---|---|---|
| 4½" | $95.00 | $185.00 |
| 6" | $185.00 | $365.00 |
| 8" | $285.00 | $565.00 |

**Molded hair**

| | | |
|---|---|---|
| 4" | $90.00 | $175.00 |
| 6½" | $175.00 | $350.00 |

Early very round face

| | | |
|---|---|---|
| 7" | $1,200.00 | $2,300.00 |

**Mold #130, 150, 160, 168, 184, 208, 602 (Kestner)**

| | | |
|---|---|---|
| 5" | $115.00 | $225.00 |
| 6" | $150.00 | $275.00 |
| 7" | $170.00 | $325.00 |
| 8" | $200.00 | $400.00 |
| 9" | $275.00 | $550.00 |
| 10½" | $415.00 | $825.00 |
| 12" | $600.00 | $1,200.00 |

*10" all bisque Wrestler, $650.00.*
*Courtesy McMasters Doll Auctions.*

## All Bisque, Slender Bodies, ca. 1880+

Slender dolls with head molded to torso, usually wire or peg jointed shoulders and hips. Allow much more for original clothes. May be in regional costumes. Add more for unusual color boots, such as gold, yellow, or orange, all in good condition

Glass eyes, open or closed mouth

| | | |
|---|---|---|
| 4" | $145.00 | $285.00 |
| 5 – 6" | $175.00 | $350.00 |

Swivel neck, closed mouth

| | | |
|---|---|---|
| 4" | $200.00 | $375.00 |
| 5 – 6" | $250.00 | $500.00 |
| 8½" | $450.00 | $900.00 |
| 10" | $650.00 | $1,300.00 |

Bent knees

| | | |
|---|---|---|
| 6" | $100.00 | $200.00 |

Jointed knees and/or elbows with swivel waist

| | | |
|---|---|---|
| 6" | $1,000.00 | $1,950.00 |
| 8" | $1,600.00 | $3,200.00 |

Swivel waist only

| | | |
|---|---|---|
| 6" | $1,000.00 | $2,000.00 |

Painted eyes, swivel neck

Open or closed mouth, painted one-strap shoes

| | | |
|---|---|---|
| 4" | $100.00 | $200.00 |
| 6" | $175.00 | $350.00 |
| 8" | $250.00 | $475.00 |
| 10" | $350.00 | $675.00 |

## All Bisque Child, Character Face, ca. 1910+

### Campbell Kids

Molded on clothes, Dutch hairstyle

| | | |
|---|---|---|
| 5" | $125.00 | $245.00 |

### Chin-chin

Made by Heubach

| | | |
|---|---|---|
| 4 ½" | $150.00 | $325.00 |

**Jeanne Orsini girls.** Designed by Orsini for Borgfeldt, produced by Alt, Beck & Gottschalck; Chi Chi, Didi, Fifi, Mimi, Vivi, ca. 1919+

*4" all bisque Little Annie Rooney with jointed arms, molded clothing, yarn braid, $250.00. Courtesy Catherine Ritter.*

Glass eyes

| | | |
|---|---|---|
| 5" | $600.00 | $1,200.00+ |

Painted eyes

| | | |
|---|---|---|
| 5" | $350.00 | $675.00+ |

## All Bisque Child, Flapper Body, ca. 1920+

One piece body and head with thin limbs, fired-in fine bisque, wig, painted eyes, painted-on long stockings, one-strap painted shoes

| | | |
|---|---|---|
| 5" | $150.00 | $300.00 |
| 7" | $225.00 | $450.00 |

Molded hair

| | | |
|---|---|---|
| 6" | $175.00 | $350.00 |
| 8" | $225.00 | $450.00 |

### Pink Bisque

Wire joints, molded hair, painted eyes

| | | |
|---|---|---|
| 4" | $35.00 | $70 |

Molded hat

| | | |
|---|---|---|
| 4" | $120.00 | $235.00 |

Aviatrix

| | | |
|---|---|---|
| 5" | $125.00 | $250.00 |

Swivel waist

| | | |
|---|---|---|
| 4½" | $200.00 | $385.00 |

# All Bisque, German (cont.)

Molded cap with rabbit ears

| | | | |
|---|---|---|---|
| 4½" | $200.00 | $385.00 | |

**ALL BISQUE IMMOBILES**

Figures with no joints

| | | | |
|---|---|---|---|
| Child | 3" | $25.00 | $50.00 |
| Adult | 5" | $75.00 | $150.00+ |
| Santa | 4" | $70.00 | $135.00 |

Child with animal on string

| | | |
|---|---|---|
| 4" | $75.00 | $150.00+ |

## BISQUE NODDERS, CA. 1920

When their heads are touched, they "nod," molded clothes, made both in Germany and Japan, decoration not fired in so wears off easily, all in good condition.

**Animals, cat, dog, rabbit**

| | | |
|---|---|---|
| 3 – 5" | $35.00 | $75.00 |

**Child/Adult, made in Germany**

| | | |
|---|---|---|
| 4 – 6" | $35.00 | $145.00 |

**Child/Adult with molded-on clothes**

| | | |
|---|---|---|
| 4" | $65.00 | $125.00+ |

**Child/Adult, Comic characters**

| | | |
|---|---|---|
| 3 – 5" | $65.00 | $245.00 |

**Child/Adult, sitting position**

| | | |
|---|---|---|
| 5" | $70.00 | $135.00 |

**Santa Claus or Indian**

| | | |
|---|---|---|
| 6" | $145.00 | $175.00 |

**Teddy Bear**

| | | |
|---|---|---|
| 5" | $85.00 | $165.00 |

**Japan/Nippon**

| | | |
|---|---|---|
| 3½" | $10.00 | $20.00 |
| 4½" | $20.00 | $40.00 |

## ALL BISQUE FIGURES, PAINTED

Top layer of paint not fired on and the color can be washed off, usually one-piece figurines, with molded hair, painted features, including clothes, shoes, and socks. Some have molded hats

First price indicates paint chips, second price is good condition with no paint chips, can be German or Japanese.

**Baby, German**

| | | |
|---|---|---|
| 3½" | $35.00 | $45.00 |
| 5" | $40.00 | $55.00 |

**Baby, Japanese**

| | | |
|---|---|---|
| 3" | $9.00 | $12.00 |
| 5" | $15.00 | $20.00 |

**Child, German**

| | | |
|---|---|---|
| 3" | $20.00 | $25.00 |
| 5" | $45.00 | $60.00 |

**Child, Japanese**

| | | |
|---|---|---|
| 3" | $7.50 | $10.00 |
| 5" | $15.00 | $20.00 |

## All Bisque, Japanese

Made by various Japanese companies. Quality varies greatly. They are jointed at shoulders and may also be jointed at hips. Good quality bisque is well painted with no chips or breaks.

The first price indicates poorer quality, flaking paint, flaws; second price indicates good quality, nicely finished.

**BABY**
Bent limbs, may or may not be jointed at hips and shoulders, very nice quality

| | | |
|---|---|---|
| 3½ | $20.00 | $35.00 |
| 5" | $35.00 | $70.00 |

**Bye-Lo-type**
Fine quality

| | | |
|---|---|---|
| 3½" | $45.00 | $85.00 |
| 5" | $70.00 | $135.00 |

Medium to poor quality

| | | |
|---|---|---|
| 3½" | $4.00 | $8.00 |
| 5" | $23.00 | $45.00 |

**Betty Boop**
Bobbed hair style, large eyes painted to side, head molded to torso

| | | |
|---|---|---|
| 4" | $20.00 | $40.00 |
| 6 – 7" | $35.00 | $65.00 |

**CHILD**
With molded clothes

| | | |
|---|---|---|
| 4½" | $23.00 | $30.00 |
| 6" | $35.00 | $45.00 |

**Child, ca. 1920s – 1930s**
Pink or painted bisque with painted features, jointed at shoulders and hips, molded hair or wig. Excellent condition.

| | | |
|---|---|---|
| 3" | $7.50 | $15.00 |
| 4 – 5" | $15.00 | $27.50 |
| 7" | $23.00 | $45.00 |

Child with Bow in hair

| | | |
|---|---|---|
| 4" | $10.00 | $20.00 |
| 7" | $23.00 | $45.00 |

**COMIC CHARACTERS**
**Jackie Coogan,** Japan

| | | |
|---|---|---|
| 6½" | $75.00 | $150.00 |

**Mr. Peanut,** made in Japan

| | | |
|---|---|---|
| 4" | $15.00 | $30.00 |

**Skippy**

| | | |
|---|---|---|
| 5" | $55.00 | $110.00 |

*3 – 7½" all bisque Japanese, left to right: Irish girl, Colonial girl, Colonial boy, $75.00 each. Courtesy Patsy Corrigan.*

*3 – 7½" all bisque Japanese, left to right: Spanish girl, Spanish boy, Russian boy, $75.00 each. Courtesy Patsy Corrigan.*

**Snow White,** Japan

| | | |
|---|---|---|
| 5" | $55.00 | $110.00 |

Boxed with Dwarfs

| | | |
|---|---|---|
| | $325.00 | $625.00+ |

**Three Bears/Goldilocks, Japan**

| | | |
|---|---|---|
| Boxed set | $165.00 | $325.00+ |

Nippon mark

| | | |
|---|---|---|
| 4" | $18.00 | $35.00 |
| 6" | $28.00 | $55.00 |

Occupied Japan mark

| | | |
|---|---|---|
| 3½" | $13.00 | $25.00 |
| 5" | $18.00 | $35.00 |
| 7" | $25.00 | $50.00 |

## Alt, Beck & Gottschalck

Established as a porcelain factory in 1854 at Nauendorf, Thuringia, Germany, Cislek reports the company imported doll heads to the United States by 1882. Made heads in both china and bisque. They made heads for other companies such as Bergman, using Wagner and Zetrsche kid bodies. Coleman reports mold numbers from 639 to 1288.

First price indicates dolls in good condition, with some flaws, nude; second price is for dolls in excellent condition, original clothes or appropriately dressed.

*Marks:*

ABG   AB.G

698※9   1235   # No 10.

**BABIES, CA. 1910+**

Open mouth, some have pierced nostrils, bent leg baby body, wigs. More for toddler body or flirty eyes, good condition, nicely dressed.

| | | |
|---|---|---|
| 12" | $300.00 | $400.00 |
| 16" | $375.00 | $500.00 |
| 21" | $600.00 | $800.00 |
| 26" | $1,200.00 | $1,600.00 |

**Character Baby, ca. 1910+**

Socket head on jointed composition body, glass or painted eyes, open mouth. Nicely dressed with good wig or molded hair, good condition.

**Mold #1322, 1342, 1346, 1352, 1361**

| | | |
|---|---|---|
| 12" | $300.00 | $400.00 |
| 15" | $395.00 | $525.00 |
| 18" | $475.00 | $625.00 |
| 22" | $645.00 | $850.00 |

## CHILD, ALL BISQUE

Rigid neck, fat tummy, jointed shoulders and hips, glass sleep eyes, open/closed mouth, molded black one-strap shoes with tan soles, white molded stockings with blue band. Similar mold dolls imported in 50s by Kimport have synthetic hair, lesser quality bisque.

Mold number appears as a fraction, with the following size numbers under 83; #83/100, 83/125, 83/150, or 83/225.

One marked 83/100 has a green label on torso reading, *"PRINCESS//MADE IN GERMANY"*

| | | | |
|---|---|---|---|
| #100 | 5¾" | $210.00 | $275.00 |
| #125 | 6¾" | $265.00 | $325.00 |
| #150 | 7½" | $300.00 | $400.00 |
| #225 | | $335.00 | $450.00 |

*19" bisque Alt, Beck & Gottschalck baby marked 1361, $225.00. Courtesy McMasters Doll Auctions.*

### Child

**Mold #632**

| | | |
|---|---|---|
| 22" | $1,800.00 | $2,400.00 |

**Mold #911, 916**

Closed mouth

| | | |
|---|---|---|
| 20" | $1,800.00 | $2,400.00 |

### Character Child, ca. 1910+

**Mold #1357, 1358, 1359**

Molded hair, center part, bun and molded ribbon, deep dimples, wide open/closed mouth

Painted eyes

| | | |
|---|---|---|
| 15" | $500.00 | $675.00 |
| 20" | $1,250.00 | $1,700.00 |

Glass eyes

| | | |
|---|---|---|
| 15" | $675.00 | $900.00 |
| 20" | $1725.00 | $2,300.00 |

**Mold #1362, Sweet Nell**

| | | |
|---|---|---|
| 16" | $510.00 | $675.00 |
| 20" | $735.00 | $975.00 |

In box

| | | |
|---|---|---|
| 27" | $945.00 | $1,250.00+ |

**Mold #1367**

| | | |
|---|---|---|
| 15" | $355.00 | $475.00 |
| 19" | $545.00 | $725.00 |

*15" bisque Alt, Beck & Gottschalck lady with molded hair, $275.00. Courtesy McMasters Doll Auctions.*

## SHOULDER HEAD, BISQUE, CA. 1880+

**Mold #639, 698, 784, 870, 890, 911, 912, 916, 990, 1000, 1008, 1028, 1032, 1044, 1046, 1064, 1123, 1127, 1142, 1210, 1234, 1235, 1254, 1304**

Cloth or kid body, bisque lower limbs, no damage and nicely dressed, allow more for molded hat or fancy hairdo

Glass eyes, closed mouth

| | | |
|---|---|---|
| 12" | $450.00 | $575.00 |
| 16" | $750.00 | $1,000.00 |
| 18" | $1,125.00 | $1,500.00 |
| 22" | $1,350.00 | $1,800.00 |
| 26" | $1,765.00 | $2,350.00 |

Open mouth

| | | |
|---|---|---|
| 16" | $375.00 | $500.00 |
| 21" | $475.00 | $625.00 |
| 25" | $525.00 | $700.00 |

Painted eyes, closed mouth

| | | |
|---|---|---|
| 14" | $300.00 | $385.00 |
| 20" | $525.00 | $700.00 |

Open mouth

| | | |
|---|---|---|
| 15" | $190.00 | $250.00 |
| 21" | $340.00 | $450.00 |

*22" bisque Alt, Beck & Gottschalck child, $525.00. Courtesy Angie Gonzales.*

## Turned Bisque Shoulder Heads

Bald head or plaster pate, kid body, bisque lower arms, all in good condition, nicely dressed. Dolls marked "DEP," or "Germany" after 1888. Some have Wagner & Zetzche marked on head, paper label inside top of body. Allow more for molded bonnet or elaborate hairdo.

Glass eyes, closed mouth

| | | |
|---|---|---|
| 15" | $600.00 | $800.00 |
| 18" | $750.00 | $1,000.00 |
| 22" | $900.00 | $1,200.00 |

Open mouth

| | | |
|---|---|---|
| 15" | $345.00 | $450.00 |
| 21" | $475.00 | $625.00 |

Painted eyes, closed mouth

| | | |
|---|---|---|
| 15" | $300.00 | $400.00 |
| 18" | $375.00 | $500.00 |
| 22 | $490.00 | $650.00 |

Open mouth

| | | |
|---|---|---|
| 15" | $190.00 | $250.00 |
| 21" | $475.00 | $625.00 |

## Shoulder Heads, China, ca. 1880+

**Mold #784, 786, 880, 882, 1000, 1003, 1008, 1028, 1046, 1112, 1142, 1144, 1210, 1214**

Blonde or black haired china heads, cloth body, china limbs, nicely dressed, all in good condition. Mark: *"1000 #10"*

| | | |
|---|---|---|
| 15" | $275.00 | $365.00 |
| 19" | $318.00 | $425.00 |
| 23" | $395.00 | $525.00 |
| 28" | $475.00 | $625.00 |

# Amberg, Louis & Sons

**Ca. 1878 – 1930.** The company began in Cincinnati, OH, and did business from 1898 in New York City. Before 1907 they used another name. They imported dolls made by other firms. First company to manufacture American-made composition dolls.

## BABY PEGGY

**Baby Peggy, composition, ca. 1923**
Portrait doll of child actress, Peggy Jean Montgomery. Composition head, arms, and legs, cloth body, molded brown bobbed hair, painted eyes with molded lower eyelids, closed mouth.

| | | |
|---|---|---|
| 15" | $85.00 | $365.00 |
| 18" | $125.00 | $500.00 |
| 23" | $175.00 | $700.00 |

**Baby Peggy, bisque, ca. 1924**
Bisque socket head, sleep-eyes, closed mouth, original wig with bangs, dimples, composition or kid body with bisque lower arms
*Mark:*
*"19 C. 24/LA & S NY/Germany"*
Mold #972 (socket head, solemn)
Mold #973 (socket head, smiling)

| | | |
|---|---|---|
| 17" | $1,725.00 | $2,300.00 |
| 22" | $1,995.00 | $2,650.00 |

Mold #982 (shoulder head, solemn)
Mold #983 (shoulder head, smiling)

| | | |
|---|---|---|
| 17" | $1,800.00 | $2,400.00 |
| 22" | $2,100.00 | $2,800.00 |

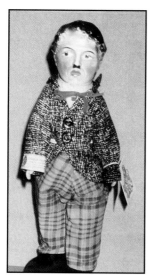

*Charlie Chaplin, 13" composition head, painted features, cloth body, cloth tag on coat sleeve, $450.00+. Courtesy Debbie Crume.*

**Baby Peggy, all bisque,** pink bisque with molded hair, painted brown eyes, closed mouth, jointed at shoulders and hips, molded and painted shoes/socks

| | | |
|---|---|---|
| 3½" | $225.00 | $400.00 |
| 5½" | $450.00 | $600.00 |

## BODY TWISTS

**(Teenie Weenies, Tiny Tots), ca. 1929**
All composition with swivel waist made from ball attached to torso. Boy or girl with molded hair and painted features. Tag attached to clothes reads: An Amberg Doll/Body Twist/Pat. Pend. #32018

| | | |
|---|---|---|
| 7½" or 8½" | $50.00 | $200.00 |

## CHARLIE CHAPLIN, CA. 1915

Composition portrait head, painted features, composition hands, cloth body and legs. Black suit, white suit, cloth label on sleeve or inside seam of coat that reads: "CHARLIE CHAPLIN DOLL/World's Greatest Comedian /Made exclusively by Louis Amberg/& Son, NY/by Special Arrangement with/Essamay Film Co."

| | | |
|---|---|---|
| 14" | $150.00 | $600.00 |

## EDWINA (SUE OR IT), CA. 1928

All composition with painted features, molded hair with side part and swirl bang across forehead, body twist (waist swivels on ball attached to torso)

Mark:
"*Amberg/Pat. Pen./L.A. & S.*"
14"    $125.00    $475.00

## HAPPINUS, 1918+

Coquette-type, all-composition with head and body molded in one piece, jointed shoulders and hips, painted molded brown hair, with molded ribbon, closed mouth, painted features, unmarked. Well modeled torso, original clothes
10"    $75.00    $300.00

## MIBS, CA. 1921

Composition turned shoulder-head designed by Hazel Drukker, with painted molded hair, painted eyes, closed mouth. Two different body styles: cork-stuffed cloth with composition arms and legs and molded shoes, painted socks; and a barefoot, swing-leg, mama-type cloth body with crier. Original dress has ribbon label that reads: "L.A.& S./Amberg Dolls/The World Standard/Created by/Hazel Drukker/Please Love Me/I'm Mibs."

*Sunny Orange Maid, 14½" Amberg, composition shoulder plate, cloth body, compo arms and legs, all original, 1924, $1,200.00. Courtesy Sherryl Shirran.*

10"    $150.00    $550.00
16"    $225.00    $875.00

### Mibs, all bisque, ca. 1921

Molded blonde hair, molded/painted socks and shoes, pink bisque, jointed at shoulders, legs molded to body

Mark:
"*C./ L.A. & S. 1921/Germany*"
3"    $185.00    $250.00
5"    $375.00    $425.00

## NEWBORN BABE, CA. 1914, REISSUED, 1924

Bisque head with cloth body, either celluloid, composition, or rubber hands, lightly painted hair, sleep eyes, closed mouth with protruding upper lip

Marks: "*L.A.& S. 1914/ G45520 Germany, L. Amberg and Son/886,*" or "*Copyright by Louis Amberg*"
8"    $275.00    $365.00
11"    $325.00    $425.00
14"    $375.00    $500. 00
18"    $655.00    $825.00

# Amberg, Louis & Sons (cont.)

Open mouth, marked L.A.& S. 371

| | | |
|---|---|---|
| 10" | $300.00 | $400.00 |
| 15" | $340.00 | $450.00 |

## VANTA BABY, CA. 1927 – 30

Bisque or composition head, sleep eyes, crier, bent limb body, distributed by Sears with advertising promotion for Vanta baby garments. In sizes from 10" to 25"

*Marks:*

Composition

| | | |
|---|---|---|
| 18" | $75.00 | $265.00 |
| 23" | $100.00 | $375.00 |

Bisque head, glass eyes, open mouth

| | | |
|---|---|---|
| 18" | $825.00 | $1,100.00 |
| 24" | $1275.00 | $1,700.00 |

Bisque head, glass eyes, closed mouth

| | | |
|---|---|---|
| 18" | $1050.00 | $1,400.00 |
| 24" | $1,500.00 | $2,000.00 |

# Arnold, Max Oscar

**ca. 1878 – 1925, Neustadt, Thuringia**
Made jointed dressed dolls and mechanical dolls including phonograph dolls
*Mark:*

*16" bisque, Max Oscar Arnold toddler, $450.00. Courtesy Matrix.*

**Baby, bisque head**

| | | |
|---|---|---|
| 12" | $125.00 | $165.00 |
| 16" | $215.00 | $285.00 |
| 19" | $375.00 | $500.00 |

**Child, Mold #150, 200, or just M.O.A.**
Excellent bisque

| | | |
|---|---|---|
| 12" | $190.00 | $250.00 |
| 15" | $265.00 | $350.00 |
| 21" | $450.00 | $600.00 |
| 30" | $750.00 | $1,000.00 |

Poor to medium quality bisque

| | | |
|---|---|---|
| 15" | $125.00 | $165.00 |
| 20" | $200.00 | $300.00 |
| 24" | $340.00 | $450.00 |

## Automatons (Mechanical Dolls)

*23" bisque, Tete Jumeau, with music box and key-wound mechanism in base. Doll nods head while bird in hand chirps when offered a piece of grain, $3,500.00. Courtesy McMasters Doll Auctions.*

*17½" bisque head by Lanternier, ca. 1910, carton bodies, papier mache hands. Multiple movements; lady nods, raises shuttle, taps foot, wheel spins, boy nods, moves spindle, $10,000.00. Courtesy Rosalie Whyel Museum of Doll Art, Bellevue, WA, photo by Charles Backus.*

*24" bisque, Simon & Halbig, Smoker, key-wound mechanism, marked 1159, $1,800.00. Courtesy McMasters Doll Auctions.*

These were made by various manufacturers using many different mediums including bisque, wood, wax, cloth, and others. Unusual complicated models performing more complex actions bring more. The unusual one-of-a-kind dolls in this category make it difficult to provide a good database range. All these auction prices are for mechanicals in good working order.

**Babies**, playing, all bisque, Heubach
    12"x7" base          $2,900.00
**Ballerina**, Simon & Halbig, by Roulelet & Decamps
       22"          $2,100.00
**Black**, "The Jubilee Champion Dancer," papier mache
      10"          $2,800.00

*18" bisque Jumeau Automaton, key wound, puts perfume bottle in hand, bows head, lifts handkerchief to smell it, $5,200.00. Courtesy McMasters Doll Auctions.*

*16" bisque Jumeau automaton, key-wound music box plays, hat twirls, doll moves right hand, $4,700.00. Courtesy McMasters Doll Auctions.*

**Boy on Tricycle,** bisque head
8½"            $1,200.00
**Child with Pony Cart,** bisque head
5"            $4,600.00
**Chinaman** drinking tea, papier mache
15"            $4,290.00
**Clown with guitar,** Simon & Halbig
16"            $4,000.00
**Cuisinier,** Tete Jumeau, with tongs and copper pan
17"            $4,180.00
**Dancers,** Waltzing Couple, Vichy Fils, Paris
13"            $6,250.00
**Fortune Telling Machine,** Madame Zita, floor model
5'            $20,000.00
**Girl, Throwing Kisses,** S.F.B.J., hairline
24"            $1,650.00
**Girl, Tea Server,** Tete Jumeau
20"            $2,200.00
**Lady,** powders nose, Tete Jumeau
19"            $6,500.00
**Man, The Drinking Waiter,** bisque head
8"            $650.00
**Musician,** K*R, papier mache
12"            $475.00

# Averill, Georgene

**MADAME HENDREN, ca. 1915+, New York City, NY.** Georgene Averill made composition and cloth dolls operating as Madame Georgene Dolls, Averill Mfg. Co., Georgene Novelties, and Madame Hendren. First line were felt dressed dolls, Lyf-Lyk, patented Mama Doll in 1918, and the Wonder line. Designed dolls for Borgfeldt, including Bonnie Babe.
**Bonnie Babe,** ca. 1926 – 30+
Designed by Georgene Averill, distributed by Borgfeldt. Bisque head, open mouth, two lower teeth, composition arms (sometimes celluloid) and legs on cloth body.
Tag on original outfit reads: "BONNIE BABE//COPYRIGHTED BY//GEORGENE AVERILL//MADE BY K AND K TOY CO."

*Bonnie Babe, 14", Georgene Averill, $700.00. Courtesy McMasters Doll Auctions.*

*Mark:*
"Copr//Georgene Averill//1005/3652//Germany"
Mold # 1368, 1402

| | | | |
|---|---|---|---|
| 12" | $465.00 | $1,000.00 | $1,100.00 |
| 14 – 15" | $950.00 | | |
| 17½" | $1,250.00 | $1,400.00 | $1,600.00 |
| 20" | $1,700.00 | $1,800.00 | $1,900.00 |

Celluloid head

| | | |
|---|---|---|
| 10" | $240.00 | $465.00 |
| 16" | $350.00 | $675.00 |

**All Bisque Bonnie Babe, see All Bisque section.**

**Cloth dolls, animals, 1930+**
Mask face with painted features, yarn hair, cloth body

| | | |
|---|---|---|
| 12" | $30.00 | $90.00 |
| 15" | $70.00 | $150.00 |
| 20" | $80.00 | $285.00 |
| 22" | $100.00 | $325.00 |

**Animals, mint condition**
B'rer Rabbit, Fuzzy Wuzzy, Nurse Jane, Uncle Wigglily, etc.

| | |
|---|---|
| 18" | $600.00+ |

Krazy Kat, 1916, felt not jointed

| | | |
|---|---|---|
| 14" | $90.00 | $350.00 |
| 18" | $125.00 | $500.00 |

**Brownies and Girl Scouts**

| | | |
|---|---|---|
| 14" | $80.00 | $250.00 |

**Comic Characters**
Alvin, Little Lulu, Nancy, Sluggo, Tubby Tom, 1944 – 51
with mask faces and painted features

| | |
|---|---|
| 14" | $500.00+ |

Little Lulu, in cowgirl outfit

| | |
|---|---|
| 14" | $585.00 |

Dolly Dingle, 1923+, designed by Grace Drayton

| | | |
|---|---|---|
| 12" | $115.00 | $450.00 |

Tear Drop Baby, one tear painted on cheek

| | | |
|---|---|---|
| 16" | $60.00 | $325.00 |

**Composition Dolls**
All composition, with jointed arms and legs, molded or wigged hair, painted or sleep eyes, open or closed mouth, all in good condition, original clothing

**Patsy-type, 1928**

| | | |
|---|---|---|
| 14" | $250.00 | $300.00 |
| 17" | $325.00 | $350.00 |

**Baby Georgene or Baby Hendren**
Composition head, arms, and lower legs. Cloth body with crier, marked with name on head

| | | |
|---|---|---|
| 16" | $75.00 | $250.00 |
| 20" | $95.00 | $325.00 |
| 26" | $200.00 | $600.00+ |

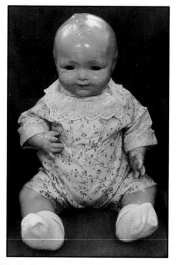

*17" baby by Georgene Averill, composition head, arms and legs with a cloth body, blue tin sleep eyes, open/closed mouth with one painted tooth, painted, molded blond hair, disk jointed, $300.00. Courtesy Janet Hill.*

*13" Whistling Dan composition, cloth body with bellows mechanism, when doll bounced on feet makes noise, painted eyes, open mouth, $300.00.*

### Character or Ethnic

Composition head, cloth or composition body, character face, painted features, composition arms and legs. Whistlers, such as Whistling Dan, Sailor, Indian, Dutch Boy, had bellows inside body that when pushed down on feet created a whistling sound. Clothes often in felt. Original tag often found in clothes reads: "I whistle when you dance me on one foot and then the other.//Patented Feb. 2 1926// Genuine Madame Hendren Doll."

|        |          |          |
|--------|----------|----------|
| 10"    | $35.00   | $145.00  |
| 14"    | $85.00   | $250.00  |
| Black  |          |          |
| 14"    | $125.00  | $450.00  |

**Dolly Dingle** (for Grace Drayton), composition

|     |          |          |
|-----|----------|----------|
| 14" | $115.00  | $450.00  |

### Dolly Record, 1922 – 28

Composition head, arms and legs, human hair wig, sleeping eyes, open mouth and teeth, record player in torso

|     |          |          |
|-----|----------|----------|
| 26" | $250.00  | $650.00  |

### Mama Doll, 1918+

Composition shoulder head and arms, cloth torso with crier, swing composition legs, molded hair or mohair wig, painted or sleep eyes, good condition, original clothes, more if MIB

|           |          |          |
|-----------|----------|----------|
| 15 – 18"  | $200.00  | $300.00  |
| 20 – 22"  | $400.00  | $500.00  |

### Snookums, 1927

Child star of Universal-Stern Bros. movie comedies, has laughing mouth, two rows of teeth, pants attached to shirt with safety pin

|     |          |          |
|-----|----------|----------|
| 14" | $100.00  | $375.00  |

# Bahr & Proschild

**Ca. 1871 – 1930+, Ohrdruf, Thuringia, Germany.** Porcelain factory, made china, bisque, and celluloid dolls and doll parts and Snow Babies. Made dolls for Kley & Hahn, Bruno Schmidt, Wiesenthal, Schindel & Kallenberg.

*Marks:*

### Baby, Character face, 1909+

Bisque socket head, solid dome or wigged, bent leg, sleep eyes, open mouth, good condition, nicely dressed

**Mold # 585, 586, 587, 602, 604, 624, 630, 678, 619, 641**

| | | |
|---|---|---|
| 13" | $340.00 | $450.00 |
| 17" | $490.00 | $650.00 |
| 22" | $640.00 | $850.00 |

Toddler body

| | | |
|---|---|---|
| 9" | $450.00 | $600.00 |
| 16" | $650.00 | $865.00 |
| 19" | $825.00 | $1,100.00 |

**Mold 526, other series #500, and 2023, 2072,** or marked *"BP"* baby body, open closed mouth

| | | |
|---|---|---|
| 14" | $2,100.00 | $2,800.00 |
| 18" | $2,625.00 | $3,500.00 |

### Dome Head or Belton-type

Mold in 200 and 300 series, with small holes, socket head or shoulder plate, composition or kid body

| | | |
|---|---|---|
| 12" | $1,050.00 | $1,400.00 |
| 16" | $1,350.00 | $1,800.00 |
| 21" | $1,690.00 | $2,250.00 |
| 24" | $2,025.00 | $2,700.00 |

*13½" bisque Bahr & Proschild, mold #619, $500.00. Courtesy Sherryl Shirran.*

### Child, Open or Closed Mouth

Mold 200 and 300 series, full cheeks, jointed composition German-type, French-type, or kid body.

**#204, 224, 239, 246, 273, 274, 275, 277, 286, 289, 293, 297, 309, 325, 332, 340, 379, 394**

| | | |
|---|---|---|
| 8" | $265.00 | $350.00 |
| 10" | $375.00 | $500.00 |
| 14" | $510.00 | $675.00 |
| 17" | $565.00 | $750.00 |
| 20" | $640.00 | $850.00 |
| 23" | $750.00 | $1,000.00 |

# Bahr & Proschild (cont.)

**Mold # 224,** open mouth, dimpled cheeks

| | | |
|---|---|---|
| 16" | $715.00 | $950.00 |
| 22" | $975.00 | $1,300.00 |

**Child, kid body, open mouth**

| | | |
|---|---|---|
| 16" | $300.00 | $400.00 |
| 18" | $415.00 | $550.00 |
| 24" | $510.00 | $675.00 |

## Barrois, E.

**Ca. 1844-77, Paris, France.** Dolls marked E.B. are attributed to this early manufacturing firm that used bisque and china heads with that mark. It is not known who made the heads for them. Bisque shoulder head with glass or painted eyes, closed mouth, kid body, may have wooden and bisque arms, good condition. China head has painted eyes and painted, molded hair.

*19" bisque Barrois fashion-type, $3,050.00. Courtesy McMasters Doll Auctions.*

*Marks:*

E 3 B

E.ᵍ DÉPOSÉ B.

E. 8 DEPOSÉ B.

| | | |
|---|---|---|
| 14" | $2,500.00 | $3,000.00 |
| 18" | $3,000.00 | $4,000.00 |
| 21" | $3,750.00 | $5,000.00+ |

## Bathing Dolls

**Bathing Beauties, ca. 1920.** All bisque figures, usually one-piece in various poses, were made by most porcelain factories in Germany and the United States in the 1920s. Beautifully detailed features, undressed, molded-on clothing, or dressed in bathing costumes. All in excellent condition, no chips or damage.

**Painted eye**

| | | |
|---|---|---|
| 3" | $190.00 | $250.00 |
| 6" | $300.00 | $400.00 |

**Glass eyes**

| | | |
|---|---|---|
| 5" | $300.00 | $400.00 |
| 6" | $490.00 | $650.00 |

*2½" all bisque Bathing Beauty; and two 3" reclining Bathing Beauties, $150.00 – $300.00. Courtesy McMasters Doll Auctions.*

*2" pink bisque bathing beauty marked, "Germany," features washed off, $100.00. 3¾" King Neptune marked, "Germay 427," $400.00. Courtesy McMasters Doll Auctions.*

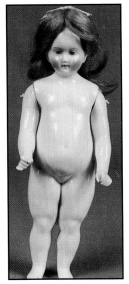

*9" china bathing doll with jointed arms and wig, $355.00. Courtesy McMasters Doll Auctions.*

| | | |
|---|---|---|
| **Swivel neck** | | |
| 5" | $510.00 | $675.00 |
| 6" | $545.00 | $725.00 |
| **With animal** | | |
| 5½" | $1,125.00 | $1,500.00 |
| Two modeled together | | |
| 4½ – 5½" | $1,600.00+ | |
| **Action figures** | | |
| 5" | $340.00 | $450.00+ |
| 7½" | $490.00 | $650.00 |
| Wigged action figure | | |
| 7" | $450.00 | $600.00 |
| **Marked Japan** | | |
| 3" | $50.00 | $75.00 |
| 5 – 6" | $65.00 | $100.00 |
| 9" | $125.00 | $175.00 |
| **Unusual** | | |
| 4" | $175.00 | $250.00 |
| 6" | $265.00 | $350.00 |

# Belton Types

No dolls marked Belton found; only mold numbers. Belton-type refers to small holes found in tops of solid bisque dolls heads; holes were used for stringing. Used by various German firms such as Bahr & Proschild, Limbach, and Simon & Halbig. Socket head, paperweight eyes, wood and composition jointed French-type body with straight wrists, appropriately dressed in good condition.

*Mark:*

None, may have Mold #100, 116, 117, 120, 125, 127, 137, 154, 183, 185, 190 or others.

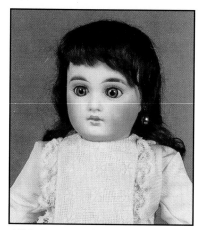

*14" Belton-type, $1,200.00. Courtesy McMasters Doll Auctions.*

**Bru-type face**

| | | |
|---|---|---|
| 16" | $1,950.00 | $2,600.00 |
| 19" | $2,250.00 | $3,000.00 |

**French-type face**, mold #125, 137

| | | |
|---|---|---|
| 9" | $825.00 | $1,100.00 |
| 13" | $1,400.00 | $1850.00 |
| 15" | $1,500.00 | $2,000.00 |
| 17" | $1,950.00 | $2,600.00 |
| 21" | $2,625.00 | $3,500.00 |
| 23" | $2,500.00 | $3,300.00 |

**German-type face**

| | | |
|---|---|---|
| 9" | $750.00 | $1,000.00 |
| 12" | $950.00 | $1,250.00 |
| 14" | $1,050.00 | $1,400.00 |
| 16" | $1,200.00 | $1,600.00 |
| 21" | $1,575.00 | $2,100.00 |
| 25" | $1,850.00 | $2,500.00 |

# Bergmann, C.M.

**Ca. 1889 – 1930+, Thuringia, Germany.** This company made dolls, but also used heads made by Alt, Beck & Gottschalck, Armand Marseille, and Simon and Halbig.

*Marks:*

C. M. B
SIMON & HALBIG
Eleonore

G.M. Bergmann
Waltershausen
Germany
1916
9

**Baby,** mold #612, open/closed mouth

| | | |
|---|---|---|
| 14" | $1,125.00 | $1,500.00 |
| 17" | $1,500.00 | $2,000.00 |

**Character Baby,** socket head, five-piece bent leg body, open mouth

| | | |
|---|---|---|
| 14" | $245.00 | $325.00 |
| 18" | $435.00 | $575.00 |
| 21" | $525.00 | $700.00 |

**Child,** head by A.M., or unknown maker; open mouth, good wig, jointed composition body

| | | |
|---|---|---|
| 10" | $245.00 | $325.00 |
| 15" | $285.00 | $375.00 |
| 20" | $300.00 | $400.00 |
| 23" | $400.00 | $535.00 |
| 29" | $600.00 | $800.00 |
| 34" | $900.00 | $1,200.00 |
| 42" | $1,500.00 | $1,950.00 |

*24" C.M. Bergmann child, sleep eyes, dolly face, open mouth, teeth, composition body, $550.00. Courtesy Angie Gonzales.*

Child, head by Simon Halbig

| | | |
|---|---|---|
| 20" | $365.00 | $500.00 |
| 23" | $475.00 | $635.00 |
| 30" | $675.00 | $1000.00 |
| 33" | $800.00 | $1,100.00 |

**Eleonore**

| | | |
|---|---|---|
| 18" | $490.00 | $650.00 |
| 25" | $640.00 | $850.00 |

**Lady,** flapper-style body with thin arms and legs

| | | |
|---|---|---|
| 12" | $470.00 | $625.00 |
| 16" | $1,125.00 | $1,500.00 |

*29" bisque C.M. Bergmann child, $650.00. Courtesy McMasters Doll Auction.*

# Bisque, French

**Ca. 1870+.** A number of French doll makers produced dolls marked with only size numbers, Paris, or France. Many are also being attributed to German makers who produced for the French trade. Unmarked, pressed bisque socket head, closed or open/closed mouth, paperweight eyes, pierced ears, excellent quality bisque and finely painted features, on French wood and composition body with straight wrists. No damage, appropriately dressed.

**Early desirable, very French-style face**

*Marks* such as J.D. (possible J. DuSerre), J.M. Paris, and H. G. (possibly Henri & Granfe-Guimonneau).

| | | |
|---|---|---|
| 14" | $6,000.00 | $8,000.00 |
| 18" | $13,500.00 | $18,000.00+ |
| 22" | $16,500.00 | $22,000.00+ |
| 26" | $19,500.00 | $26,000.00+ |

*26" bisque Petite Francaise by J. Verlingue, $650.00. Courtesy McMasters Doll Auctions.*

*11" pale bisque with closed mouth, bald head and fur wig, bisque forearms, $1,300.00. Courtesy Amanda Hash.*

**Jumeau- or Bru-style face,** may be marked W. D. or R. R.

| | | |
|---|---|---|
| 15" | $2,025.00 | $2,700.00 |
| 18" | $2,200.00 | $3,000.00 |
| 21" | $3,300.00 | $4,400.00 |
| 24" | $3,750.00 | $5,000.00 |
| 27" | $3,975.00 | $5,300.00 |

*Marked: "F.1, F.2, J, #137, 136"* or others

Excellent quality, closed mouth, unusual face

| | | |
|---|---|---|
| 10" | $1,250.00 | $1,700.00 |
| 15" | $3,000.00 | $4,000.00 |
| 18" | $3,600.00 | $4,750.00 |
| 23" | $4,500.00 | $6,000.00 |
| 27" | $5,250.00 | $7,000.00 |

Standard quality, closed mouth, excellent bisque

| | | |
|---|---|---|
| 15" | $2,100.00 | $2,800.00 |
| 18" | $2,600.00 | $3,450.00 |
| 23" | $3,375.00 | $4,500.00 |

Medium quality, closed mouth, may have poor painting and/or blotches on cheeks

| | | |
|---|---|---|
| 15" | $900.00 | $1,200.00 |
| 21" | $1,350.00 | $1,800.00 |
| 26" | $1,725.00 | $2,300.00 |

Excellent quality, open mouth, ca. 1890+, French body

| | | |
|---|---|---|
| 15" | $1,125.00 | $1,500.00 |
| 18" | $1,725.00 | $2,300.00 |
| 21" | $1,800.00 | $2,400.00 |
| 25" | $2,400.00 | $3,200.00 |

*8½" bisque, marked "39.17//S," in old sailor outfit, $500.00. Courtesy Sherryl Shirran.*

Open mouth, high cheek color, ca. 1920s, may have five-piece papier mache body

| | | |
|---|---|---|
| 16" | $490.00 | $650.00 |
| 20" | $625.00 | $825.00 |
| 24" | $750.00 | $1,000.00 |

**Little-known German factories, ca. 1860+**

*Marks:*

May be only a mold or size number or "Germany"

**American Schoolboy (so called)**

Side-part molded, painted hair swept across forehead like bangs, glass eyes, closed mouth

Jointed composition body

| | | |
|---|---|---|
| 12" | $415.00 | $550.00 |
| 16" | $525.00 | $700.00 |

Kid or cloth body

| | | |
|---|---|---|
| 12" | $325.00 | $425.00 |
| 16" | $415.00 | $550.00 |
| 20" | $525.00 | $700.00 |

**Baby, cloth body**

Bisque head, molded/painted hair, composition or celluloid hands, glass eyes, good condition, appropriately dressed

| | | |
|---|---|---|
| 12" | $245.00 | $325.00 |
| 15" | $360.00 | $475.00 |
| 18" | $475.00 | $625.00 |

**Baby, composition body**

Solid dome or wigged, five-piece baby body, open mouth, good condition, appropriately dressed

Glass eyes

| | | |
|---|---|---|
| 9" | $165.00 | $225.00 |
| 14" | $360.00 | $475.00 |
| 17" | $400.00 | $600.00 |
| 22" | $575.00 | $765.00 |

Painted eyes

| | | |
|---|---|---|
| 9" | $125.00 | $165.00 |
| 14" | $210.00 | $275.00 |
| 17" | $320.00 | $425.00 |

*Allow more for closed or open/closed mouth, unusual face, or toddler body.

**Child, character face, glass eyes, closed or open/closed mouth**

Unidentified, may have wig or solid dome, excellent quality bisque, good condition, appropriately dressed.

| | | |
|---|---|---|
| 16" | $3,000.00 | $4,000.00 |
| 20" | $3,600.00 | $4,800.00 |

*8" bisque socket head, open mouth, teeth, papier mache body, molded shoes and socks, all original with box, $425.00. Courtesy Sue Kinkade.*

*10" bisque German American School Boy, $115.00. Courtesy McMasters Doll Auctions.*

*24" German solid dome bisque head, bent limb baby body, open mouth, sleep eyes, $800.00. Courtesy Angie Gonzales.*

*16" Dream Baby type, $275.00.
Courtesy McMasters Doll Auctions.*

*Bisque shoulder head, painted, molded hair, bisque lower arms, cloth body, $525.00.
Courtesy McMasters Doll Auctions.*

*German bisque child, made for the French market, $300.00. Courtesy McMasters Doll Auctions.*

*20" bisque German fashion-type lady, $975.00.
Courtesy McMasters Doll Auctions.*

Mold #128, 134, and others of this quality, closed mouth, glass eyes

| | | |
|---|---|---|
| 16" | $5,750.00 | $7,500.00+ |
| 22" | $7,500.00 | $10,000.00+ |

Painted eyes

| | | |
|---|---|---|
| 16" | $4,000.00 | $6,000.00+ |
| 22" | $6,150.00 | $8,200.00+ |

**Mold #111, glass eyes**

| | | |
|---|---|---|
| 22" | $16,500.00 | $22,000.00+ |

Mold #111, painted eyes

| | | |
|---|---|---|
| 21" | $9,750.00 | $12,500.00+ |

**Mold #116**

| | | |
|---|---|---|
| 18" | $7,125.00 | $9,500.00 |

**Mold #163**

| | | |
|---|---|---|
| 16" | $750.00 | $1,000.00 |

*25" bisque socket head, marked only "15," closed mouth, glass eyes, human hair wig, composition jointed body, $3,500.00. Courtesy Shirlee Larson.*

**Child, closed mouth**

Excellent bisque, appropriately dressed, jointed composition body

| | | |
|---|---|---|
| 12" | $525.00 | $700.00 |
| 16" | $750.00 | $1,000.00 |
| 21" | $1,125.00 | $1,500.00 |
| 25" | $1,500.00 | $2,000.00 |

Kid, or cloth body, may, have slighted turned head, bisque lower arms

| | | |
|---|---|---|
| 12" | $435.00 | $575.00 |
| 15" | $600.00 | $800.00 |
| 20" | $900.00 | $1,200.00 |
| 24" | $1,050.00 | $1,400.00 |
| 26" | $1,200.00 | $1,600.00 |

**Child, open mouth, ca. 1880+**

Excellent pale bisque, glass eyes, good condition, appropriately dressed
Jointed composition body

| | | |
|---|---|---|
| 12" | $135.00 | $185.00 |
| 15" | $215.00 | $285.00 |
| 20" | $340.00 | $450.00 |
| 22" | $375.00 | $500.00 |
| 25" | $435.00 | $575.00 |
| 28" | $475.00 | $625.00 |

Kid body

| | | |
|---|---|---|
| 12" | $110.00 | $145.00 |
| 15" | $135.00 | $180.00 |
| 18" | $165.00 | $215.00 |
| 22" | $200.00 | $265.00 |

**Molded Hair Doll, ca. 1880+**

Bisque shoulder head with well modeled hair, often blonde, painted or glass eyes, closed mouth, kid or cloth body, bisque lower arms, good condition, appropriately dressed. Mold # 890, 1000, 1008, 1028, 1064, 1142, 1256, 1288, may be made by Alt, Beck & Gottschalck.

*23" German bisque lady, marked "136," in original outfit, $1,800.00. Courtesy McMasters Doll Auctions.*

### Boy
Glass eyes

| | | |
|---|---|---|
| 17" | $640.00 | $850.00 |
| 20" | $750.00 | $1,000.00 |
| 23" | $1,125.00 | $1,500.00 |

Painted eyes

| | | |
|---|---|---|
| 17" | $525.00 | $700.00 |
| 20" | $640.00 | $850.00 |
| 23" | $750.00 | $1,000.00 |

### Child, closed mouth
Glass eyes

| | | |
|---|---|---|
| 6" | $110.00 | $145.00 |
| 10" | $170.00 | $225.00 |
| 16" | $400.00 | $525.00 |
| 21" | $715.00 | $950.00 |
| 24" | $1,125.00 | $1,500.00 |

Painted eyes

| | | |
|---|---|---|
| 10" | $95.00 | $125.00 |
| 15" | $265.00 | $350.00 |
| 21" | $395.00 | $525.00 |
| 24" | $600.00 | $800.00 |
| 26" | $1,000.00 | |

### Decorated shoulder plate, fancy hairdo
Glass eyes

| | | |
|---|---|---|
| 20" | $2,075.00 | $2,750.00+ |

Painted eyes

| | | |
|---|---|---|
| 20" | $1,125.00 | $1,500.00 |

### Small unmarked doll, open mouth
Head of good quality bisque, glass eyes, on five-piece papier mache or composition body, good condition, appropriately dressed.

| | | |
|---|---|---|
| 6" | $140.00 | $185.00 |
| 9" | $190.00 | $250.00 |
| 12" | $285.00 | $375.00 |

Jointed body

| | | |
|---|---|---|
| 6" | $170.00 | $225.00 |
| 9" | $285.00 | $375.00 |
| 12" | $375.00 | $500.00 |

*18" German tinted bisque lady, antique dress, $750.00. Courtesy McMasters Doll Auctions.*

Poorly painted

| | | |
|---|---|---|
| 6" | $65.00 | $85.00 |
| 9" | $95.00 | $125.00 |
| 12" | $135.00 | $175.00 |

**Closed mouth**

Jointed body

| | | |
|---|---|---|
| 6" | $245.00 | $325.00 |
| 9" | $340.00 | $450.00 |
| 12" | $470.00 | $625.00 |

Five-piece body

| | | |
|---|---|---|
| 6" | $170.00 | $225.00 |
| 9" | $245.00 | $325.00 |
| 12" | $300.00 | $400.00 |

## Bisque, Japanese

**Ca. 1915 – 1926+.** Various Japanese firms such as Morimura and Yamato made dolls for export when supplies were cut off from Germany during World War I. Some were marked Nippon or J.W. Quality varies greatly.

*Marks:*

*20" Nippon #70018 with red wig, composition body, $525.00. Courtesy Angie Gonzales.*

**Baby, Character Face**

Good to excellent quality bisque, well painted, nice body, and appropriately dressed

| | | |
|---|---|---|
| 10" | $135.00 | $175.00 |
| 12" | $175.00 | $235.00 |
| 15" | $225.00 | $300.00 |
| 21" | $435.00 | $575.00 |
| 24" | $600.00 | $800.00 |

Poor quality bisque

| | | |
|---|---|---|
| 12" | $95.00 | $125.00 |
| 16" | $135.00 | $175.00 |
| 20" | $200.00 | $265.00 |
| 25" | $340.00 | $450.00 |

*12" bisque Oriental baby, marked "FY, N/1," $425.00. Courtesy McMasters Doll Auctions.*

### Hilda-type
Excellent quality, glass eyes, open mouth with two upper teeth

| | | |
|---|---|---|
| 15" | $565.00 | $750.00 |
| 18" | $675.00 | $900.00 |

Closed mouth

| | | |
|---|---|---|
| 14" | $565.00 | $750.00 |

Medium quality

| | | |
|---|---|---|
| 15" | $360.00 | $475.00 |
| 18" | $525.00 | $700.00 |

### Child, Character Face
Good to excellent quality bisque, good condition, and appropriately dressed.

| | | |
|---|---|---|
| 14" | $190.00 | $250.00 |
| 17" | $243.00 | $325.00 |
| 22" | $375.00 | $500.00 |

Poor quality bisque

| | | |
|---|---|---|
| 15" | $95.00 | $125.00 |
| 19" | $170.00 | $225.00 |
| 23" | $245.00 | $325.00 |

### Mold #600, marked "Fy"

| | | |
|---|---|---|
| 14" | $265.00 | $350.00 |
| 17" | $375.00 | $500.00 |

*21" bisque with sleep eyes, pre-World War II, $975.00; small 5" all bisque baby, pre-World War I, $225.00. Courtesy Amanda Hash.*

*15" Morimura bisque with composition bent limb body, $300.00. Courtesy Angie Gonzales.*

# Black or Brown

Black or brown dolls can have fired-in color or be painted bisque, composition, cloth, or papier mache. The color can be from very black to a light tan. They can have typical open mouth dolly faces or ethnic features. The quality of this group of dolls varies greatly and the prices are based on the quality of dolls in good condition, appropriately dressed.

The first price indicates dolls in good condition, but with flaws, perhaps nude; the second price indicates dolls in excellent condition with original clothes or appropriately dressed.

## ALL BISQUE

Glass eyes, head molded to torso
| | | |
|---|---|---|
| 4 – 5" | $200.00 | $385.00+ |

Glass eyes, swivel neck
| | | |
|---|---|---|
| 5 – 6" | $300.00 | $500.00+ |

Painted eyes, head molded to torso
| | | |
|---|---|---|
| 5" | $125.00 | $245.00 |

Painted eyes, swivel head
| | | |
|---|---|---|
| 5" | $250.00 | $500.00 |

French-type
| | | |
|---|---|---|
| 4" | $300.00 | $500.00 |

All bisque, marked by known maker such as JDK, S&H
| | | |
|---|---|---|
| 6 – 7" | $975.00 | $1,300.00+ |

### Frozen Charlie/Charlotte
| | | |
|---|---|---|
| 3" | $100.00 | $135.00 |
| 6" | $190.00 | $250.00 |
| 8 – 9" | $265.00 | $350.00 |

Jointed at shoulder
| | | |
|---|---|---|
| 3" | $150.00 | $200.00 |
| 6" | $265.00 | $350.00 |

## BISQUE

### Bahr & Proschild, open mouth, mold #277
| | | |
|---|---|---|
| 12" | $525.00 | $700.00 |
| 16" | $1,250.00 | $1,650.00 |

### Belton-type, closed mouth
| | | |
|---|---|---|
| 12" | $1.350.00 | $1,800.00 |
| 15" | $2,025.00 | $2,700.00 |

## BISQUE, FRENCH

### Bru (circle dot or Brevette)
| | | |
|---|---|---|
| 17" | $19,875.00 | $26,500.00+ |
| 19" | $22,500.00 | $30,000.00+ |

### Bru-Jne
| | | |
|---|---|---|
| 19" | $19,500.00 | $26,000.00+ |
| 23" | $26,250.00 | $35,000.00+ |

### E.D., open mouth
| | | |
|---|---|---|
| 16" | $1,725.00 | $2,300.00 |
| 22" | $1,950.00 | $2,600.00 |

### Fashion type
Swivel neck, articulated body, original
| | | |
|---|---|---|
| 16" | $9,750.00 | $12,750.00 |

Shoulder head, original
| | | |
|---|---|---|
| 16" | $4,500.00 | $6,000.00 |

**F.G., open/closed mouth**
| | | |
|---|---|---|
| 17 – 18" | $2,850.00 | $3,800.00 |

**F.G., fashion**
Kid body, swivel neck
| | | |
|---|---|---|
| 14" | $1,800.00 | $2,400.00 |
| 17" | $,2800.00 | $3,800.00 |

**French, unmarked or marked DEP**
Closed mouth
| | | |
|---|---|---|
| 11 – 12" | $1,350.00 | $1,800.00+ |
| 15" | $2,250.00 | $3,000.00 |
| 20" | $3,150.00 | $4,200.00 |

Open mouth
| | | |
|---|---|---|
| 10" | $450.00 | $600.00 |
| 15" | $825.00 | $1,100.00 |
| 22" | $1,650.00 | $2,200.00 |

**Painted bisque**
Closed mouth
| | | |
|---|---|---|
| 15" | $735.00 | $975.00 |
| 20" | $800.00 | $1,200.00 |

Open mouth
| | | |
|---|---|---|
| 15" | $375.00 | $500.00 |
| 20" | $750.00 | $1,000.00 |

With ethnic features
| | | |
|---|---|---|
| 18" | $3,450.00 | $4,600.00+ |

**Jumeau**

**Tete Jumeau, closed mouth**
| | | |
|---|---|---|
| 15" | $3,525.00 | $4,700.00 |
| 18" | $3,825.00 | $5,100.00 |
| 23" | $4,575.00 | $6,100.00 |

**Tete Jumeau, open mouth**
| | | |
|---|---|---|
| 10" | $1,650.00 | $2,200.00 |
| 15" | $2,025.00 | $2,700.00 |
| 18" | $2,250.00 | $3,000.00 |
| 23" | $2,625.00 | $3,500.00 |

**E. J., closed mouth**
| | | |
|---|---|---|
| 15" | $5,400.00 | $7,200.00 |
| 17" | $6,225.00 | $8,300.00 |
| 19" | $6,525.00 | $8,700.00 |

**Character face, very rare**
| | |
|---|---|
| 20" | $90,000.00 |

*too few to give a complete range*

**Jumeau-type**
Closed mouth
| | | |
|---|---|---|
| 12" | $1,950.00 | $2,600.00 |
| 15" | $2,700.00 | $3,600.00 |
| 19" | $3,600.00 | $4,800.00 |

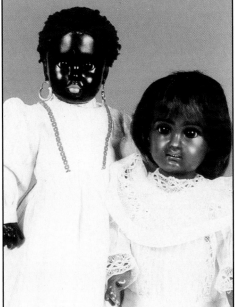

*Left: 18" black bisque Belton-type, $2,700.00; right: 12" black bisque Jumeau child, $2,000.00. Courtesy McMasters Doll Auctions.*

Open mouth

| | | |
|---|---|---|
| 12" | $825.00 | $1,100.00 |
| 15" | $1,575.00 | $2,100.00 |
| 19" | $2,400.00 | $3,200.00 |

**Paris Bebe**

| | | |
|---|---|---|
| 16" | $3,450.00 | $4,600.00 |
| 19" | $4,125.00 | $5,500.00 |

## S.F.B.J.

**Mold #226**

| | | |
|---|---|---|
| 16" | $2,175.00 | $2,900.00 |

**#235, open/closed mouth**

| | | |
|---|---|---|
| 15" | $1,950.00 | $2,600.00 |
| 17" | $2,212.50 | $2,950.00 |

## S & Q (Schuetzmeister & Quendt) Mold #251

| | | |
|---|---|---|
| 9" | $450.00 | $600.00 |
| 15" | $1,500.00 | $2,000.00 |

**#252, baby**

| | | |
|---|---|---|
| 20" | $1,250.00 | $1,650.00 |

**#252, child**

| | | |
|---|---|---|
| 20" | $1,350.00 | $1,800.00 |

## Jules Steiner

**A series, closed mouth**

| | | |
|---|---|---|
| 18" | $4,425.00 | $5,900.00 |
| 22" | $4,875.00 | $6,500.00 |

**A series, open mouth**

| | | |
|---|---|---|
| 13" | $3,225.00 | $4,300.00 |
| 16" | $3,600.00 | $4,800.00 |
| 19" | $4,050.00 | $5,400.00 |

**C series**

| | | |
|---|---|---|
| 18" | $4,000.00 | $6,000.00 |
| 21" | $4,650.00 | $6,200.00 |

**Unis**

**Mold # 301, or 60, open mouth**

| | | |
|---|---|---|
| 14" | $340.00 | $450.00 |
| 17" | $600.00 | $800.00 |

## Bisque, German

**Unmarked**

Closed mouth

| | | |
|---|---|---|
| 10 – 11" | $225.00 | $300.00 |
| 14" | $300.00 | $400.00 |
| 17" | $395.00 | $525.00 |
| 21" | $600.00 | $800.00 |

Open mouth

| | | |
|---|---|---|
| 10" | $375.00 | $500.00 |
| 13" | $490.00 | $650.00 |
| 15" | $640.00 | $850.00 |

**Painted Bisque**

Closed mouth

| | | |
|---|---|---|
| 16" | $265.00 | $350.00 |
| 19" | $375.00 | $500.00 |

*14" early primitive black cloth doll with oil painted face, unmarked, $1,800.00. Courtesy Sherryl Shirran.*

Open mouth

| | | |
|---|---|---|
| 14" | $225.00 | $300.00 |
| 18" | $375.00 | $500.00 |

**Ethnic features**

| | | |
|---|---|---|
| 15" | $2,250.00 | $3,000.00 |
| 18" | $2,850.00 | $3,800.00 |

**Marked Bye-Lo**

| | | |
|---|---|---|
| 16" | $2,250.00 | $3,000.00 |

**Cameo Doll Company**

**Kewpie (Hottentot) bisque**

| | |
|---|---|
| 4" | $400.00 |
| 5" | $565.00 |
| 9" | $985.00 |

**Kewpie, composition**

| | |
|---|---|
| 12" | $400.00 |
| 15" | $725.00 |

**Kewpie, papier mache**

| | |
|---|---|
| 8" | $265.00 |

**Scootles, composition, original outfit**

| | |
|---|---|
| 13" | $750.00 |

*7" black German bisque, $180.00. Courtesy Mc Masters Doll Auctions.*

**Heinrick, Handwerck**
Open mouth

| | | |
|---|---|---|
| 18" | $1,200.00 | $1,600.00 |
| 22" | $1,425.00 | $1,900.00 |
| 29" | $1,950.00 | $2,600.00 |

**Gebruder Heubach, Sunburst mark**
Boy, eyes to side, open/closed mouth

| | | |
|---|---|---|
| 12" | $1,875.00 | $2,500.00 |

**Mold #7657, 7658, 7668, 7671**

| | | |
|---|---|---|
| 9" | $950.00 | $1,250.00 |
| 13" | $1,275.00 | $1,700.00 |

**Mold # 7661, 7686**

| | | |
|---|---|---|
| 10" | $900.00 | $1,200.00 |
| 14" | $1,950.00 | $2,600.00 |
| 17" | $2,850.00 | $3,800.00 |

**Heubach, Ernst (Koppelsdorf)**
**Mold # 320, 339, 350**

| | | |
|---|---|---|
| 10" | $325.00 | $425.00 |
| 13" | $400.00 | $535.00 |
| 18" | $525.00 | $700.00 |

**#399, Allow more for toddler**

| | | |
|---|---|---|
| 10" | $300.00 | $400.00 |
| 14" | $415.00 | $550.00 |
| 17" | $525.00 | $700.00 |

**#414**

| | | |
|---|---|---|
| 9" | $340.00 | $450.00 |
| 14" | $525.00 | $700.00 |
| 17" | $715.00 | $950.00 |

**#418 (grin)**

| | | |
|---|---|---|
| 9" | $510.00 | $675.00 |
| 14" | $525.00 | $700.00 |

**#444, 451**

| | | |
|---|---|---|
| 9" | $300.00 | $400.00 |
| 14" | $525.00 | $700.00 |

**#452, brown**

| | | |
|---|---|---|
| 7½" | $285.00 | $375.00 |
| 10" | $360.00 | $475.00 |
| 15" | $510.00 | $675.00 |

**#458**

| | | |
|---|---|---|
| 10" | $350.00 | $465.00 |
| 15" | $525.00 | $700.00 |

**#463**

| | | |
|---|---|---|
| 12" | $450.00 | $600.00 |
| 16" | $715.00 | $950.00 |

**#1900**

| | | |
|---|---|---|
| 14" | $375.00 | $500.00 |
| 17" | $450.00 | $600.00 |

## Black or Brown (cont.)

**Kammer & Reinhardt (K*R)**
**Child, no mold number**

| | | |
|---|---|---|
| 7½" | $340.00 | $450.00 |
| 14" | $515.00 | $675.00 |
| 17" | $660.00 | $875.00 |

**Mold #100**

| | | |
|---|---|---|
| 10" | $525.00 | $700.00 |
| 14" | $825.00 | $1,100.00 |
| 17" | $1,200.00 | $1,600.00 |

**#101, painted eyes**

| | | |
|---|---|---|
| 15" | $3,300.00 *at auction | |

Glass eyes

| | | |
|---|---|---|
| 17" | $3,700.00 | $4,925.00 |

**#114**

| | | |
|---|---|---|
| 13" | $3,150.00 | $4,200.00 |

**#116, 116a**

| | | |
|---|---|---|
| 15" | $2,250.00 | $3,000.00 |
| 19" | $2,800.00 | $3,725.00 |

**#126, baby body**

| | | |
|---|---|---|
| 12" | $565.00 | $750.00 |
| 18" | $845.00 | $1,125.00 |

Toddler

| | | |
|---|---|---|
| 18" | $1,200.00 | $1,600.00 |

**Kestner, J.D.**
**Child, no mold number**
Closed mouth

| | | |
|---|---|---|
| 14" | $475.00 | $625.00 |
| 17" | $715.00 | $950.00 |

Open mouth

| | | |
|---|---|---|
| 12" | $340.00 | $450.00 |
| 16" | $490.00 | $650.00 |

**Five-piece body**

| | | |
|---|---|---|
| 9" | $215.00 | $285.00 |
| 12" | $265.00 | $350.00 |

**Hilda, Mold #245**

| | | |
|---|---|---|
| 14" | $4,125.00 | $5,500.00 |

**Konig & Wernicke (KW/G)**

| | | |
|---|---|---|
| 18" | $565.00 | $750.00 |

Ethnic features

| | | |
|---|---|---|
| 17" | $750.00 | $1,000.00 |

**Kuhnlenz, Gebruder**
Closed mouth

| | | |
|---|---|---|
| 15" | $675.00 | $900.00 |
| 18" | $1,350.00 | $1,800.00 |

Open mouth, Mold #34.14, 34.16, 34.24, etc.

| | | |
|---|---|---|
| 12" | $415.00 | $550.00 |
| 16" | $490.00 | $650.00 |

Ethnic features
| | | |
|---|---|---|
| 16" | $3,000.00 | $4,000.00 |

**Marseille, Armand**
**Mold #341, 351**
| | | |
|---|---|---|
| 10" | $275.00 | $365.00 |
| 13" | $425.00 | $565.00 |
| 16" | $545.00 | $725.00 |
| 20" | $825.00 | $1,100.00 |

**#390, 390n**
| | | |
|---|---|---|
| 16" | $415.00 | $550.00 |
| 19" | $585.00 | $775.00 |
| 23" | $675.00 | $895.00 |
| 28" | $825.00 | $1,100.00 |

**#451, 458 (Indians)**
| | | |
|---|---|---|
| 9" | $265.00 | $350.00 |
| 12" | $375.00 | $500.00 |

**#970, 971, 992, 995 (Baby or Toddler)**
| | | |
|---|---|---|
| 9" | $200.00 | $265.00 |
| 14" | $415.00 | $550.00 |
| 18" | $660.00 | $875.00 |

**#1894, 1897, 1912, 1914**
| | | |
|---|---|---|
| 12" | $245.00 | $325.00 |
| 14" | $415.00 | $550.00 |

**Recknagel**
**Marked R.A., #138**
| | | |
|---|---|---|
| 16" | $545.00 | $725.00 |
| 22" | $1,075.00 | $1,430.00 |

**Schoenau & Hoffmeister (S PB H)**
**Hanna**
| | | |
|---|---|---|
| 8" | $285.00 | $375.00 |
| 10 – 12" | $415.00 | $550.00 |
| 15" | $525.00 | $700.00 |
| 18" | $640.00 | $850.00 |

**#1909**
| | | |
|---|---|---|
| 16" | $400.00 | $525.00 |
| 19" | $525.00 | $700.00 |

**SIMON & HALBIG**
**Mold #639**
| | | |
|---|---|---|
| 14" | $5,100.00 | $6,800.00 |
| 18" | $7,500.00 | $10,000.00 |

**#739, open mouth**
| | | |
|---|---|---|
| 16" | $1,650.00 | $2,175.00 |

Closed mouth
| | | |
|---|---|---|
| 17" | $1,950.00 | $2,600.00 |
| 22" | $2,775.00 | $3,700.00 |

**#939, closed mouth**
| | | |
|---|---|---|
| 18" | $2,475.00 | $3,300.00 |
| 21" | $3,375.00 | $4,500.00 |

Open mouth

| | | |
|---|---|---|
| 17" | $1,050.00 | $1,400.00 |
| 21" | $1,575.00 | $2,100.00 |

**#949, closed mouth**

| | | |
|---|---|---|
| 18" | $2,550.00 | $3,400.00 |
| 21" | $3,000.00 | $3,950.00 |

Open mouth

| | | |
|---|---|---|
| 18" | $1,275.00 | $1,700.00 |
| 21" | $1,500.00 | $2,000.00 |

Kid body

| | | |
|---|---|---|
| 18" | $975.00 | $1,300.00 |
| 21" | $1,325.00 | $1,750.00 |

**#969, open mouth, fat cheeks**

| | | |
|---|---|---|
| 18" | $1,425.00 | $1,900.00 |

**#1009, 1039, 1079, open mouth**

| | | |
|---|---|---|
| 12" | $900.00 | $1,200.00 |
| 16" | $1,200.00 | $1,600.00 |
| 19" | $1,425.00 | $1,900.00 |

**Pull string sleep eyes**

| | | |
|---|---|---|
| 19" | $1,725.00 | $2,300.00 |

**#1248, open mouth**

| | | |
|---|---|---|
| 15" | $1,125.00 | $1,500.00 |
| 18" | $1,350.00 | $1,800.00 |
| 16" | $4,100.00 * at auction | |

**#1302, closed mouth**

Glass eyes, black character face

| | | |
|---|---|---|
| 18" | $5,250.00 | $7,000.00 |

Indian, sad expression, brown face

| | | |
|---|---|---|
| 18" | $5,500.00 | $7,400.00 |

**#1303, Indian, thin face, man or woman**

| | | |
|---|---|---|
| 16" | $4,574.00 | $6,100.00 |
| 21" | $6,000.00 | $8,000.00 |

**#1339, 1358, 1368**

| | | |
|---|---|---|
| 16" | $4,350.00 | $5,800.00 |
| 20" | $5,700.00 | $7,600.00 |

*22" black bisque Simon & Halbig child, marked "739," $3,400.00. Courtesy McMasters Doll Auctions.*

## CELLULOID

The first price indicates dolls in good condition, but with flaws, perhaps nude; the second price indicates dolls in excellent condition with original clothes or appropriately dressed.

**All celluloid**

| | | |
|---|---|---|
| 10" | $150.00 | $200.00 |
| 15" | $265.00 | $350.00 |
| 18" | $400.00 | $600.00 |

**Celluloid shoulder head, kid body, add more for glass eyes**

| | | |
|---|---|---|
| 17" | $265.00 | $350.00 |
| 21" | $340.00 | $450.00 |

**French type, marked SNF**

| | | |
|---|---|---|
| 14" | $265.00 | $350.00 |
| 18" | $400.00 | $600.00 |

**Parsons Jackson baby (Biskoline)**

| | | |
|---|---|---|
| 13" | $340.00 | $450.00 |

Toddler

| | | |
|---|---|---|
| 14" | $435.00 | $575.00 |

## CLOTH

The first price indicates dolls in good condition, but with flaws, perhaps nude; the second price indicates dolls in excellent condition with original clothes or appropriately dressed.

**Alabama**

See Cloth Dolls

**Bruckner**

See Cloth Dolls

**Chase, Martha**

| | | |
|---|---|---|
| 24" | $5,500.00 | $7,400.00 |
| 28" | $6,900.00 | $9,200.00 |

**Stockinette**

Oil painted features, excellent condition

| | | |
|---|---|---|
| 16" | $1,800.00 | $2,400.00 |
| 22" | $2,475.00 | $3,300.00 |

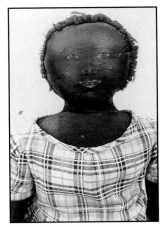

*18" black cloth Arnold Print Works child with printed on underwear, stockings, and shoes, $550.00. Courtesy Sherryl Shirran.*

*26" early black cloth Lettie Jane, unmarked, $4,000.00. Courtesy Sherryl Shirran.*

## COMPOSITION

The first price indicates dolls with heavy crazing, perhaps nude; the second price indicates dolls in excellent condition with original clothes or appropriately dressed.

**Effanbee**

### Baby Grumpy

Original clothing, very good condition

| | | |
|---|---|---|
| 10" | $75.00 | $265.00 |
| 16" | $115.00 | $450.00 |

# Black or Brown (cont.)

**Bubbles**
Original clothing, very good condition

| | | |
|---|---|---|
| 17" | $110.00 | $425.00+ |
| 22" | $165.00 | $650.00+ |

**Candy Kid,** with original shorts, robe, and gloves

| | | |
|---|---|---|
| 12" | $75.00 | $285.00 |

**Skippy,** with original outfit

| | | |
|---|---|---|
| 14" | $225.00 | $900.00 *at auction |

**Tony Sarg**
Mammy with baby

| | | |
|---|---|---|
| 18" | $145.00 | $575.00 |

## HARD PLASTIC
**Terri Lee**
Patty-Jo

| | | |
|---|---|---|
| 16" | $450.00 | $600.00+ |

## PAPIER MACHE
**Leo Moss, late 1880s, early 1900s**
Papier mache head and lower limbs, molded hair or wig, inset glass eyes, closed mouth, full lips, brown twill body filled with excelsior, may have tear on cheek.

| | | |
|---|---|---|
| 17" | $5,475.00 | $7,300.00 |
| 21" | $6,675.00 | $8,900.00 |

**Ethnic features**

| | | |
|---|---|---|
| 8" | $210.00 | $275.00 |
| 13" | $400.00 | $525.00 |
| 17" | $625.00 | $825.00 |

**Others**

| | | |
|---|---|---|
| 15" | $245.00 | $325.00 |
| 22" | $525.00 | $685.00 |

# Bonnet Head

**1860-1940+.** Dolls heads of various materials with painted, molded bonnets, hats, or headgear.

**All Bisque**
One-piece body and head, painted or glass eyes, Germany

| | | |
|---|---|---|
| 5" | $135.00 | $175.00 |
| 7" | $175.00 | $235.00 |
| 8" | $215.00 | $285.00 |
| 10" | $285.00 | $375.00 |

**Bisque Head, Glass Eyes**
Hat or bonnet, molded hair, five-piece papier mache, kid, or cloth body.

| | | |
|---|---|---|
| 7" | $140.00 | $185.00 |
| 9" | $225.00 | $300.00 |
| 12" | $325.00 | $425.00 |
| 15" | $490.00 | $650.00 |
| 18" | $750.00 | $1,000.00 |
| 21" | $940.00 | $1,250.00 |

8½" bisque Gerbruder Heubach, Baby Stuart, marked "7977," in original outfit, $800.00. Courtesy McMasters Doll Auctions.

13" bisque shoulder head, cloth body, bisque limbs, $425.00; 11½" bisque shoulder head, cloth body, bisque limbs, $375.00. Courtesy McMasters Doll Auctions.

**With bisque lower arms, fully jointed composition, kid or cloth body**

| | | |
|---|---|---|
| 7" | $150.00 | $200.00 |
| 9" | $265.00 | $350.00 |
| 12" | $365.00 | $485.00 |
| 15" | $545.00 | $725.00 |
| 21" | $900.00 | $1,200.00 |

**Molded shirt or top**

| | | |
|---|---|---|
| 15" | $625.00 | $825.00 |
| 21" | $1,015.00 | $1,350.00 |

**Stone bisque**

| | | |
|---|---|---|
| 8 – 9" | $125.00 | $165.00 |
| 12" | $170.00 | $225.00 |
| 15" | $290.00 | $385.00 |
| 18" | $400.00 | $600.00 |
| 21" | $640.00 | $850.00 |

**Googly: see that section**

Left: 13½" child shoulder head, painted blonde hair, poke bonnet, cloth body, china limbs, $500.00; right: 13" bisque shoulder head, cloth body, bisque limbs, $475.00. Courtesy McMasters Doll Auc-

51

# Bonnet Head (cont.)

## Japan

| | | |
|---|---|---|
| 8 – 9" | $55.00 | $75.00 |
| 12" | $95.00 | $125.00 |

## Borgfeldt, George

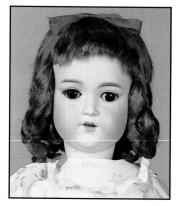

*24" George Borgfeldt bisque child, open mouth, sleep eyes, $375.00. Courtesy McMasters Doll Auctions.*

*24" bisque George Borgfeldt Pansy IV, $105.00. Courtesy McMasters Doll Auctions*

**Ca. 1881 – 1930+, New York.** Assembled and distributed dolls. Used dolls from many companies and employed designers such as Rose O'Neill, Grace Cory, Grace Storey Putnam, Joseph L. Kallus, Georgene Averill, and others. Konig & Wernicke made dolls for Borgfeldt.

*Marks: G. B.*

**Baby, 1910+**

Five-piece, bent leg baby body, open mouth

| | | |
|---|---|---|
| 10" | $225.00 | $300.00 |
| 14" | $350.00 | $475.00 |
| 17" | $425.00 | $575.00 |
| 22" | $550.00 | $725.00 |
| 27" | $675.00 | $900.00+ |

**Baby BoKaye**

Designed by Joseph Kallus, made by Alt, Beck & Gottschalck for Borgfeldt, molded hair, open mouth, glass eyes, cloth body, composition limbs

| | | |
|---|---|---|
| 15" | $1,725.00 | $2,300.00 |
| 18" | $2,025.00 | $2,700.00 |

**Babykins, 1931**

Made for G. Borgfeldt by Grace S. Putnam, round face, glass eyes, pursed lips

| | | |
|---|---|---|
| 14" | $735.00 | $980.00 |
| 17" | $900.00 | $1,190.00+ |

**Child mold #325, 327, 329, or marked G.B.**

1910 – 22, fully jointed composition body, open mouth, good condition, and appropriately dressed

| | | |
|---|---|---|
| 10" | $255.00 | $340.00 |
| 13" | $340.00 | $450.00 |
| 15" | $400.00 | $525.00 |
| 17" | $450.00 | $600.00 |
| 20" | $525.00 | $700.00 |
| 22" | $550.00 | $750.00 |
| 25" | $640.00 | $850.00 |

## Boudoir Dolls

**Ca. 1915 – 40.** Bed dolls, originally used as decorations to sit on the bed, usually French, with extra long arms and legs, heads of cloth, composition, ceramics, wax, and suede, with mohair or silk floss wigs, painted features, some with real lashes, cloth or composition bodies, dressed in fancy period costumes. Other manufacturers were Italian, British, or American.

*28" cloth French bed doll with beautiful coloring, mohair wig, painted features, lashes, elaborate costume, $475.00. Courtesy Sharon Kolibaba.*

*28" cloth, French boudoir doll with inset eyelashes, painted silk face, and original clothes, $325.00. Courtesy of Matrix.*

**Standard quality, dressed**

| | | |
|---|---|---|
| 16" | $95.00 | $125.00 |
| 28" | $125.00 | $165.00 |
| 32" | $170.00 | $225.00 |

**Excellent quality, with glass eyes**

| | | |
|---|---|---|
| 15" | $225.00 | $300.00 |
| 28" | $365.00 | $475.00 |
| 32" | $75.00 | $500.00 |

# Boudoir Dolls (cont.)

**Lenci**

| | | |
|---|---|---|
| 18" – 26" | $1,500.00 | $2,000.00+ |

**Smoker, Cloth**

| | | |
|---|---|---|
| 16" | $215.00 | $285.00 |
| 25" | $350.00 | $475.00 |

Composition

| | | |
|---|---|---|
| 25" | $185.00 | $245.00 |
| 28" | $285.00 | $375.00 |

**Black**

| | | |
|---|---|---|
| | $450.00 | $600.00+ |

# Bru

**Bru Jne. & Cie., ca. 1867 – 99.** Paris and Montreuil-sous-Bous, France, factories, eventually succeeded by Societe Francaise de Fabrication de Bebe & Jouets (S.F.B.J.), 1899 – 1953. Bebe Bru with kid bodies are one of the most collectible dolls, highly sought after because of the fine quality of bisque, delicate coloring, and fine workmanship.

Identifying characteristics: Brus are made of pressed bisque and have a metal spring stringing mechanism in the neck. Add more for original clothes and rare body styles.

*Mark:*

**Bebe**

*19" bisque, Bru Brevete Bebe, paperweight eyes with shaded lids, kid body with bisque lower arms, $18,000.00+. Courtesy of Matrix.*

BRU Jⁿⁱet CⁱNº1

DEPOSE

BÉBÉ BRU
Nº 1

BRU      E
6

**Brevete, ca. 1879 – 1883**

Bisque swivel head, shoulder plate, mohair or human hair wig, cork pate, paperweight eyes, multi-stroke eyebrows, closed mouth with space between lips, full cheeks, pierced ears, kid or wooden articulated bodies. Head marked with size number only; kid body may have paper Bebe Brevete label, good condition, nicely dressed.

First price is for dolls in good condition, but with some flaws; second price is for dolls in excellent condition, appropriately dressed, add more for original clothes and marked shoes.

| | | |
|---|---|---|
| 13" | $9,375.00 | $12,500.00 |
| 18" | $13,000.00 | $17,250.00 |

## Bru Jne, 1879 – 1880

Bisque swivel head marked Bru Jne, with size number on head, kid over wood body marked with rectangular paper label, deep shoulder molded breast plate, mohair or human hair wig, cork pate, paperweight eyes, multi-stroke eyebrows, open/closed mouth with painted/molded teeth, pierced ears, bisque lower arms, good condition, nicely dressed. Add more for original clothes and marked shoes.

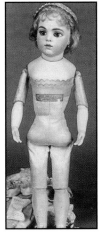

*22" Bru Jne, $19,000.00. Courtesy McMasters Doll Auctions.*

| | | |
|---|---|---|
| 12" | $8,750.00 | $11,500.00 |
| 14" | $10,250.00 | $13,500.00 |
| 17" | $12,000.00 | $16,000.00 |
| 20" | $14,250.00 | $19,000.00 |
| 23" | $16,250.00 | $21,500.00 |
| 27" | $19,250.00 | $25,500.00 |

## Bru Jne R, 1892+

Bisque swivel head marked Bru. JneR, with size number on head, articulated wood and composition body stamped in red, "Bebe Bru," and size number, mohair or human hair wig, cork pate, paperweight eyes, multi-stroke eyebrows, open mouth with four or six upper teeth or closed mouth, pierced ears, good condition, nicely dressed. Add more for original clothes.

Closed mouth

| | | |
|---|---|---|
| 12" | $1,850.00 | $2,450.00 |
| 14" | $2,200.00 | $2,900.00 |
| 16" | $2,500.00 | $3,250.00 |
| 19" | $2,900.00 | $3,850.00 |
| 23" | $3,500.00 | $4,650.00 |

Open mouth

| | | |
|---|---|---|
| 12" | $1,000.00 | $1,350.00 |
| 14" | $1,100.00 | $1,500.00 |
| 16" | $1,600.00 | $2,100.00 |
| 20" | $2,250.00 | $3,000.00 |

## Circle Dot Bebe, 1879 – 1884+

Bisque swivel head marked dot within a circle or half-circle, deep shoulder molded breast plate, mohair or human hair wig, cork pate, paperweight eyes, multi-stroke eyebrows, open/closed mouth with painted/molded teeth, pierced ears, gusseted kid body, bisque lower arms, good condition, nicely dressed. Add more for original clothes.

*17" bisque Bru Jne on jointed wooden body, socket head, paperweight eyes, open/closed mouth, cork pate, human hair wig, $14,000.00. Courtesy McMasters Doll Auctions.*

*30" bisque Bru Jne Bebe with paperweight eyes, shaded lids, kid with bisque lower arms, and wooden lower legs, $28,000.00+. Courtesy Matrix.*

| | | |
|---|---|---|
| 13" | $9,000.00 | $12,000.00 |
| 15" | $10,350.00 | $13,800.00 |
| 19" | $13,125.00 | $17,500.00 |
| 24" | $17,250.00 | $23,000.00 |
| 27" | $18,750.00 | $25,000.00 |
| 30" | $21,000.00 | $28,000.00 |

### Fashion-type (poupee), 1867 – 1877+

All bisque swivel heads, shoulder plate, kid body, painted or glass eyes, pierced ears, cork pate, mohair wig. Add more for original clothes.

| | | |
|---|---|---|
| 14" | $1,875.00 | $2,500.00 |
| 16" | $2,175.00 | $2,900.00 |

### Fashion-type, Smiler (poupee), 1872+

Pressed bisque swivel head, shoulder plate, articulated wood, wood and kid or kid gusseted lady body, marked "A" through "M," 11" to 28," cork pate, mohair or human hair wig, glass paperweight eyes, pierced ears, closed smiling mouth, nicely dressed. Some incised "Depose" on forehead. Add more for original clothes.

| | | |
|---|---|---|
| 14" | $2,300.00 | $3,050.00+ |
| 16" | $2,625.00 | $3,500.00 |
| 20" | $3,300.00 | $4,375.00 |

Kid body, bisque lower arms

| | | |
|---|---|---|
| 20" | $3,750.00 | $5000.00 |

Wood arms, kid body

| | | |
|---|---|---|
| 18" | $3,400.00 | $4,500.00+ |

Wood articulated body

| | | |
|---|---|---|
| 18" | $4,125.00 | $5,500.00+ |

## Variants

### Bebe Teteur (nursing), 1879

Open mouth to insert bottle, usually with screw-type key on back of head to allow the doll to drink.

| | |
|---|---|
| 14" | $7,000.00 |
| 17" | $9,200.00 |
| 20" | $9,600.00 |

### Bebe Gourmand (eater), 1880

Open mouth with tongue to take food, which fell into throat and out through bottom of feet, and had shoes specially designed with hinged soles to take out food.

*\*Not enough samples in database to qualify*

**Bebe Modele, 1880**
Carved wooden body
*Not enough samples in database to qualify*
**Bebe Automate** (breather, talker),1892+
With key or lever in torso, activates talking and breathing mechanism.
| | |
|---|---|
| 19" | $15,000.00 |
| 24" | $17,000.00 |

**Bebe Marchant (walker), 1892**
Clockwork walking mechanism which allows head to move and talk, has articulated body with key in torso.
| | |
|---|---|
| 17" | $6,800.00 |
| 21" | $7,400.00 |
| 25" | $8,200.00 |

**Bebe Baiser (kiss thrower), 1892**
A simple pull string mechanism allows doll's arm to raise to appear to throw kisses.
| | |
|---|---|
| 11" | $4,100.00 *at auction |

**Accessories**
Bru Shoes (marked), $500.00 – $800.00+

*Early Brevete Bru Teteur, paperweight eyes, shaded lids, open mouth for nursing apparatus, mechanism in head to retrieve liquid, early kid body with bisque arms, $9,500.00+. Courtesy Matrix.*

## Bye-Lo

**1922 – 1952.** Designed by Grace Storey Putnam to represent a three-day-old baby, manufactured by various firms, such as Kestner, Alt, Beck & Gottschalck, Hertel & Schwab, and others; body made by K&K, a subsidiary of George Borgfeldt, NY, the sole licensee. Composition dolls were made by Cameo Doll Company, and came in 10", 12", 14", and 16½" sizes.

First price is for dolls in good condition with some flaws; second price is for dolls in excellent condition, nicely dressed, add more for tagged original clothes, labels, and pin-back button.

*Marks:*

BYE - LO - BABY
PAT. APPL'D FOR
COPY
    BY GRACE
        STOREY
            PUTNAM

© 1923 by
Grace S. Putnam
MADE IN GERMANY
7372/45

BYE-LO
BABY

**Bisque Head**
Bisque head, molded painted hair, sleeping blue eyes, closed mouth, flange neck, cloth baby-shaped "frog" body, some stamped "Bye-Lo Baby"; celluloid hands.

| | | |
|---|---|---|
| 9" | $325.00 | $450.00 |
| 11" | $400.00 | $525.00 |
| 14" | $500.00 | $675.00 |
| 16" | $600.00 | $775.00 |
| 18" | $650.00 | $875.00 |
| 20" | $725.00 | $1,000.00 |

*10" bisque Grace S. Putnam Bye Lo Baby dressed in old white baby dress, $250.00. Courtesy McMasters Doll Auctions.*

### Composition Head

Painted, molded hair, sleeping or painted eyes, closed mouth, cloth body.

First price indicates dolls with crazing, flaws; second price is for dolls in excellent condition, with good color, and original clothes or appropriately dressed.

| | | |
|---|---|---|
| 10" | $85.00 | $325.00 |
| 12" | $95.00 | $375.00 |
| 14" | $115.00 | $450.00 |
| 16" | $150.00 | $575.00 |

### All Bisque

All bisque versions made by J.D. Kestner were 4" to 8" and marked G.S. Putnam on back with dark green sticker on chest that read "Bye-Lo Baby."

| | | |
|---|---|---|
| 4" | $350.00 | $475.00 |
| 6" | $500.00 | $675.00 |
| 8" | $700.00 | $950.00 |

\* original paper label, with original gown, bed, $800.00 at auction

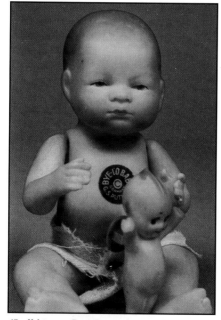

*6" all bisque Bye-Lo with round green sticker on tummy, $500.00; with 2" bisque button hole Kewpie, $175.00. Courtesy McMasters Doll Auctions.*

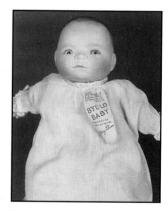

*10" bisque Grace S. Putnam Bye Lo Baby in tagged dress, $500.00. Courtesy McMasters Doll Auctions.*

### Celluloid

All celluloid

| | | |
|---|---|---|
| 4" | $75.00 | $150.00 |

Celluloid head, cloth body

| | | |
|---|---|---|
| 12" | $175.00 | $350.00 |
| 15" | $245.00 | $465.00 |

## Variations

**Fly-Lo Baby, 1926 – 30+.** Ceramic, bisque, or composition head, glass or metal sleeping eyes, painted molded hair, flange type neck, cloth body. Marked "Copr. by//Grace S. Putnam." Cloth bodies with celluloid hands, satin wings in green, gold, or pink.

Bisque

| | | |
|---|---|---|
| 11" | $3,000.00 | $4,000.00 |
| 13" | $3,750.00 | $5,000.00 |

Composition

| | | |
|---|---|---|
| 14" | $300.00 | $900.00 |
| 16" | $400.00 | $1,200.00 |

**Vinyl, ca. 1950s,** head vinyl, cloth stuffed limbs, marked "Grace Storey Putnam" on head

| | | |
|---|---|---|
| 16" | $65.00** | $225.00 |

# Catterfelder Puppenfabrik

**1894 – 1930+, Catterfeld, Thuringia, Germany.** Made dolls using Kestner bisque head on composition bodies.

*Marks:*

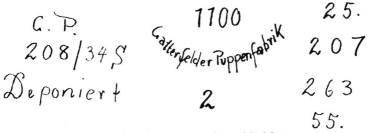

**Baby, 1909 and after,** wigged, or painted, molded hair, bent leg body, glass or painted eyes. Add more for toddler body.

**Mold #200** (similar to K*R #100), domed head, painted eyes, open/closed mouth, also black version.

**#201,** domed head, painted eyes, open/closed mouth.

**#207,** character head, painted eyes, closed mouth.

**#208,** character baby or toddler with domed head, or wigged, sleep eyes, open mouth, two teeth, movable tongue.

**#209,** character baby, movable tongue.

**#218,** character baby, domed head, sleep eyes, open mouth, movable tongue.

**#262,** character baby, sleep eyes, open mouth, movable tongue, only marked with mold number.

**#263,** character baby.

| | |
|---|---|
| 14" | $485.00 |
| 16" | $600.00 |
| 20" | $775.00 |
| 23" | $985.00 |
| 26" | $1,200.00 |

*Too few examples in database.*

# Catterfelder Puppenfabrik (cont.)

**Child, character face,** composition body, open or open/closed mouth.
#210, painted eyes, closed mouth.
#212, wide open/closed laughing mouth, painted teeth and eyes.
#215, #219, character face, wig, painted eyes.
#220, character doll, sleeping eyes, open/closed mouth with two molded teeth.
#264, character face, socket head, sleep eyes, open mouth. #270, character face, socket head, open mouth, sleep eyes. Molds 1100, 1200, and 1357 were used for ball jointed dolls.

| | | |
|---|---|---|
| **#210** | 14" | $5,000.00 *at auction |
| **#215** | 16" | $8,600.00 * |
| **#219** | 16" | $3,850.00 * |
| **#220** | 17" | $7,300.00 * |

*21" bisque, mold #1100, Catterfelder Puppenfabrik socket head child, open mouth, jointed composition body, $750.00. Courtesy McMasters Doll Auctions.*

## Celluloid

* *Too few examples in database*

**1869+.** Celluloid became more durable after 1905, and in 1910 better production methods were found. Dolls were made in England, France, Japan, Germany, Poland, and the U.S. When short hair became popular, the demand for celluloid hair ornaments decreased and companies produced more dolls.

**American manufacturers:** Averill, Bo Peep (H. J. Brown), Du Pont Viscoloid Co., Horsman, Irwin, Marks Bros., Parsons Jackson Co. (stork mark), Celluloid Novelty Co.

**English celluloid manufactures:** Wilson Doll Co. and Cascelloid Ltd. (Palitoy)

**French celluloid manufacturers:** Peticolin (profile head of an eagle mark), Widow Chalory, Convert, Cie, Parisienne de Cellulosine, Neuman & Marx (Dragon), Societe Industrielle de Celluloid (S.I.C.), Sicoine, Societe Nobel Francaise (S N F in diamond)

*18" celluloid, all jointed with painted features, open/closed mouth, only size mark, $275.00.*

**German celluloid manufacturers:** Bahr & Proschild, Buschow & Beck (helmet), Minerva, Catterfelder Puppenfabrik Co., Cuno & Otto Dressel, E. Maar & Sohn (3 M) Emasco, Kammer & Reinhardt, Kestner, Konig & Wernicke, Hagendorfer Celluloid Warenfabrik, Dr. Paul Hunaeus, Kohn & Wengenroth, Rheinsche Gummi and Celluloid Fabrik Co. (turtle mark), Max Rudolph, Bruno Schmidt, Franz Schmidt & Co., Schoberl & Becker (Mermaid) Celba, Karl Standfuss, Albert Wacker

**Japanese celluloid manufacturers:** Various firms, may be marked Japan

**Polish celluloid manufacturers:** Zast (A.S.K. in triangle)

ALL CELLULOID

First price is for dolls with some flaws or nude; second price is for dolls in perfect condition.

**Baby**

Painted eyes

| | | |
|---|---|---|
| 8" | $20.00 | $75.00 |
| 12" | $35.00 | $125.00 |
| 14" | $45.00 | $175.00 |
| 16" | $50.00 | $185.00 |
| 20" | $75.00 | $300.00 |
| 24" | $90.00 | $350.00 |

Glass eyes

| | | |
|---|---|---|
| 14" | $50.00 | $200.00 |
| 16" | $70.00 | $265.00 |
| 20" | $60.00 | $425.00 |
| 24" | $125.00 | $485.00 |

**Child, all celluloid, jointed neck, shoulders, hips**

Painted eyes

| | | |
|---|---|---|
| 6" | $12.00 | $45.00 |
| 8" | $20.00 | $70.00 |
| 12" | $35.00 | $125.00 |
| 15" | $50.00 | $200.00 |
| 18" | $100.00 | $375.00 |

Jointed neck and shoulders only

| | | |
|---|---|---|
| 5" | $7.50 | $25.00 |
| 7" | $12.00 | $45.00 |
| 10" | $25.00 | $85.00 |

Glass eyes

| | | |
|---|---|---|
| 13" | $45.00 | $165.00 |
| 15" | $60.00 | $225.00 |
| 18" | $110.00 | $425.00 |

Marked France

| | | |
|---|---|---|
| 8" | $40.00 | $150.00 |
| 10" | $50.00 | $200.00 |
| 16" | $75.00 | $300.00 |
| 19" | $140.00 | $550.00 |

Molded on clothes, all celluloid, jointed shoulders only

| | | |
|---|---|---|
| 4" | $15.00 | $55.00 |
| 6" | $20.00 | $70.00 |
| 9" | $35.00 | $125.00 |

# Celluloid (cont.)

Immobile, all celluloid, no joints

| | | |
|---|---|---|
| 4" | $5.00 | $20.00 |
| 6" | $10.00 | $36.00 |

Black, all celluloid: See section on Black Dolls
Carnival dolls, all celluloid, may have feathers glued to body/head, some have top hats.

| | | |
|---|---|---|
| 8" | $10.00 | $40.00 |
| 12" | $20.00 | $80.00 |
| 17" | $45.00 | $175.00+ |

## CELLULOID

Shoulder head, painted eyes, 1900+, Germany, molded hair, or wigged, open or closed mouth, kid, kidaleen, or cloth bodies, may have arms of other materials.

| | | |
|---|---|---|
| 14" | $90.00 | $175.00 |
| 17" | $125.00 | $225.00 |
| 19" | $200.00 | $385.00 |

Shoulder head, glass eyes

| | | |
|---|---|---|
| 14" | $100.00 | $200.00 |
| 16" | $175.00 | $350.00 |
| 19" | $225.00 | $450.00 |
| 23" | $250.00 | $500.00 |

12½" celluloid Kammer & Reinhardt Marie, circa 1901, painted brown eyes, marked (turtle) "K*R701/30," $750.00. Courtesy Sherryl Shirran.

**Bye-Lo**

| | | |
|---|---|---|
| 4" | $45.00 | $165.00 |
| 6" | $100.00 | $200.00 |

**Celluloid/Plush,** early 1910, teddy bear body, can have half or full celluloid body with hood half head.

| | | |
|---|---|---|
| 12" | $325.00 | $650.00 |
| 14" | $400.00 | $785.00 |
| 17" | $475.00 | $925.00 |

**Hitler youth group**

| | | |
|---|---|---|
| 8" | $90.00 | $175.00 |

**Heubach Koppelsdorf, Mold 399 (brown or black). See that section.**

**Japan**

| | | |
|---|---|---|
| 4" | $7.50 | $15.00 |
| 8" | $10.00 | $35.00 |
| 10" | $12.00 | $45.00 |
| 12" | $20.00 | $75.00 |
| 16" | $40.00 | $175.00 |
| 19" | $90.00 | $350.00 |
| 22" | $115.00 | $425.00 |

**Jumeau,** marked on head, jointed body

| | | |
|---|---|---|
| 12" | $225.00 | $450.00 |
| 16" | $275.00 | $550.00 |

**Kammer & Reinhardt (K*R)**
   Mold #406, 700, child or baby
      14"    $250.00      $475.00
   Mold #701
      14"    $475.00      $950.00
   Mold #714, 715
      15"    $300.00      $685.00
   Mold #717
      15"    $250.00      $485.00
      22"    $350.00      $700.00
   Mold #728, 828
      16"    $250.00      $500.00
      20"    $350.00      $700.00
   Toddler
      15"    $325.00      $650.00
   All celluloid toddler body
      15"    $365.00      $725.00
   Mold #225, 255, 321, 406, 826, 828
   Baby
      12"    $95.00      $190.00
      14"    $185.00      $370.00
      17"    $250.00      $485.00
      20"    $300.00      $600.00
   Kathe Kruse child all original
      14"    $250.00      $475.00
      17"    $350.00      $675.00

*Front: 7" bisque Kestner toddler, mold 260, original outfit, $180.00. Back: 14" celluloid Parsons-Jackson baby, original outfit, $100.00. Courtesy McMasters Doll Auctions*

**Kewpie:** See that section.

**Konig & Wernicke (K&W)**
   Toddler
      15"    $165.00      $325.00
      19"    $250.00      $500.00
**Max and Moritz, each**
      7"    $150.00      $300.00
**Parson - Jackson**
   Baby
      12"    $100.00      $200.00
      14"    $150.00      $285.00
   Toddler
      15"    $200.00      $385.00
   Black
      14"    $250.00      $485.00

*21" German celluloid doll, $300.00. Courtesy McMasters Doll Auctions.*

**Century Doll Co., 1909 – 30, New York City.** Founded by Max Scheuer and sons. They used bisque heads on many later dolls. In about 1929 they merged with Domec to become the Doll Corporation of America.

*Marks:*

CENTURY DOLL C°.
Kestner Germany

CENTURY
DOLL CO.
N. Y.

## BISQUE
**Baby, ca. 1926,** bisque head, painted, molded hair, sleep eyes, open/closed mouth, cloth body, nicely dressed, good condition.
    17"    $750.00
  **Mold #275**
    14"    $950.00
**Child,** bisque socket head, glass eyes, open mouth, wig, ball jointed
    23"    $725.00

## COMPOSITION
**Chuckles, 1927 – 29,** composition shoulder head, arms, and legs, cloth body with crier, marked on back "Chuckles A Century Doll," open mouth, molded short hair, painted or sleep eyes, two upper teeth, dimples in cheeks. Came as a bent leg baby or toddler.
    16"    $75.00    $300.00

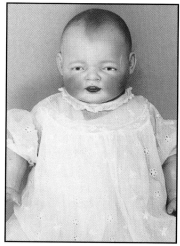

*13" bisque Century baby made by Kestner, circa 1925, marked "Century Doll Co.//Kestner Germany," $475.00. Courtesy Sherryl Shirran.*

*17" Century Baby made by Kestner, $750.00. Courtesy McMasters Doll Auctions.*

**Mama dolls, ca. 1920,** composition head, tin sleep eyes, cloth body with crier, composition swing legs and arms, nicely dressed, very good condition.

| | | |
|---|---|---|
| 16" | $65.00 | $245.00 |
| 23" | $120.00 | $465.00 |

## Chase

**Martha Chase, ca. 1889 – 1930+, Pawtucket, RI.** Heads were made from stockinet covered masks reproduced from bisque dolls, heavily painted features including thick lashes, closed mouth, sometimes open nostrils, painted textured hair, jointed shoulders, elbows, knees, and hips; later dolls were jointed only at shoulders and hips.

First price indicates dolls in good condition with some flaws; second price indicates dolls in excellent condition with original or appropriate clothes.

*Marks:*
**"Chase Stockinet Doll"** on left leg or under left arm. Paper label, if there, reads:

**PAWTUCKET, R.I**
**MADE IN U.S.A.**

**Baby**

| | | |
|---|---|---|
| 16" | $425.00 | $575.00 |
| 19" | $495.00 | $700.00 |
| 24" | $625.00 | $875.00 |

Hospital-type

| | | |
|---|---|---|
| 24" | $320.00 | $425.00 |
| 29" | $450.00 | $575.00 |

**Child**

Molded bobbed hair

| | | |
|---|---|---|
| 12" | $900.00 | $1,200.00 |
| 16" | $1,200.00 | $1,600.00 |
| 22" | $1,650.00 | $2,200.00 |

*Chase baby with weighted body, painted features, open nostrils, $600.00.*

Solid dome, painted hair

| | | |
|---|---|---|
| 15" | $365.00 | $485.00 |
| 18" | $475.00 | $625.00 |

Unusual hairdo, molded bun

| | |
|---|---|
| 15" | $1,200.00 *at auction |

**Characters**

*too few examples in database to give reliable range*

Alice in Wonderland

| | |
|---|---|
| 15" | $1,700.00 |

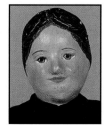

15" Martha Chase lady, $1,200.00. Courtesy McMasters Doll Auctions.

24" cloth Martha Chase baby dressed in old outfit, $475.00. Courtesy McMasters Doll Auctions.

Benjamin Franklin
15"    $6,875.00 *at auction
Frog Footman
15"    $1,900.00+
George Washington
26"    $4,500.00+
Mad Hatter
5"    $2,000.00
Tweedle-dee and Tweedle-dum
15"    $2,000.00+

**Later Dolls**

Baby

| | | |
|---|---|---|
| 14" | $150.00 | $200.00 |
| 15" | $190.00 | $250.00 |
| 19" | $300.00 | $400.00 |

Child

| | | |
|---|---|---|
| 15" | $215.00 | $285.00 |
| 20" | $300.00 | $400.00 |

19" Chase hospital child, $675.00. Courtesy McMasters Doll Auctions.

## China

**Ca. 1840+.** Most china shoulder-head dolls were made in Germany by many firms. Prior to 1880, most china heads were pressed into the mold; later ones poured. Pre-1880 china heads were sold separately. The purchaser then bought a commercial body or made one at home. Original commercial costumes are rare; most clothing was homemade. Early unusual features are glass eyes or eyes painted brown. After 1870, pierced ears and blonde hair were found. After 1880 china dolls, with shorter hair and shorter necks were popular. Common during this period were flat tops and low brows. The latter were made until the mid-1900s. Later innovations were china arms and legs with molded boots. Most heads are unmarked or marked with size or mold number only, usually on the back shoulder plate. Hairstyles help date the doll

*24" apple cheeked, flat top china doll with high brow center-part hairdo, cloth body, circa 1860, $425.00.*

First price indicates dolls in good condition with some flaws; second price indicates dolls in excellent condition with original or appropriate clothes.

**Child,** swivel neck, shoulder plate, may have china lower limbs.

| | | |
|---|---|---|
| 12" | $1,850.00 | $2,450.00 |

**Child or boy,** short black or blonde curly hairdo with exposed ears

| | | |
|---|---|---|
| 15" | $225.00 | $300.00 |
| 21" | $325.00 | $425.00 |

**French,** glass or painted eyes, open crown, cork pate, wig, kid body, china arms.

| | | |
|---|---|---|
| 16" | $2,700.00 | $3,600.00 |
| 19" | $3,200.00 | $4,275.00 |

**Japanese,** ca. 1910 – 20, marked or unmarked, black or blonde hair

| | | |
|---|---|---|
| 12" | $110.00 | $145.00 |
| 14" | $130.00 | $175.00 |

**Jenny Lind,** black hair pulled back into a bun or coronet

| | | |
|---|---|---|
| 17" | $1,315.00 | $1,750.00 |

**Kling,** marked with bell and number

| | | |
|---|---|---|
| 14" | $285.00 | $375.00 |
| 17" | $345.00 | $460.00 |
| 22" | $450.00 | $600.00 |

**Man, curls**

| | | |
|---|---|---|
| 16" | $1,165.00 | $1,550.00 |
| 20" | $1,450.00 | $1,950.00 |

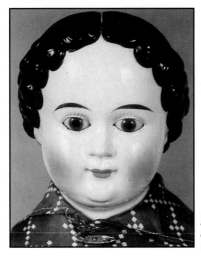

**Man or boy, glass eyes**

| | | |
|---|---|---|
| 15" | $1,850.00 | $2,475.00 |
| 17" | $2,100.00 | $2,800.00 |
| 21" | $2,625.00 | $3,500.00 |

**Man, or boy, side part, brown hair**

| | | |
|---|---|---|
| 14" | $1,500.00 | $2,000.00 |
| 17" | $1,850.00 | $2,450.00 |
| 21" | $2,250.00 | $3,000.00 |

**Pierced ears,** various common hairstyles

| | | |
|---|---|---|
| 13" | $335.00 | $450.00 |
| 17" | $450.00 | $600.00 |

*27" glass-eyed china shoulder head, cloth body, kid lower arms, $2,550.00. Courtesy McMasters Doll Auctions*

With elaborate hairstyle

| | | |
|---|---|---|
| 13" | $975.00 | $1,300.00 |
| 17" | $1,250.00 | $1,650.00+ |

**Queen Victoria,** young

| | | |
|---|---|---|
| 16" | $1,275.00 | $1,700.00 |
| 21" | $1,685.00 | $2,250.00 |
| 25" | $2,025.00 | $2,700.00 |

**Sophia Smith,** straight sausage curls that end in a ridge around head rather than curved to head shape.

| | | |
|---|---|---|
| 15" | $775.00 | $1,025.00 |
| 17" | $850.00 | $1,175.00 |
| 21" | $1,100.00 | $1,450.00+ |

**Spill curls,** with or without headband, lots of single curls across forehead, to ringlets in back, may or may not have head band.

| | | |
|---|---|---|
| 15" | $375.00 | $500.00 |
| 17" | $500.00 | $650.00 |
| 22" | $625.00 | $825.00 |
| 26" | $700.00 | $925.00 |

*11" china with solid dome and black spot on top is so-called Beidermeir, with hat and mohair wig removed to show black circle on solid dome, $600.00.*

**Swivel neck, flange type**

| | | |
|---|---|---|
| 9" | $1,400.00 | $1,875.00 |
| 12" | $1,875.00 | $2,500.00 |

## 1840s STYLES

China shoulder head with long neck, painted features, black or brown molded hair, may have exposed ears and pink complexion, with red-orange facial detail, may have bust modeling, cloth, leather, or wood body, nicely dressed, good condition.

**Bun or coronet, brown hair**

| | | |
|---|---|---|
| 17" | $2,400.00 | $3,200.00 |

**Early marked china (Nuremberg, Rudolstadt)**

| | | |
|---|---|---|
| 16" | $1,950.00 | $2,600.00+ |
| 18" | $2,250.00 | $3,000.00 |

**Brown hair, bun**

| | | |
|---|---|---|
| 16" | $2,800.00 | $3,750.00 |

**Boy, smiling, side part brown hair**

| | | |
|---|---|---|
| 21" | $3,450.00 | $4,600.00 |

**Child head** with windblown styled black hair, brushmarks around face, cloth body leather arms.

**Covered wagon,** center part, combed back to form sausage curls

| | | |
|---|---|---|
| 9" | $185.00 | $250.00 |
| 13" | $275.00 | $365.00 |
| 16" | $400.00 | $450.00 |
| 19" | $400.00 | $535.00 |
| 23" | $485.00 | $650.00 |
| 35" | $750.00 | $1,000.00+ |

**Wood Body**

| | | |
|---|---|---|
| 6" | $825.00 | $1,100.00 |
| 8" | $1,050.00 | $1,400.00 |
| 12" | $1,500.00 | $2,000.00 |
| 15" | $1,875.00 | $2,500.00 |
| 18" | $2,325.00 | $3,100.00+ |

*Left: 21" Covered Wagon china shoulder head, with pink tint, cloth body, china limbs, $500.00. Right: 22" Flat Top china shoulder head, cloth body, china limbs, $165.00. Courtesy McMasters Doll Auctions.*

**1850s STYLES**

China shoulder head, painted features, bald or black molded hair, may have pink complexion, cloth, leather, or wood body, china arms, china legs, nicely dressed, good condition.

**Alice in Wonderland,** snood, head band

| | | |
|---|---|---|
| 13" | $245.00 | $325.00 |
| 15" | $285.00 | $375.00 |
| 19" | $350.00 | $475.00 |

**Flange neck,** Motchmann style body

| | | |
|---|---|---|
| 10" | $1,125.00 | $1,500.00 |
| 13" | $1,600.00 | $2,100.00 |
| 15" | $1,750.00 | $2,350.00 |

**Bald head, glazed china with black spot** (formerly called Biedermier), human hair or mohair wig

| | | |
|---|---|---|
| 13" | $525.00 | $700.00 |
| 15" | $600.00 | $800.00 |
| 17" | $675.00 | $900.00 |

**With black spot, glass eyes**

| | | |
|---|---|---|
| 15" | $1,350.00 | $1,800.00 |
| 20" | $1,800.00 | $2,400.00 |

**Frozen Charlies or Charlottes, see that section**

# China (cont.)

**Glass eyes with painted black eyelashes,** various hair-dos

| | | |
|---|---|---|
| 14" | $2,000.00 | $2,650.00 |
| 18" | $2,550.00 | $3,400.00 |
| 23" | $3,275.00 | $4,350.00 |

## 1860s STYLES

China shoulder head, center part, smooth, black curls, painted features, seldom seen with brushmarks or pink-tones, all cloth bodies, or cloth with china arms and legs, may have leather arms. Decorated chinas with fancy hairstyles embellished with flowers, ornaments, snoods, bands, ribbons, may have earrings.

*11" china with solid dome and black spot on top is so-called Bei- dermeir, china forearms and feet, cloth body, original outfit, $600.00.*

**Flat top Civil War,** black hair, center part, curls on sides and back

| | | |
|---|---|---|
| 9" | $100.00 | $150.00 |
| 13" | $175.00 | $225.00 |
| 15" | $200.00 | $255.00 |
| 18" | $225.00 | $300.00 |
| 21" | $275.00 | $350.00 |
| 25" | $325.00 | $425.00 |
| 26" | $350.00 | $450.00 |
| 30" | $400.00 | $525.00 |
| 35" | $450.00 | $600.00 |

Swivel neck

| | | |
|---|---|---|
| 14" | $675.00 | $900.00 |
| 21" | $1,000.00 | $1,350.00 |

Molded necklace

| | | |
|---|---|---|
| 21" | $525.00 | $700.00+ |

**Highbrow,** similar to covered wagon, with high forehead, round face

| | | |
|---|---|---|
| 14" | $375.00 | $500.00 |
| 20" | $545.00 | $725.00 |
| 24" | $650.00 | $875.00+ |

**Grape Lady** (with cluster of grape leaves and blue grapes)

| | | |
|---|---|---|
| 15" | $975.00 | $1,300.00 |
| 22" | $1,275.00 | $1,700.00 |

**Mary Todd Lincoln** (black hair, gold snood, with gold luster bows at ears)

| | | |
|---|---|---|
| 16" | $500.00 | $650.00 |
| 20" | $600.00 | $800.00 |

Blonde with black snood

| | | |
|---|---|---|
| 18" | $1,275.00 | $1,700.00 |

**Morning Glory** (with flowers behind the ears)

| | | |
|---|---|---|
| 21" | $4,200.00 | $5,600.00 |

## 1870s STYLES

China shoulder head, poured, finely painted, well molded, black or other color hair, cloth or cloth and leather bodies, pink facial details instead or earlier red-orange.

**Adelina Patti,** hair pulled up and away, center part, brush stroked at temples, partly exposed ears, ringlets across back of head.

| | | |
|---|---|---|
| 15" | $210.00 | $275.00 |
| 19" | $350.00 | $475.00 |
| 24" | $395.00 | $525.00 |

**Bangs,** full cut across forehead, sometimes called **Highland Mary**

Black hair

| | | |
|---|---|---|
| 13" | $215.00 | $285.00 |
| 18" | $300.00 | $400.00 |
| 22" | $365.00 | $485.00 |

Blonde hair

| | | |
|---|---|---|
| 14" | $265.00 | $325.00 |
| 22" | $400.00 | $525.00 |
| 24" | $415.00 | $550.00 |

**Curly Top,** black overall curls, coming to points across forehead.

*12" china doll with cloth body, china lower legs with molded high heel shoes, ca. 1870, $300.00. Courtesy Karen Koch.*

### 1880s STYLES

Now may also have blonde as well as black hair, more curls, and overall curls, narrower shoulders, fatter cheeks, irises outlined with black paint, may have bangs. China legs have fat calves and molded boots.

**Dolly Madison,** black molded hair, two separate clusters of curls on forehead, molded ribbon and bow across top, ears partially exposed, painted blue eyes, irises and eyes outlined with black, black eyebrows

| | | |
|---|---|---|
| 13" | $225.00 | $325.00 |
| 17" | $335.00 | $445.00 |
| 20" | $400.00 | $525.00 |
| 23" | $450.00 | $600.00 |
| 27" | $525.00 | $700.00 |

### 1890s STYLES

Shorter, fatter arms and legs, may have printed body with alphabet, emblems, flags

**Common or lowbrow,** black or blonde center part wavy hairdo that comes down low on forehead

| | | |
|---|---|---|
| 9" | $75.00 | $100.00 |
| 13" | $100.00 | $145.00 |
| 15" | $125.00 | $165.00 |
| 18" | $150.00 | $200.00 |
| 22" | $185.00 | $245.00 |
| 25" | $225.00 | $300.00 |

With jewel necklace

| | | |
|---|---|---|
| 14" | $175.00 | $225.00 |
| 20" | $245.00 | $325.00 |

With molded bonnet

| | | |
|---|---|---|
| 9" | $135.00 | $175.00 |
| 14" | $185.00 | $250.00 |

71

Open mouth

| | | |
|---|---|---|
| 15" | $365.00 | $485.00 |
| 19" | $600.00 | $775.00 |

## PET NAMES, CA. 1899 – 1930 +

Agnes, Bertha, Daisy, Dorothy, Edith, Esther, Ethel, Florence, Helen, Mabel, Marion, Pauline, and Ruth. Made for Butler Brothers by various German firms. China head and limbs on cloth body. Molded blouse marked in front with name in gold lettering, molded blonde or black over all curls.

| | | |
|---|---|---|
| 10" | $95.00 | $125.00 |
| 15" | $150.00 | $200.00 |
| 17" | $195.00 | $225.00 |
| 20" | $200.00 | $265.00 |
| 22" | $225.00 | $300.00 |
| 25" | $325.00 | $425.00 |

*8½" Dresden-type ballet dancer, music box top, has hole in one toe for mounting, molded and painted features, painted ballet slippers, $1,000.00. Courtesy Amanda Hash.*

*Two 15" china dolls with printed cloth bodies, ca. 1880, $175.00 each. Courtesy Sue Kinkade.*

First price is for dolls in good condition with some wear or soiled; second price is for dolls that are in very good condition and are clean and bright.

**ALABAMA INDESTRUCTIBLE DOLLS, CA. 1900 – 25, ROANOKE, AL.** Ella Gauntt Smith made all cloth dolls with painted features that were jointed at shoulders and hips. Head construction may include round "monk's cap" on top of head. Painted feet varied, some had stitched toes, but most had one button slippers, or low boots. Shoes were painted black, brown, pink, or blue; they came in seven heights, from 12" to 27". Body Marks: *"Mrs. S.S. Smith//Manufacturer and Dealer in//The Alabama Indestructible Doll//Roanoke, ALA// Patented//Sept 26, 1905."*

*30" cloth Ella Smith Doll Co. Alabama Indestructible Doll, circa 1905, marked "#4C patented, Sept. 26, 1905," $3,000.00. Courtesy Sherryl Shirran.*

**Baby**

| | | |
|---|---|---|
| 15" | $850.00 | $1,700.00 |
| 21" | $1,100.00 | $2,200.00 |

Black Baby

| | | |
|---|---|---|
| 20" | $3,200.00 | $6,200.00 |

Barefoot Baby, rare

| | | |
|---|---|---|
| 23" | $1,500.00 | $3,000.00 |

**Child**

| | | |
|---|---|---|
| 15" | $800.00 | $1,600.00 |
| 22" | $1,200.00 | $2,400.00 |

Black Child

| | | |
|---|---|---|
| 18" | $3,100.00 | $6,200.00 |
| 23" | $3,400.00 | $6,800.00 |

**ART FABRIC MILLS**

**1899 – 1910+, New York, New Haven, and London.** They made cloth cut-out dolls that were lithographed in color, and marked "Art Fabric Mills, NY, Pat. Feb. 13th, 1900" on shoe or bottom of foot.

**Improved Life Size Doll,** with printed underwear

| | | |
|---|---|---|
| 20" | $75.00 | $275.00 |
| 30" | $100.00 | $400.00 |

**Punch and Judy,** pair

| | |
|---|---|
| 27" | $800.00 |

*18" cloth Improved Foot Cloth Doll by Arnold Print Works, Ca. 1901 +, printed on underwear, stockings, and shoes, $275.00. Courtesy Sherryl Shirran*

*14" cloth child with mask face by Albert Bruckner, NJ, sold by Horsman as part of their Babyland Rag line, original, $325.00. Courtesy Sherryl Shirran.*

## BABYLAND RAG, 1893 – 1928

Babyland Dolls made by E. I. Horsman with oil painted or lithographed faces.

**Lithographed**

| | | |
|---|---|---|
| 14½" | $175.00 | $335.00 |
| 16½" | $200.00 | $400.00 |
| 24" | $275.00 | $550.00 |

Black

| | | |
|---|---|---|
| 14½" | $240.00 | $480.00 |
| 16½" | $275.00 | $550.00 |
| 24" | $400.00 | $800.00 |

**Molded Painted Faces**

| | | |
|---|---|---|
| 13" | $350.00 | $700.00 |

**Flat Painted Faces**

| | | |
|---|---|---|
| 16½" | $450.00 | $900.00 |
| 20" | $540.00 | $1,080.00 |
| 30" | $810.00 | $1,620.00 |

Black

| | | |
|---|---|---|
| 16½" | $490.00 | $975.00 |
| 20" | $590.00 | $1,180.00 |
| 30" | $885.00 | $1,770.00 |

## BEECHER, JULIA JONES

Ca. 1893 – 1910, Elmira, NY. Wife of Congregational Church pastor Thomas K., sister-in-law of Harriet Beecher Stowe. Made **Missionary Ragbabies** of old silk jersey underwear with flat hand-painted and needle-sculpted features. All proceeds used for missionary work. Sizes 16" to 23" and larger.

| | | |
|---|---|---|
| 16" | $1,725.00 | $3,450.00 |
| 23" | $2,500.00 | $5,000.00 |

Black

| | | |
|---|---|---|
| 16" | $1,750.00 | $3,500.00 |
| 23" | $2,800.00 | $5,600.00 |

**Beecher-type**

| | | |
|---|---|---|
| 20" | $550.00 | $2,200.00 |

## BING ART

**Bing Werke, Germany, 1921 – 1932,** all cloth, felt, or composition head with cloth body. Molded face, oil painted features, wigged or painted hair, pin jointed cloth body, seams down front of legs, mitt hands.

**Painted hair,** cloth or felt, unmarked or Bing on bottom of foot

| | | |
|---|---|---|
| 13" | $275.00 | $550.00 |
| 15" | $325.00 | $650.00 |

**Wigged**

| | | |
|---|---|---|
| 10" | $175.00 | $350.00 |
| 16" | $325.00 | $650.00 |

**Composition head**

| | | |
|---|---|---|
| 8" | $40.00 | $145.00 |
| 12" | $45.00 | $175.00 |
| 16" | $60.00 | $225.00 |

**BLACK, 1830+**

Black cloth doll patterns in *American Girls Book*, describe how to make doll of black silk or crepe, gingham or calico dress, apron and cap. Beecher, Bruckner, Chad Valley, Chase, and Lenci made black cloth dolls. Horsman advertised black cloth Topsy and Dinah cloth dolls, ca. 1912. In about 1921, black cloth dolls were made by Grace Cory for Century Doll Co. Many cloth dolls were homemade one-of-a-kind. Patterns were available to make mammy doll toaster covers during the forties.

**Mammy-style,** with painted or embroidered features

| 1910 – 20s | | | |
|---|---|---|---|
| | 12" | $65.00 | $200.00 |
| | 16" | $85.00 | $285.00 |
| 1930s | | | |
| | 15" | $55.00 | $165.00+ |

**Topsy-Turvey**

Cloth dolls with two heads. Some had a black doll in one skirt, that when turned over revealed a white doll under the other skirt.

| Oil painted | $200.00 | $650.00 |
|---|---|---|
| Printed | $150.00 | $425.00 |

*Bruckner Topsy Turvy

| 13" | $950.00 at auction |
|---|---|

**BROWNIES**

**By Palmer Cox, 1892 – 1907**

Printed cloth dolls based on copyrighted figures of Palmer Cox; twelve different figures, including Canadian, Chinaman, Dude, German, Highlander, Indian, Irishman, John Bull, Policeman, Sailor, Soldier, and Uncle Sam. Marked **"Copyright 1892 by Palmer Cox"** on right foot.

Set of three uncut, one yard length

| 7½" | $350.00 |
|---|---|
| 7½" | $100.00 |

Set of twelve with book

$825.00 *at auction

**BRUCKNER, ALBERT**

**Ca. 1901 – 1930+, Jersey City, NJ**

Obtained patent for cloth dolls using printed, molded face mask, marked *"PAT'D. JULY 8TH 1901"* on right front shoulder edge. Made dolls for Horsman.

| 14" | $165.00 | $325.00 |
|---|---|---|

Black

| 14" | $215.00 | $425.00 |
|---|---|---|

**CHAD VALLEY**

**1917 – 30+, Harbonne, England.** Founded by Johnson Bros., made all types of cloth dolls, early ones had stockinette faces, later felt, with velvet body, jointed neck, shoulders, hips, glass or painted eyes, mohair wig.

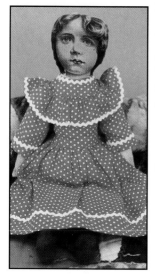

*14" printed cloth, maker unknown, $200.00. Courtesy Sherryl Shirran.*

Mabel Lucie Atwell was an early designer.
*Marks:* Usually on sole of foot, *"THE CHAD VALLEY CO. LTD//(BRITISH ROYAL COAT OF ARMS)//TOYMAKER TO//H.M. or HYGENIC TOYS//MADE IN ENGLAND BY//CHAD VALLEY CO. LTD."*

**Animals**

**Cat**

| | | |
|---|---|---|
| 12" | $75.00 | $215.00+ |

**Bonzo,** cloth dog with painted eyes, almost closed and smile

| | | |
|---|---|---|
| 4" | $65.00 | $210.00 |
| 13" | $110.00 | $415.00 |

Bonzo, eyes open

| | | |
|---|---|---|
| 5½" | $80.00 | $275.00 |
| 14" | $150.00 | $575.00 |

**Dog,** plush

| | | |
|---|---|---|
| 12" | $65.00 | $260.00 |

**Characters**

**Captain Bly, Fisherman, Long John Silver, Pirate, Policeman, Train Conductor, etc.**

Glass eyes

| | | |
|---|---|---|
| 18" | $325.00 | $1,000.00 |
| 20" | $375.00 | $1,300.00 |

Painted eyes

| | | |
|---|---|---|
| 18" | $225.00 | $775.00 |
| 20" | $250.00 | $875.00 |

**Ghandi/India**

| | | |
|---|---|---|
| 13" | $175.00 | $675.00 |

**Rahmah-Jah**

| | | |
|---|---|---|
| 26" | $225.00 | $900.00 |

**Child,** glass eyes

| | | |
|---|---|---|
| 14" | $165.00 | $625.00 |
| 16" | $200.00 | $725.00 |
| 18" | $225.00 | $775.00 |

Painted eyes

| | | |
|---|---|---|
| 9 – 10" | $40.00 | $150.00 |
| 12" | $65.00 | $225.00 |
| 15" | $115.00 | $425.00 |
| 18" | $160.00 | $625.00 |

**Royal Family,** all with glass eyes, 16" – 18"

**Princess Alexandra**

| | |
|---|---|
| $400.00 | $1,500.00 |

**Prince Edward**

| | |
|---|---|
| $400.00 | $1,500.00 |

**Prince Edward, Duke of Kent**
$350.00    $1,500.00
**Prince Edward, Duke of Windsor**
$400.00    $1,500.00
**Princess Elizabeth**
$425.00    $1,700.00
**Princess Margaret Rose**
$400.00    $1,500.00
**Story Book Dolls**
  **Ding Dong Dell**
  14"    $125.00        $475.00
  **Dwarfs**
  9½" each   $165.00      $675.00
  **My Elizabeth, My Friend**
  14"    $165.00        $675.00
  **Snow White**
  17"    $250.00      $1,000.00
  **Red Riding Hood**
  14"    $125.00        $500.00

**CHASE, MARTHA:** see that section.

**COLUMBIAN**

Emma E. Adams made rag dolls, distributed by Marshall Field, that won awards at the 1893 Chicago Worlds' Fair. Succeeded by her sister Marietta Adams Ruttan. Cloth dolls with hand-painted features, stitched fingers and toes. Stamped "Columbian Doll, Emma E. Adams, Oswego, NY."

  15"    $2,225.00      $4,500.00
  19"    $2,850.00      $5,700.00
  15"    $6,250.00 *at auction
**Columbian-type**
  16"    $650.00      $1,280.00
  22"    $1,100.00      $2,200.00
**Comic Characters**
  15"    $150.00        $450.00

**DEANS RAG BOOK CO.**
  **1903 – 25+, London**
Henry Samuel Dean, publisher; Horsman distributor in U.S.

Bing Art: Made cloth dolls in sheets of calico, linen, or other material, lithographed in bright colors, had dolls of many nations, including U.S. and Japan.

*19" Columbian Rag by Emma Marietta Adams, Oswego Center, NY, ca. 1891 – 1910, oil painted features, body marked "Columbian Doll//Emma E. Adams// Oswega Center// NY," $6,000.00. Courtesy Sherryl Shirran.*

**Child**

| | | |
|---|---|---|
| 10" | $100.00 | $285.00 |
| 16" | $185.00 | $550.00 |
| 17" | $250.00 | $750.00 |

**Lithographed face**

| | | |
|---|---|---|
| 9" | $30.00 | $85.00 |
| 15" | $55.00 | $165.00 |
| 16" | $75.00 | $225.00 |

**Mask face, velvet, with cloth body and limbs**

| | | |
|---|---|---|
| 12" | $45.00 | $125.00 |
| 18" | $90.00 | $265.00 |
| 24" | $125.00 | $385.00 |
| 30" | $155.00 | $475.00 |
| 34" | $185.00 | $565.00 |
| 40" | $225.00 | $695.00 |

**Golliwogs** (English black character doll)

| | | |
|---|---|---|
| 13" | $85.00 | $250.00 |
| 15" | $150.00 | $450.00 |

## DRAYTON, GRACE

### 1909 – 29, Philadelphia, PA

An illustrator, her designs were used for cloth and other dolls. Made printed dolls with big eyes, flat faces, marked "G.G. Drayton ©."

**Chocolate Drop,** 1923, Averill Mfg. Corp., brown cloth, printed features, three tufts yarn hair

| | | |
|---|---|---|
| 10" | $135.00 | $400.00 |
| 14" | $185.00 | $550.00 |

**Dolly Dingle,** 1923, Averill Mfg. Corp., cloth, printed features, marked on torso

| | | |
|---|---|---|
| 11" | $115.00 | $385.00 |
| 15" | $165.00 | $550.00 |

**Double face or topsy turvy**

| | | |
|---|---|---|
| 15" | $190.00 | $625.00 |

**Hug Me Tight,** Colonial Toy Mfg. Co., 1916, printed cloth with boy standing behind girl, one-piece

| | | |
|---|---|---|
| 12" | $75.00 | $250.00 |
| 16" | $150.00 | $435.00 |

**Kitty Puss,** all cloth, cat face, wired poseable limbs and tail

| | | |
|---|---|---|
| 15" | $135.00 | $400.00 |

**Peek-A-Boo,** Horsman, 1913 – 1915, printed features

| | | |
|---|---|---|
| 9" | $55.00 | $175.00 |
| 12" | $75.00 | $225.00 |
| 15" | $90.00 | $275.00 |

## FANGEL, MAUD TOUSEY

### 1920 – 30+

Designed cloth dolls, with flat printed faces, some with mitten hands. Some had three-piece heads and feet.

**Baby**

| | | |
|---|---|---|
| 13" | $150.00 | $425.00 |
| 17" | $200.00 | $600.00 |

**Child, Peggy Ann, Rosy, Snooks, Sweets**

| | | |
|---|---|---|
| 9" | $100.00 | $300.00 |
| 12" | $165.00 | $500.00 |
| 15" | $200.00 | $625.00 |
| 21" | $250.00 | $800.00 |

**FARNELL'S ALPHA TOYS**
Marked with label on foot "Farnell's Alpha Toys//Made in England."

**Baby**

| | | |
|---|---|---|
| 15" | $150.00 | $475.00 |
| 18" | $200.00 | $600.00 |

**Child**

| | | |
|---|---|---|
| 10" | $85.00 | $250.00 |
| 15" | $165.00 | $500.00 |

**King George VI, "H.M. The King"**

| | | |
|---|---|---|
| 15" | $400.00 | $1,000.00 |

**Palace Guard, "Beefeater"**

| | | |
|---|---|---|
| 15" | $225.00 | $700.00 |

**KAMKINS, 1919 – 28**
Cloth doll made by Louise R. Kampes Studio, made by cottage industry workers at home. *Marks*, heart-shaped sticker: *"KAMKINS// A DOLLY MADE TO LOVE//PATENTED//FROM//L.R. KAMPES//STUDIOS//ATLANTIC CITY //N.J.,"* All cloth, molded mask face, painted features, swivel head, jointed shoulders hips, mohair wig.

| | | |
|---|---|---|
| 19" | $600.00 | $1,600.00 |

**KRUSE, KATHE: SEE THAT SECTION.**

**KRUEGER, RICHARD**
**1917+.** Made many cloth dolls, some of oilcloth or with oilcloth clothing, oil painted face mask, yarn or mohair wig, label marked: "Krueger NY// Reg. U.S. Pat. Off//Made in U.S.A." on body or clothing seam.

**Child**

| | | |
|---|---|---|
| 12" | $40.00 | $135.00 |
| 16" | $60.00 | $195.00 |
| 20" | $80.00 | $240.00 |

**Walt Disney and other characters**

Dwarf

| | | |
|---|---|---|
| 12½" | $65.00 | $200.00 |

Pinocchio

| | | |
|---|---|---|
| 16" | $125.00 | $425.00+ |

**LENCI, SEE THAT SECTION**

**LIBERTY OF LONDON, 1939+**
Handmade needle sculptured cloth dolls dressed as historical and story-book characters.

| | | |
|---|---|---|
| 10" | $60.00 | $175.00 |

**MOLLYE'S**
**1929–30+.** Trademark used by Molly Goldman of International Doll Co. of Philadelphia, PA, made clothes for cloth dolls with mask faces (and composition dolls), dressed in international costumes.

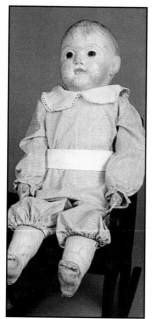

*21" cloth Philadelphia Baby by J.B. Sheppard, $1,000.00. Courtesy McMasters Doll Auctions.*

**Child**

| | | |
|---|---|---|
| 13" | $90.00 | $130.00 |
| 17" | $45.00 | $150.00 |
| 22" | $65.00 | $200.00 |
| 27" | $85.00 | $275.00 |

**Lady,** in long dresses or gowns

| | | |
|---|---|---|
| 16" | $55.00 | $175.00 |
| 21" | $75.00 | $250.00 |

**Internationals**

| | | |
|---|---|---|
| 13" | $30.00 | $90.00 |
| 15" | $45.00 | $135.00 |
| 27" | $100.00 | $300.00 |

**Princess, Thief of Bagdad,** blue painted Oriental-style eyes, harem outfit

| | | |
|---|---|---|
| 14" | $100.00 | $300.00 |

**PHILADELPHIA BABIES, J.B. SHEPPARD & CO., ca. 1860 – 1935.** Shoulder head, stockinette rag doll with molded eyelids, stitched fingers and toes, painted features, sizes 18" – 22", also known as Sheppard Dolls.

| | | |
|---|---|---|
| 18" | $1,200.00 | $3,500.00 |
| 22" | $1,320.00 | $4,000.00 |
| 21" | $4,730.00 *at auction | |

## PETZOLD, DORA

**Germany, 1919 – 30+.** Made and dressed dolls, molded head, painted features, wig, stockinette body, sawdust filled, short torso, free-formed thumbs, stitched fingers, shaped legs

| | | |
|---|---|---|
| 18" | $200.00 | $600.00 |
| 22" | $225.00 | $775.00 |
| 26" | $250.00 | $850.00 |

## PRINTED CLOTH

**Ca 1876 +.** Made by various firms such as Arnold Print Works, North Adams, MA (some marked Cocheoco Manufacturing Co.), and Art Fabric Mills, New Haven CT, NY, and London (see that category), made printed fabric for making cutout dolls, to be sewn together, and stuffed.

**Aunt Jemima,** set of 4 dolls, $100.00 each

**Black Child**

| | | |
|---|---|---|
| 16" | $150.00 | $425.00 |

**Cream of Wheat, Rastus**

| | | |
|---|---|---|
| 16" | $40.00 | $125.00 |

**With printed underwear,** Dolly Dear, Flaked Rice, Merry Marie, etc.
Cut and sewn

| | | |
|---|---|---|
| 7" | $35.00 | $95.00 |
| 16" | $60.00 | $175.00 |
| 19" | $70.00 | $200.00 |

Uncut

| | | |
|---|---|---|
| 7" | $125.00 | |
| 16" | $200.00 | |
| 19" | $275.00 | |

**With printed clothing, ca. 1903**

Cut and sewn

| | | |
|---|---|---|
| 9" | $30.00 | $90.00 |
| 14" | $65.00 | $200.00 |
| 19" | $115.00 | $325.00 |

Uncut

| | | |
|---|---|---|
| 9" | $125.00 | |
| 14" | $200.00 | |
| 19" | $350.00 | |

**Santa Claus/St. Nicholas,** marked "Pat. Dec 18, 1886//Made by E.S.Peck NY"

Cut and sewn

| | | |
|---|---|---|
| 15" | $100.00 | $325.00 |

Uncut

| | | |
|---|---|---|
| 15" | $600.00 | |

## RAYNAL

**1922 – 30 +, Paris.** Edouard Raynal made dolls of felt, cloth, or with celluloid head with widely spaced eyebrows. Dressed, some resemble Lenci, except fingers were together or hands of celluloid; marked Raynal on soles of shoes and/or pendant. Trade*Mark:* Poupees Raynal.

| | | |
|---|---|---|
| 14½" | $165.00 | $500.00 |
| 17" | $225.00 | $700.00 |

## ROLLISON, GERTRUDE F.

**1916 – 29. Holyoke, MA.** Designed and made cloth dolls, with molded faces treated to be washable, painted features, cloth torso has diamond stamp, "Rollison Doll//Holyoke, Mass." Dolls were produced by Utley Co., distributed by Borgfeldt, L. Wolf and Strobel and Wilken.

Molded painted hair

| | | |
|---|---|---|
| 20" | $400.00 | $1,150.00 |

Wigged

| | | |
|---|---|---|
| 19" | $650.00 | $1,300.00 |

## RUSSIAN, 1920+

All cloth, molded painted stockinette head, hands, in regional costumes. Marked **"Made in Soviet Union"**

| | | |
|---|---|---|
| 7" | $25.00 | $70.00 |
| 15" | $50.00 | $150.00 |
| 18" | $60.00 | $180.00 |

## STEIFF: SEE THAT SECTION.

## WALKER, IZANNAH

**Ca. late 1800s, Central Fall, RI.** Made cloth stockinette dolls, with pressed mask face, oil painted features, applied ears, some marked "Patented Nov. 4, 1873." Brush-stroked or corkscrew curls, stitched hands and feet, some with painted boots.

*14" cloth, softly painted mask face, "14" on front neck, maker unknown, $300.00. Courtesy Sherryl Shirran.*

*14" ink etched, unmarked cloth doll, legs are made of red horizontal striped material, $250.00. Courtesy Sherryl Shirran.*

First price indicates very worn; second price for good condition. More for unusual hair style.

*Marks:*

```
I.F. WALKER'S
    PATENT
NOV. 4TH 1873.
```

|  |  |  |
|---|---|---|
| 16" | $4,500.00 | $18,000.00 |

**WELLINGS, NORAH**

**Victoria Toy Works, 1926 – 30+, Wellington, Shropshire, England.**

Chief designer for Chad Valley, she and brother Leonard started own factory. Made cloth dolls of velvet, velveteen, plush, and felt, specializing in sailors souvenir dolls for steamship lines. The line included children, adults, blacks, ethnic, and fantasy dolls. Cloth label usually on sole of the foot reads: "**Made in England//by//Norah Wellings.**"

**Baby,** molded face, oil painted features, some papier mache covered by stockinette, stitched hip and shoulder joints.

|  |  |  |
|---|---|---|
| 15" | $200.00 | $600.00 |
| 22" | $300.00 | $900.00 |

**Child,** painted eyes

|  |  |  |
|---|---|---|
| 13" | $125.00 | $400.00 |
| 18" | $200.00 | $600.00 |
| 22" | $235.00 | $700.00 |
| 28" | $300.00 | $900.00 |

Glass eyes

|  |  |  |
|---|---|---|
| 15" | $175.00 | $550.00 |
| 18" | $275.00 | $850.00 |
| 22" | $425.00 | $1,300.00 |

**Characters in uniform, regional dress:** Mounties, Policemen, others

|  |  |  |
|---|---|---|
| 13" | $125.00 | $385.00 |
| 17" | $250.00 | $750.00 |
| 24" | $350.00 | $1,100.00 |

Black Islander, or Scot

|  |  |  |
|---|---|---|
| 9" | $30.00 | $90.00 |
| 13" | $61.00 | $185.00 |
| 16" | $75.00 | $225.00 |

*10½" glass-eyed composition Creche lady, $350.00. 11" Creche man, $270.00. Courtesy McMasters Doll Auctions.*

*14½" composition glass-eyed Creche man, $175.00. Courtesy McMasters Doll Auctions.*

These include figures of various materials made especially for religious scenes such as the Christmas manger scene. They are usually not jointed. Some have elaborate costumes. Early created figures were gesso over wooden head and limbs, fabric covered bodies with wire frames, later figures made of terra-cotta, or other materials. Some with inset eyes.

*Too few in database for reliable range.*

Man, carved wooden shoulder head, glass eyes, wire body
 8"        $115.00
Lady, carved wooden shoulder head, glass eyes, wire body
 10½"        $350.00
Lady, gesso over wood, hand carved, glass eyes, open mouth, pierced ears, wire frame
 14½"        $500.00
Lady, wood, on base
 23"        $1,000.00

# C.S.F.J.

**Chambre Syndicale des Fabricants de Jouets et Jeux et Engrins Sportif, 1886 – 1928+, Paris, France,** was a trade organization composed of French toymakers. Numbers refer to numbered list of manufacturers.

First price is for dolls in good condition, but with flaws; second price indicates dolls in excellent condition with original or appropriate clothing.

*Marks:*

**Child,** closed mouth, excellent quality bisque

| | | |
|---|---|---|
| 12" | $700.00 | $925.00 |
| 16" | $975.00 | $1,300.00 |

## Danel & CIE

**1889 – 95, Paris,** Danel, once director of the Jumeau factory, was sued by Jumeau for copying Bebes Jumeau.

*Marks:* **E. (size number) D. on head, "Eiffel Tower Paris Bebe," on body; shoes with "Paris Bebe," in star.**

**Paris Bebe,** bisque socket head, appropriate wig, pierced ears, paperweight eyes, closed mouth, nicely dressed in good condition.

First price is for dolls in good condition, but with flaws; second price indicates dolls in excellent condition with original or appropriate clothing.

| | | |
|---|---|---|
| 17" | $3,375.00 | $4,500.00 |
| 21" | $4,125.00 | $5,500.00 |

## DEP

The "DEP" mark on the back of bisque heads stands for the French "Depose" or the German "Deponirt," which means "registered claim." Some dolls made by Simon and Halbig have the S&H mark hidden above the DEP under the wig. Bisque head, swivel neck, appropriate wig, paperweight eyes, open or closed mouth, good condition, nicely dressed, on French style wood and composition body.

First price is for dolls in good condition, but with flaws; second price indicates dolls in excellent condition with original or appropriate clothing.

*Mark:*

### DEP
**(size number)**

| | | |
|---|---|---|
| Closed mouth | | |
| 14" | $1,500.00 | $2,000.00 |
| 21" | $2,100.00 | $2,800.00 |
| 24" | $2,400.00 | $3,200.00 |
| Open mouth | | |
| 11" | $525.00 | $700.00 |
| 15" | $575.00 | $775.00 |
| 17" | $825.00 | $1,100.00 |
| 20" | $1,000.00 | $1,350.00 |
| 24" | $1,350.00 | $1,800.00 |
| 29" | $1,950.00 | $2,600.00 |
| 32" | $2,250.00 | $3,000.00 |

*32" bisque, DEP child re-dressed, $1,400.00. Courtesy McMasters Doll Auctions.*

*21" DEP child, $600.00. Courtesy McMasters Doll Auctions.*

## Doll House

Small dolls generally under 8" were usually dressed as members of a family or representing household-related occupations. They were often sold as a group. Made of any material, but usually with a bisque head by 1880.

First price is for doll in good condition, but with flaws; second price is for doll in excellent condition with original clothes.

**Adult, man or woman, painted eyes, molded hair, wig**

| | | |
|---|---|---|
| 6" | $125.00 | $225.00 |

Glass eyes, molded hair

| | | |
|---|---|---|
| 6" | $300.00 | $400.00 |

Wigged

| | | |
|---|---|---|
| 6" | $400.00 | $600.00 |

**Black man or woman, molded hair, original clothes**

| | | |
|---|---|---|
| 6" | $360.00 | $475.00 |

**Chauffeur, molded cap**

| | | |
|---|---|---|
| 6" | $200.00 | $285.00 |

**Children, all bisque**

| | | |
|---|---|---|
| 4" | $40.00 | $75.00 |

**China, with early hairdo**

| | | |
|---|---|---|
| 4" | $225.00 | $300.00 |

With lowbrow or common hairdo, ca. 1900s and after

| | | |
|---|---|---|
| 4" | $115.00 | $150.00 |

*Bisque Doll House dolls, left: 6" man, middle: 5" bisque lady, right: 5" bisque lady, $335.00 set. Courtesy McMasters Doll Auctions.*

*4" doll house dolls with papier mache heads, cloth covered wire armature limbs and body, painted features, molded hair, dressed in old costumes, $180.00. Courtesy Ruth Brown.*

**Grandparents, or with molded on hats**
    6"        $200.00        $265.00

**Military man,** mustache, original clothes
    6"        $435.00        $575.00+

With molded on helmet
    6"        $525.00        $700.00+

# Door of Hope

**1901 – 50, Shanghai, China.** Corneilia Bonnell started the Door of Hope Mission in Shanghi to help poor girls who were sold by their families. As a means to learn sewing skills, the girls dressed carved pearwood heads from Ning-po. The heads and hands were left with their natural finish, stuffed cloth bodies were then dressed in correct representation for the 26 different Chinese classes. Carved wooden head, cloth or wooden arms, original handmade costumes, in very good condition.

First price indicates dolls with faded clothing or soiled; second price is for dolls in excellent condition with clean, bright clothing.

*11" Door of Hope woman, $350.00. 12" Door of Hope man, $395.00. Courtesy McMasters Doll Auctions.*

**Adult,** man or woman
    12"    $225.00    $550.00

**Schoolchild**
    8"    $300.00    $600.00

**Bride**
    12"    $325.00    $650.00

**Groom**
    12"    $325.00    $650.00

    *Bridal couple in fancy dress, $1,500.00 * at auction

**Amah with Baby**
        $375.00    $750.00

**Manchu** lady or man
    12"    $500.00    $1,000.00

**Mourner**
        $325.00    $750.00

**Policeman**
        $325.00    $750.00

*11" Door of Hope man, wood carved head and hands, $450.00. Courtesy Amanda Hash.*

**Dressel, Otto & Cunel, 1873 – 1945, Sonnenberg, Thuringia, Germany.** The Dressels made wood, wax over composition, papier mache, composition, china, and bisque heads for their dolls which they produced, distributed, and exported. Their bisque heads were made by Simon & Halbig, Armand Marseille, Ernst F. Heubach, Schoenau & Hoffmeister, and others.

*Marks:*

6/0X

*A M*
*C 0D93-A-DEP*
*made in Germany*

*S & H*

*1349*
*D ressel*

**BISQUE**
**Baby,** 1910 + marked "*C.O.D.*," more for toddler body

| | | |
|---|---|---|
| 14" | $200.00 | $265.00 |
| 16" | $375.00 | $500.00 |
| 21" | $500.00 | $650.00 |

**Child,** open mouth, jointed composition body

| | | |
|---|---|---|
| 15" | $250.00 | $325.00 |
| 19" | $450.00 | $475.00 |
| 22" | $400.00 | $525.00 |
| 26" | $435.00 | $575.00 |

**Child, character face, closed mouth,** jointed child or toddler body
Painted eyes

| | | |
|---|---|---|
| 13" | $1,200.00 | $1,625.00 |
| 14" | $1,850.00 | $2,450.00 |
| 18" | $2,300.00 | $3,000.00 |
| 23" | $2,600.00 | $3,450.00 |

Glass eyes

| | | |
|---|---|---|
| 15" | $2,300.00 | $2,500.00 |
| 18" | $2,400.00 | $3,400.00 |
| 25" | $2,700.00 | $3,600.00 |

**Flapper,** closed mouth, five-piece composition body with thin legs and high heel feet, painted on hose up entire leg, marked #1469

| | | |
|---|---|---|
| 12" | $2,500.00 | $3,300.00 |
| 15" | $2,850.00 | $3,800.00 |

**Jutta baby,** open mouth, bent leg body

| | | |
|---|---|---|
| 13" | $325.00 | $435.00 |
| 15" | $400.00 | $500.00 |
| 18" | $500.00 | $675.00 |
| 21" | $600.00 | $800.00 |
| 24" | $1,000.00 | $1,400.00 |
| 27" | $1,350.00 | $1,800.00 |

**Jutta child,** open mouth, marked with "Jutta" or "S&H #1914," "1348," "1349," etc., 1906 – 1921

| | | |
|---|---|---|
| 14" | $300.00 | $425.00 |
| 16" | $425.00 | $575.00 |
| 20" | $525.00 | $700.00 |
| 24" | $625.00 | $850.00 |
| 26" | $700.00 | $950.00 |
| 30" | $900.00 | $1,200.00 |
| 38" | $1,875.00 | $2,500.00 |

**Jutta toddler**

| | | |
|---|---|---|
| 8" | $400.00 | $550.00 |
| 15" | $500.00 | $675.00 |
| 18" | $700.00 | $950.00 |
| 22" | $925.00 | $1,250.00 |
| 25" | $1,150.00 | $1,550.00 |
| 27" | $1,350.00 | $1,850.00 |

**Portrait Dolls**

1896+, bisque head, glass eyes, composition body

Admiral Dewey, Admiral Byrd

| | | |
|---|---|---|
| 8" | $500.00 | $700.00 |
| 12" | $1,100.00 | $1,475.00 |

Buffalo Bill

| | | |
|---|---|---|
| 10" | $575.00 | $765.00 |

Farmer, Old Rip, Witch

| | | |
|---|---|---|
| 8" | $475.00 | $650.00 |
| 14" | $1,125.00 | $1,500.00 |

Father Christmas

| | | |
|---|---|---|
| 12" | $1,125.00 | $1,500.00+ |

Uncle Sam

| | | |
|---|---|---|
| 8" | $550.00 | $735.00 |
| 14" | $1,200.00 | $1,600.00 |

*24" Jutta in red cape, mold #1349, by Cuno & Otto Dressel, $525.00. Courtesy McMasters Doll Auctions.*

*12" Cunno & Otto Dressel character child, painted eyes, closed mouth, $800.00. Courtesy McMasters Doll Auctions.*

## COMPOSITION

**Holz-Masse, 1875+,** composition shoulder head, wigged or molded hair, painted or glass eyes, cloth body, composition limbs, molded on boots.

Molded hair

|  | | |
|---|---|---|
| 13" | $65.00 | $250.00 |
| 17" | $100.00 | $400.00 |
| 24" | $150.00 | $565.00 |

Wigged

|  | | |
|---|---|---|
| 16" | $80.00 | $325.00 |
| 24" | $110.00 | $425.00 |

# E.D.

Some E.D. dolls may have been made by either Etienne Denamure, 1857 – 99, Paris, or Danel & Cie (see that section). Other marked E.D. (no Depose mark) dolls that have the Jumeau look may have been made when Emile Douillet was director of Jumeau and should be priced as Jumeau dolls. Denamure made porcelain-head dolls with either open or closed mouths. Probably some of the bisque heads marked E.D. were made by Denamur.

First price indicates dolls in good condition, but with some flaws; second price indicated dolls in excellent condition, with original clothes or appropriately dressed.

Mark:

E1D
DEPOSE

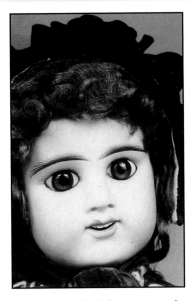

*22" bisque E.D. Bebe, open mouth, mohair wig, $2,000.00. Courtesy McMasters Doll Auctions.*

*25" bisque E.D. Bebe marked "E 10 D" on back of head, closed mouth, jointed composition body, jointed wrists, $3,000.00. Courtesy McMasters Doll Auctions.*

**Closed Mouth**

| | | |
|---|---|---|
| 13" | $1,500.00 | $2,000.00 |
| 15" | $1,800.00 | $2,400.00 |
| 21" | $2,400.00 | $3,150.00 |
| 25" | $2,800.00 | $3,750.00 |
| 27" | $3,000.00 | $4,100.00 |
| 31" | $3500.00 | $4,700.00 |

**Open mouth**

| | | |
|---|---|---|
| 14" | $975.00 | $1,300.00 |
| 16" | $1,200.00 | $1,600.00 |
| 20" | $1,575.00 | $2,100.00 |
| 23" | $1,800.00 | $2,400.00 |

Black

| | | |
|---|---|---|
| 16" | $1,700.00 | $2,250.00 |
| 22" | $1,950.00 | $2,600.00 |

## Eden Bebe

**1890 – 99, made by Fleischmann & Blodel; 1899 – 1953 made by Societe Francaise de Fabrication de Bebes & Jouet (S.F.B.J.).** Dolls had bisque heads, jointed composition bodies.

First price indicates dolls in good condition, but with some flaws; second price indicated dolls in excellent condition, with original clothes or appropriately dressed.

*Marks:*

E DEN BEBE
PARIS
7
DEPOSÉ

EDEN·BEBE
PARIS
N

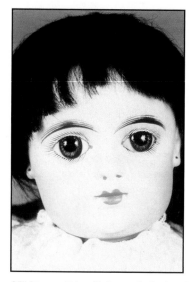

*27" bisque Eden Bebe with Gesland type stockinette padded body with wire armature, wooden lower arms, composition hands and legs, $3,600.00. Courtesy McMasters Doll Auctions.*

*24" bisque socket head, paperweight eyes, closed mouth, pierced ears, jointed French body, $3,200.00. Courtesy McMasters Doll Auctions.*

**Closed Mouth, pale bisque**

| | | |
|---|---|---|
| 15" | $2,250.00 | |
| 18" | $2,700.00 | |
| 22" | $3,000.00 | |
| 25" | $3,400.00 | |

High color, five-piece body

| | | |
|---|---|---|
| 12" | $750.00 | $1,000.00 |
| 16" | $900.00 | $1,200.00 |
| 17" | $1,200.00 | $1,600.00 |
| 21" | $1,350.00 | $1,850.00 |
| 25" | $1,800.00 | $2,400.00 |

**Open Mouth**

| | | |
|---|---|---|
| 14" | $1,000.00 | $1,400.00 |
| 17" | $1,250.00 | $1,700.00 |
| 21" | $1,550.00 | $2,100.00 |
| 26" | $1,950.00 | $2,600.00 |

**Walking, Talking, Kissing,** jointed body, walker mechanism, head turns, arm throws a kiss, heads by Simon & Halbig using mold #1039 and others, bodies assembled by Fleischmann & Bloedel. Price for perfect working doll.

| | |
|---|---|
| 21" | $1,600.00 |

*too few in database to give relevant range*

# Fashion Type

**French Poupee, 1869+.** Unmarked or with size number only, glass eyes, dolls modeled as an adult lady, with bisque shoulder head, stationary or swivel neck, closed mouth, earrings, kid or kid and cloth, body, nicely dressed, good condition.

**COLLECTOR ALERT:** French fashion-types are being reproduced, made to look old. Collectors need to arm themselves with knowledge before purchasing. Quality information is available to members of the United Federation of Doll Clubs (UFDC). Continuing research is being conducted by them.

*15" bisque, similar to Bru, fashion-type, $1,600.00. Courtesy McMasters Doll Auctions.*

| | | |
|---|---|---|
| 12" | $1,100.00 | $1,450.00 |
| 14" | $1,275.00 | $1,700.00 |
| 16" | $1,450.00 | $1,900.00 |
| 18" | $1,600.00 | $2,150.00 |
| 21" | $1,900.00 | $2,500.00 |
| 27" | $2,500.00 | $3,250.00 |

**Painted eyes,** kid body

| | | |
|---|---|---|
| 14 | $700.00 | $950.00 |
| 17" | $1,000.00 | $1,400.00 |
| 22" | $1,350.00 | $1,800.00 |

**Black, glass eyes,** kid body

| | | |
|---|---|---|
| 14" | $1,350.00 | $1,800.00+ |

**Wooden articulated body, glass eyes**

| | | |
|---|---|---|
| 13" | $2,000.00 | $2,600.00 |
| 15" | $2,800.00 | $3,700.00 |
| 18" | $3,300.00 | $4,400.00 |

# Fashion Type (cont.)

**BARROIS (E.B.), glass eyes**

| | | |
|---|---|---|
| 16" | $2,800.00 | $3,750.00 |
| 18" | $3,550.00 | $4,750.00 |

**BRU**

Swivel head of pressed bisque, bisque shoulder plate, metal spring stringing mechanism in neck, marked "A" through "M" on back of head

| | | |
|---|---|---|
| 13" | $2,100.00 | $2,800.00 |
| 15" | $2,400.00 | $3,250.00 |

**Bru, Smiler** (smiling face some call "Mona Lisa")

Cloth body

| | | |
|---|---|---|
| 18" | $2,300.00 | $3,100.00 |

Kid body, kid or bisque arms, allow more for wooden arms

| | | |
|---|---|---|
| 12" | $2,100.00 | $2,800.00 |
| 14" | $2,400.00 | $3,200.00 |
| 17" | $2,900.00 | $3,900.00 |
| 19" | $3,675.00 | $4,900.00 |
| 22" | $4,275.00 | $5,700.00 |

Wooden body

| | | |
|---|---|---|
| 14" | $3,700.00 | $4,900.00 |
| 19" | $4,900.00 | $6,500.00 |

**F.G. 1860+, marked one-piece shoulder head,** glass eyes, kid body

| | | |
|---|---|---|
| 12" | $700.00 | $925.00 |
| 15" | $900.00 | $1,175.00 |
| 17" | $1,275.00 | $1,700.00 |

Painted eyes

| | | |
|---|---|---|
| 11" | $500.00 | $650.00 |
| 15" | $825.00 | $1,100.00 |
| 17" | $1,000.00 | $1,300.00 |

**Marked swivel head on bisque shoulder plate,** kid body, may have bisque lower arms, glass eyes

| | | |
|---|---|---|
| 12" | $1,300.00 | $1,400.00 |
| 14" | $2,000.00 | $2,100.00 |
| 18 | $2,500.00 | $2,600.00 |
| 23" | $2,400.00 | $3,150.00 |
| 27" | $3,450.00 | $4,600.00 |

Black

| | | |
|---|---|---|
| 16" | $2,500.00 | $3,400.00 |
| 20" | $3,500.00 | $4,650.00 |

**Fortune Teller**

Fashion-type head with swivel neck, glass or painted eyes, kid body, skirt made to hold many paper "fortunes."

**Closed mouth**

| | | |
|---|---|---|
| 17" | $3,450.00 | $4,600.00+ |

**Open mouth**

| | | |
|---|---|---|
| 18" | $2,250.00 | $3,000.00+ |

**China, glazed finish,** 1870 – 1880 hair style

| | | |
|---|---|---|
| 15" | $1,250.00 | $1,700.00 |

*16" French fashion-type, blue glass eyes, mohair wig, gusseted leather body, with trunk and two extra outfits, $3,500.00.*

*12" French Fashion, $2,650.00. Courtesy McMasters Doll Auctions.*

**Wood, German**, with tuck comb

| | | |
|---|---|---|
| 16" | $2,300.00 | $3,100.00 |

## Gesland

**Marked F.G.**, stockinette covered metal articulated body, bisque lower arms and legs

| | | |
|---|---|---|
| 15" | $3,800.00 | $5,150.00 |
| 18" | $4,600.00 | $6,150.00 |
| 23" | $4,950.00 | $6,600.00 |
| 25" | $5,600.00 | $7,300.00 |

**HURET,** bisque or china glazed shoulder head, kid body with bisque lower arms, glass eyes

| | | |
|---|---|---|
| 14" | $4,400.00 | $5,800.00 |
| 19" | $5,900.00 | $7,900.00 |

**Swivel neck**

| | |
|---|---|
| 18" | $30,000.00+ |

* *too few in database to give reliable range*

**Wood body**

| | |
|---|---|
| 18" | $20,000.00+ |

* *too few in database to give reliable range*

**Gutta percha body**

| | |
|---|---|
| 19" | $20,000.00+ |

* *too few in database to give reliable range*

**Painted eyes, kid body**

| | | |
|---|---|---|
| 15" | $11,000.00 | $15,250.00 |
| 19" | $14,250.00 | $19,000.00 |

**Portrait adult,** painted eyes, articulated wooden body, metal hands

| | |
|---|---|
| 18" | $17,500.00 |

*too few in database to give reliable range.*

# Fashion Type (cont.)

\* A rare mulatto pressed bisque swivel head 'Madagascar' doll thought to be by Jumeau, circa 1876, marked 3, 24½" tall, pierced ears, kid body, black silk outfit, brought $89,270.00 at a recent auction.

## JUMEAU

Marked with size number on swivel head, stamped kid body

| | | |
|---|---|---|
| 12" | $1,800.00 | $2,400.00 |
| 15" | $2,400.00 | $3,200.00 |
| 19" | $2,700.00 | $3,600.00 |

Wooden body, bisque lower arms

| | | |
|---|---|---|
| 18" | $4,300.00 | $5,700.00 |
| 22" | $5,100.00 | $6,800.00 |

Extra large eyes

| | | |
|---|---|---|
| 12" | $1,800.00 | $2,400.00 |
| 16" | $2,100.00 | $2,800.00 |

**Jumeau portrait**

| | | |
|---|---|---|
| 15" | $2,550.00 | $3,400.00 |
| 18" | $4,200.00 | $5,600.00 |
| 22" | $4,800.00 | $6,400.00 |
| 26" | $5,600.00 | $7,500.00 |
| 28" | $6,250.00 | $8,350.00 |

Wooden body

| | | |
|---|---|---|
| 15" | $4,200.00 | $5,625.00 |
| 18" | $6,500.00 | $8,700.00 |
| 26" | $9,000.00 | $12,000.00 |

## ROHMER

**Glass eyes**, bisque or china glazed shoulder or swivel head on shoulder plate, kid body, bisque or wooden lower arms. *Marks:* green oval stamp on torso.

| | | |
|---|---|---|
| 14" | $4,800.00 | $6,400.00 |
| 17" | $7,200.00 | $9,500.00 |

**Painted eyes**

| | | |
|---|---|---|
| 14" | $4,200.00 | $5,600.00 |
| 18" | $6,000.00 | $8,000.00 |

**Wooden body**

| | | |
|---|---|---|
| 16" | $5,550.00 | $7,400.00 |
| 19" | $9,000.00 | $12,000.00 |

## ACCESSORIES

**Dress** $500.00+
**Shoes** marked by maker, $500.00+, unmarked, $250.00
**Trunk** $250.00+
**Wig** $250.00 +

## Frozen Charlie/Charlotte

**Ca. 1860 – 1940.** Most porcelain factories made all china dolls in one piece molds with molded or painted black or blonde hair, eyes, and usually undressed. Sometimes called Bathing Dolls they were dubbed "Frozen Charlotte" from a song about a girl who went dancing lightly dressed and froze in the snow. Victorians found them immoral. They range in size from under 1" to over 19". Some were reproduced in Germany in the '70s. Allow more for pink tint, extra decoration, or hairdo.

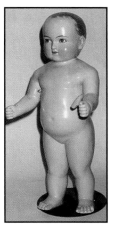

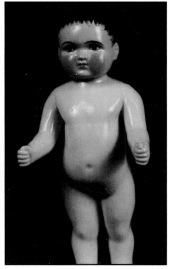

*14" china pink-tone Frozen Charlie with painted blond hair and blue eyes, $400.00. Private collection.*

*15" Frozen Charlie, unmarked china, flesh-tinted head, molded blond hair, $525.00. Courtesy McMasters Doll Auctions.*

*12" china Frozen Charlie with black hair and flesh-toned face, $165.00. Courtesy McMasters Doll Auctions.*

**All China**

| | | |
|---|---|---|
| 2" | $65.00 | $85.00 |
| 5" | $75.00 | $100.00 |
| 7" | $150.00 | $200.00 |
| 9" | $200.00 | $275.00 |
| 15" | $350.00 | $450.00 |

**Black, china**

| | | |
|---|---|---|
| 6" | $200.00 | $275.00 |
| 8" | $275.00 | $375.00 |

**Black Hair, flesh tones head and neck**

| | | |
|---|---|---|
| 12" | $300.00 | $400.00 |
| 15" | $400.00 | $550.00 |

**Jointed Shoulders**

| | | |
|---|---|---|
| 5" | $110.00 | $145.00 |
| 7" | $165.00 | $225.00 |

**Molded Boots**

| | | |
|---|---|---|
| 4" | $135.00 | $185.00 |
| 8" | $200.00 | $275.00 |

**Molded Clothes or hats**

| | | |
|---|---|---|
| 3" | $185.00 | $250.00 |
| 6" | $225.00 | $300.00 |
| 8" | $325.00 | $425.00 |

**Pink Tint, hairdo**

| | | |
|---|---|---|
| 3" | $200.00 | $225.00 |
| 5" | $300.00 | $350.00 |

**Pink Tint, bonnet-head**

| | | |
|---|---|---|
| 3" | $350.00 | $375.00 |
| 5" | $425.00 | $475.00 |

**Stone Bisque, molded hair, one piece**

| | | |
|---|---|---|
| 3" | $20.00 | $25.00 |
| 6" | $30.00 | $40.00 |

**Untinted Bisque, ca. 1860s, molded hair, jointed shoulders**

| | | |
|---|---|---|
| 4" | $100.00 | $135.00 |
| 7" | $120.00 | $160.00 |

Parian-type

| | | |
|---|---|---|
| 5" | $135.00 | $185.00 |
| 7" | $200.00 | $250.00 |

## Fulper

**Fulper Pottery Co., 1918 – 22+, Flemington, NJ,** made dolls with bisque heads and all bisque dolls. They sold dolls to Amberg, Colonial Toy Mfg. Co. and Horsman. M.S. monogram stood for Martin Stangl, in charge of production.

First price indicates dolls in good condition, with flaws; second price indicates dolls in excellent condition with original or appropriate clothes.

*Marks:*

*30" bisque, Fulper Amberg Victory Doll, marked "Amberg Dolls, The World Standard, Made in USA, 70" back head, celluloid eyes, real lashes, $525.00. Courtesy McMasters Doll Auctions.*

**Baby,** bisque socket head, glass eyes, open mouth, teeth, mohair wig, bent leg body

| | | |
|---|---|---|
| 17" | $450.00 | $600.00 |
| 19" | $500.00 | $700.00 |

**Toddler,** straight leg body

| | | |
|---|---|---|
| 19" | $550.00 | $750.00 |
| 25" | $750.00 | $1,000.00+ |

**Child,** socket head, glass eyes, open mouth, teeth, mohair or human hair wig

Composition body

| | | |
|---|---|---|
| 14" | $225.00 | $300.00 |
| 16" | $335.00 | $450.00 |
| 20" | $450.00 | $600.00 |

Kid body

| | | |
|---|---|---|
| 15" | $250.00 | $350.00 |
| 21" | $400.00 | $550.00 |

## Gans & Seyforth

**1908 – 1922, Waltershausen, Germany,** made bisque dolls and had a patent for flirty and googly eyes. The partners separated in 1922, and Otta Gans opened his own factory.

*Marks:*

Gansz Seyfarth.

Germany

ℂ. & S
3

**Baby,** bent leg baby, original clothes or appropriately dressed

| | | |
|---|---|---|
| 16" | $375.00 | $525.00 |
| 20" | $465.00 | $625.00 |
| 25" | $575.00 | $775.00 |

**Child,** open mouth, composition body, original clothes, or appropriately dressed

| | | |
|---|---|---|
| 15" | $375.00 | $500.00 |
| 21" | $500.00 | $675.00 |
| 28" | $675.00 | $900.00 |

## Gaultier

**Gaultier, Francois, 1860 – 99,** was located near Paris and made porcelain doll heads and parts for lady dolls and for bebes, and sold to many French makers of dolls. Also made all-bisque dolls marked F.G. In 1899 they became part of S.F.B.J.

*Marks:*

**F.1.G**

**9**

◄•F.G•►

**Bebe (child), F.G. in block letters**
    Closed mouth, excellent quality bisque socket head, glass eyes, pierced ears, cork pate

**Composition and wooden body** with straight wrists

| | | |
|---|---|---|
| 10" | $2,700.00 | $3,600.00 |
| 12" | $2,850.00 | $3,800.00 |
| 16" | $3,500.00 | $4,500.00 |
| 21" | $4,400.00 | $5,900.00 |
| 30" | $5,900.00 | $7,150.00 |

**Kid body,** may have bisque forearms

| | | |
|---|---|---|
| 15" | $3,300.00 | $4,450.00 |
| 17" | $3,800.00 | $5,000.00 |

*18" French Fashion by F. Gaultier, replaced arms $1,200.00. Courtesy McMasters Doll Auctions.*

*25½" bisque Francois Gualtier fashion-type with leather gusseted body, blue glass eyes, wig, $3,300.00. Courtesy Waneta Jost.*

All wood body
22"      $10,450.00 *at auction

**Bebe (child), F.G. in scroll letters**
**Composition Body, closed mouth**

| | | |
|---|---|---|
| 12" | $975.00 | $1,300.00 |
| 17" | $2,200.00 | $2,950.00 |
| 23" | $2,800.00 | $3,700.00 |
| 28" | $3,400.00 | $4,500.00 |

Open mouth

| | | |
|---|---|---|
| 11" | $475.00 | $650.00 |
| 16" | $1,350.00 | $1,800.00 |
| 24" | $2,000.00 | $2,700.00 |

**Poupee, Marked F.G. on shoulder plate**

Fashion-type body, bisque swivel head, bisque shoulder plate, kid body, may have bisque lower arms, glass eyes, appropriate wig, closed mouth, pierced ears, nicely dressed.

**F.G., 1860+,** marked one-piece shoulder head, glass eyes, kid body

| | | |
|---|---|---|
| 12" | $700.00 | $925.00 |
| 15" | $900.00 | $1,175.00 |
| 17" | $1,275.00 | $1,700.00 |

Painted eyes

| | | |
|---|---|---|
| 11" | $500.00 | $650.00 |
| 15" | $825.00 | $1,100.00 |
| 17" | $1,000.00 | $1,300.00 |

*24" Gaultier, open mouth, marked "9 F.G." with scroll mark, $3,250.00. Courtesy Sherryl Shirran.*

**F.G.,** marked swivel head on bisque shoulder plate, kid body, may have bisque lower arms, glass eyes

| | | |
|---|---|---|
| 12" | $1,300.00 | $1,400.00 |
| 14" | $2,000.00 | $2,100.00 |
| 18" | $2,500.00 | $2,600.00 |
| 23" | $2,400.00 | $3,150.00 |
| 27" | $3,450.00 | $4,600.00 |

Black

| | | |
|---|---|---|
| 16" | $2,500.00 | $3,400.00 |
| 20" | $3,500.00 | $4,650.00 |

**1860 – 1928, Paris,** made, repaired, exported, and distributed dolls, patented a doll body and used heads from Francois Gaultier with F.G. block or scroll mark. Gesland's unusual body had metal articulated armature covered with padding and stockinette, with bisque or wood/composition hands and legs.

*Marks:*

Bisque socket head marked "F.G," in scroll, with marked Gesland stockinet body with wire armature, $5,000.00. Courtesy McMasters Doll Auctions.

**E. GESLAND**

**B**ᵀᴱ S. G. D. G.

**PARIS**

**Bebe (child) on marked Gesland body**
Closed mouth

|       |            |            |
| ----- | ---------- | ---------- |
| 14"   | $3,375.00  | $4,500.00  |
| 17"   | $3,825.00  | $5,100.00  |
| 21"   | $3,950.00  | $5,200.00  |

Open mouth

|       |            |            |
| ----- | ---------- | ---------- |
| 16"   | $1,875.00  | $2,500.00  |
| 20"   | $2,250.00  | $3,000.00  |
| 25"   | $2,850.00  | $3,800.00  |

**Poupee (fashion-type) Gesland, marked F.G.,** stockinette covered metal articulated body, bisque lower arms and legs

|       |            |            |
| ----- | ---------- | ---------- |
| 15"   | $3,800.00  | $5,150.00  |
| 18"   | $4,600.00  | $6,150.00  |
| 23"   | $4,950.00  | $6,600.00  |
| 25"   | $5,600.00  | $7,300.00  |

# Gladdie

**1928 – 30+.** Gladdie was the trade name of doll designed by Helen Webster Jensen and made in Germany. The body was made by K&K, for Verleger and Borgfeldt. Heads made of biscaloid, an imitation bisque and composition that is like ceramic, with molded hair, glass or painted eyes, open /closed mouth with two upper teeth, laughing expression, compo arms and lower legs, cloth torso and upper legs, some with crier. Mark "copyriht" misspelled.

*Mark:*

Gladdie
Copyright By
Helen W. Jensen
Germany

**Biscaloid ceramic head**

| | | |
|---|---|---|
| 18" | $875.00 | $1,150.00 |
| 20" | $1,050.00 | $1,400.00 |

**Bisque head, mold #1410**

| | | |
|---|---|---|
| 14" | $,2,600.00 | $3,450.00 |
| 18" | $3,300.00 | $4,400.00 |
| 21" | $4,150.00 | $5,400.00 |
| 26" | $5,100.00 | $6,800.00 |

*18" Gladdie, $825.00. Courtesy McMasters Doll Auctions.*

# Goebel

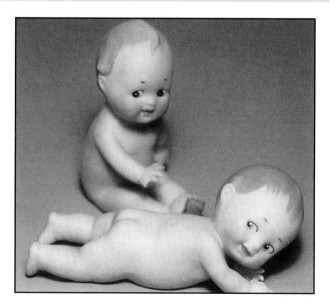

*Two rare Goebel position babies with incised markings, $225.00+ each. Courtesy of Matrix.*

**Goebel Wm. and F & W., 1871 – 1930+. Oeslau, Bavaria.** Made porcelain and glazed china dolls, as well as bathing dolls, Kewpie-types, and others. Earlier mark was triangle with half-moon.

First price indicates dolls in good condition, with flaws; second price indicates dolls in excellent condition appropriately dressed or original clothes.

*Marks:*

*Left: 4" Goebel child with molded flowers in hair and original clothes, $325.00. Right: 6" Ernst Heubach googly, $450.00. Courtesy of Matrix.*

**Character baby,** after 1909, open mouth, sleep eyes, five-piece bent limb baby body.

| | | |
|---|---|---|
| 15" | $365.00 | $485.00 |
| 18" | $450.00 | $600.00 |
| 21" | $575.00 | $775.00 |
| 26" | $725.00 | $975.00 |

Toddler body

| | | |
|---|---|---|
| 14" | $425.00 | $550.00 |
| 17" | $525.00 | $700.00 |
| 22" | $775.00 | $1,050.00 |

**Child, 1895+, open mouth,** composition body, sleep or set eyes

| | | |
|---|---|---|
| 6" | $115.00 | $150.00 |
| 14" | $225.00 | $300.00 |
| 19" | $375.00 | $500.00 |
| 21" | $450.00 | $600.00 |

**Child, open/closed mouth,** shoulder plate, wig, molded teeth, kid body, bisque hands

| | | |
|---|---|---|
| 17" | $625.00 | $850.00 |
| 20" | $850.00 | $1,150.00 |

**Character child, after 1909,** molded hair, may have molded flowers or ribbons, painted features on five-piece papier mache body.

| | | |
|---|---|---|
| 9" | $300.00 | $400.00 |
| 11" | $375.00 | $500.00 |
| 14" | $465.00 | $625.00 |

**Molded on bonnet or hat,** closed mouth, five-piece papier mache body, painted features

| | | |
|---|---|---|
| 7" | $250.00 | $350.00 |
| 9" | $375.00 | $500.00 |
| 12" | $450.00 | $600.00 |

## Googly

Side-glancing eyes that were sometimes round, painted, glass, tin, or celluloid. When they move to the side they are called flirty eyes. They were popular from 1900 to 1925. Most doll manufacturers made dolls with googly eyes. Painted eyes could be found painted looking to the side or straight ahead. If the eyes were inserted, the same head mold can be found with/or without flirty eyes. May have closed smiling mouth, composition or papier mache body, molded hair or wigged.

First price is for dolls in good condition with flaws; second price is for dolls in excellent condition appropriately dressed or with original clothes.

**ALL BISQUE**

Jointed shoulders and hips, molded shoes and socks

*7" bisque Goebel Googly, five-piece composition body, $650.00. Courtesy McMasters Doll Auctions.*

**Rigid neck,** glass eyes

| | | |
|---|---|---|
| 3" | $195.00 | $265.00 |
| 5" | $350.00 | $450.00 |

Painted eyes

| | | |
|---|---|---|
| 3" | $150.00 | $200.00 |
| 5" | $250.00 | $335.00 |

**Swivel neck, glass eyes**

| | | |
|---|---|---|
| 5" | $400.00 | $550.00 |
| 7" | $650.00 | $875.00 |

With jointed elbows, knees

| | | |
|---|---|---|
| 5" | $1,624.00 | $2,200.00 |
| 7" | $2,000.00 | $2,600.00 |

**Marked by maker: Mold #217, 330, 501**

| | | |
|---|---|---|
| 5" | $435.00 | $575.00 |
| 7" | $550.00 | $725.00 |

**Mold #189, 292**

| | | |
|---|---|---|
| 5" | $675.00 | $900.00 |
| 7" | $1,050.00 | $1,400.00 |

**Mold #222, "Our Fairy," Hertel & Schwab, ca. 1914, glass eyes,** sticker on torso, all bisque, wig, open/closed mouth with teeth, movable arms

| | | |
|---|---|---|
| 11" | $1,700.00 | $2,250.00 |

Our Fairy, painted eyes

| | | |
|---|---|---|
| 7" | $900.00 | $1,250.00 |

## BAHR & PROSCHILD
*Marked B.P.*
### Bisque
**Mold #401**

| | | |
|---|---|---|
| 6" | $350.00 | $475.00 |

**Mold #686,** baby

| | | |
|---|---|---|
| 16" | $1,200.00 | $1,600.00 |

Child

| | | |
|---|---|---|
| 13" | $1,850.00 | $2,500.00 |
| 15" | $2,250.00 | $3,000.00 |

## DEMOCOL
Bisque socket head, closed watermelon mouth, mohair wig, five-piece composition toddler body

| | | |
|---|---|---|
| 10" | $900.00 | $1,200.00 |

## HANDWERK, MAX
*Marked Elite,* bisque socket head, molded helmet or hat

| | | |
|---|---|---|
| 11" | $1,350.00 | $1,800.00 |

## HERTEL & SCHWAB
**#163, 164, 165**

| | | |
|---|---|---|
| 11" | $3,075.00 | $4,100.00 |
| 16" | $4,700.00 | $6,250.00 |

## HEUBACH, ERNST
**#262,** "EH" character, painted eyes, closed mouth
**#264** character

| | | |
|---|---|---|
| 8" | $300.00 | $400.00 |
| 11" | $375.00 | $500.00 |

**#291,** "EH" character, glass eyes, closed mouth

| | | |
|---|---|---|
| 9" | $1,000.00 | $1,350.00 |

**#318,** "EH" character, closed mouth

| | | |
|---|---|---|
| 11" | $960.00 | $1,285.00 |
| 14" | $1,500.00 | $2,050.00 |

**#319** "EH" character, tearful features

| | | |
|---|---|---|
| 8" | $425.00 | $575.00 |
| 11" | $850.00 | $1,150.00 |

**#322** character, closed smiling mouth

| | | |
|---|---|---|
| 10" | $500.00 | $650.00 |

**#417**

| | | |
|---|---|---|
| 9" | $900.00 | $1,250.00 |

*too few in database to determine reliable range*
**#419**

| | | |
|---|---|---|
| 8" | $1,450.00 | $1,700.00 |

*too few in database to determine reliable range*
** Rare examples may bring much higher prices*

## HEUBACH, GEBRUDER
**Mold #8556**

| | | |
|---|---|---|
| 15" | $6,000.00 | $8,000.00 |

**#8676**

| | | |
|---|---|---|
| 9" | $650.00 | $850.00 |
| 11" | $775.00 | $1,050.00 |

**#8723, #8995,** glass eyes

| | | |
|---|---|---|
| 13" | $2,100.00 | $2,800.00 |

**#9056,** full bangs, hair rolled under around head

| | | |
|---|---|---|
| 9" | $775.00 | $1,050.00 |
| 14" | $1,090.00 | $1,450.00 |

**#9573**

| | | |
|---|---|---|
| 9" | $675.00 | $900.00 |
| 11" | $1,050.00 | $1,400.00 |

**#9578, #11173,** "Tiss Me"

| | | |
|---|---|---|
| 10" | $1,050.00 | $1,450.00 |
| 14" | $1,200.00 | $1,600.00 |

**#9743,** sitting, wide open/closed mouth, top knot, star-shaped hands

| | | |
|---|---|---|
| 7" | $450.00 | $600.00 |

**Winker,** one eye painted closed

| | | |
|---|---|---|
| 14" | $1,600.00 | $2,200.00 |

## KAMMER & REINHARDT

**Mold #131, "S&H/K&R"** character, closed mouth

| | | |
|---|---|---|
| 9" | $2,100.00 | $2,800.00 |
| 13" | $4,150.00 | $5,500.00 |
| 16" | $5,850.00 | $7,800.00 |

*13" Kestner mold #221 Googly, $2,900.00. Courtesy McMasters Doll Auctions.*

## KESTNER

**Mold #221, ca. 1913, "JDK ges. gesch,"** character, smiling closed mouth

| | | |
|---|---|---|
| 12" | $3,500.00 | $4,730.00 |
| 19" | $6,450.00 | $8,600.00 |

## KLEY & HAHN

**#180 "K&H"** made by Hertel & Schwab & Co. for K&H, character, laughing open/closed mouth

| | | |
|---|---|---|
| 15" | $2,025.00 | $2,700.00 |
| 17" | $2,550.00 | $3,400.00 |

## LIMBACH

Marked with crown and cloverleaf, socket head, large round glass eyes, pug nose, closed smiling mouth

| | | |
|---|---|---|
| 8" | $3,600.00 * at auction |

## ARMAND MARSEILLE

**Mold #200, "AM 243"** character, closed mouth, molded tongue

| | | |
|---|---|---|
| 8" | $925.00 | $1,240.00 |
| 12" | $1,500.00 | $2,000.00 |

**#210, "AM 243"** character, solid dome head, painted eyes, closed mouth

| | | |
|---|---|---|
| 8" | $1,400.00 | $1,850.00 |
| 12" | $2,000.00 | $2,700.00 |

*Left: 7½" bisque Googly mold #320 by Armand Marseille, five-piece composition body, $600.00. Right: 7" Armand Marseille Googly mold #323, five-piece composition body, $875.00. Courtesy McMasters Doll Auctions.*

**#223,** ca. 1913, character, closed mouth

| | | |
|---|---|---|
| 7" | $550.00 | $750.00 |
| 11" | $725.00 | $950.00 |

**#240, "AM"** character, solid dome, painted eyes, closed mouth

| | | |
|---|---|---|
| 11" | $1,500.00 | $2,000.00 |
| 15" | $2,000.00 | $2,700.00 |

**#252, "AM 248"** ca. **1912,** character, solid dome, molded tuft, painted eyes, closed mouth

| | | |
|---|---|---|
| 9" | $1,350.00 | $1,800.00 |
| 12" | $1,800.00 | $2,400.00 |

**#253, "AM Nobbikid Reg. U.S. Pat. 066 Germany,"** ca. **1925,** character, closed mouth

| | | |
|---|---|---|
| 6" | $675.00 | $900.00 |
| 10" | $2,500.00 | $3,400.00 |

**#254, "AM"** character, solid dome, painted eyes, closed mouth

| | | |
|---|---|---|
| 10" | $600.00 | $800.00 |

**#310, "AM JUST ME,"** ca. **1929,** character, closed mouth for Geo. Borgfeldt & Co.

| | | |
|---|---|---|
| 9" | $750.00 | $950.00 |
| 12" | $1,350.00 | $1,800.00 |

Painted bisque

| | | |
|---|---|---|
| 9" | $525.00 | $700.00 |
| 12" | $825.00 | $1,100.00 |

**#320, "AM 255," ca. 1913,** character, solid dome, painted eyes, closed mouth

| | | |
|---|---|---|
| 9" | $575.00 | $775.00 |
| 12" | $700.00 | $950.00 |

**#322, "AM," ca. 1914,** character, solid dome, painted eyes, closed mouth

| | | |
|---|---|---|
| 8" | $500.00 | $675.00 |
| 11" | $650.00 | $875.00 |

**#323, ca. 1914 – 25,** character, glass eyes, closed mouth, also made in compo

| | | |
|---|---|---|
| 7" | $650.00 | $875.00 |
| 11" | $965.00 | $1,275.00 |
| 16" | $1,375.00 | $1,800.00 |

Baby body

| | | |
|---|---|---|
| 13" | $700.00 | $950.00 |
| 15" | $845.00 | $1,125.00 |

Painted bisque baby

| | | |
|---|---|---|
| 11" | $350.00 | $475.00 |
| 16" | $500.00 | $675.00 |

**#325, ca. 1915,** character, closed mouth

| | | |
|---|---|---|
| 9" | $548.00 | $725.00 |
| 14" | $750.00 | $1,000.00 |

## P.M. POZELLANFABRIK MENGERSGEREUTH

Ca. 1926

"PM" character, closed mouth (previously thought to be made by Otto Reinecke.)

**#950**

| | | |
|---|---|---|
| 8" | $725.00 | $975.00 |
| 11" | $825.00 | $1,100.00 |
| 15" | $1,200.00 | $1,600.00 |
| 18" | $1,400.00 | $1,850.00 |

## S.F.B.J.

**#245**

| | | |
|---|---|---|
| 8" | $975.00 | $1,300.00 |

Fully jointed body

| | | |
|---|---|---|
| 10" | $1,200.00 | $1,600.00 |
| 14" | $3,300.00 | $4,400.00 |

## STEINER, HERM

**#133, "HS"** character, closed mouth, five-piece papier mache body

| | | |
|---|---|---|
| 7" | $500.00 | $700.00 |

## WALTER & SOHN

**#208, ca. 1920,** "W&S" character, closed mouth, bisque socket head, five-piece papier mache body, painted socks and shoes

| | | |
|---|---|---|
| 8" | $525.00 | $700.00 |

# Greiner

**Greiner, Ludwig 1840 – 74,** succeeded by sons, 1890 – 1900, Philadelphia, PA. Papier mache shoulder head dolls with molded hair, painted/glass eyes, usually made up to be large dolls, 13" – 38".

First price is for dolls in good condition with flaws; second price is for dolls in excellent condition appropriately dressed or with original clothes.

*Marks:*

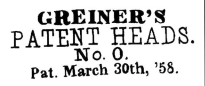

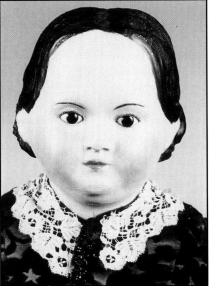

*33" glass-eyed pre-Greiner, papier mache, $2,000.00. Courtesy McMasters Doll Auctions.*

*30" papier mache, Greiner lady in red print dress, $975.00. Courtesy McMasters Doll Auctions.*

**With '58 label**

| | | |
|---|---|---|
| 17" | $400.00 | $550.00 |
| 23" | $525.00 | $725.00 |
| 26" | $600.00 | $825.00 |
| 30" | $725.00 | $975.00 |
| 35" | $975.00 | $1,300.00 |
| 38" | $1,350.00 | $1,800.00 |

**With '72 label**

| | | |
|---|---|---|
| 18" | $335.00 | $450.00 |
| 21" | $400.00 | $525.00 |
| 26" | $475.00 | $650.00 |
| 30" | $700.00 | $1,000.00 |

Glass eyes

| | | |
|---|---|---|
| 21" | $1,200.00 | $1,600.00 |
| 26" | $1,725.00 | $2,300.00 |

**Unmarked,** glass eyes, ca. 1850, pre-Greiner, papier mache shoulder head, cloth body, leather, wood, or cloth limbs, painted hair, black eyes, no pupils

| | | |
|---|---|---|
| 18" | $900.00 | $1,200.00 |
| 26" | $1,200.00 | $1,600.00 |
| 30" | $1,425.00 | $1,900.00 |

Painted eyes

| | | |
|---|---|---|
| 18" | $335.00 | $450.00 |
| 26" | $475.00 | $650.00 |
| 30" | $600.00 | $825.00 |

*Left: 25" bisque Armand Marseille Florodora, $200.00. Right: 29" bisque, Heinrich Handwerck child, $650.00. Courtesy McMasters Doll Auctions.*

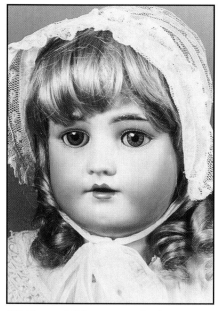

*30" bisque child, open mouth, glass eyes, composition body, human hair wig, $1,000.00.*

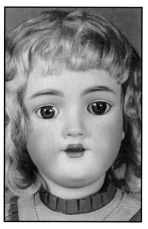

*26½" bisque Heinrich Handwerck child marked "119," $450.00. Courtesy McMasters Doll Auctions.*

**1876 – 1930, Gotha, Germany.** Made composition dolls' bodies, sent Handwerck molds to Simon and Halbig to make bisque heads. Trademarks included an eight-point star with French or German wording, a shield and *"Bebe Cosmopolite," "Bebe de Reclame,"* and *"Bebe Superior."* Sold dolls through Gimbels, Macy's, Montgomery Wards, and others. Bodies marked Handwerk in red on lower back torso. Patented a straight wrist body.

First price is for dolls in good condition with flaws; second price is for dolls in excellent condition appropriately dressed or with original clothes.

*Marks:*

119 - 13
HANDWERCK
5
Germany

110

W
Heinrich Handwerck
Simon & Halbig
Germany
0 1/2

11 1/2
99
DEP
Germany
HANDWERCK

Hch 2/0 H

**Child, no mold number, open mouth**, sleep or set eyes, ball jointed body, bisque socket head, appropriate wig, nicely dressed

| | | |
|---|---|---|
| 15" | $285.00 | $375.00 |
| 17" | $350.00 | $465.00 |
| 21" | $450.00 | $600.00 |
| 25" | $500.00 | $675.00 |
| 27" | $600.00 | $800.00 |
| 29" | $700.00 | $950.00 |
| 33" | $1,050.00 | $1,400.00 |
| 36" | $1,350.00 | $1,800.00 |
| 40" | $1,950.00 | $2,600.00 |

**Child with mold number, open mouth, Mold #69, 79, 89, 99, 109, 119, 139, 199**

| | | |
|---|---|---|
| 13" | $335.00 | $450.00 |
| 15" | $350.00 | $475.00 |
| 18" | $525.00 | $700.00 |
| 22" | $525.00 | $725.00 |
| 25" | $550.00 | $750.00 |
| 29" | $700.00 | $950.00 |
| 32" | $975.00 | $1,300.00 |
| 36" | $1,150.00 | $1,550.00 |
| 40" | $2,300.00 | $3,100.00 |

**Kid body, shoulder head, open mouth**

| | | |
|---|---|---|
| 14" | $175.00 | $235.00 |
| 17" | $250.00 | $330.00 |
| 24" | $350.00 | $475.00 |
| 26" | $500.00 | $675.00 |

**Mold #79, 89, closed mouth**

| | | |
|---|---|---|
| 15" | $1,275.00 | $1,700.00 |
| 18" | $1,500.00 | $2,000.00 |
| 22" | $1,800.00 | $2,400.00 |

*\* too few in database to determine reliable range*

**#189, open mouth**

| | | |
|---|---|---|
| 15" | $600.00 | $800.00 |
| 18" | $700.00 | $950.00 |
| 22" | $900.00 | $1,200.00 |

## Handwerk, Max

*24" Max Handwerk child, mold #283, $300.00. Courtesy McMasters Doll Auctions.*

**1899 – 1930, Walthershausen, Germany.** Made dolls and doll bodies, registered trademark, "Bebe Elite." Used heads made by Goebel.

*Marks:*

Max Handwerk
Bebe Elite
286/3
Germany

283/28,5
MAJC.
HANDWERCK
GERMANY.
2 1/4

**Child**

Bisque socket head, open mouth, sleep or set eyes, jointed composition body

Mold #283, 287, 291 and others

| | | |
|---|---|---|
| 23" | $400.00 | $550.00 |

**Bebe Elite**

Bisque socket head, mohair wig, glass sleep eyes, mohair lashes, open mouth, pierced ears, jointed composition/wood body. *Marks:* "Max Handwerk Bebe Elite 286 12 Germany" on back of head.

| | | |
|---|---|---|
| 16" | $450.00 | $600.00 |
| 24" | $700.00 | $950.00 |
| 29" | $800.00 | $1,050.00 |

Bebe Elite, flange neck, cloth body

| | | |
|---|---|---|
| 15" | $350.00 | $445.00 |
| 20" | $475.00 | $650.00 |

**Googly**

Bisque socket head, molded painted helmet and hair, glass eyes, smiling mouth, marked *"DEP Elite"*

| | | |
|---|---|---|
| 11" | $900.00 | $1,200.00 |

# Hartman, Karl

**1889 – 1930, Neustadt, Germany.** Made and exported bisque and celluloid dolls, especially small dolls in regional costumes, called Globe Babies. Kammer & Reinhardt made heads for Hartman.

*Marks:*

Globe Baby
DEP
Germany
C 3 H

DEP
CH
10/0
GERMANY

### Child
Bisque socket head, open mouth, jointed composition and wood body

| | | |
|---|---|---|
| 22" | $225.00 | $375.00 |
| 32" | $735.00 | $975.00 |

### Globe Baby
Bisque socket head, glass sleep eyes, open mouth, four teeth, mohair or human hair wig, five-piece papier mache or composition body with painted shoes and stockings.

| | | |
|---|---|---|
| 8" | $315.00 | $450.00 |
| 9" | $375.00 | $500.00 |

*22" Karl Hartman child, $275.00. Courtesy McMasters Doll Auctions.*

# Hertel Schwab & Co.

**1910 – 30+, Stutzhaus, Germany.** Founded by August Hertel and Heinrich Schwab, who both designed doll heads. They were used by Borgfeldt, Kley and Hahn, Konig & Wernicke, Louis Wolf, and others. Made china and bisque heads as well as all porcelain; most with character faces. Molded hair or wig, painted blue or glass eyes (often blue gray), open mouth with tongue, or closed mouth, socket or shoulder heads. Usually marked with mold number and *"Made in Germany,"* or mark of company that owned the mold.

*Marks:*

2046
151
3

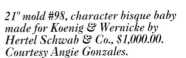

*21" mold #98, character bisque baby made for Koenig & Wernicke by Hertel Schwab & Co., $1,000.00. Courtesy Angie Gonzales.*

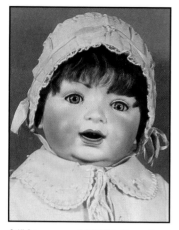

*26" bisque, mold #152, five-piece composition bent limb body, glass eyes, mohair wig, $1,000.00.*

*22" bisque, Hertel, Schwab & Co. boy marked "152," $425.00. Courtesy McMasters Doll Auctions.*

## Baby

Bisque head, molded hair or wig, open or open/closed mouth, teeth, sleep or painted eyes, bent limb composition baby body

**Mold #142, 150, 151, 152, 154**

| | | |
|---|---|---|
| 11" | $335.00 | $450.00 |
| 13" | $400.00 | $525.00 |
| 15" | $450.00 | $600.00 |
| 22" | $675.00 | $900.00 |
| 24" | $700.00 | $950.00 |

Toddler body

| | | |
|---|---|---|
| 14" | $375.00 | $500.00 |
| 20" | $550.00 | $750.00 |

## Child

**#127,** ca. 1915, character face, solid dome with molded hair, sleep eyes, open mouth, Patsy-type

| | | |
|---|---|---|
| 15" | $1,000.00 | $1,350.00 |
| 17" | $1,500.00 | $2,000.00 |

*9" all bisque Our Fairy marked "222," made by Hertel & Schwab, $400.00. Courtesy McMasters Doll Auctions.*

**#131,** character face, solid dome, painted closed mouth

| | |
|---|---|
| 18" | $1,300.00 * at auction |

**#134,** character face, sleep eyes, closed mouth

| | |
|---|---|
| 11" | $3,500.00 * at auction |

**#136,** "Made in Germany," character face, sleep eyes, open mouth

| | | |
|---|---|---|
| 24" | $900.00 | $1,200.00 |

**#140,** character, glass eyes, open/closed laughing mouth

| | | |
|---|---|---|
| 12" | $2,550.00 | $3,400.00 |
| 16" | $3,525.00 | $4,700.00 |
| 18" | $4,275.00 | $5,700.00 |

**#141,** character, painted eyes, open/closed mouth

| | | |
|---|---|---|
| 12" | $2,325.00 | $3,100.00 |
| 24" | $5,500.00 | $7,500.00 |

**#167, "K&H"** character, sleep eyes, open/closed or closed mouth, made for Kley & Hahn

| | | |
|---|---|---|
| 15" | $1,500.00 | $2,000.00 * at auction |

**Googly**

**#163**

| | |
|---|---|
| 16" | $6,250.00 * at auction |

**#222, Our Fairy,** all bisque, wigged glass eyes

| | | |
|---|---|---|
| 11" | $1,350.00 | $1,800.00 |

Painted eyes, molded hair

| | | |
|---|---|---|
| 8" | $650.00 | $850.00 |
| 12" | $1,100.00 | $1,500.00 |

# Heubach, Ernst

*16" bisque Ernst Heubach newborn baby, mold #340, $700.00. Courtesy Sherryl Shirran.*

*22" Ernst Heubach, mold #320, with composition toddler body, $750.00. Courtesy Amanda Hash.*

*15" Ernst Heubach character, $450.00. Courtesy McMasters Doll Auctions.*

**1886 – 1930+, Koppelsdorf, Germany**. In 1919, the son of Armand Marseille married the daughter of Ernst Heubach, and merged the two factories. Mold numbers range from 250 to 452; made porcelain heads for Dressel (Jutta), Revalo, and others.

Marks:

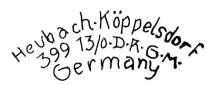

Heubach. 1900 7/0

**250·12/0**

**Koppelsdorf**

**Thuringia**

### Baby

Open mouth, glass eyes, socket head, wig, five-piece bent limb compo body, add more for toddler body, flirty eyes. **Mold #267, 300, 320, 321, 342**

| | | |
|---|---|---|
| 11" | $170.00 | $230.00 |
| 14" | $275.00 | $375.00 |
| 16" | $375.00 | $500.00 |
| 27" | $725.00 | $975.00 |

Fully jointed body

| | | |
|---|---|---|
| 19" | $450.00 | $600.00 |
| 24" | $525.00 | $725.00 |

**Baby, newborn, ca. 1925+,** solid dome, molded, painted hair, glass eyes, closed mouth, cloth body, composition or celluloid hands. **Mold #339, 340, 348, 349, 399**

| | | |
|---|---|---|
| 12" | $300.00 | $425.00 |
| 14" | $425.00 | $575.00 |
| 16" | $525.00 | $700.00 |
| 18" | $600.00 | $800.00 |

**Black, #444**

| | | |
|---|---|---|
| 12" | $300.00 | $400.00 |

### Child, 1888+

Open mouth, glass eyes, kid or cloth body, bisque lower arms

| | | |
|---|---|---|
| 14" | $125.00 | $175.00 |
| 20" | $225.00 | $310.00 |
| 24" | $325.00 | $450.00 |
| 30" | $550.00 | $750.00 |

Painted bisque

| | | |
|---|---|---|
| 10" | $100.00 | $140.00 |
| 14" | $150.00 | $200.00 |

**Mold #250, 275 (shoulder head), 302, kid body**

| | | |
|---|---|---|
| 8" | $125.00 | $175.00 |
| 11" | $150.00 | $200.00 |
| 15" | $215.00 | $250.00 |
| 18" | $325.00 | $425.00 |
| 24" | $450.00 | $600.00 |
| 29" | $550.00 | $750.00 |
| 34" | $750.00 | $1,000.00 |
| 38" | $1,000.00 | $1,350.00 |

**1820 – 1945, Lichte, Thuringia, Germany.** Made bisque heads and all bisque dolls, characters after 1910, either socket or shoulder head, molded hair or wigs, sleeping or intaglio eyes, in heights from 4" to 26". Mold numbers from 556 to 10633. Sunburst or square marks; more dolls with square marks.

*Marks:*

*12" #5842 Gebruder Heubach with bisque head and deep shoulder plate with sew holes on shoulder for attachment of cloth for arms; cloth mid-section with bisque limbs, $1,000.00. Courtesy Amanda Hash.*

**Marked "Heubach," No Mold Number**
Open/closed mouth, dimples
| | | |
|---|---|---|
| 18" | $3,300.00 | $4,450.00 |
| 24" | $4,700.00 | $6,300.00 |

Adult, open mouth, glass eyes
| | | |
|---|---|---|
| 14" | $3,350.00 | $4,500.00 |

Smile, painted eyes
| | | |
|---|---|---|
| 15" | $2,700.00 | $3,500.00 |

**Character Child, Shoulder Head**
**#6688,** solid dome, molded hair, intaglio eyes, closed mouth
| | | |
|---|---|---|
| 10" | $450.00 | $625.00 |

**#6692,** sunburst mark, intaglio eyes, closed mouth
| | | |
|---|---|---|
| 14" | $650.00 | $875.00 |

**#6736,** square mark, painted eyes, laughing mouth, boy
| | | |
|---|---|---|
| 13" | $800.00 | $1,100.00 |
| 16" | $1,400.00 | $1,900.00 |

**#7345,** sunburst, pink-tinted bisque, glass eyes, closed mouth, wig, kid body
| | |
|---|---|
| 17" | $1,150.00 |

*\*too few examples in database to give reliable range*

**#7644,** sunburst or square mark, molded hair, painted eyes, open/closed laughing mouth
| | | |
|---|---|---|
| 14" | $650.00 | $865.00 |
| 17" | $875.00 | $1,200.00 |

*13" bisque Gebruder Heubach with square mark, molded hair, open/closed mouth with teeth, $750.00. Courtesy Amanda Hash.*

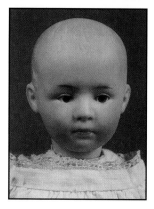

9" bisque Gebruder
Heubach baby, $300.00.
Courtesy McMasters Doll
Auctions.

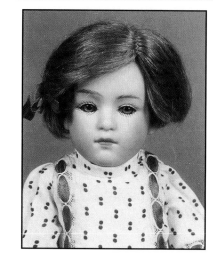

10½" bisque Gebruder Heubach,
mold #6979, $1,100.00. Courtesy
McMasters Doll Auctions.

20½" bisque, Gebruder
Heubach child, marked "8319"
(sunburst), $3,500.00. Courtesy

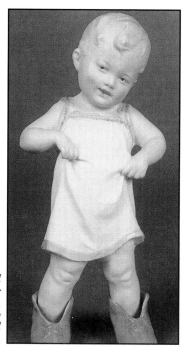

8" all
bisque Gebruder
Heubach figurine,
$400.00. Courtesy
McMasters Doll
Auction.

10" Gebruder Heubach Screamer, $350.00. Courtesy
McMasters Doll Auctions.

**#7850, "Coquette,"** molded hair with ribbon, open/closed mouth with teeth.

| | | |
|---|---|---|
| 11" | $550.00 | $750.00 |
| 15" | $800.00 | $1,100.00 |

**#7926,** glass eyes, smiling open mouth, lady

| | | |
|---|---|---|
| 15" | $1,500.00 | $2,000.00 |

* *too few examples in database to give reliable range*

**#7972,** molded hair, intaglio eyes, closed mouth

| | | |
|---|---|---|
| 20" | $1,500.00 | $2,000.00 |

* *too few examples in database to give reliable range*

**#8221,** square mark, solid dome, intaglio yes, open/closed mouth

| | | |
|---|---|---|
| 14" | $500.00 | $675.00 |

* *too few examples in database to give reliable range*

**#8764,** Einco, produced for Eisenmann & Co. googly eyes, closed mouth

| | | |
|---|---|---|
| 21" | $3,900.00 | $5,250.00 |

* *too few examples in database to give reliable range*

**#9355, "Dolly Dimple"** square mark, glass eyes, open mouth

| | | |
|---|---|---|
| 13" | $650.00 | $850.00 |
| 19" | $925.00 | $1,250.00 |

## Character Baby/Child, Socket Head

**Mold #5636,** glass eyes, open/closed laughing mouth, two teeth

| | | |
|---|---|---|
| 13" | $1,500.00 | $2,000.00 |
| 15" | $1,800.00 | $2,400.00 |

**Mold #5689,** sunburst mark, glass eyes, open mouth

| | | |
|---|---|---|
| 14" | $1,350.00 | $1,800.00 |
| 17" | $1,700.00 | $2,250.00 |
| 22" | $2,200.00 | $2,900.00 |

**#5730, "Santa,"** sunburst mark, glass eyes, open mouth, made for Hamburger & Co.

| | | |
|---|---|---|
| 16" | $1,250.00 | $1,700.00 |
| 19" | $1,900.00 | $2,500.00 |
| 26" | $2,100.00 | $2,800.00 |

**#5777, "Dolly Dimple,"** sleep eyes, open mouth, made for Hamburger & Co.

| | | |
|---|---|---|
| 14" | $1,725.00 | $2,300.00 |
| 16" | $1,900.00 | $2,500.00 |
| 24" | $2,600.00 | $3,450.00 |

**#6894, 7759,** baby, sunburst or square mark, intaglio eyes, closed mouth, molded hair

| | | |
|---|---|---|
| 7" | $275.00 | $375.00 |
| 9" | $375.00 | $500.00 |
| 12" | $525.00 | $700.00 |

**#6969,** square mark, glass eyes, closed mouth

| | | |
|---|---|---|
| 13" | $1,450.00 | $1,950.00 |
| 16" | $1,800.00 | $2,400.00 |
| 19" | $2,400.00 | $3,300.00 |
| 25" | $3,250.00 | $4,400.00 |

**#6970,** sunburst, glass eyes, closed mouth

| | | |
|---|---|---|
| 10" | $1,300.00 | $1,800.00 |
| 13" | $1,700.00 | $2,300.00 |
| 16" | $2,350.00 | $3,000.00 |
| 21" | $3,000.00 | $4,000.00 |

**#7246, 7247, 7248** sunburst or square mark, glass eyes, closed mouth

| | | |
|---|---|---|
| 9" | $1,200.00 | $1,700.00 |
| 11" | $1,600.00 | $2,100.00 |
| 15" | $2,100.00 | $2,900.00 |
| 20" | $2,900.00 | $3,800.00 |

**#7268,** square mark, glass eyes, closed mouth, wig

| | |
|---|---|
| 12" | $5,000.00 * at auction |

**#7602,** molded or tufts of hair, intaglio eyes, closed mouth

| | | |
|---|---|---|
| 14" | $1,500.00 | $2,050.00 |
| 17" | $1,875.00 | $2,500.00 |

Glass eyes

| | | |
|---|---|---|
| 17" | $2,100.00 | $2,700.00 |
| 22" | $2,600.00 | $3,450.00 |

**#7604,** laughing open/closed mouth, painted or molded hair, intaglio eyes

| | | |
|---|---|---|
| 10" | $400.00 | $550.00 |
| 14" | $625.00 | $850.00 |
| 15" | $525.00 | $700.00 |

2½" bisque clown in egg, square Gebruder Heubach mark #2604, $175.00. Courtesy Amanda Hash.

**#7622,** sunburst mark, molded hair, intaglio eyes, closed mouth

| | | |
|---|---|---|
| 15" | $1,400.00 | $1,900.00 |
| 20" | $2,300.00 | $2,600.00 |

**#7711,** sunburst mark, glass eyes, open mouth, flapper body

| | | |
|---|---|---|
| 10" | $525.00 | $700.00 |
| 13" | $650.00 | $900.00 |

**#7911,** intaglio eyes, laughing open/closed mouth

| | | |
|---|---|---|
| 9" | $525.00 | $700.00 |
| 15" | $900.00 | $1,200.00 |
| 17" | $1,000.00 | $1,350.00 |

**#7975** "Stuart Baby," glass eyes, removable molded bisque bonnet, sunburst or square mark, closed mouth

| | | |
|---|---|---|
| 13" | $1,425.00 | $1,900.00 |

**#7977,** "Baby Stuart," sunburst or square mark, molded bonnet, closed mouth, painted eyes

| | | |
|---|---|---|
| 8" | $600.00 | $800.00 |
| 10" | $750.00 | $1,000.00 |
| 14" | $1,300.00 | $1,700.00 |
| 16" | $1,600.00 | $2,150.00 |

**#8191,** "Crooked Smile," square mark, character, intaglio eyes, laughing, boy

| | | |
|---|---|---|
| 14" | $375.00 | $500.00 |
| 17" | $475.00 | $650.00 |
| 22" | $550.00 | $750.00. |

**#8192,** sunburst or square mark, sleep eyes, open mouth
| | | |
|---|---|---|
| 13" | $675.00 | $900.00 |
| 15" | $775.00 | $1,050.00 |
| 18" | $1,100.00 | $1,500.00 |

**#8316, "Grinning Boy,"** square mark, wig, open/closed mouth, eight molded teeth, glass eyes
| | | |
|---|---|---|
| 16" | $2,500.00 | $3,400.00 |
| 19" | $3,600.00 | $4,800.00 |

**#8381, "Princess Juliana,"** square mark, molded hair, ribbon, painted eyes, closed mouth
| | | |
|---|---|---|
| 14" | $5,000.00 | $6,600.00+ |
| 18" | $6,400.00 | $8,500.00+ |

**#8413,** square mark, wig, sleep eyes, open/closed mouth, molded tongue, two upper teeth
| | |
|---|---|
| 19" | $2,400.00 |
| 24" | $,3600.00 |

*\* too few examples in database to give reliable range*

**#8420,** square mark, sleep eyes, closed mouth
| | | |
|---|---|---|
| 15" | $2,100.00 | $2,800.00 |

*\* too few examples in database to give reliable range*

**#8429,** square mark, glass eyes, closed mouth
| | | |
|---|---|---|
| 14" | $1,150.00 | $1,525.00 |

*\* too few examples in database to give reliable range*

**#8774, "Whistling Jim"** smoker or whistler, flange neck, square mark, intaglio eyes, molded hair, cloth body with bellows
| | | |
|---|---|---|
| 13" | $900.00 | $1,200.00 |

**#8819,** square mark, intaglio eyes, open/closed mouth
| | | |
|---|---|---|
| 9" | $1,050.00 | $1,400.00 |

*\* too few examples in database to give reliable range*

**#9027,** bisque solid dome, molded hair, intaglio eyes, closed mouth
| | | |
|---|---|---|
| 13" | $900.00 | $1,200.00 |

*\* too few examples in database to give reliable range*

**#9055,** molded hair, intaglio eyes, closed mouth
| | | |
|---|---|---|
| 11" | $275.00 | $375.00 |

*\* too few examples in database to give reliable range*

**#9056,** square mark, googly painted eyes, molded hair, closed mouth
| | | |
|---|---|---|
| 8" | $525.00 | $700.00 |

*\* too few examples in database to give reliable range*

**#9457,** square mark, solid dome, intaglio eyes, closed mouth, Indian
| | | |
|---|---|---|
| 15" | $1,875.00 | $2,500.00 |
| 18" | $3,000.00 | $4,000.00 |

**#9573,** square mark, glass googly eyes, closed mouth
| | | |
|---|---|---|
| 7" | $850.00 | $1,100.00 |

*\* too few examples in database to give reliable range*

**#9746,** square mark, painted eyes, closed mouth
| | | |
|---|---|---|
| 7½" | $600.00 | $800.00 |

**#10532** square mark, glass eyes, open mouth
| | | |
|---|---|---|
| 13½" | $450.00 | $600.00 |

# Heubach, Gebruder (cont.)

| | | |
|---|---|---|
| 25" | $1,125.00 | $1,500.00 |

**#11010, marked "Revalo,"** sleep eyes, open mouth, made for Gebr. Ohlhaver

| | | |
|---|---|---|
| 19" | $525.00 | $700.00 |
| 24" | $650.00 | $850.00 |

**#11173, "Tiss Me,"** wig,

| | | |
|---|---|---|
| 8" | $1,500.00 | $2,000.00 |

**Figurines**

**Piano Baby, #7287, 9693 and others**

| | | |
|---|---|---|
| 5" | $400.00 | $525.00 |
| 9" | $525.00 | $700.00 |

**#8455,** cupid in auto figurine

| | |
|---|---|
| 10" | $375.00 |

## Hulss, Adolph

**Hulss, Adolph, 1915 – 30+, Waltershausen, Germany.** Made dolls with bisque heads, jointed composition bodies, trademark, Nesthakchen. The "h" in mold mark often resembles a "b." Made babies, toddlers, and child dolls with ball joints.

*Marks:*

*15" bisque, Adolph Hulss toddler with flirty eyes and active crier, head made by Simon Halbig, mold 156, $750.00. Courtesy of Matrix.*

**Baby**

Bisque socket head, sleep eyes, open mouth, teeth, wig, bent leg baby composition body, add more for flirty eyes

**Mold #156**

| | | |
|---|---|---|
| 16" | $475.00 | $650.00 |
| 21" | $925.00 | $1,250.00 |

Toddler

| | | |
|---|---|---|
| 14" | $625.00 | $825.00 |
| 18" | $675.00 | $900.00 |

## Child

Bisque socket head, wig, sleep eyes, open mouth, teeth, tongue, jointed composition body

**Mold #176**

| | | |
|---|---|---|
| 18" | $675.00 | $900.00 |
| 24" | $975.00 | $1,350.00 |

## Huret, Maison

**1812 – 1930+, France.** Bisque, china heads, painted or glass eyes, closed mouth, bodies of composition, gutta-percha, kid, or wood, sometimes metal hands. Used fur or mohair for wigs, dressed as ladies or children.

*Marks:*

BREVET D'INV: S.G.D.G.
MAISON HURET
Boulevard Montmartre, 22
PARIS.

HURET
34 Bould Haussmann
PARIS

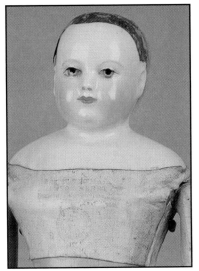

*18" china shoulder head fashion by Mme. Huret, mark stamped on kid over wood upper body, jointed lower body, ca. 1870, 18,000.00+. Courtesy Rosalie Whyel Museum of Doll Art. Photo by Charles Backus.*

**Huret,** bisque or china glazed shoulder head, kid body with bisque lower arms, glass eyes

| | | |
|---|---|---|
| 14" | $4,400.00 | $5,800.00 |
| 19" | $5,900.00 | $7,900.00 |

**Swivel neck**

18"  $30,000+

* *too few in database to give reliable range*

**Wood body,** shoulder plate, painted eyes, on labeled body

17"  $21,000.00 at auction

* *too few in database to give reliable range*

**Gutta percha body**

19"  $20,000.00+

* *too few in database to give reliable range*

Child with provenance, glass eyes

18"  $62,000.00 at auction

* *too few in database to give reliable range*

## Huret, Maison (cont.)

**Kid body,** painted eyes

| | | |
|---|---|---|
| 15" | $11,000.00 | $15,250.00 |
| 19" | $14,250.00 | $19,000.00 |

**Portrait adult,** painted eyes, articulated wooden body, metal hands

| | |
|---|---|
| 18" | $17,500.00 |

*too few in database to give reliable range.*

**Child**

| | |
|---|---|
| 17" | $25,000.00 |
| 22" | $30,000.00 |

*too few in database to give reliable range.*

## Jullien

**1827 – 1904, Paris, Conflans, St. Leonard.** Had a porcelain factory, won some awards, purchased bisque heads from Francois Gaultier.

*Marks:*

# 5
# JULLIEN

Bisque socket head, wig, glass eyes, pierced ears, open mouth with teeth or closed mouth, on jointed composition body

*20" open mouth Jullien, $1,700.00. Courtesy McMasters Doll Auctions.*

**Closed mouth**

| | | |
|---|---|---|
| 18" | $2,700.00 | $3,600.00 |
| 25" | $3,300.00 | $4,400.00 |

**Open mouth**

| | | |
|---|---|---|
| 20" | $1,275.00 | $1,700.00 |
| 28" | $1,800.00 | $2,400.00 |

## Jumeau

**1842 – 1899, Paris and Monttreuil-sous-Bois; succeeded by S.F.B.J. through 1958.** Founder Pierre Francois Jumeau made fashion dolls with kid or wood bodies, head marked with size number; bodies stamped "JUMEAU//MEDAILLE D'OR//PARIS." Early Jumeau heads were pressed pre – 1890. By 1878, Pierre's son, Emile Jumeau was the head of the company and made Bebe Jumeau. It was marked on the back of head, the chemise, and with a band on the arm of the dress. Tete Jumeaus have poured heads. Bebe Protige and Bebe Jumeau were registered trademarks in 1886; Bebe mark in 1891; Bebe Marcheur in 1895; Bebe Francaise in 1896.

First price is for dolls in good condition, but with some flaw; second price is for dolls in excellent condition, nicely wigged, and with appropriate clothing.

Mold Numbers of marked EJs and Tetes approximate the following heights: 1 – 10", 2 – 11", 3 – 12", 4 – 13", 5 – 14", 6 – 16", 7 – 7", 8 – 18", 9 – 20", 10 – 21", 11 – 24", 12 – 26", 13 – 30

*Marks:*
*On heads:*

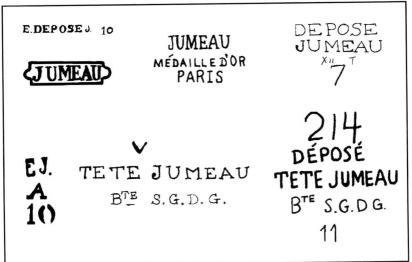

*Marks after 1900:*

*Marks on bodies:*

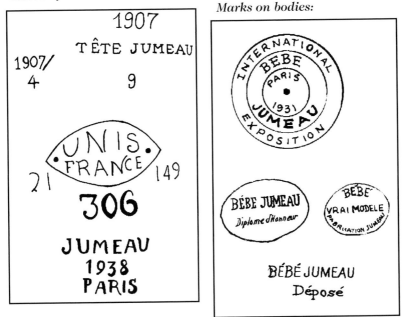

*Marks on shoes:*

**BÉBE JUMEAU**

MED.OR 1878

PARIS

DÉPOSÉ

## Fashion Type
Marked with size number on swivel head, stamped kid body

| | | |
|---|---|---|
| 12" | $1,800.00 | $2,400.00 |
| 15" | $2,400.00 | $3,200.00 |
| 19" | $2,700.00 | $3,600.00 |

**Wood Body, bisque lower arms**

| | | |
|---|---|---|
| 18" | $4,300.00 | $5,700.00 |
| 22" | $5,100.00 | $6,800.00 |

**Extra Large Eyes**

| | | |
|---|---|---|
| 12" | $1,800.00 | $2,400.00 |
| 16" | $2,100.00 | $2,800.00 |

**Jumeau Portrait**

| | | |
|---|---|---|
| 15" | $2,550.00 | $3,400.00 |
| 18" | $4,200.00 | $5,600.00 |
| 22" | $4,800.00 | $6,400.00 |
| 26" | $5,600.00 | $7,500.00 |
| 28" | $6,250.00 | $8,350.00 |
| 30" | $18,000.00 | |

**Wooden Body**

| | | |
|---|---|---|
| 15" | $4,200.00 | $5,625.00 |
| 18" | $6,500.00 | $8,700.00 |
| 26" | $9,000.00 | $12,000.00 |

**Almond Eye,** early style, eyes are larger and more round

| | | |
|---|---|---|
| 13" | $4,800.00 | $6,400.00 |
| 15" | $5,250.00 | $7,000.00 |
| 18" | $6,000.00 | $8,050.00 |
| 23" | $9,000.00 | $12,000.00 |

**E.J. Bebe, 1881 – 86**
*Marks:*

8

**E J**

**Earlier EJ mark, above,** socket head, wig, paperweight eyes, pierced ears, closed mouth jointed body with straight wrists

| | | |
|---|---|---|
| 17" | $7,500.00 | $10,000.00 |
| 22" | $12,000.00 | $16,000.00 |

**EJ/A marked Bebe**

| | | |
|---|---|---|
| 14" | $12,500.00 | $16,000.00 |
| 22" | $19,000.00 | $26,000.00 |
| 26" | $24,500.00 | $31,000.00 |

**Mid EJ mark** has size number centered between the E and J *(E 8 J)*

| | | |
|---|---|---|
| 9 – 10" | $4,275.00 | $5,700.00 |
| 15" | $4,450.00 | $5,950.00 |
| 18" | $4,875.00 | $6,500.00 |
| 20" | $5,250.00 | $7,000.00 |
| 22" | $5,550.00 | $7,400.00 |
| 26" | $6,450.00 | $8,600.00 |

**Later EJ mark** is preceded by DEPOSE *(DEPOSE/E 8 J)*

| | | |
|---|---|---|
| 18" | $4,125.00 | $5,500.00+ |
| 22" | $4,800.00 | $6,400.00+ |
| 26" | $5,700.00 | $7,600.00+ |

**Depose Jumeau**

Marked head, ca. 1886 – 89, composition and wood body with straight wrists, *marked "Medaille d'Or Paris,"* pierced ears, closed mouth, paperweight eyes

| | | |
|---|---|---|
| 14" | $3,750.00 | $5,000.00 |
| 18" | $4,400.00 | $5,900.00 |
| 23" | $5,200.00 | $6,900.00 |

**Long Face Triste Bebe, 1879 – 1886**

Head marked with number only, applied pierced ears, closed mouth, paperweight eyes, straight wrists on Jumeau marked body

| | | |
|---|---|---|
| 19" | $14,000.00 | $18,500.00+ |
| 27" | $22,500.00 | $27,000.00+ |

*19" open mouth Jumeau, $1,900.00. Courtesy McMasters Doll Auctions.*

**Tete Jumeau, ca. 1885+**

Red stamp on head, stamp or sticker on body, wig, glass eyes, pierced ears, closed mouth, jointed composition body with straight wrists

**Bebe (child),** closed mouth

| | | |
|---|---|---|
| 10" | $4,500.00 | $6,000.00 |
| 12" | $2,500.00 | $3,300.00 |
| 15" | $2,625.00 | $3,500.00 |
| 17" | $3,000.00 | $4,000.00 |
| 19" | $3,400.00 | $4,500.00 |
| 23" | $3,600.00 | $4,800.00 |
| 26" | $3,825.00 | $5,100.00 |
| 30" | $4,500.00 | $6,000.00 |
| 32" | $4,650.00 | $6,200.00 |
| 35" | $5,625.00 | $7,500.00 |

*22" Jumeau 1907, $2,700.00. Courtesy McMasters Doll Auctions.*

*20" bisque Long Face Jumeau, rare size 9 with original wig, jewelry, and factory chemise, $20,000.00+. Courtesy of Matrix.*

Open mouth

| | | |
|---|---|---|
| 17" | $1,725.00 | $2,300.00 |
| 22" | $2,100.00 | $2,800.00 |
| 25" | $2,400.00 | $3,200.00 |
| 28" | $2,625.00 | $3,500.00 |
| 32" | $3,000.00 | $4,000.00 |

**Adult body,** closed mouth

| | | |
|---|---|---|
| 20" | $4,500.00 | $6,000.00 |
| 25" | $4,875.00 | $6,500.00 |

Open mouth

| | | |
|---|---|---|
| 14" | $1,650.00 | $2,200.00 |
| 16" | $1,950.00 | $2,600.00 |
| 19" | $2,175.00 | $2,900.00 |
| 20" | $2,325.00 | $3,100.00 |
| 22" | $2,475.00 | $3,300.00 |
| 24" | $2,625.00 | $3,500.00 |
| 28" | $3,000.00 | $4,000.00 |
| 30" | $3,300.00 | $4,400.00 |
| 34" | $3,600.00 | $4,800.00 |

**1907, Marked Jumeau**

Some with Tete Jumeau stamp, sleep or set eyes, open mouth, jointed French body

| | | |
|---|---|---|
| 14" | $875.00 | $1,750.00 |
| 17" | $,1750.00 | $2,350.00 |
| 20" | $2,100.00 | $2,800.00 |
| 23" | $2,325.00 | $3,100.00 |
| 26" | $2,625.00 | $3,500.00 |
| 29" | $2,900.00 | $3,800.00 |
| 32" | $3,000.00 | $4,050.00 |

**B/L. Bebe, ca. 1880s**

Marked B. L. for the Louver department store, socket head, wig, pierced ears, paperweight eyes, closed mouth, jointed composition body

| | | |
|---|---|---|
| 32" | $3,000.00 | $4,050.00 |

*Too few examples in database for reliable range*

**R. Bebe, ca 1880s**

Wig, pierced ears, paperweight eyes, closed mouth, jointed composition body with straight wrists

| | | |
|---|---|---|
| 22" | $3,825.00 | $5,100.00 |

*too few examples in database for reliable range*

## Character Child

**200 series,** marked with mold number and Jumeau,

| | | |
|---|---|---|
| 15" | $36,000.00+ | |
| 21" | $58,000.00+ | |

**#230,** open mouth

| | | |
|---|---|---|
| 16" | $1,080.00 | $1,450.00 |
| 20" | $1,350.00 | $1,800.00 |

**Two-Faced Jumeau**

| | |
|---|---|
| 18" | $10,500.00 *at auction |

**Phonograph Jumeau**

Bisque head, open mouth, phonograph in torso, working condition.

| | |
|---|---|
| 20" | $7,800.00 |
| 27" | $11,400.00 |

*Too few examples in database to give reliable range.*

*18" bisque Jumeau child, marked "E.J.," $4,500.00. Courtesy McMasters Doll Auctions.*

## Princess Elizabeth

**#306** Made after Jumeau joined S.F.B.J. and adopted Unis label, *mark* will be *"71 Unis//France 149//306//Jumeau//1938//Paris."* Bisque socket head with high color, closed mouth, flirty eyes, jointed composition body

| | | |
|---|---|---|
| 18" | $1,600.00 | $2,100.00 |
| 30" | $2,900.00 | $3,900.00 |

*too few examples in database to give reliable range*

Accessories

Marked shoes

| | | |
|---|---|---|
| #5 – #6 | $225.00 | $300.00 |
| #7 – #10 | $450.00 | $600.00 |

# Kammer & Reinhardt

**1886 – 1930+, Waltershausen, Germany.** Registered trademark K&R, Majestic Doll, Mein Leibling, Die Kokette, Charakterpuppen (Character Dolls). Designed doll heads, most bisque were made by Simon & Halbig; in 1918, Schuetzmeister & Quendt also supplied heads; Rheinische Gummi und Celluloid Fabric Co. made celluloid heads for Kammer & Reinhardt. Kammer & Reinhardt dolls were distributed by Bing, Borgfeldt, B. Illfelder, L. Rees & Co., Strobel & Wilken, and Louis Wolf. Also made heads of wood and composition, later cloth and rubber dolls. Mold numbers identify heads starting with 1. bisque socket heads; 2. shoulder heads, as well as socket heads of black or mulatto babies; 3. bisque socket heads or celluloid shoulder heads; 4. heads having eyelashes; 5. googlies, black heads, pincushion heads; 6. mulatto heads; 7. celluloid heads, bisque head walking dolls; 8. rubber heads; 9. composition heads, some rubber heads. Other letters refer to style or material of wig or clothing.

*Marks:*

$$Germany$$
$$1126 - 21$$

**(all bisque)**

$$K\ R$$
$$x$$
$$10$$

$$K \boxtimes R$$
$$SIMON \& HALBIG$$
$$126$$
$$36$$

## Child, Dolly Face
Open mouth sleep eyes, jointed body

**Mold #191,** open mouth, sleep eyes, jointed child body

| | | |
|---|---|---|
| 17" | $650.00 | $865.00 |
| 30" | $900.00 | $1,200.00 |

**Mold #192,** open mouth, sleep eyes, jointed child body

| | | |
|---|---|---|
| 9" | $750.00 | $1,000.00 |
| 18" | $750.00 | $1,000.00 |
| 22" | $800.00 | $1,200.00 |

With trunk and wardrobe

| | |
|---|---|
| 9" | $1,800.00 * at auction |

Closed mouth

| | | |
|---|---|---|
| 18" | $2,325.00 | $3,100.00 * at auction |

**No mold numbers, or marked only K\*R or size number in centimeters, or**

**Mold #401, #402, #403,** socket head, glass eyes, open mouth,

| | | |
|---|---|---|
| 12" | $400.00 | $550.00 |
| 15" | $450.00 | $625.00 |
| 19" | $550.00 | $750.00 |
| 25" | $825.00 | $1,100.00 |
| 32" | $1,350.00 | $1,800.00 |

## Characters
**Mold #100** (Formerly called Kaiser Baby, but no connection has been found.) Character baby with dome head, jointed bent leg body, intaglio eyes, open /closed mouth, appropriate dress, good condition.

| | | |
|---|---|---|
| 11 – 12" | $400.00 | $525.00 |
| 15" | $600.00 | $800.00 |
| 18" | $750.00 | $1,000.00 |
| 21" | $1,100.00 | $1,500.00 |

**#101 Peter or Marie,** painted eyes, closed mouth

| | | |
|---|---|---|
| 8 – 9" | $1,500.00 | $2,000.00 |
| 11 – 12" | $1,800.00 | $2,400.00 |
| 15" | $2,250.00 | $3,000.00+ |
| 18" | $2,900.00 | $3,900.00+ |
| 23" | $4,500.00 | $6,000.00 |

*12" bisque Kammer & Reinhardt child marked*
*"100," $410.00.Courtesy McMasters Doll Auctions.*

With glass eyes

| 14" | $4,700.00 | $6,250.00 |
|-----|-----------|-----------|
| 19" | $5,900.00 | $7,900.00 |
| 23" | $7,700.00 | $10,300.00 |

*too few examples in database to give reliable range*

**#102 Elsa or Walter,** painted eyes, molded hair, closed mouth, very rare

| 14" | $32,000.00 |
|-----|-----------|
| 17" | $37,000.00 |
| 22" | $54,000.00 |

*too few examples in database to give reliable range*

**#103** painted eyes, closed mouth

| 19" | $60,000.00 |
|-----|-----------|

*too few examples in database to give reliable range*

**#104** painted eyes, laughing closed mouth, very rare

| 18" | $58,000.00+ |
|-----|-----------|
| 21" | $72,000.00 |

*too few examples in database to give reliable range*

*6" bisque socket head, mold #126, sleep eyes, open mouth, teeth, composition body, wigged, in original costume, $750.00. Courtesy Sue Kinkade.*

**#105** painted eyes, open/closed mouth, very rare

| 17" | $73,000.00+ |
|-----|-----------|

*too few examples in database to give reliable range*

**#106** painted intaglio eyes to side, slightly closed mouth, very rare

| 20" | $65,000.00 |
|-----|-----------|

*too few examples in database to give reliable range*

**#107 Carl,** painted intaglio eyes, closed mouth

| 15" | $15,900.00+ |
|-----|-----------|
| 21" | $40,000.00+ |

*too few examples in database to give reliable range*

**#108,** only one example reported

$275,000.00 * at auction

**#109 Elise,** Painted eyes, closed mouth

| 8" | $2,000.00 | $2,600.00 |
|----|-----------|-----------|
| 14" | $6,000.00 | $8,000.00 |
| 20" | $10,500.00 | $14,000.00 |

**#112** painted open/closed mouth

| 14" | $7,200.00 | $9,700.00 |
|-----|-----------|-----------|

Glass eyes

| 15" | $11,250.00 | $15,000.00 |
|-----|-----------|-----------|

**#114 Hans or Gretchen,** painted eyes, closed mouth

| 12" | $2,175.00 | $2,900.00 |
|-----|-----------|-----------|
| 18" | $4,000.00 | $5,400.00 |
| 24" | $6,150.00 | $8,200.00 |

*19" bisque, Kammer & Reinhardt character sometimes known as Elsa, painted eyes, open/closed mouth and jointed body, $45,000.00+. Courtesy Matrix.*

*12" bisque Kammer & Reinhardt Carl with painted blue eyes, marked "K*R 107/30," ca. 1910, old clothes, $12,000.00+. Courtesy Sherryl Shirran.*

Glass eyes

| | | |
|---|---|---|
| 18" | $6,225.00 | $8,300.00 |
| 24" | $11,550.00 | $15,400.00 |
| 27" | $15,500.00 | $21,000.00 |

Hans, brown glass eyes

| | |
|---|---|
| 9" | $5,900.00 * at auction |

**#115,** solid dome, painted hair, sleeping eyes, closed mouth

| | | |
|---|---|---|
| 15" | $3,750.00 | $5,000.00 |

**#115A,** bisque socket head, sleep eyes, closed mouth, wig

Bent leg baby body

| | | |
|---|---|---|
| 19" | $2,625.00 | $3,500.00 |

Composition jointed toddler body

| | | |
|---|---|---|
| 15 – 16" | $3,750.00 | $5,000.00 |

**#116** Bisque solid dome head, sleeping eyes, open/closed mouth, bent limb baby body

| | |
|---|---|
| 17" | $3,200.00 |

**#116A** Bisque socket head, sleep eyes, open/closed mouth or open mouth, wigged, bent limb baby body

| | | |
|---|---|---|
| 15" | $2,000.00 | $2,750.00 |

Toddler body

| | | |
|---|---|---|
| 16" | $2,400.00 | $3,200.00 |
| 22" | $3,200.00 | $4,250.00 |

**#117 Mein Leibling** (My Darling), glass eyes, closed mouth

| | | |
|---|---|---|
| 15" | $3,225.00 | $4,300.00 |
| 18" | $4,000.00 | $5,300.00 |
| 23" | $5,000.00 | $6,750.00 |

**#117A,** glass eyes, closed mouth with flapper body

| | | |
|---|---|---|
| 8, | $3,500.00 *at auction | |
| 16" | $3,075.00 | $4,100.00 |
| 23" | $6,000.00 | $8,000.00 |
| 30" | $6,375.00 | $8,500.00 |

**#117N, Mein neum Liebling** (My new Darling), flirty eyes, open mouth

| | | |
|---|---|---|
| 20" | $1,350.00 | $1,800.00 |
| 30" | $2,300.00 | $3,050.00 |

**#117X,** bisque socket head, sleep eyes, open mouth, compo/wood ball jointed body

| | |
|---|---|
| 14" | $3,700.00 * auction |

**#118, 118A,** sleep eyes, open mouth, bent limb baby body

| | | |
|---|---|---|
| 15" | $1,125.00 | $1,500.00 |
| 18" | $1,700.00 | $2,275.00 |

*19" 115A baby, $3,500.00. Courtesy McMasters Doll Auctions.*

*19" bisque Kammer & Reinhardt character baby, marked "K*R Simon & Halbig 116/A," ca. 1909, replaced clothes, $3,600.00. Courtesy Sherryl Shirran.*

**#119** Bisque socket head, sleep eyes, open/closed mouth, marked "Baby," five-piece baby body

25"    $16,000.00 * at auction

**#121** Sleep eyes, open mouth, bent limb baby body

| | | |
|---|---|---|
| 14" | $600.00 | $800.00 |
| 19" | $750.00 | $1,000.00 |
| 25" | $1,050.00 | $1,400.00 |

Toddler body

| | | |
|---|---|---|
| 16" | $975.00 | $1,300.00 |
| 25" | $1,600.00 | $2,100.00 |

**#122** sleep eyes, bent limb baby body

| | | |
|---|---|---|
| 11" | $525.00 | $700.00 |
| 16" | $635.00 | $850.00 |
| 20" | $825.00 | $1,100.00 |

Original, with wicker layette basket and accessories

22"    $2,800.00 * at auction

Toddler body

| | | |
|---|---|---|
| 13" | $825.00 | $1,100.00 |
| 19" | $975.00 | $1,300.00 |
| 22" | $1,125.00 | $1,500.00 |

**#123 Max** and **#124 Moritz,** flirting, sleep eyes, laughing/closed mouth

Max

16"    $15,500.00 *at auction

Moritz

16"    $23,000.00 * at auction

*30" 117A K*R Mein Leibling, $8,100.00. Courtesy McMasters Doll Auctions.*

*31" bisque socket head, marked only "K*R," open mouth, sleep eyes, $1,750.00. Courtesy Harriet Wagner.*

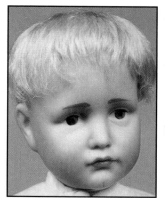

*13" bisque Kammer & Reinhardt mold #114 character boy, closed mouth, painted eyes, $3,000.00. Courtesy McMasters Doll Auctions.*

**#126 Mein Liebling Baby** (My Darling Baby), sleep or flirty eyes, bent leg baby, 1914 – 1930s

| | | |
|---|---|---|
| 14" | $550.00 | $750.00 |
| 18" | $800.00 | $1,200.00 |
| 22" | $1,125.00 | $1,500.00 |
| Toddler body | | |
| 6" | $400.00 | $500.00 |
| 8" | $1,000.00 | $1,350.00 |
| 17" | $750.00 | $1,000.00 |
| 22" | $1,050.00 | $1,400.00 |
| 24" | $1,425.00 | $1,900.00 |
| Child body | | |
| 22" | $750.00 | $1,000.00 |
| 32" | $1,300.00 | $1,725.00 |

**#127, 127N** domed head like model #126, bent leg baby body, add more for flirty eyes

| | | |
|---|---|---|
| 14" | $800.00 | $1,200.00 |
| 18" | $1,200.00 | $1,600.00 |
| Toddler body | | |
| 20" | $1,650.00 | $2,200.00 |
| 26" | $1,950.00 | $2,600.00 |

**#128** sleep eyes, open mouth, bent limb baby body

| | | |
|---|---|---|
| 18" | $1,100.00 | $1,450.00 |

Original clothes, with layette in wicker basket

| | | |
|---|---|---|
| 10" | $1,600.00 * at auction | |

**#131,** See Googly category

**#135** Sleep eyes, open mouth, bent limb baby body

| | | |
|---|---|---|
| 13" | $625.00 | $850.00 |
| Toddler body | | |
| 18" | $1,050.00 | $1,450.00 |

**#171 Klein Mammi** (Little Mammy), solid dome, open mouth, sleep eyes

| | | |
|---|---|---|
| 18" | $1,500.00 * at auction | |

**#214** bisque shoulder head, painted eyes, closed mouth, similar to mold #114, muslin stitch jointed body

| | | |
|---|---|---|
| 12" | $2,600.00 * at auction | |

## Kestner, J.D.

**1805 – 1930+, Waltershausen, Germany.** Supplied bisque heads to Catterfelder Puppenfabrik. Kestner was one of the first firms to make dressed dolls. Borgfeldt, Butler Bros., Century Doll Co., Horsman, R.H. Macy, Sears, Siegel Cooper, F.A.O.Schwarz and others were distributors for

Kestner. Besides wooden dolls, papier mache, wax over composition, and Frozen Charlottes, Kestner made bisque dolls with leather or composition bodies, chinas, and all bisque dolls. Early bisque heads with closed mouths marked X or XI, and turned shoulder head and swivel heads on shoulder plates are thought to be Kestners. After 1892, dolls were marked "made in Germany" with mold numbers. Bisque heads with early mold numbers are stamped Excelsior DRP No. 70 685; heads of 100 number series are marked "dep." Some early characters are unmarked or only marked with the mold number. After 211 on, it is believed all dolls were marked "JDK," or "JDK, Jr.," Register the Crown Doll (Kronen Puppe) in 1915, used on label on bodies and dolls. The Kestner Alphabet is registered in 1897 as a design patent. It is possible to identify the sizes of doll heads by this key. Letter and number always go together: B/6, C/7, D/8, E/9, F/10, G/11, H/12, H – 3/4/ 12 – 3/4, J/13, J – 3/4/13 – 3/4, K/14, K – 1/2/14 – 1/2, L/15, L – 1/2/15 – 1/2, M/16, N/17. It is believed all dolls with plaster pates were made by Kestner.

First price is for dolls in good condition with some flaw; second price is for dolls in excellent condition with original clothes or appropriately dressed.

*Marks:*

B½ made in Germany

C½ made in Germany

F made in Germany 843     10

J.D.K.

Dep. 195.6½
+

12
A. made in Germany 5
143.

J made in Germany. 13.
247.
J.D.K.

made in Germany.
E.198.9.

*25" bisque Kestner solid dome baby marked "109," $750.00. Courtesy McMasters Doll Auctions.*

*10" bisque Kestner, solid dome baby, $400.00. Courtesy McMasters Doll Auctions.*

**Early Baby**

**Unmarked, or only JDK, made in Germany or with size number, open or closed mouth,** solid dome bisque socket head, glass sleep eyes, molded and/or painted hair, composition bent limb baby body. Add more for body with crown label, original clothes

| | | |
|---|---|---|
| 10" | $450.00 | $625.00 |
| 12" | $650.00 | $850.00 |
| 14" | $700.00 | $950.00 |
| 17" | $750.00 | $1,000.00 |

**Early Child**

**Bisque shoulder head, closed or open/closed mouth,** plaster pate, may be marked with size numbers only, glass eyes, may sleep, kid body, bisque lower arms, appropriate wig and dress, in good condition, more for original clothes

| | | |
|---|---|---|
| 11" | $375.00 | $500.00 |
| 15" | $525.00 | $700.00 |
| 17" | $600.00 | $800.00 |

**Open mouth, mold #145, 147, 148, 154, 166, 195**

| | | |
|---|---|---|
| 25" | $300.00 | $400.00 |
| 29" | $450.00 | $600.00 |

**Turned shoulder head, closed mouth,** no mold number, size number only

| | | |
|---|---|---|
| 12" | $265.00 | $350.00 |
| 16" | $300.00 | $425.00 |
| 18" | $375.00 | $500.00 |
| 22" | $450.00 | $600.00 |
| 25" | $525.00 | $700.00 |

**Early child doll, bisque socket head,** open mouth, glass eyes, Kestner ball jointed body, add more for square cut teeth, on body marked only with number and letter

**#142, 144, 146, 164, 167, 171**

| | | |
|---|---|---|
| 8" | $450.00 | $600.00 |
| 12" | $525.00 | $725.00 |
| 18" | $700.00 | $950.00 |
| 25" | $1,075.00 | $1,450.00 |

**Mold #171 "Daisy,"** 18" size only

| | | |
|---|---|---|
| 18" | $750.00 | $1,000.00 |

**A.T. type,** bisque socket head, closed mouth, glass eyes, mohair wig over plaster pate, early compo and wood ball jointed body with straight wrists. Marked only with size number such as 15 for 24".

| | |
|---|---|
| 24" | $19,000.00 at auction |

**#XI, 103** pouty face, closed mouth, less for kid body

| | | |
|---|---|---|
| 30" | $1,950.00 | $2,600.00 |
| 32" | $2,625.00 | $3,500.00 |

**#128, 169,** bisque socket head, pouty closed mouth, glass eyes, composition and wood ball jointed body, nicely wigged,

| | | |
|---|---|---|
| 14" | $1,425.00 | $1,900.00 |
| 26" | $2,700.00 | $3,400.00 |

**#129, 149, 152, 155, 160, 161, 168,173 174 196, 214,** bisque socket head, open mouth, glass eyes, composition wood jointed body, add more for fur eyebrows

| | | |
|---|---|---|
| 12" | $400.00 | $550.00 |
| 16" | $475.00 | $650.00 |
| 18" | $600.00 | $825.00 |
| 22" | $675.00 | $900.00 |
| 24" | $725.00 | $975.00 |
| 26" | $875.00 | $1,175.00 |
| 30" | $1,200.00 | $1,600.00 |

**#143,** open mouth, glass eyes, compo and wood jointed body, mohair wig,

| | | |
|---|---|---|
| 8" | $450.00 | $600.00 |
| 9" | $625.00 | $850.00 |
| 13" | $750.00 | $1,000.00 |
| 18" | $825.00 | $1,100.00 |

**#155,** open mouth, glass eyes, five-piece or fully jointed body, mohair wig

| | |
|---|---|
| 7" | $1,300.00 *at auction |

*18" all original Daisy, bisque socket head, blonde mohair wig, original outfit, crown paper tag, composition body, only size that can be called Daisy, $1,000.00.*

*23" bisque Hilda, solid dome socket head, sleep eyes, open mouth, composition bent limb baby body, $4,750.00.*

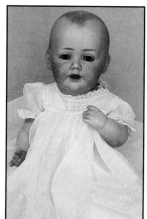

*13" bisque J.D. Kestner Baby Jean marked "J.D.K. Made in 10 Germany," $900.00. Courtesy Sherryl Shirran.*

*30" bisque Kestner child marked "103," $2,300.00. Courtesy McMasters Doll Auctions.*

*16½" closed mouth Kestner, $1,300.00. Courtesy McMasters Doll Auctions.*

**Character Baby, 1910+**

Socket head with wig or solid dome with painted hair, glass eyes, open mouth, bent limb baby body.

**#211, 226, 236, 260, 262, 263**

| | | |
|---|---|---|
| 11" | $500.00 | $675.00 |
| 14" | $600.00 | $800.00 |
| 16" | $675.00 | $900.00 |
| 18" | $750.00 | $1,000.00 |
| 22" | $800.00 | $1,200.00+ |
| 25" | $1,200.00 | $1,600.00+ |

**#210, #234, 235,** shoulder head, solid dome, sleep eyes, open/closed mouth, or open mouth

| | | |
|---|---|---|
| 12" | $400.00 | $550.00 |
| 15" | $500.00 | $700.00 |
| 18" | $675.00 | $900.00 |
| 22" | $775.00 | $1,050.00 |
| 24" | $850.00 | $1,150.00 |

**#220,** sleep eyes, open/closed mouth

| | | |
|---|---|---|
| 14" | $3,225.00 | $4,300.00 |
| 18" | $4,200.00 | $5,600.00 |
| Toddler | | |
| 19" | $4,650.00 | $6,200.00 |
| 25" | $4,900.00 | $6,500.00 |

**#237, 245 (#1070, bald solid dome), Hilda,** sleep eyes, open mouth

| | | |
|---|---|---|
| 14" | $2,100.00 | $2,800.00 |
| 17" | $2,550.00 | $3,400.00 |
| 20" | $3,000.00 | $4,000.00 |
| 22" | $3,375.00 | $4,500.00 |
| 25" | $4,000.00 | $6,000.00 |

**#243, Oriental baby,** socket head, sleep eyes, open mouth, Oriental outfit

| | | |
|---|---|---|
| 13" | $2,625.00 | $3,550.00 |
| 14" | $3,900.00 | $5,200.00 |
| 16" | $4,275.00 | $5,700.00 |
| 19" | $4,950.00 | $6,600.00 |

**#247,** socket head, open mouth, sleep eyes

| | | |
|---|---|---|
| 16" | $1,050.00 | $1,400.00 |
| 18" | $1,425.00 | $1,900.00 |

**#249,** socket head, open mouth, sleep eyes

| | | |
|---|---|---|
| 15" | $775.00 | $1,050.00 |
| 18" | $1,300.00 | $1,800.00 |
| 22" | $1,400.00 | $1,900.00 |

**#255,** marked "O.I.C. made in Germany," solid dome, flange neck, tiny glass eyes, large open/closed crying mouth, cloth body

| | |
|---|---|
| 15" | $1,500.00 |

* *too few in database to give a reliable range.*

*28" Kestner mold #128, closed mouth, $4,000.00. Courtesy Chantal Jeschien.*

*18" bisque Kestner turned-head child, $500.00. Courtesy McMasters Doll Auctions.*

**#257,** bisque socket head, sleep eyes, open mouth

| | | |
|---|---|---|
| 10" | $450.00 | $625.00 |
| 14" | $675.00 | $900.00 |
| 17" | $775.00 | $1,025.00 |
| 23" | $1,050.00 | $1,400.00 |
| 25" | $1,800.00 | $2,400.00 |

Toddler body

| | | |
|---|---|---|
| 16" | $700.00 | $950.00 |
| 24" | $1,350.00 | $1,800.00 |

**Character Child, ca. 1910+**

Socket head, wig, closed mouth, glass eyes, compo and wood jointed body; add more for painted eyes

*Kestner #241, $7,500.00. Courtesy Chantal Jeschien.*

**#175, 176, 177, 178, 179, 180, 181, 182, 182, 184, 185, 187, 188, 189, 190**

| | | |
|---|---|---|
| 15" | $3,000.00 | $4,000.00 |
| 18" | $3,375.00 | $4,500.00 |
| 20" | $3,750.00 | $5,000.00 |

**#206,** fat cheeks, closed mouth, glass eyes, child or toddler

| | | |
|---|---|---|
| 12" | $5,000.00 | $6,600.00 |
| 15" | $6,700.00 | $8,900.00 |
| 17" | $7,500.00 | $10,000.00 |
| 21" | $11,900.00 | $15,750.00 |
| 25" | $13,500.00 | $18,500.00 |

**#208,** glass eyes

| | | |
|---|---|---|
| 16" | $6,750.00 | $9,000.00 |
| 22" | $7,900.00 | $10,500.00 |

*26" bisque Kestner, AT child, $700.00. Courtesy McMasters Doll Auctions.*

7" bisque socket head, mold #260, sleep eyes, red mohair wig, open mouth, composition body, appropriately dressed, $600.00. Courtesy Elaine Beling.

21" bisque Kestner closed mouth child, $625.00. Courtesy McMasters Doll Auctions.

**#208,** painted eyes

| | | |
|---|---|---|
| 12" | $2,500.00 | $3,300.00 |
| 16" | $4,400.00 | $5,800.00 |
| 20" | $7,000.00 | $9,300.00 |
| 26" | $9,350.00 | $12,500.00 |

**#211, #260,** socket head, open mouth, sleep eyes, jointed, toddler, or baby body

| | | |
|---|---|---|
| 7½" | $500.00 | $675.00 |
| 12" | $600.00 | $800.00 |
| 18" | $1,400.00 | $1,900.00 |
| 25" | $1,950.00 | $2,600.00 |
| 42" | $3,000.00 | $4,000.00 |

**#220,** socket head, sleep eyes, open or closed mouth, toddler jointed compo body

| | | |
|---|---|---|
| 15" | $3,800.00 | $5,200.00 |
| 18" | $4,700.00 | $6,200.00 |

19" bisque Kestner child, mold 152, $250.00. Courtesy McMasters Doll Auctions.

**#239,** socket head, open mouth, sleep eyes, toddler, also comes as baby

| | | |
|---|---|---|
| 17" | $2,550.00 | $3,400.00 |
| 21" | $3,300.00 | $4,400.00 |
| 26" | $4,500.00 | $6,000.00 |

**#241,** socket head, open mouth, sleep eyes

| | | |
|---|---|---|
| 18" | $3,300.00 | $4,500.00 |
| 25" | $4,500.00 | $6,000.00 |

# Kestner, J.D. (cont.)

**Adult**

**#162,** bisque socket head, open mouth, glass eyes, compo body with slender waists and molded breasts

| | | |
|---|---|---|
| 18" | $1,150.00 | $1,525.00 |
| 22" | $1,800.00 | $2,400.00 |

**#172, Gibson Girl,** shoulder head, closed mouth, glass eyes, kid body, bisque forearms

| | | |
|---|---|---|
| 10" | $625.00 | $825.00 |
| 15" | $1,250.00 | $1,650.00 |
| 18" | $1,500.00 | $2,000.00 |
| 20" | $3,800.00 *at auction | |

**Wunderkind**

Set includes doll body with four interchangeable heads, some with extra apparel, one set included heads with mold #174 178, 184, and 185.

| | | |
|---|---|---|
| 11" | $7,500.00 | $10,000.00 |
| 15" | $9,375.00 | $12,500.00 |

# Kewpie

1912+, designed by Rose O'Neill. Manufactured by Borgfeldt, later Joseph Kallus, and then Jesco in 1984, and various companies with special license, as well as unlicensed companies. They were made of all bisque, celluloid, cloth, composition, rubber, vinyl, zylonite, and other materials. Kewpie figurines (action Kewpies) have mold numbers 4843 through 4883. Kewpies were also marked with a round paper sticker on the back: "KEWPIES DES. PAT. III, R. 1913; Germany; REG. US. PAT. OFF." On the front, was a heart-shaped sticker marked: "KEWPIE//REG. US. // PAT. OFF." May also be incised on the soles of the feet, "O'Neill."

*Marks:*

**O'Neill**

First price indicates dolls in good condition, with some flaws; second price indicates dolls in excellent condition with no chips. Add more for label, accessories, original box.

**All Bisque**

*Made in Germany*
*1377*

**Immobiles**

Standing, legs together, immobile, no joints, blue wings, painted molded hair, painted side glancing eyes

| | | |
|---|---|---|
| 2" | $55.00 | $110.00 |
| 2½" | $70.00 | $135.00 |
| 4½" | $75.00 | $150.00 |
| 5" | $90.00 | $175.00 |
| 6" | $150.00 | $275.00 |

**KEWPIE**
Germany

**Jointed shoulders**

| | | |
|---|---|---|
| 2" | $50.00 | $95.00 |
| 4½" | $65.00 | $130.00 |
| 6" | $100.00 | $195.00 |
| 8½" | $200.00 | $400.00 |
| 10" | $350.00 | $625.00 |
| 12" | $500.00 | $975.00 |

Carnival chalk Kewpie with jointed shoulders

| | | |
|---|---|---|
| 13" | $50.00 | $165.00 |

**CAMEO DOLL**

**Jointed shoulders with any article of molded clothing**

| | | |
|---|---|---|
| 2½" | $100.00 | $200.00 |
| 6" | $115.00 | $330.00 |
| 8" | $190.00 | $375.00 |
| 10" | $325.00 | $625.00 |

With Mary Jane shoes

| | | |
|---|---|---|
| 6½" | $250.00 | $500.00 |

**Jointed hips and shoulders**

| | | |
|---|---|---|
| 5" | $265.00 | $525.00 |
| 7" | $375.00 | $750.00 |
| 10" | $500.00 | $1,000.00 |
| 12½" | $650.00 | $1,300.00 |

**Bisque Action Figures**

**Arms folded**

| | | |
|---|---|---|
| 6" | $300.00 | $600.00 |

**Aviator**

| | | |
|---|---|---|
| 8½" | $425.00 | $850.00 |

**Back, kicking one foot**

| | | |
|---|---|---|
| 4" | $100.00 | $200.00 |

**Basket and ladybug, Kewpie seated**

| | | |
|---|---|---|
| 4" | $900.00 | $1,800.00 |

*Two 10" all bisque Kewpie Bride & Groom dolls, $1,300.00. Courtesy McMasters Doll Auctions.*

**Bear holding Kewpie**

| | | |
|---|---|---|
| 3½" | $110.00 | $220.00 |

**"Blunderboo," Kewpie falling down**

| | | |
|---|---|---|
| 1¾" | $240.00 | $465.00 |

**Bottle**, green beverage, with Kewpie standing next to it and kicking out

| | | |
|---|---|---|
| 2½" | $330.00 | $660.00 |

**Bottle stopper**

| | | |
|---|---|---|
| 2" | $75.00 | $150.00 |

**Box, heart shaped, with Kewpie kicker atop**

| | | |
|---|---|---|
| 4" | $440.00 | $880.00 |

**Bride and Groom**

| | | |
|---|---|---|
| 3½" | $175.00 | $350.00 |

**Boutonnière**

| | | |
|---|---|---|
| 1¼" | $55.00 | $110.00 |
| 2" | $70.00 | $135.00 |

**Candy container**

| | | |
|---|---|---|
| 4" | $250.00 | $500.00 |

**Card holder**

| | | |
|---|---|---|
| 2" | $250.00 | $500.00 |

With label

| | | |
|---|---|---|
| 2½" | $330.00 | $660.00 |

**Carpenter, wearing tool apron**

| | | |
|---|---|---|
| 8½" | $550.00 | $1,100.00 |

**Cowboy**

| | | |
|---|---|---|
| 10" | $400.00 | $800.00 |

**Cat, black with Kewpie**
2¼"    $150.00      $300.00
**Cat, gray on lap of seated Kewpie**
2¼"    $850.00 * at auction
**Cat, gray with Kewpie on back**
3"    $275.00      $525.00
**Cat, tan with Kewpie**
3"    $150.00      $300.00
**Cat, white with Kewpie**
3"    $220.00      $440.00
**Chick with seated Kewpie**
2"    $300.00      $600.00
**Crawler, Dog, with Kewpie on stomach**
3 x 14" long    $3,000.00 * at auction
**Dog, with Red Cross Kewpie**
4"    $300.00
**Doodle Dog alone**
1½ "    $350.00      $700.00
3"    $625.00      $1,350.00
**Doodle Dog with Kewpie**
2½"    $125.00      $250.00
**Drum on brown stool, with Kewpie**
3½"    $1,200.00      $2,400.00
**Farmer**
6½"    $300.00      $600.00
**Flowers, Kewpie with bouquet in right hand**
5"    $475.00      $935.00
**Fly on foot of Kewpie**
3"    $300.00      $600.00
**Governor**
2½"    $150.00      $275.00
3¾"    $250.00      $500.00
**Hottentot, black Kewpie**
3½"    $225.00      $425.00
5"    $300.00      $575.00
9"    $450.00      $950.00
12"    $4,500.00+
**Huggers**
2½"    $65.00      $125.00
3½ "    $75.00      $150.00
4½ "    $100.00      $200.00
**Inkwell, with writer Kewpie**
4½"    $250.00      $500.00
**Jack-O-Lantern between legs of Kewpie**
2"    $250.00      $500.00
**Jester, with white hat on head**
4½"    $300.00      $575.00

**Kneeling**
   4"      $375.00      $750.00
**Mandolin, green basket, and seated Kewpie**
   2"      $150.00      $275.00
**Mandolin held by seated Kewpie in blue chair**
   4"      $475.00      $925.00
**Mandolin, with Kewpie seated on moon swing**
   2½"   $4,400.00 * at auction
**Mayor, seated Kewpie in green wicker chair**
   4½"   $475.00      $950.00
**Minister**
   5"      $125.00      $250.00
**Nursing bottle, with Kewpie**
   3½"   $300.00      $600.00
**Reader Kewpie seated with book**
   2"      $125.00      $250.00
   3½"   $165.00      $325.00
   4"      $250.00      $500.00

*2½" bisque Military Kewpies, $275.00 each. Courtesy McMasters Doll Auctions.*

**Sack, held by Kewpie with both hands**
   4½"      $1,430.00 * at auction
**Salt Shaker**
   2"         $165.00
**Seated in fancy chair**
   4"         $200.00         $400.00
**Soldier, Confederate**
   4"         $200.00         $400.00
**Soldier taking aim with rifle**
   3½"       $500.00         $990.00
**Soldier, with red hat, sword, and rifle**
   3½"       $150.00         $300.00
   4½"       $220.00         $440.00
   5¼"       $415.00         $825.00
**Soldier, with black hat, sword, and rifle**
   4½"       $200.00         $385.00
**Soldier with helmet**
   2¾"       $300.00         $400. 00
   4½"       $300.00         $600.00
**Soldier bursting out of egg**
   4"         $6,900.00 * at auction
**Soldier in egg**
   3½"       $6,600.00 * at auction
**Soldier vase**
   6½ "      $330.00         $660.00

145

*Left: 3½" all bisque Kewpie Sweeper, marked "O'Neill," (faint) on feet, $245.00. Right: 3½" all bisque Kewpie Traveler, marked "O'Neill" on bottom of valise, $225.00. Courtesy McMasters Doll Auctions.*

*4½" Kewpie Thinker, $275.00. Courtesy McMasters Doll Auctions.*

**Stomach, Kewpie laying flat with arms and legs out**

| | | |
|---|---|---|
| 4" | $225.00 | $450.00 |

**Thinker**

| | | |
|---|---|---|
| 4 – 5" | $150.00 | $275.00 |

**Traveler with dog and umbrella**

| | | |
|---|---|---|
| 3½ " | $1,300.00 * at auction | |

**Traveler with umbrella and bag**

| | | |
|---|---|---|
| 4" | $175.00 | $350.00 |
| 5" | $300.00 | $600.00 |

**Vase with farmer Kewpie**

| | | |
|---|---|---|
| 6½" | $1,045.00 * at auction | |

**Vase with huggers**

| | | |
|---|---|---|
| 3¾" | $325.00 | $650.00 |

**Vase with card holder and Kewpie**

| | | |
|---|---|---|
| 2½" | $165.00 | $330.00 |

**Writer, seated Kewpie with pen in hand**

| | | |
|---|---|---|
| 2" | $255.00 | $475.00 |
| 4" | $265.00 | $550.00 |

**Bisque Shoulder Head**

**Cloth, or stockinette body**

| | | |
|---|---|---|
| 7" | $285.00 | $565.00 |

**Head only**

| | | |
|---|---|---|
| 3" | $165.00+ | |

**Celluloid**

**Bride and Groom**

| | | |
|---|---|---|
| 2½" | $10.00 | $35.00 |
| 4" | $15.00 | $40.00 |

**Jointed arms, heart label on chest**

| | | |
|---|---|---|
| 12" | $175.00 | $325.00 |

**China**

**Perfume holder, one piece with opening at back of head**

| | | |
|---|---|---|
| 4½" | $550.00 | $1,100.00 |

**Salt Shaker**

| | | |
|---|---|---|
| 1¼" | $85.00 | $165.00 |

**Cloth Head and Body**

**"Cuddle Kewpie," silk screened face**, satin body, tagged

| | |
|---|---|
| 12" | $825.00 |

**Plush,** with stockinette face, tagged

| | |
|---|---|
| 8" | $115.00 | $225.00 |

**Composition**

**Hottentot, all composition,** heart decal to chest, jointed arms, red winks, ca. 1946

| | | |
|---|---|---|
| 11" | $300.00 | $575.00 |

**Kewpie, all composition**, jointed body, blue wings

| | | |
|---|---|---|
| 13" | $200.00 | $450.00 |

**Kewpie, composition head, cloth body,** flange neck, jointed composition forearms, original tagged floral print dress

| | | |
|---|---|---|
| 11" | $250.00 | $875.00 |

**Talcum container,** one piece composition with talcum shaker, heart label on chest

| | | |
|---|---|---|
| 7" | $35.00 | $65.00 |

With box

| | | |
|---|---|---|
| 7" | $65.00 | $125.00 |

**Hard Plastic**

**Kewpie** in original box, ca. 1950, with Kewpie design, five-piece hard plastic body

| | | |
|---|---|---|
| 8½" | $200.00 | $385.00 |

**Kewpie,** sleep eyes, five-piece hard plastic body with starfish hands

| | | |
|---|---|---|
| 14" | $150.00 | $300.00 |

**Metal**

**Figurine,** cast steel on square base, excellent condition

| | | |
|---|---|---|
| 5½" | $30.00 | $55.00 |

**Soap**

Figure with cotton batting, colored label with rhyme, marked "R.O. Wilson, 1917"

| | | |
|---|---|---|
| 4" | $55.00 | $110.00 |

*10" Kestner googly, bisque Kewpie, $6,400.00. Courtesy McMasters Doll Auctions.*

# Kley & Hahn

**1902 – 30+, Ohrdruf, Thuringia, Germany.** Bisque heads, jointed composition or leather bodies; exporter, bought heads from Kestner (Walkure), and Hertel & Schwab. Also made composition and celluloid head dolls.

First price indicates dolls in good condition, but with some flaw; second price indicates dolls in excellent condition, with original clothes, or appropriately dressed.

*Marks:*

```
525
  6
Germany
)K & H(
```

```
)K & H(
Germany
  526
    6
```

```
   282
   ★
S)KH(H
    2½
 Germany
```

## Character Baby

**Mold #133** (made by Hertel & Schwab), solid dome, painted eyes, closed mouth

**#135** (made by Hertel & Schwab), solid dome, painted eyes, open/closed mouth

**#138** (made by Hertel & Schwab), solid dome, painted eyes, open/closed mouth

**#158** (made by Hertel & Schwab), painted eyes, open mouth

**#160** (made by Hertel & Schwab), sleep eyes, open/closed mouth

**#161** (made by Hertel & Schwab), character face, sleep eyes, open/closed mouth

**#167** (made by Hertel & Schwab), sleep eyes, open/closed or open mouth

**#571** "K&H" (made by Bahr & Proschild), character, solid dome, glass eyes, open/closed mouth, laughing, giant baby

| | | |
|---|---|---|
| 12" | $400.00 | $550.00 |
| 15" | $450.00 | $600.00 |
| 17" | $525.00 | $700.00 |
| 21" | $725.00 | $975.00 |
| 25" | $900.00 | $1,225.00 |

Toddler body

| | | |
|---|---|---|
| 19" | $725.00 | $975.00 |
| 21" | $975.00 | $1,300.00 |
| 25" | $1,100.00 | $1,500.00 |
| 27" | $1,425.00 | $1,900.00 |

**#567** (made by Bahr & Proschild), character, multi-face, laughing face, glass eyes, open mouth; crying face, painted eyes, open/closed mouth

| | | |
|---|---|---|
| 15" | $1,475.00 | $1,950.00 |
| 17" | $1,875.00 | $2,500.00 |
| 19" | $2,550.00 | $3,400.00 |

**#680** "K & CO K&H" with "266 K&H" (made by Kestner & Comp.), character, sleep eyes, open mouth

| | | |
|---|---|---|
| 17" | $700.00 | $925.00 |

Toddler

| | | |
|---|---|---|
| 19" | $975.00 | $1,300.00 |

## Child

**#250 Walkure** (made by J.D. Kestner, Jr.), dolly face, sleep eyes, open mouth

**#282 Walkure** (made by J. D. Kestner, Jr.), dolly face, sleep eyes, open mouth

| | | |
|---|---|---|
| 25" | $550.00 | $750.00 |
| 27" | $675.00 | $900.00 |
| 31" | $865.00 | $1,100.00 |
| 33" | $900.00 | $1,200.00 |
| 35" | $1,125.00 | $1,500.00 |

## Character Child

**#154** (made by Hertel & Schwab), solid dome, glass eyes, closed mouth

**#166** (made by Hertel & Schwab), solid dome, sleep eyes, closed mouth

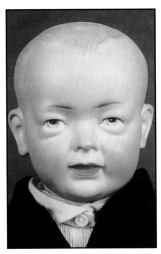

*19" bisque Kley & Hahn boy,
marked 525, $650.00. Courtesy
McMasters Doll Auctions.*

*28" bisque Kley & Hahn child
walkure, $400.00. Courtesy
McMasters Doll Auctions.*

**#169** (made by Hertel & Schwab), sleep eyes, with closed or open/closed mouth

| | | |
|---|---|---|
| 17" | $2,000.00 | $2,600.00 |
| 21" | $2,400.00 | $3,200.00 |
| 31" | $3,000.00 | $4,000.00 |

Baby body with bent limbs

| | | |
|---|---|---|
| 12" | $1,300.00 | $1,750.00 |

**#162** (made by Hertel & Schwab), sleep eyes, open mouth, cut out for voice

| | | |
|---|---|---|
| 17" | $1,100.00 | $1,500.00 |

**#178** (made by Hertel & Schwab), solid dome, molded hair, googly eyes, open mouth

**#180** (made by Hertel & Schwab), googly eyes, laughing open/closed mouth

| | | |
|---|---|---|
| 15" | $2,025.00 | $2,700.00 |
| 17" | $2,550.00 | $3,400.00 |

**#292** "KH 1930" ( made by J. D. Kestner, Jr.), character face

**#520** "K&H"(made by Bahr & Proschild), painted eyes, closed mouth

**#525** "K&H" (made by Bahr & Proschild), solid dome, painted eyes, open/closed mouth

**#526** "K&H" (made by Bahr & Proschild), painted eyes, closed mouth

**#531** "K&H" (made by Bahr & Proschild), solid dome, painted eyes, open/closed mouth

| | | |
|---|---|---|
| 15" | $1,600.00 | $2,100.00 |
| 17" | $1,800.00 | $2,400.00 |
| 21" | $2,250.00 | $3,000.00 |
| 25" | $2,700.00 | $3,600.00 |

# Kley & Hahn (cont.)

**#546** "K&H" (made by Bahr & Proschild), glass eyes, closed mouth, child body

**#549** "K&H" (made by Bahr & Proschild), painted eyes, closed mouth, also in celluloid

| | | |
|---|---|---|
| 16" | $3,150.00 | $4,200.00 |
| 18" | $3,375.00 | $4,500.00 |

**#554** "K&H" (made by Bahr & Proschild), glass eyes, open/closed mouth, crying voice

**#568** (made by Bahr & Proschild), solid dome, sleep eyes, smiling

| | | |
|---|---|---|
| 15" | $525.00 | $700.00 |
| 17" | $635.00 | $850.00 |
| 21" | $7,509.00 | $1,000.00 |

# Kling, C.F. & Co.

**1836 – 1930+, Ohrdruf, Thuringia, Germany.** Porcelain factory that made chinas, bisque dolls, all bisque, and Snow Babies. Often mold number marks are followed by size number.

First price indicates dolls in good condition, but with some flaw; second price indicates dolls in excellent condition, with original clothes, or appropriately dressed.

*Marks:*

186 Ⓚ 2          188 Ⓚ 0

**Bisque Shoulder Head**

Wig or molded hair, painted eyes, cloth or kid body

| | | |
|---|---|---|
| 15" | $300.00 | $400.00 |
| 19" | $465.00 | $625.00 |
| 21" | $475.00 | $650.00 |

Glass eyes

| | | |
|---|---|---|
| 13" | $400.00 | $525.00 |

**Mold #123**, incised with bell mark, shoulder head, glass eyes, closed mouth

| | | |
|---|---|---|
| 15" | $650.00 | $850.00 |

**Mold #131,** incised bell, shoulder head, glass eyes, closed mouth

**Mold #167,** incised bell, shoulder head, solid dome, with wig, closed mouth

*Parian-type Lady by Kling with fancy decorations in hair and heavily decorated shoulder plate, $1,075.00. Courtesy Chantal Jeshien.*

**Mold #178,** shoulder head, molded hair, glass eyes, closed mouth
**Mold #186,** shoulder head, molded hair, painted eyes, closed mouth
**Mold #182,** shoulder head, molded hair, painted eyes, closed mouth

| | | |
|---|---|---|
| 15" | $800.00 | $1,075.00 |

**Mold #370, #372, #373, #377** shoulder head, dolly face, sleep eyes, open mouth

| | | |
|---|---|---|
| 15" | $360.00 | $485.00 |
| 21" | $515.00 | $700.00 |

**Bisque Socket Head,** open mouth, jointed body

| | | |
|---|---|---|
| 13" | $300.00 | $400.00 |
| 17" | $425.00 | $550.00 |
| 21" | $550.00 | $725.00 |

## China Shoulder Head

Cloth or kid body, china limbs, blonde or black molded hair
**Mold #131,** painted eyes, closed mouth
**Mold #188,** molded hair, glass eyes, closed mouth
**Mold #189,** molded hair, painted eyes, closed mouth
**Mold #202,** molded hair, painted eyes, closed mouth

| | | |
|---|---|---|
| 13" | $200.00 | $275.00 |
| 18" | $335.00 | $450.00 |
| 21" | $375.00 | $500.00 |

## Knoch, Gebruder

**1887 – 1918+, Neustad, Thuringia, Germany.** Made bisque doll heads and doll joints with cloth or kid body. Succeeded in 1918 by Max Oscar Arnold.

*Marks:*

Mold #s 179, 181, 190, 192, 193, 201, 204 socket heads #203, 205, 216, domed head, character face, painted eyes, open/closed mouth. #223 shoulder head

**Shoulder Head**
**Mold #203,** character face, painted eyes, closed mouth, stuffed cloth body

| | | |
|---|---|---|
| 12" | $600.00 | $800.00 |

**Mold #205** "GKN," character face, painted eyes, open/closed mouth, molded tongue

| | | |
|---|---|---|
| 14" | $750.00 | $1,000.00 |

**Mold #216,** "GKN," solid dome, painted eyes, laughing open/closed mouth

| | | |
|---|---|---|
| 12" | $1,425.00 | $1,900.00 |

*14" bisque solid dome character mold #217 with open/closed laughing mouth, $1,100.00. Courtesy Amanda Hash.*

# Knoch, Gebruder (cont.)

**Mold #223,** "GKN GES. NO. GESCH," character face, solid dome, painted eyes, molded tears, closed mouth

*\*too few in database to give reliable range*

**Socket Head**

**Mold #179, #181, #190, #192, #193, #201** (also came as black), dolly face, glass eyes, open mouth

| | | |
|---|---|---|
| 13" | $185.00 | $250.00 |
| 17" | $300.00 | $425.00 |
| 19" | $400.00 | $525.00 |

**Mold #204,** character face

| | | |
|---|---|---|
| 15" | $865.00 | $1,150.00 |

**#230** Molded bonnet, character shoulder head, painted eyes, laughing open/closed mouth

**#232** Molded bonnet, character shoulder head, laughing mouth

| | | |
|---|---|---|
| 13" | $675.00 | $900.00 |
| 15" | $1,200.00 | $1,600.00 |

# Konig & Wernicke

**1912 – 1930+, Waltershausen, Germany.** This was a doll factory that made bisque or celluloid dolls with composition bodies, later dolls had hard rubber heads.

*Marks:*

K&W
HARTGUMMI
555 o
GERMANY

K & W
1070
15

**Bisque Baby**

**Mold #98, 99** "made in Germany" (made by Hertel & Schwab), socket head, sleep eyes, open mouth, teeth, tremble tongue, wigged, composition bent leg baby body

| | | |
|---|---|---|
| 22" | $600.00 | $800.00 |
| 27" | $900.00 | $1,200.00 |

**Mold #1070,** socket head, open mouth, bent leg baby body

| | | |
|---|---|---|
| 12" | $400.00 | $550.00 |
| 16" | $500.00 | $650.00 |

Toddler

| | | |
|---|---|---|
| 17" | $1,000.00 | $1,350.00 |
| 19" | $1,125.00 | $1,525.00 |

*13½" bisque toddler, by Konig & Wernicke, has unusual straight legs, marked "KW" in circle, $900.00. Courtesy Amanda Hash.*

## Composition Child

Composition head on five piece or fully jointed body, open mouth, sleep eyes, add more for flirty eyes,

|      |          |          |
|------|----------|----------|
| 14"  | $225.00  | $300.00  |
| 16"  | $350.00  | $450.00  |

*15" painted bisque Konig & Wernicke baby, marked "201," $145.00. Courtesy McMasters Doll Auctions.*

## Kruse, Kathe

**1910 – 80+ Prussia, after W.W.II, Bavaria.** Kruse made dolls of waterproof muslin, wool, and stockinette. Heads and hair were hand painted with oil. Dolls had a skeleton frame, with rigid and movable parts. Early dolls are stuffed with deer hair. Early thumbs are part of the hand, after 1914 they are attached separately, and later, were again part of the hand. Usually marked on the bottom of the foot with number and name Kathe Kruse, in black, red, or purple ink. In 1946 dolls had wigs, but some had painted hair and wigs. Original doll modeled after Dutch bust sculpture *Fiamingo* by Francois Duquesnois.

First price is for fair condition; second price is for good condition, third price is for excellent condition.

Marks:

*Left: 18" hard plastic Kathy Kruse boy, all original in box, $180.00. Right: Girl, all original in box, $205.00. Courtesy McMasters Doll Auctions.*

33947

**Cloth**

|  |  |  |  |
|---|---|---|---|
| 19" | $250.00 | $375.00 | $500.00 |

**Series I, 1910+,** wide hips, painted hair, early model, jointed hips, shoulders

|  |  |  |  |
|---|---|---|---|
| 17" | $1,600.00 | $3,450.00 | $4,600.00 |

Jointed knees

|  |  |
|---|---|
| 17" | $5,000.00+ |

*\* too few examples in database to give reliable range*

**Series I,** 1929+, like above but with slim hips

|  |  |  |  |
|---|---|---|---|
| 17" | $1,400.00 | $2,100.00 | $2,800.00 |

Wigged

|  |  |  |
|---|---|---|
| $1,300.00 | $1,950.00 | $2,600.00 |

**Series II,** ca. 1922 – 36, smiling baby with stockinette covered body and limbs

|  |  |  |  |
|---|---|---|---|
| 14" | $1,400.00 | $2,100.00 | $2,800.00 |

**Series V, VI Sandbabies,** made in 1920s+, "Traumchen" has weighted five-pound, stockinette-covered wire frame body with closed eyes, navel on body. "Du Mein" came with open eyes, both weighted and not weighted body. Other heads of a composition type material called magnesit were produced in the 30s.

|  |  |  |  |
|---|---|---|---|
| 20" | $1,800.00 | $2,700.00 | $3,600.00 |

Magnesit head

|  |  |  |  |
|---|---|---|---|
| 20" | $325.00 | $650.00 | $1,300.00 |

**Series VII,** ca. 1927 – 52, "Hampelchen," with loose legs

|  |  |  |  |
|---|---|---|---|
| 14" | $1,000.00 | $1,500.00 | $2,000.00 |

**Series VII,** 1946

|  |  |  |  |
|---|---|---|---|
| 20½" | $1,200.00 | $1,800.00 | $2,400.00 |

**Series VIII,** 1929+, Deutsche Kind "German Child," wigged, swivel head, slim body

|  |  |  |  |
|---|---|---|---|
| 20½ " | $1,200.00 | $1,800.00 | $2,400.00 |

**Series IX,** 1929+, wigged swivel head

|  |  |  |  |
|---|---|---|---|
| 14" | $1,000.00 | $1,500.00 | $2,000.00 |

**Series X,** ca. 1935 – 52

|  |  |  |  |
|---|---|---|---|
| 14" | $1,000.00 | $1,500.00 | $2,000.00 |

**U. S. Zone,** ca. 1946 – 1951

Cloth

|  |  |  |  |
|---|---|---|---|
| 14" | $650.00 | $975.00 | $1,300.00 |

Magnesit (composition – type)

|  |  |  |  |
|---|---|---|---|
| 14" | $400.00 | $600.00 | $800.00 |

**Hard Plastic**

**1952 – 1975**

Glued on wigs, sleep or painted eyes, pink muslin body

|  |  |  |  |
|---|---|---|---|
| 18" | $200.00 | $350.00 | $600.00 |
| 21" | $250.00 | $500.00 | $750.00 |

**1975 to date**

|  |  |
|---|---|
| 9" | $165.00+ |
| 14" | $350.00+ |
| 17" | $465.00+ |

# Kuhnlenz, Gebruder

**1884 – 1930, Kronach, Bavaria.** Made dolls, doll heads, movable children, and swimmers. Butler Bros. and Marshall Field distributed their dolls.

*Marks:*

$$Q^{br} \, 30\,5 \atop 165 \, K \atop 9$$

Germany
9

**Mold #32,** bisque socket head, closed mouth, glass eyes, pierced ears, wig, wood, composition jointed body

| | | |
|---|---|---|
| 19" | $1,800.00 | $2,400.00 |
| 23" | $2,175.00 | $2,900.00 |

**Mold #34,** Bru type, paperweight eyes, closed mouth, pierced ears, compo jointed body

| | | |
|---|---|---|
| 12½" | $1,650.00 | $2,200.00 |

**Mold #38,** solid dome shoulder head, glass eyes, closed mouth, pierced ears, kid body

| | | |
|---|---|---|
| 20" | $900.00 | $1,200.00 |

**Mold #41,** all bisque (marked "GK" on torso), swivel head, kid lined torso, glass sleep eyes, open mouth, teeth, mohair wig,

| | | |
|---|---|---|
| 8½" | $525.00 | $700.00 |
| 10" | $900.00 | $1,200.00 |

**Mold #44,** small dolls marked "Gbr. K" in sunburst, socket head, glass eye, open mouth, five-piece compo body, painted, molded socks and shoes

| | | |
|---|---|---|
| 7" | $250.00 | $325.00 |

with trunk and wardrobe

| | |
|---|---|
| 6" | $1,600.00 * at auction |

*33" bisque Gebruder Kuhnlenz child, open mouth, composition jointed body, $1,500.00. Courtesy McMasters Doll Auctions.*

**1915 – 24, Limoges, France.** Porcelain factory made dolls and heads, including heads marked Caprice, Cherie, Favorite, La Georgienne, Lorraine, and Toto. Lady dolls were dressed in French provincial costumes, bodies by Ortyz; dolls were produced for Association to Aid War Widows.

*Marks:*

**Adult, ca. 1915**

Marked Caprice, Cherie, Favorite, La Georgienne, Lorraine, or Toto, bisque socket head, open/closed mouth with teeth, composition adult body

JE masson
S.C.
LORRAINE
N°0
ALEC°
LIMOGES

*28" bisque Lanternier child, named Favorite, with original wig, clothes, and paperweight eyes, $1,750.00+. Courtesy Matrix.*

| 17" | $975.00 | $1,300.00 |
| 23" | $1,200.00 | $1,750.00 |

**Child**

Bisque socket head, open mouth with teeth, wig, composition jointed body

| 17" | $525.00 | $725.00 |
| 23" | $700.00 | $950.00 |
| 28" | $1,125.00 | $1,500.00 |

# Leather

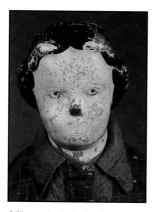

*25" rawhide lady, $165.00. Courtesy McMasters Doll Auctions.*

*12" leather doll with the name "Maxine" incised into the back, manufactured by M.S. Davis Co., patented by Gussie Decker, Chicago, IL, ca. 1902 – 09, $275.00. Courtesy Sherryl Shirran.*

Leather was an available resource for native Americans to use for making doll heads, bodies, or entire dolls. Some examples of Gussie Decker's dolls were advertised as "impossible for child to hurt itself" and leather was fine for teething babies.

    12"      $275.00
*too few examples to give reliable range*
    25"      $325.00
*two few examples to give reliable range*

# Lenci

**1918 – 80+, Turine, Italy.** Trademark and name of a firm started by Enrico and Elenadi Scavini that made felt dolls with pressed faces, composition head dolls, wooden dolls, and porcelain figurines and dolls. Early Lenci dolls have tiny metal button, hangtags with "Lenci//Torino//Made in Italy." Ribbon strips marked "Lenci//Made in Italy" were found in the clothes ca. 1925 – 1950. Some dolls have Lenci marked in purple or black ink on the sole of the foot; otherwise unmarked. Dolls have felt swivel heads, oil painted features, side glancing eyes, jointed shoulders and hips, sewn together third and fourth fingers, sewn on felt ears, often dressed in felt and organdy original clothes, excellent condition.

*Marks:* With button, paper tag, ribbon strips, or on bottom of foot.

First price indicates dolls in poor condition, perhaps worn, soiled or faded, prices in this condition should reflect 25% of dolls in excellent condition; second price indicates dolls in excellent condition, clean, with colors still bright. Add more for tags, boxes, or accessories. Rare examples may go much higher.

**Baby**

| | | |
|---|---|---|
| 13" | $350.00 | $1,400.00 |
| 18" | $500.00 | $2,000.00 |

**Child**

| | | |
|---|---|---|
| 13" | $175.00 | $700.00 |
| 17" | $325.00 | $1,100.00 |
| 21" | $375.00 | $1,500.00 |

**SMALL DOLLS**

(Mascottes) under 9"

| | | |
|---|---|---|
| 6" | $55.00 | $225.00 |
| 8" | $80.00 | $325.00 |

In rare outfit

| | | |
|---|---|---|
| 8" | $115.00 | $450.00 |

*25" cloth Lenci, Oriental Butterfly, ca. 1925 – 27, all original, $4,800.00. Courtesy Sherryl Shirran.*

**Lady**

With adult face, flapper or boudoir body with long slim limbs.

| | | |
|---|---|---|
| 17" | $265.00 | $1,050.00 |
| 26" | $500.00 | $2,000.00 |
| 32" | $650.00 | $2,600.00 |
| 35" | $750.00 | $3,000.00 |
| 42" | $900.00 | $3,600.00 |
| 48" | $1,250.00 | $5,000.00 |

**Celebrities**

**Bach**

| | | |
|---|---|---|
| 17" | $715.00 | $2,850.00 |

**Jack Dempsey**

| | | |
|---|---|---|
| 18" | $875.00 | $3,500.00 |

**Tom Mix**

| | | |
|---|---|---|
| 18" | $875.00 | $3,500.00 |

**Mendel**

| | | |
|---|---|---|
| 22" | $925.00 | $3,700.00 |

**Mozart**

| | | |
|---|---|---|
| 20" | $850.00 | $3,350.00 |

**Characters**

**Aladdin**

| | | |
|---|---|---|
| 14" | $1,925.00 | $7,750.00 |

**Athlete**

Golfer

| | | |
|---|---|---|
| 16" | $650.00 | $2,650.00 |

**Aviator,** girl with felt helmet

| | | |
|---|---|---|
| 18" | $800.00 | $3,200.00 |

**Bernadetta**

| | | |
|---|---|---|
| 19" | $260.00 | $1,050.00 |

**Butterfly**

| | | |
|---|---|---|
| 17" | $800.00 | $3,200.00 |

**Clown**

| | | |
|---|---|---|
| 19" | $450.00 | $1,800.00 |

**Cupid**

| | | |
|---|---|---|
| 17" | $1,300.00 | $5,200.00 |

**Flower Girl**

| | | |
|---|---|---|
| 20" | $250.00 | $1,000.00 |

**Henriette**

| | | |
|---|---|---|
| 26" | $625.00 | $2,500.00 |

**Hitler youth**

| | | |
|---|---|---|
| 16" | $375.00 | $1,500.00 |

**Indian**

| | | |
|---|---|---|
| 17" | $900.00 | $3,600.00 |

Squaw with papoose

| | | |
|---|---|---|
| 17" | $1,050.00 | $4,200.00 |

**Li Tia Guai**

| | | |
|---|---|---|
| 17" | $7,000.00 | * at auction |

**Lucia**
14"    $225.00    $900.00
**Merry Widow**
20"    $360.00    $1,450.00
**Oriental**
17"    $900.00    $3,600.00
Chinese man
15"    $600.00    $2,400.00
Hu Sun
22"    $575.00    $2,300.00
Oriental lady
21"    $5,800.00 *at auction
**Pan, hooved feet**
10"    $500.00    $2000.00
**Sailor**
17"    $360.00    $1,450.00
**Salon Lady**
40"    $725.00    $2,900.00
**Series 300 Children**
Eastern European boy
17"    $275.00    $1,100.00
Turkish boy
17"    $375.00    $1,500.00
**Smoker**
Painted eyes
28"    $600.00    $2,400.00
Glass eyes
24"    $975.00    $3,900.00
**Spanish Girl**
14"    $200.00    $800.00
17"    $250.00    $1,000.00
**Tirol Boy or Girl**
14"    $200.00    $800.00
**Val Gardena**
19"    $225.00    $900.00
**Winking Bellhop with Love Letter**
11"    $175.00    $700.00
**Young Flower Merchant**
on wood bases
9"    $1,300.00 * at auction
**Ethnic or Regional Costume**
  **Bali Dancer**
15"    $375.00    $1,500.00
  **South Seas Girl**
17"    $710.00    $2,850.00
  **Eugenia**
25"    $275.00    $1,100.00

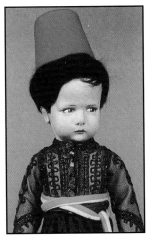

*17" felt Lenci Turkish Boy, jointed felt body with hollow torso, elaborate original felt Turkish outfit, $1,500.00. Courtesy McMasters Doll Auctions.*

*17" Lenci Salome, ca. 1920, jointed shoulders and hips with unusual felt ball at waist to allow doll to swivel, $3,500.00. Courtesy Sherryl Shirran.*

# Lenci (cont.)

**Eye Variations**
  **Glass Eyes**
| | | |
|---|---|---|
| 16" | $400.00 | $1,600.00 |
| 22" | $750.00 | $3,000.00 |

  **Flirty Glass Eyes**
| | | |
|---|---|---|
| 15" | $550.00 | $2,200.00 |
| 20" | $700.00 | $2,800.00 |

  **Surprise Eye,** "O" shaped eyes, and mouth
| | | |
|---|---|---|
| 16" | $400.00 | $1,200.00 |

**Accessories**
  Lenci Catalogs $900.00 – $1,200.00

## Lenci-Type

**1920 – 50.** These were made by many English, French or Italian firms. They were felt or cloth with painted features, mohair wig, original clothes. These must be in very good condition, tagged or unmarked.

*15" cloth Lenci-type girl, $145.00. Courtesy McMasters Doll Auctions.*

*7" cloth Lenci-type man dressed in ethnic costume, $30.00.*

**Child**
| | | |
|---|---|---|
| 15" | $35.00 | $145.00 |
| 25" | $65.00 | $275.00 |
| Regional costume | | |
| 19" | $115.00 | $450.00 |

## Limbach

**1772 – 1927+, Alsbach, Thuringia, Germany.** This porcelain factory made bisque head dolls, china dolls, bathing dolls, and all bisque dolls. Usually marked with three leaf clover.

  *Marks:*

*Rita*
3/0

Germany
🍀
4

**All Bisque**

**Child,** small doll, molded or wigged hair, painted eyes, painted molded shoes and socks

| | | |
|---|---|---|
| 6" | $95.00 | $125.00 |

Glass eyes

| | | |
|---|---|---|
| 6" | $200.00 | $275.00 |

**Baby**

**#8682, character face,** bisque socket head, glass eyes, clover mark, bent leg baby body, wig, open/closed mouth

| | | |
|---|---|---|
| 15" | $535.00 | $700.00 |

**Child,** may have name above mold mark, such as Norm or Rita, bisque socket head, glass eyes, clover mark, wig, open mouth

| | | |
|---|---|---|
| 20" | $700.00 | $950.00 |

*8" Limbach baby, mold #8682, $300.00. Courtesy McMasters Doll Auctions.*

# Marottes

*16" all original German composition stick toy, $475.00+. Courtesy of Matrix.*

*27" bisque doll made for the French market, $700.00. 11" celluloid head Marotte with cloth body, "Germany" on handle with whistle, $250.00. Courtesy McMasters Doll Auctions.*

**Ca. 1860** on. Doll's head on wooden or ivory stick, sometimes with whistle; when twirled some play music. Bisque head on stick made by various French and German companies. Add more for marked head.

**Bisque,** open mouth
11 – 12"          $700.00     $1,000.00
Closed mouth
11 – 12"          $1,000.00   $1,300.00
**Celluloid**
11"              $190.00     $250.00

*30" bisque C.M. Bergmann child, marked "Bergmann, S&H 13.5" on back of head. Right: 13" Marotte bisque head on music box, stick with whistle, $1,250.00. Courtesy McMasters Doll Auctions.*

## Marseille, Armand

**1885 – 1930+, Sonneberg, Koppelsdorf, Thuringia, Germany.** One of largest suppliers of bisque doll heads from 1900 to 1930, they supplied to such companies as Amberg, Arranbee, Bergmann, Borgfeldt, Butler Bros., Dressel, Montgomery Ward, Sears, Steiner, Wiegand, and Louis Wolf and others. They made some doll heads that had no mold numbers, but did have names, such as Alma, Baby Betty, Baby Gloria, Baby Florence, Baby Phyllis, Beauty, Columbia, Duchess, Ella, Florodora, Jubilee, Mabel, Majestic, Melitta, My Playmate, Nobbi Kid, our Pet, Princess, Queen Louis, Rosebud, Superb, Sunshine, and Tiny Tot. Some Indian dolls had no mold numbers. Often used Superb kid bodies with bisque hands.

*Marks:*

Queen Louise          Armand Marseille          Baby Gloria
Germany               Germany                   Germany
7.                    390
                      A. 4. M.

First price indicates dolls in good condition with flaw; second price indicates dolls in excellent condition with original clothes, or appropriately dressed. Add $50.00 more for composition body; add $100.00 more for toddler body.

Made in Germany
Florodora
A 5 M

### BABY

**Newborn,** bisque solid dome socket head or flange neck, may have wig, glass eyes, closed mouth, cloth body with celluloid or composition hands.

20" bisque Armand Marseille baby, with flirty eyes and wobble tongue, composition bent limb baby body, mold #259, $625.00. Courtesy Angie Gonzales.

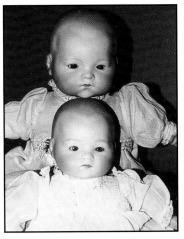

13" and 15" bisque solid dome Dream Babies with cloth body, mold #341, $375.00 – $475.00. Courtesy Angie Gonzales.

**Mold #341, My Dream Baby, #351, Rock-A-Bye Baby** marked AM in original presentation basket with layette

| | | |
|---|---|---|
| 5½" | $900.00 * at auction | |
| 9" | $165.00 | $225.00 |
| 13" | $300.00 | $400.00 |
| 16" | $375.00 | $500.00 |

**Mold #345, Kiddiejoy, #352,** bisque solid dome socket head or flange neck, may have wig, glass eyes, closed mouth, cloth body with celluloid or composition hands.

| | | |
|---|---|---|
| 8" | $140.00 | $185.00 |
| 10" | $185.00 | $250.00 |
| 15" | $350.00 | $475.00 |
| 20" | $500.00 | $685.00 |
| 28" | $900.00 | $1,200.00 with toddler body |
| Hand puppet | | |
| | $245.00 | $325.00 |

16" Kiddiejoy Baby, $300.00. Courtesy McMasters Doll Auctions.

**BABY, CHARACTER FACE**
**Baby Betty,** usually found on composition child body, some on bent leg baby body

| | | |
|---|---|---|
| 13" | $275.00 | $375.00 |
| 17" | $400.00 | $545.00 |
| 21" | $465.00 | $625.00 |

**Baby Gloria, #240**

| | | |
|---|---|---|
| 11" | $300.00 | $415.00 |
| 15" | $475.00 | $625.00 |
| 18" | $700.00 | $925.00 |

*10" Armand Marseille, mold
#550, $1,000.00. Courtesy
McMasters Doll Auctions.*

*16" bisque character baby by
Armand Marseille, $500.00.
Courtesy Angie Gonzales.*

**Baby Phyllis,** painted hair, closed mouth

| | | |
|---|---|---|
| 11" | $285.00 | $385.00 |
| 15" | $425.00 | $560.00 |
| 19" | $780.00 | $1,045.00 |

**Fanny, with mold #230, 231** (can be child, toddler, or baby), more for molded hair

| | | |
|---|---|---|
| 16" | $3,425.00 | $4,575.00 |
| 19" | $4,625.00 | $6,175.00 |

**Mold #256, 259, 326, 327, 328, 329, 360a, 750, 790, 900, 927, 970, 971, 975, 980, 984, 985, 990, 991, 992 Our Pet, 995, 996.**

Bisque solid dome or socket head, open mouth, glass eyes, composition bent limb baby body, add more for toddler body or flirty eyes

| | | |
|---|---|---|
| 10" | $185.00 | $250.00 |
| 12" | $225.00 | $300.00 |
| 15" | $335.00 | $450.00 |
| 17" | $425.00 | $575.00 |
| 20" | $485.00 | $650.00 |
| 23" | $585.00 | $785.00 |

## CHILD

**No mold number, or just marked A.M.** bisque socket head, open mouth, glass eyes, wig, composition jointed body

| | | |
|---|---|---|
| 17" | $300.00 | $400.00 |
| 32" | $700.00 | $925.00 |
| 42" | $1,500.00 | $2,000.00 |

**Mold #1890, 1892, 1893** (made for Cuno & Otto Dressel), **1894, 1897, 1898** (made for Cuno & Otto Dressel), **1899, 1900, 1901, 1902, 1903, 1909, and 3200,** bisque shoulder or socket head, glass eyes, open mouth with teeth, wig, kid body, add more for original clothes, labels.

| | | |
|---|---|---|
| 12" | $150.00 | $200.00 |
| 16" | $140.00 | $185.00 |
| 19" | $210.00 | $280.00 |
| 22" | $255.00 | $340.00 |
| 26" | $330.00 | $445.00 |

Composition body

| | | |
|---|---|---|
| 8" | $245.00 | $325.00 |
| 12" | $190.00 | $265.00 |
| 15" | $225.00 | $300.00 |
| 19" | $365.00 | $450.00 |
| 21" | $375.00 | $500.00 |
| 24" | $465.00 | $624.00 |
| 27" | $545.00 | $725.00 |
| 30" | $675.00 | $900.00 |

**Alma, Duchess, Floradora, Lilly, Mabel, My Playmate, and Mold #3700, open mouth, glass eyes**

Kid body

| | | |
|---|---|---|
| 13" | $135.00 | $180.00 |
| 16" | $200.00 | $265.00 |
| 19" | $255.00 | $345.00 |
| 23" | $545.00 | $735.00 |

Composition body

| | | |
|---|---|---|
| 13" | $200.00 | $270.00 |
| 17" | $275.00 | $365.00 |
| 20" | $355.00 | $475.00 |
| 25" | $450.00 | $600.00 |
| 28" | $580.00 | $775.00 |
| 30" | $710.00 | $975.00 |

**Beauty, Columbia, Melitta, My Companion, Princess, Queen Louise, Rosebud**

Kid body

| | | |
|---|---|---|
| 13" | $175.00 | $235.00 |
| 15" | $255.00 | $350.00 |
| 20" | $355.00 | $475.00 |
| 25" | $425.00 | $575.00 |
| 30" | $545.00 | $725.00 |
| 34" | $750.00 | $1,000.00 |

Composition body

| | | |
|---|---|---|
| 14" | $215.00 | $290.00 |
| 17" | $275.00 | $365.00 |
| 20" | $415.00 | $550.00 |
| 23" | $430.00 | $575.00 |
| 27" | $470.00 | $625.00 |
| 29" | $740.00 | $950.00 |
| 32" | $845.00 | $1,125.00 |

*30" bisque Armand Marseille Queen Louise, marked "32," $375.00. Courtesy McMasters Doll Auctions.*

*20" bisque Armand Marseille toddler, marked "996," $325.00. Courtesy McMasters Doll Auctions.*

*35" bisque Armand Marseille child, marked "390," $750.00. Courtesy McMasters Doll Auctions.*

## CHILD, CHARACTER FACE

**Mold #225,** bisque socket head, glass eyes, open mouth, two rows of teeth, composition jointed body

| | | |
|---|---|---|
| 15" | $2,900.00 | $3,850.00 |
| 18" | $3,300.00 | $4,400.00 |

**Mold #250**

| | | |
|---|---|---|
| 12" | $475.00 | $635.00 |
| 14" | $425.00 | $550.00 |
| 19" | $775.00 | $1,055.00 |

**Mold #251,** open/closed mouth

| | | |
|---|---|---|
| 15" | $1,265.00 | $1,675.00 |
| 18" | $1,500.00 | $2,000.00 |

Open mouth

| | | |
|---|---|---|
| 15" | $665.00 | $900.00 |

**Mold #310, Just Me,** bisque socket head, wig, flirty eyes, closed mouth, compo body

| | | |
|---|---|---|
| 7½" | $750.00 | $1,000.00 |
| 9" | $800.00 | $1,200.00 |
| 11" | $1,200.00 | $1,600.00 |
| 13" | $1,500.00 | $2,000.00 |

Painted bisque, Vogue labeled outfits

| | | |
|---|---|---|
| 8" | $625.00 | $850.00 |
| 10" | $750.00 | $1,000.00 |

**Mold #340**

| | | |
|---|---|---|
| 14" | $2,100.00 | $2,800.00 |

*not enough examples in database to give reliable range*

**Mold #345,** closed mouth, intaglio eyes,

| | | |
|---|---|---|
| 13" | $900.00 | $1,200.00 |
| 17" | $1,500.00 | $2,000.00 |

**Mold #350,** socket head, glass eyes, closed mouth

| | | |
|---|---|---|
| 12" | $1,000.00 | $1,300.00 |
| 16" | $1,650.00 | $2,250.00 |
| 20" | $2,100.00 | $2,850.00 |
| 25" | $2,600.00 | $3,600.00 |

**Mold #360**

| | | |
|---|---|---|
| 12" | $300.00 | $400.00 |
| 16" | $550.00 | $725.00 |

**Mold #372 Kiddiejoy,** ca. 1925, shoulder head, molded hair, painted eyes, open/closed mouth, two upper teeth, kid body

| | | |
|---|---|---|
| 12" | $300.00 | $400.00 |
| 18" | $500.00 | $650.00 |
| 21" | $775.00 | $1,025.00 |

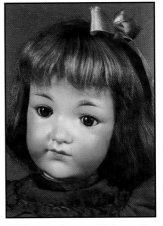

*19" bisque Armand Marseille character girl, marked "400," made in Germany, $2,400.00. Courtesy McMasters Doll Auctions.*

**Mold #400, 401,** bisque socket head, glass eyes, closed mouth

| | | |
|---|---|---|
| 13" | $1,450.00 | $1,950.00 |
| 16" | $1,885.00 | $2,500.00 |
| 22" | $2,500.00 | $3,300.00 |

Flapper body, thin limbs

| | | |
|---|---|---|
| 14" | $1,475.00 | $1,975.00 |

**Mold #449,** bisque socket head, painted eyes, closed mouth

| | | |
|---|---|---|
| 12" | $436.00 | $585.00 |
| 16" | $800.00 | $1,075.00 |
| 21" | $1,150.00 | $1,500.00 |

Painted bisque

| | | |
|---|---|---|
| 10" | $225.00 | $315.00 |
| 15" | $500.00 | $675.00 |
| 20" | $785.00 | $1,050.00 |

**Mold #450,** bisque socket head, glass eyes, closed

| | | |
|---|---|---|
| 13" | $500.00 | $675.00 |
| 16" | $900.00 | $1,225.00 |
| 19" | $1,200.00 | $1,625.00 |

**Mold #500, 620, 630, 640,** domed shoulder head, painted molded hair, painted intaglio eyes, closed mouth

| | | |
|---|---|---|
| 11" | $450.00 | $600.00 |
| 15" | $700.00 | $950.00 |

**Mold #520,** domed head, glass eyes, open mouth

Composition body

| | | |
|---|---|---|
| 11" | $465.00 | $715.00 |
| 16" | $950.00 | $1,275.00 |
| 20" | $1,750.00 | $2,300.00 |

Kid body

| | | |
|---|---|---|
| 11" | $450.00 | $600.00 |
| 15" | $700.00 | $950.00 |
| 21" | $1,175.00 | $1,575.00 |

# Marseille, Armand (cont.)

**Mold #550,** domed head, glass eyes, closed mouth
| | | |
|---|---|---|
| 10" | $1,000.00 | $1,300.00 |
| 14" | $1,750.00 | $2,300.00 |
| 20" | $2,600.00 | $3,500.00 |

**Mold #570, 590,** bisque socket head, sleep eyes, open mouth
| | | |
|---|---|---|
| 12" | $435.00 | $575.00 |
| 15" | $625.00 | $850.00 |

Open/closed mouth
| | | |
|---|---|---|
| 16" | $1,400.00 | $1,900.00 |

**Mold #600,** domed shoulder head, painted eyes, closed mouth
**Mold #640a,** shoulder head, painted eyes, closed mouth
| | | |
|---|---|---|
| 10" | $625.00 | $850.00 |
| 17" | $1,350.00 | $1,800.00 |

**Mold #700,** socket head, painted or sleep eyes, closed mouth
Painted eyes
| | | |
|---|---|---|
| 12½" | $1,500.00 | $1870.00 |

*too few examples in database to give reliable range*
Glass eyes
| | | |
|---|---|---|
| 14" | $4,200.00 | * at auction |

**Mold 701, 711** socket or shoulder head, sleep eyes, closed mouth
| | | |
|---|---|---|
| 12" | $1,080.00 | $1,400.00 |
| 16" | $1,835.00 | $2,450.00 |

* *too few in database to give reliable range*
**Mold #800,** socket head, glass eyes, open mouth
**Mold #820,** shoulder head, glass eyes, open/closed mouth
| | | |
|---|---|---|
| 15" | $1,200.00 | $1,600.00 |
| 18" | $1,800.00 | $2,400.00 |
| 22" | $2,100.00 | $2,850.00 |

* *too few in database to give reliable range*

## Mascotte

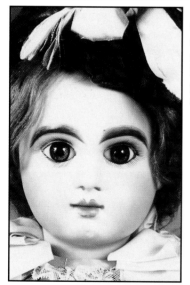

**(Bebe Mascotte) 1882 – 1901,** trademark of May Freres Cie, using sizes similar to Bebes Jumeau. Became part of Jules Steiner in 1898. Bisque socket head, wig over cork pate, closed mouth, paperweight eyes, pierced ears, jointed composition French style body.
*Marks:*
On head:
*MASCOTTE*
On body:
*Bebe Mascotte//Paris*
**Child,** marked "Mascotte" on head
| | | |
|---|---|---|
| 14" | $2,300.00 | $3,200.00 |
| 18" | $3,200.00 | $4,250.00 |
| 21" | $3,500.0 | $4,700.00 |

*25" bisque Mascotte Bebe, marked "Mascotte, J" on back of head, $5,000.00. Courtesy McMasters Doll Auctions.*

# Metal Heads

**Ca. 1850 – 1930+.** Often called "Minerva," because of a style of metal shoulder head widely distributed in the United States. Dolls with metal heads were made by various manufactures including Buschow & Beck, Alfred Heller who made Diana metal heads, and Karl Standfuss who made Juno metal heads. In the United States, Art Metal Works made metal head dolls. Various metals used were aluminum, brass, and others. They might be marked with just a size and country of origin or they may unmarked.

*21" German tin head child, glass eyes, $325.00. Courtesy Angie Gonzales.*

**Metal shoulder head,** cloth or kid body, molded, painted hair

Glass eyes

| | | |
|---|---|---|
| 16" | $160.00 | $215.00 |
| 18" | $215.00 | $290.00 |
| 21" | $250.00 | $335.00 |

Painted eyes

| | | |
|---|---|---|
| 14" | $100.00 | $140.00 |
| 20" | $185.00 | $250.00 |

**Child,** all metal or with composition body, metal limbs

| | | |
|---|---|---|
| 15" | $335.00 | $445.00 |
| 20" | $475.00 | $625.00 |

**Swiss,** all metal jointed dolls, ca. 1921 – 40, metal ball joints

Man

| | | |
|---|---|---|
| 7" | $100.00 | $145.00 |
| 10" | $140.00 | $190.00 |

# Mothereau

**Ca. 1880 – 95.** Bebe Mothereau was made by Alexandre C. T. Mothereau who patented a joint for doll bodies, with wooden upper arms and legs. Lower arms and legs have a rounded joint and metal bracket for stringing. Pressed bisque socket head, glass eyes, closed mouth, pierced ears, cork pate, jointed composition body.

*Mark:*

6

B. M.

**Child**

12"     $12,000.00 * auction

*too few examples in database to give reliable range*

# Multi-Face, Multi-Head

**1866 – 1930+.** Various firms made dolls with two or more faces, or more than one head.

**Bisque, French**

**Bru, Surprise poupee,** awake, asleep faces

12"     $9,500.00

* *too few examples in database to give reliable range*

**Jumeau,** bisque head, crying, laughing faces, under cardboard cap hides knob

    18"    $10,500.00 * at auction

**Bisque, German**

**Bergner, Carl,** bisque socket head, with three faces, sleeping, laughing, crying, molded tears, glass eyes, on composition jointed body, may have molded bonnet or hood, marked C.B. or Designed by Carl Bergner

    12"    $900.00       $1,200.00
    15"    $1050.00     $1,400.00

*15" two-faced wax doll, two faces swivel in molded bonnet, $300.00. Courtesy McMasters Doll Auctions.*

**Kestner, J. D.** ca. 1900+, Wunderkind, bisque doll with set of several different mold number heads that could be attached to body. Set of one doll and body with additional three heads, and wardrobe

    including heads #174, 178, 184, & 185
        11"    $10,000.00 * at auction
    including heads, 171, 179, 182, & 183
        14½"    $12,650.00 * at auction

**Kley and Hahn,** solid dome bisque socket head, painted hair, smiling baby and frowning baby, closed mouth, tongue, glass eyes, baby body

    13"    $1,100.00 * at auction

**Simon and Halbig,** bisque socket head, smiling, sleeping, crying, turn ring at top of head to change faces, glass and painted eyes, closed mouth

    14½"    $935.00 * at auction

**Cloth**

**Topsy-Turvy,** one black head, one white head. See Cloth section.

**Composition**

**Berwick Doll Co., Famlee Dolls,** ca. 1926+, composition head and limbs, cloth body with crier, neck with screw joint, allowing different heads to be screwed into the body, painted features, mohair wigs and/or painted molded hair. Came in sets of two to twelve heads, with different costumes for each head

Five heads, including baby, girl in fancy dress, girl in sports dress, Indian, and clown

| | | |
|---|---|---|
| 16" | $600.00 | $800.00 |

**Effanbee,** Johnny Tu-Face, composition

| | |
|---|---|
| 16" | $275.00 |

*too few examples in database to give reliable range*

**Ideal,** 1923, Soozie Smiles, composition, sleep or painted eyes on happy face, two faces, smiling, crying, cloth body composition hands, cloth legs, original romper and hat

| | | |
|---|---|---|
| 15½" | $300.00 | $400.00 |

**Three in One Doll Corp.,** Trudy, 1946+, composition head with turning knob on top, cloth body and limbs, three faces, "Sleepy, Weepy, Smiley," dressed in felt or fleece snowsuit, or sheer dresses.

| | | |
|---|---|---|
| 15½" | $85.00 | $300.00 |

## Munich Art

**1908 – 20s.** Marion Kaulitz hand painted heads designed by Marc – Schnur, Vogelsanger, and Wackerle, dressed in German or French regional costumes. Usually composition heads and bodies distributed by Cuno & Otto Dressell and Arnoldt Doll Co.

**Compo character** with painted features, wigged, composition body, unmarked

| | |
|---|---|
| 19" | $2,100.00 * at auction |

*18" Munich Art Doll by Marion Kaulitz with original painted features, wig, and fully jointed body, $2,000.00. Courtesy Matrix.*

## Ohlhaver, Gebruder

**1913 – 30, Sonneberg, Germany.** Had Revalo (Ohlhaver spelled backwards omitting the two H's) line; made bisque socket and shoulder head and composition dolls. Ernst Heubach supplied some heads to Ohlhaver. Marked: **"Revalo."**

**Baby or Toddler, character face,** bisque socket head, glass eyes, open mouth, teeth, wig, compo and wood ball jointed body (bent limb for baby)

Baby

| | | |
|---|---|---|
| 16" | $425.00 | $575.00 |
| 20" | $525.00 | $700.00 |

# Ohlhaver, Gebruder (cont.)

Toddler
| | | |
|---|---|---|
| 14" | $525.00 | $700.00 |
| 18" | $675.00 | $900.00 |

**Child,** bisque socket head, open mouth, sleep eyes, composition body
| | | |
|---|---|---|
| 16" | $425.00 | $575.00 |
| 19" | $500.00 | $675.00 |
| 26" | $675.00 | $925.00 |

## Oriental

**ALL BISQUE**
**Kestner**
| | | |
|---|---|---|
| 6" | $1,050.00 | $1,400.00 |
| 8" | $1,200.00 | $1,600.00 |

**S&H**
| | | |
|---|---|---|
| 6" | $965.00 | $1,275.00 |
| 9" | $1,400.00 | $1,850.00 |

**BSW**
| | | |
|---|---|---|
| 6" | $600.00 | $800.00 |

**Unmarked or unknown maker, presumed German or French**
| | | |
|---|---|---|
| 6" | $400.00 | $550.00 |

**EUROPEAN BISQUE**
Bisque head, jointed body
**Amusco, mold #1006**
| | | |
|---|---|---|
| 17" | $900.00 | $1,200.00 |

**Belton-type, #193, 206**
| | | |
|---|---|---|
| 10" | $1,550.00 | $2,075.00 |
| 14" | $2,000.00 | $2,700.00 |
| 17" | $2,800.00 | $3,775.00 |

**Schmidt, Bruno (BSW)**
Mold **#500** glass eyes, open mouth
| | | |
|---|---|---|
| 14" | $1,600.00 | $2,100.00 |
| 16" | $1,835.00 | $2,450.00 |

**Bru,** pressed bisque swivel head, glass eyes, closed mouth, original outfit
| | | |
|---|---|---|
| 20" | $26,000.00 * at auction | |

**Kestner. J. D., 1899 – 1930+, #243,** bisque socket head, open mouth, wig, bent limb baby body; add more for original clothing
| | | |
|---|---|---|
| 14" | $3,400.00 | $4,550.00 |
| 19" | $4,950.00 | $6,600.00 |

**Solid dome,** painted hair
| | | |
|---|---|---|
| 15" | $3,750.00 | $5,000.00 |

**Armand Marseille, ca. 1925**
**#353** Solid dome bisque socket head, glass eyes, closed mouth
Baby body
| | | |
|---|---|---|
| 7½" | $900.00 | $1,200.00 |
| 14" | $925.00 | $1,225.00 |
| 16" | $1,050.00 | $1,400.00 |

Toddler
| | | |
|---|---|---|
| 16" | $975.00 | $1,300.00 |

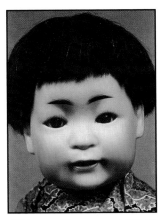

*13" bisque Kestner, mold #243, Oriental baby, $4,000.00. Courtesy McMasters Doll Auctions.*

*14" bisque Oriental child, mold #4900, Schoenau & Hoffmeister, open mouth, $750.00. Courtesy McMasters Doll Auctions.*

*13" bisque Oriental child, Bruno Schmidt, mold #500, $2,000.00. Courtesy McMasters Doll Auctions.*

Painted bisque

| | | |
|---|---|---|
| 7" | $350.00 * at auction | |

**Schoenau & Hoffmeister**

**Mold #4900,** bisque socket head, glass eyes, open mouth, tinted composition and wood jointed body

| | | |
|---|---|---|
| 10" | $350.00 | $475.00 |

**Simon & Halbig**

**Mold #1099,** bisque socket head, glass eyes, open mouth, pierced ears, original outfit

| | | |
|---|---|---|
| 16" | $9,000.00 * at auction | |

**Mold #1129, #1199, #1329,** bisque socket head, glass eyes, open mouth, pierced ears, composition and wood jointed body

| | | |
|---|---|---|
| 13" | $1,350.00 | $1,800.00 |
| 30" | $1,875.00 | $2,500.00 |

**Unknown maker,** bisque socket head, jointed body

Closed mouth

| | | |
|---|---|---|
| 14" | $975.00 | $1,300.00 |
| 20" | $2,200.00 | $2,800.00 |

**JAPANESE BISQUE**

Various makers including Morimura and Yamato, made dolls when doll production was halted in Europe during World War I. They were marked "FY," "Nippon," or "J.W."

*9" Armand Marseille bisque Oriental baby, marked "A.Ellar (in star) M," closed mouth, painted hair, five-piece composition body, $1,000.00. Courtesy McMasters Doll Auctions.*

*14½" bisque Bahr & Proschild Oriental child, mold #220, $750.00. Courtesy McMasters Doll Auctions.*

**Baby,** marked Japan or Nippon or by other maker

| | | |
|---|---|---|
| 11" | $135.00 | $180.00 |
| 13" | $180.00 | $245.00 |
| 15" | $225.00 | $300.00 |
| 19" | $400.00 | $525.00 |
| 24" | $585.00 | $785.00 |

**Child,** marked Nippon or Japan or other

| | | |
|---|---|---|
| 14" | $195.00 | $250.00 |
| 17" | $250.00 | $330.00 |
| 22" | $415.00 | $550.00 |

## COMPOSITION
### Effanbee

**Patsy,** painted Oriental features including black bangs, straight across the forehead, brown side-glancing eyes, dressed in silk Chinese pajamas and matching shoes, excellent condition

| | | |
|---|---|---|
| 14" | $200.00 | $750.00+ |

**Butin-nose,** in basket with wardrobe, painted Oriental features including black bobbed hair, with bangs, side-glancing eyes, excellent color and condition

| | | |
|---|---|---|
| 8" | $125.00 | $500.00 |

### Horsman

*9" French celluloid Oriental baby, $475.00. Courtesy McMasters Doll Auctions.*

**Baby Butterfly,** ca. 1911 – 13, composition head and hands, cloth body, painted hair and features

| | | |
|---|---|---|
| 13" | $75.00 | $300.00 |

**Quan-Quan Co.,** California
   **Ming Ming Baby**, all composition jointed baby, painted features, original costume, yarn que, painted shoes
   | 11" | $50.00 | $200.00 |

**TRADITIONAL CHINESE**
   Man or woman, composition-type head, cloth wound bodies, may have carved arms and feet, in traditional costume
   | 11" | $115.00 | $350.00 |
   | 14" | $175.00 | $525.00 |

**TRADITIONAL JAPANESE**
**Papier mache** swivel head and shoulder plate, cloth midsection, upper arms, and legs, limbs and torso are papier mache, glass eyes, pierced nostrils, original dress. Early dolls have jointed wrists and ankles. Many of the later dolls imported by Kimport.
   **Traditional, early, fine quality, ca. 1890s**
   | 16" | $200.00 | $400.00 |
   | 19" | $275.00 | $545.00 |
   | 25" | $550.00 | $1,100.00 |

   **Traditional, early boy, painted hair**
   | 15" | $280.00 | $560.00 |
   | 20" | $425.00 | $950.00 |
   | 24" | $650.00 | $1,300.00 |

   Traditional boy, 1930s
   | 14" | $80.00 | $155.00 |
   | 19" | $150.00 | $300.00 |

   Traditional boy, 1940s
   | 15" | $50.00 | $100.00 |

   **Traditional lady, 1920s**
   | 14" | $135.00 | $270.00 |
   | 16" | $165.00 | $325.00 |

   Traditional lady, 1940s – 50s
   | 14" | $50.00 | $95.00 |
   | 16" | $70.00 | $135.00 |

   **Emperor or Empress, seated,** ca. 1890s,
   | 8" | $285.00 | $575.00 |

   Ca. 1920s
   | 6" | $90.00 | $180.00 |
   | 8" | $115.00 | $225.00 |

   **Warrior, 1880 – 1890s**
   | 16" | $500.00 | $650.00 |
   * *too few in database to give reliable range*
   On horse
   | 15" | $1,100.00+ |
   * *too few in database to give reliable range*
   Warrior, 1920s
   | 15" | $400.00 |
   * *too few in database to give reliable range*

On horse
13"        $850.00+
* too few in database to give reliable range

**Japanese baby, ca. 1920s,** bisque head, sleep eyes, closed mouth, papier mache body

| | | |
|---|---|---|
| 8" | $50.00 | $70.00 |
| 14" | $65.00 | $90.00 |

Glass eyes

| | | |
|---|---|---|
| 8" | $95.00 | $125.00 |
| 14" | $200.00 | $265.00 |

**Japanese baby,** crushed oyster shell head, painted flesh color, papier mache body, glass eyes and original clothes

| | | |
|---|---|---|
| 8" | $25.00 | $50.00 |
| 14" | $45.00 | $95.00 |
| 18" | $95.00 | $185.00 |

## WOOD

**Door of Hope (see that section).**
**Schoenhut (see that section).**

# Papier Mache

**Pre-1600 on.** Varying types of composition made from paper or paper pulp could be mass produced in molds for heads after 1810, reached heights of popularity by mid 1850s and was also used for bodies. Papier mache shoulder head, glass or painted eyes, painted molded, hair, sometimes in fancy hairdos.

First price indicates dolls in good condition with flaws, less if poorly repainted; second price is for dolls in very good condition, nicely dressed.

*10" papier mache Milliner's Model, unmarked shoulder head, kid body, wooden lower arms and legs, $600.00. Courtesy McMasters Doll Auctions.*

*24" papier mache, unmarked shoulder head, home-made cloth body, $1,250.00. Courtesy McMasters Doll Auctions.*

**EARLY TYPE**

**Ca. 1840s – 1860s.** Cloth body, wooden limbs, top knot, bun, puff curls or braided hair styles, dressed in original clothing or excellent copy, may have some wear

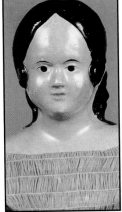

Painted eyes

| | | |
|---|---|---|
| 9" | $225.00 | $450.00 |
| 12" | $340.00 | $675.00 |
| 18" | $525.00 | $1,050.00 |
| 21" | $575.00 | $1,150.00 |
| 26" | $700.00 | $1,400.00 |
| 32" | $985.00 | $1,975.00 |

Glass eyes

| | | |
|---|---|---|
| 22" | $1,000.00 | $2,000.00 |
| 26" | $1,400.00 | $2,800.00 |

Long curls

| | | |
|---|---|---|
| 9" | $235.00 | $475.00 |
| 15" | $350.00 | $700.00 |
| 25" | $725.00 | $1,450.00 |

Covered Wagon or Flat Top hair style

| | | |
|---|---|---|
| 9" | $150.00 | $300.00 |
| 13" | $200.00 | $400.00 |
| 15" | $225.00 | $550.00 |

*16" paper mache Milliner's Model, painted eyes, kid body, leather lower limbs, $1,000.00. Courtesy McMasters Doll Auctions.*

**Milliner's Models**

**Ca. 1820 _ 1860s.** Contemporary collectors have used this term "Milliner's models" to describe dolls with a shapely waist, kid body, and wooden limbs

Apollo top knot, (beehive) side curls

| | | |
|---|---|---|
| 12" | $485.00 | $965.00 |
| 15" | $915.00 | $1,825.00 |
| 18" | $1,200.00 | $2,400.00 |

Braided bun, side curls

| | | |
|---|---|---|
| 9" | $450.00 | $900.00 |
| 13" | $750.00 | $1,400.00 |

Center part, molded bun

| | | |
|---|---|---|
| 9" | $325.00 | $650.00 |
| 13" | $500.00 | $1,000.00 |

Center part, sausage curls

| | | |
|---|---|---|
| 15" | $315.00 | $625.00 |
| 20" | $450.00 | $900.00 |

Coiled braids over ears, braided bun

| | | |
|---|---|---|
| 16" | $850.00 | $1700.00 |
| 20" | $1,100.00 | $2,200.00 |

**Molded bonnet,** kid body, wooden limbs, bonnet painted to tie under chin, very rare

| | |
|---|---|
| 15" | $1,700.00 |

*14" German papier mache shoulder head, glass eyes, cloth body, hinged derriere with cloth tabs attached to the legs to keep doll sitting, not marked, ca. 1830s–40s, original outfit, $1,750.00+. Courtesy Rosalie Whyel Museum of Doll Art, Bellevue, WA, photo by Charles Backus.*

*\* too few examples in database to give reliable range*

# Papier Mache (cont.)

**Molded comb**, side curls, braided coronet

| | | |
|---|---|---|
| 16" | $1,650.00 | $3,300.00 |

*\* too few examples in database to give reliable range*

## FRENCH TYPE

Painted black hair, brushmarks, solid dome, some have nailed on wigs, open mouth, bamboo teeth, kid or leather body, appropriately dressed

**Glass eyes**

| | | |
|---|---|---|
| 16" | $725.00 | $1,450.00 |
| 19" | $975.00 | $1,950.00 |
| 23" | $1,100.00 | $2,200.00 |
| 26" | $1,200.00 | $2,400.00 |
| 30" | $1,400.00 | $2,800.00 |

**Painted eyes**

| | | |
|---|---|---|
| 15" | $325.00 | $650.00 |
| 20" | $515.00 | $1,025.00 |

**Wooden jointed body**

| | | |
|---|---|---|
| 8" | $385.00 | $765.00 |

## GERMAN TYPE

**"M&S Superior,"** Muller & Strassburger of Sonneberg, Germany, ca. 1844 – 1892, shoulder head with blonde or molded hair, painted blue or brown eyes, cloth body with kid or leather arms and boots. Mold numbers on stickers reported are 1020, 2020, 2015, and 4515

| | | |
|---|---|---|
| 16" | $200.00 | $400.00 |
| 20" | $325.00 | $650.00 |
| 26" | $400.00 | $815.00 |

**Glass eyes**

| | | |
|---|---|---|
| 22" | $435.00 | $865.00 |

**Wigged**

| | | |
|---|---|---|
| 20" | $430.00 | $860.00 |

**German type, 1879 – 1900s**

Molded blonde or black hairstyles, closed mouth

**Painted eyes**

| | | |
|---|---|---|
| 14" | $120.00 | $235.00 |
| 17" | $175.00 | $350.00 |
| 25" | $225.00 | $450.00 |
| 30" | $375.00 | $750.00 |

**Glass eyes**

| | | |
|---|---|---|
| 14" | $255.00 | $515.00 |
| 17" | $375.00 | $750.00 |

**Turned shoulder head,** solid dome, glass eyes, closed mouth, cloth body, composition forearms

| | | |
|---|---|---|
| 16" | $350.00 | $700.00 |
| 22" | $465.00 | $925.00 |

**Character heads,** molded like the bisque ones, glass eyes, closed mouth, on fully jointed body

| | | |
|---|---|---|
| 15" | $515.00 | $1,025.00 |
| 21" | $815.00 | $1,625.00 |

## PAPIER MACHE, 1920+

Head has brighter coloring, wigged, child often in ethnic costume, stuffed cloth body and limbs, or papier mache arms

**French**

| | | |
|---|---|---|
| 8" | $55.00 | $110.00 |
| 12" | $95.00 | $185.00 |
| 14" | $135.00 | $265.00 |

**German**

| | | |
|---|---|---|
| 8" | $40.00 | $75.00 |
| 14" | $890.00 | $155.00 |

**Unknown maker**

| | | |
|---|---|---|
| 8" | $30.00 | $60.00 |
| 12" | $60.00 | $115.00 |
| 16" | $90.00 | $175.00 |

**Clowns,** papier mache head with painted clown features, open or closed mouth, molded or wigged hair, cloth body, composition or papier mache arms, or five-piece jointed body

| | | |
|---|---|---|
| 8" | $120.00 | $235.00 |
| 14" | $245.00 | $485.00 |
| 20" | $395.00 | $785.00 |
| 26" | $460.00 | $925.00 |

**Eden Clown,** socket head, open mouth, blue glass eyes, blonde mohair wig, five-piece jointed body, all original with labeled box

| | |
|---|---|
| 16" | $4,000.00 * at auction |

# Parian Type – Untinted Bisque

**Ca. 1850 – 1900+, Germany.** Refers to very white color of untinted bisque dolls, often with molded blonde hair, some with fancy hair arrangements and ornaments or bonnets; can have glass or painted eyes, pierced ears, molded jewelry or clothing. Occasionally solid dome with wig. Cloth body, nicely dressed in good condition.

*Mark:*

Seldom any mark; may have number inside shoulder plate.

*16" unmarked untinted bisque Parian-type shoulder head, molded net on hair, cloth body, kid lower arms, $250.00. Courtesy McMasters Doll Auctions.*

*25" Countess Dagmar Parian-type, untinted bisque shoulder head, pierced ears, cloth body, kid arms, $475.00. Courtesy McMasters Doll Auctions.*

*25" bisque shoulder head, blue glass eyes, molded hair with ribbon, cloth body, bisque lower arms, pierced ears, $575.00. Courtesy McMasters Doll Auctions.*

*24" bisque Parian-type, glass eyes, swivel neck, cloth body, leather lower arms, $3,200.00. Courtesy McMasters Doll Auctions.*

**Fancy hairstyle,** with molded combs, ribbons, flowers, bands, or snoods, cloth body, untinted bisque limbs

Glass eyes, pierced ears

| | | |
|---|---|---|
| 16" | $1,275.00 | $1,700.00 |
| 21" | $2,200.00 | $2,900.00 |

Painted eyes, pierced ears

| | | |
|---|---|---|
| 15" | $650.00 | $850.00 |
| 20" | $1,175.00 | $1,575.00 |

Painted eyes, ears not pierced

| | | |
|---|---|---|
| 14½" | $2,090.00 | * at auction |
| 18" | $7,800.00 | $10,400.00 |

*\*not enough examples in database to give reliable range*

**Men or Boys,** center or side part hairstyle, cloth body, decorated shirt and tie

Glass eyes

| | | |
|---|---|---|
| 16" | $2,100.00 | $2,825.00 |

Painted eyes

| | | |
|---|---|---|
| 16" | $700.00 | $950.00 |
| 19" | $950.00 | $1,250.00 |

**Molded hat,** with blonde or black painted hair

Glass eyes

| | | |
|---|---|---|
| 16" | $2,100.00 | $2,825.00 |
| 18" | $2,500.00 | $3,350.00 |

Painted eyes

| | | |
|---|---|---|
| 15" | $1,600.00 | $2,150.00 |
| 18" | $2,050.00 | $2,750.00 |

**Molded headband or comb,** "Alice in Wonderland" hairstyle has band

| | | |
|---|---|---|
| 12" | $300.00 | $400.00 |
| 15" | $425.00 | $585.00 |
| 18" | $525.00 | $700.00 |

**Molded necklace,** jewels or standing ruffles

Glass eyes, pierced ears

| | | |
|---|---|---|
| 16" | $1,250.00 | $1,700.00 |
| 21" | $1,650.00 | $2,200.00 |

Painted eyes, ears not pierced

| | | |
|---|---|---|
| 16" | $700.00 | $950.00 |
| 19" | $1,000.00 | $1,350.00 |

With large stones, painted scenes behind them

| | |
|---|---|
| 17" | $9,700.00+ |

*\* too few examples in database to give reliable range*

**Swivel neck, glass eyes**

| | | |
|---|---|---|
| 15" | $1,950.00 | $2,625.00 |
| 19" | $2,275.00 | $3,000.00 |

| | | |
|---|---|---|
| 21" | $2,400.00 | $3,200.00 |
| **Undecorated, plain style** | | |
| 13" | $135.00 | $175.00 |
| 15" | $225.00 | $300.00 |
| 21" | $325.00 | $425.00 |
| 25" | $400.00 | $525.00 |
| **Wigged,** solid dome, ca. 1850s, molded ear | | |
| 16" | $625.00 | $850.00 |
| 18" | $700.00 | $950.00 |
| 21" | $1,025.00 | $1,350.00 |

## P.D.

**Frederic Petit & Andre Dumontier, 1878 – 90, Paris.** Made dolls with bisque heads from Francois Gaultier factory. Pressed bisque socket head, rounded face, glass eyes, closed mouth, pierced ears, wig over cork pate, French composition and wooden jointed body.

*Marks:*

P 3 D

| | | |
|---|---|---|
| 19" | $9,000.00 | $12,000.00 |
| 25" | $11,450.00 | $15,250.00 |

## Piano Babies

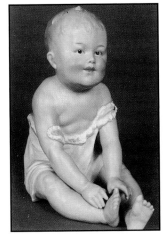

*8" bisque Gebruder Heubach Piano Baby, $650.00. Courtesy McMasters Doll Auctions.*

*6" Heubach Piano Baby, $900.00. Courtesy McMasters Doll Auctions.*

**Ca. 1880 – 1930+, Germany.** Theses all bisque figurines were made by Gebruder Heubach, Kestner, Dressel, Limbach, and others. May have molded on clothes; came in a variety of poses. Some were reproduced during the 60s and 70s and the skin tones are paler than the others.

First price indicates figurine in good condition with flaws; second price indicates figurine in excellent condition.

# Piano Babies (cont.)

**Excellent quality or marked Heubach,** fine details

| | | |
|---|---|---|
| 4" | $235.00 | $300.00 |
| 6" | $350.00 | $475.00 |
| 9" | $525.00 | $700.00 |
| 16" | $850.00 | $1,125.00 |

**Black**

| | | |
|---|---|---|
| 5" | $300.00 | $425.00 |
| 9" | $375.00 | $500.00 |
| 14" | $675.00 | $900.00 |

**With animal, pot, flowers, chair, or other items**

| | | |
|---|---|---|
| 5" | $195.00 | $260.00 |
| 8" | $315.00 | $425.00 |
| 10" | $400.00 | $525.00 |
| 15" | $750.00 | $1,000.00 |

**Medium quality or unmarked,** may not have painted finished on back

| | | |
|---|---|---|
| 4" | $75.00 | $100.00 |
| 8" | $150.00 | $200.00 |
| 12" | $225.00 | $300.00 |

## Pincushion or Half Dolls

*5" china half doll, made in France, mounted on wire frame, $275.00. Courtesy McMasters Doll Auctions.*

**Ca. 1900 – 1930s, Germany, Japan.** Half dolls can be made of bisque, china, composition, or papier mache and were used not only for pin cushions but on tops of jewelry or cosmetic boxes, brushes, lamps, and other decorative uses. The most sought after have arms molded away from the body. These were easier to break with the limbs in this position, and thus fewer survived.

*Left: 4½" German half doll with Schneider mark, 14274, hands away, arms close to body, $125.00. Right: 6½" Goebel half doll with legs on base, hands away, $120.00. Courtesy McMasters Doll Auctions.*

**Arms away from china or bisque figure, bald head with wig**

| | | |
|---|---|---|
| 4" | $105.00 | $140.00 |
| 6" | $155.00 | $210.00 |

Arms away, marked by maker or with mold number

| | | |
|---|---|---|
| 4" | $150.00 | $200.00 |
| 6" | $225.00 | $300.00 |
| 8" | $300.00 | $400.00 |
| 12" | $675.00 | $900.00 |

Arms away holding items, such as letter, flower, etc.

| | | |
|---|---|---|
| 4" | $135.00 | $185.00 |
| 6" | $200.00 | $275.00 |

**Arms in, close to figure, bald head with wig**

| | | |
|---|---|---|
| 4" | $55.00 | $75.00 |
| 6" | $80.00 | $110.00 |

Arms in, marked by maker or with mold number

| | | |
|---|---|---|
| 5" | $80.00 | $105.00 |
| 7" | $110.00 | $150.00 |

Arms in, hands attached

| | | |
|---|---|---|
| 3" | $19.00 | $25.00 |
| 5" | $25.00 | $35.00 |
| 7" | $45.00 | |

Arms in, papier mache or composition

| | | |
|---|---|---|
| 4" | $25.00 | $35.00 |
| 6" | $60.00 | $80.00 |

**Jointed shoulders, china or bisque, molded hair**

| | | |
|---|---|---|
| 5" | $110.00 | $145.00 |
| 7" | $150.00 | $200.00 |

Jointed shoulders, solid dome, mohair wig

| | | |
|---|---|---|
| 4" | $165.00 | $220.00 |
| 6" | $330.00 | |

**Man or child**

| | | |
|---|---|---|
| 4" | $90.00 | $120.00 |
| 6" | $120.00 | $160.00 |

**Marked Germany**

| | | |
|---|---|---|
| 4" | $150.00 | $200.00 |
| 6" | $375.00 | $500.00 |

**Marked Japan**

| | | |
|---|---|---|
| 3" | $10.00 | $15.00 |
| 6" | $38.00 | $50.00 |

*4¾" Dressel & Kister half doll, one arm extended and one away, $175.00. Courtesy McMasters Doll Auctions.*

**Other items**

Brush with porcelain figurine for handle, molded hair

| | | |
|---|---|---|
| 9" | $55.00 | $75.00 |

Dresser Box, unmarked, with figurine on lid

| | | |
|---|---|---|
| 7" | $265.00 | $350.00 |
| 9" | $345.00 | $450.00 |

Dresser box, marked with mold number, country, or manufacturer

| | | |
|---|---|---|
| 5" | $210.00 | $285.00 |
| 6" | $275.00 | $350.00 |

Perfume bottle, stopper is half doll, skirt is bottle

| | | |
|---|---|---|
| 6½" | $165.00 * at auction | |

**1856 – 1930 and later, Paris.** Became S.F.B.J. in 1899. Some heads pressed and some poured. Also purchased heads from Francois Gaultier.

*Marks:*

# R.1.D

# R.3.D

### Child

**Closed mouth,** bisque socket head, paperweight eyes, pierced ears, mohair wig over cork pate, French wooden and compo jointed body

| | | |
|---|---|---|
| 11" | $2,400.00 | $3,200.00 |
| 18" | $2,500.00 | $3,300.00 |
| 23" | $3,150.00 | $4,200.00 |

**Open mouth**

| | | |
|---|---|---|
| 18" | $975.00 | $1,300.00 |
| 25" | $1,350.00 | $1,800.00 |
| 29" | $1,575.00 | $2,100.00 |

*22" bisque socket head Bebe, glass eyes, open/closed mouth, jointed wood and composition body, marked "Rabery Paris" on soles of shoes, $4,000.00. Courtesy McMasters Doll Auctions.*

---

## Recknagel

**1886 – 1930+, Thuringia, Germany.** Made bisque heads of varying quality, incised or raised mark, wigged or molded hair, glass or painted eyes, open or closed mouth, flange neck or socket head.

*Marks:*

**1909
DEP
R22/₀A**

### Baby

**Bent limb baby body,** glass eyes

| | | |
|---|---|---|
| 9" | $140.00 | $185.00 |
| 12" | $180.00 | $250.00 |
| 16" | $325.00 | $425.00 |
| 20" | $375.00 | $500.00 |

**Bonnethead Baby,** painted eyes, open/closed mouth, teeth, molded white boy's cap, bent leg baby body

9"  $250.00 * at auction

**Oriental Baby,** solid dome bisque socket head, sleep eyes, closed mouth, five-piece, yellow tinted body

11"  $2,300.00 * at auction

**Child, ca. 1890s – 1914**
**Glass eyes,** open mouth, painted shoes and socks on small dolls.

| | | |
|---|---|---|
| 8" | $85.00 | $115.00 |
| 12" | $155.00 | $210.00 |
| 18" | $275.00 | $375.00 |
| 22" | $375.00 | $500.00 |
| 25" | $500.00 | $650.00 |

**Mold #1907, 1909, 1914,** etc. dolly face, open mouth, glass eyes

| | | |
|---|---|---|
| 8" | $100.00 | $125.00 |
| 13" | $200.00 | $275.00 |
| 16" | $260.00 | $350.00 |
| 22" | $415.00 | $550.00 |
| 25" | $525.00 | $700.00 |

**Painted eyes,** open/closed mouth, some with molded bonnet or ribbon

| | | |
|---|---|---|
| 9" | $550.00 | $750.00 |
| 12" | $675.00 | $900.00 |

**Boy,** character face, solid dome bisque socket head, painted brush stroked hair, intaglio eyes, closed mouth, composition and wooden fully jointed body

| | |
|---|---|
| 18" | $1,700.00 * at auction |

# Rohmer

**1857 – 80, Paris.** Mme. Rohmer held patents for doll bodies made of various materials.

*Mark:*

**Fashion-type,** bisque swivel head, rounded face, kid lined shoulder plate, mohair wig over cork pate, gusseted kid body, kid over wooden arms, dowel jointed on stamped Rohmer body

| | | |
|---|---|---|
| 17" | $4,200.00 | $5,600.00 |
| 16" | $7,400.00 | * at auction |

China head, painted eyes

| | | |
|---|---|---|
| 17" | $2,800.00 | $3,700.00 |

*16" Rohmer fashion, bisque head, kid leather body, china lower arms, ca. 1860s, $6,500.00+. Courtesy Rosalie Whyel Museum of Doll Art, Bellevue, WA., photo by Charles Backus.*

# Schmidt, Bruno

**1900 – 1930+, Waltershausen, Germany.** Made bisque, composition and wooden head dolls, after 1913 they also made celluloid dolls. Acquired Bahr and Proschild in 1918. Often used a heart-shaped tag.

*Marks:*

**BSW** (in heart)

♡
425
15

5

**Baby**

Marked "BSW" in heart, no mold number, bisque socket head, glass eyes, open mouth, wig, compo bent limb baby body, add more for flirty eyes and toddler body

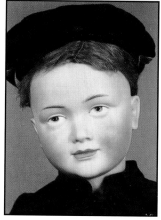

*21" bisque Bruno Schmidt boy, marked "2025," $4,750.00. Courtesy McMasters Doll Auctions.*

**Mold #2095, #2097**

| | | |
|---|---|---|
| 11" | $375.00 | $500.00 |
| 13" | $400.00 | $600.00 |
| 18" | $600.00 | $800.00 |
| 23" | $775.00 | $1,050.00 |
| 28" | $945.00 | $1,250.00 |

**Child**

Bisque socket head, jointed body, sleep eyes, open mouth, add $50.00 more for flirty eyes

| | | |
|---|---|---|
| 14" | $335.00 | $450.00 |
| 18" | $475.00 | $625.00 |
| 23" | $625.00 | $850.00 |

**Oriental, Mold #500,** yellow tinted bisque socket head, glass eyes, open mouth with teeth, pierced ears, wig, yellow tinted composition jointed body

| | | |
|---|---|---|
| 11" | $940.00 | $1,250.00 |
| 18" | $1,350.00 | $1,800.00 |

**Mold #529, 539, 2023, 2025,** solid dome, or with wig, painted eyes, closed mouth

| | | |
|---|---|---|
| 16" | $1,450.00 | $1,925.00 |
| 20" | $2,700.00 | $3,600.00 |

**Mold #537, 2033,** character face, sleep eyes, closed mouth

| | | |
|---|---|---|
| 13" | $6,900.00 | $9,200.00 |
| 15" | $12,000.00 | $16,000.00 |
| 17" | $12,750.00 | $17,000.00 |

\* *too few in database to give reliable range*

*12" bisque baby made for Bruno Schmidt by Bahr & Proschild, $475.00. Courtesy McMasters Doll Auctions.*

**Mold #2048, 2094, 2096,** solid dome, painted molded hair, sleep eyes, open or closed mouth, composition jointed body

Open mouth

| | | |
|---|---|---|
| 13" | $850.00 | $1,100.00 |
| 16" | $1,050.00 | $1,400.00 |
| 20" | $1,250.00 | $1,700.00 |

Closed mouth

| | | |
|---|---|---|
| 16" | $1,560.00 | $2,050.00 |
| 20" | $2,050.00 | $2,700.00 |
| 25" | $2,500.00 | $3,300.00 |

**Mold #2072,** character face, sleep eyes, open or closed mouth

Closed mouth

| | | |
|---|---|---|
| 18" | $2,700.00 | $3,600.00 |

* *too few examples in database to give reliable range*

**Mold #2097, baby**

| | | |
|---|---|---|
| 15" | $400.00 | $550.00 |
| 19" | $625.00 | $850.00 |

**Mold #2097, child or toddler**

| | | |
|---|---|---|
| 15" | $500.00 | $675.00 |
| 21" | $750.00 | $1,000.00 |

## Schmidt, Franz

**1890 – 1930+, Georgenthal, Germany.** Made, produced, and exported dolls with bisque, composition, wooden, and celluloid heads. Used some heads made by Simon Halbig.

*Marks:*

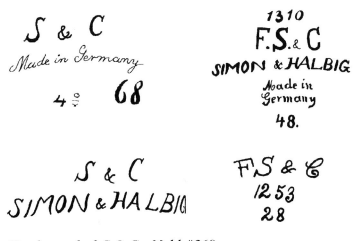

Heads marked S & C.: Mold #269, 293, 927, 1180, 1310

Heads marked F.S. & C.: Mold #1250, 1253, 1259, 1262, 1263, 1266, 1267, 1270, 1271, 1272, 1274, 1293, 1295, 1296, 1297, 1298 1310.

*Walkers: Mold #1071, 1310*

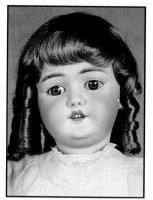

*31" bisque Franz Schmidt child, marked "S&7C," on back of head, pierced ears, open mouth, jointed wood and composition body, $1,250.00+. Courtesy McMasters Doll Auctions.*

## Baby

Bisque head, solid dome or cut out for wig, bent limb body, sleep or set eyes, open mouth, some pierced nostrils. Add more for flirty eyes.

**Mold #1271, 1272, 1295, 1296, 1297, 1310**

| | | |
|---|---|---|
| 12" | $300.00 | $400.00 |
| 14" | $325.00 | $450.00 |
| 19" | $500.00 | $650.00 |
| 24" | $950.00 | $1,250.00 |
| Toddler | | |
| 12" | $625.00 | $825.00 |
| 18" | $900.00 | $1,200.00 |
| 23" | $1,100.00 | $1,475.00 |
| 25" | $1,325.00 | $1,800.00 |

**Mold #1267,** character face, solid dome, painted eyes, closed mouth

| | | |
|---|---|---|
| 14" | $2,050.00 | $2,750.00 |
| 19" | $2,800.00 | $3,700.00 |

**Mold #1270,** painted eyes, open/closed mouth painted with teeth, bald head, large ears

| | | |
|---|---|---|
| 16" | $650.00 | $875.00 |

*too few examples in database to give reliable range*

With two faces

| | | |
|---|---|---|
| 16" | $1,075.00 | $1,450.00 |

## Child

**Mold #23, small child,** bisque socket head, glass eyes, open mouth, mohair wig, five-piece papier mache body

| | | |
|---|---|---|
| 6" | $1,400.00 * at auction | |

Child, dolly face, open mouth, glass eyes

| | | |
|---|---|---|
| 14" | $335.00 | $450.00 |
| 19" | $500.00 | $650.00 |
| 23" | $625.00 | $850.00 |
| 27" | $800.00 | $1,050.00 |

**Mold #1262, 1263,** character face, painted eyes, closed mouth, jointed body

| | | |
|---|---|---|
| 14" | $4,350.00 | $5,800.00 |
| 19" | $7,500.00 | $10,000.00 |

*too few examples in database to give reliable range*

**Mold #1071, 1310**

Walker, papier mache and composition body, walker mechanism of rollers on feet, open mouth, sleep eyes. Working mechanism.

| | | |
|---|---|---|
| 16" | $540.00 | $725.00 |
| 22" | $725.00 | $950.00 |

*too few examples in database to give reliable range*

# Schmitt & Fils

*31" bisque Schmitt & Fils, marked "SCH" in shield, paperweight eyes, open/closed mouth, pierced ears, jointed composition body, $10,500.00. Courtesy McMasters Doll Auctions.*

*20" bisque Schmitt & Fils child, marked "10," crossed hammers, and "SCH" in shield on back of head, $9,000.00+. Courtesy McMasters Doll Auctions.*

**1854 – 91, Paris.** Made bisque, wax over bisque, or wax over composition dolls. Heads were pressed. Used neck socket like on later Patsy dolls.

*Marks:*

Shield on head, "SCH" in shield on bottom of flat cut derriere.

**Child**

Pressed bisque head, closed mouth, glass eyes, pierced ears, mohair or human hair wig, French compo and wooden jointed body with straight wrists

**Early round face**

| | | |
|---|---|---|
| 12" | $6,375.00 | $8,500.00 |
| 19" | $6,000.00 | $8,000.00 |
| 24" | $12,850.00 | $17,125.00 |

**Long face modeling**

| | | |
|---|---|---|
| 24" | $11,400.00 | $15,250.00 * at auction |

**Wax over papier mache,** swivel head, cup and saucer type neck, glass eyes, closed mouth, compo and wooden body

| | | |
|---|---|---|
| 22" | $825.00 | $1,100.00 |

**Schmitt body only,** eight ball joints, straight wrists, separated fingers, marked SCH in shield

| | |
|---|---|
| 15" | $1,400.00 * at auction |

# Schoenau & Hoffmeister

**1901 – 53, Sonneberg, and Burggrub, Bavaria.** Had a porcelain factory, produced bisque heads for dolls, also supplied other manufacturers, including Bruckner, Dressel, E. Knoch, and others.

*17" Schoenau & Hoffmeister Princess Elizabeth, $7,500.00. Courtesy McMasters Doll Auctions.*

*36" bisque socket head, sleep eyes, open mouth, dimple in chin, human hair wig, composition body, $1,500.00.*

Mark:

## Baby

Bisque solid dome or wigged socket head, sleep eyes, teeth, compo bent limb body.

**Closed mouth,** newborn, solid dome, painted hair, cloth body, may have celluloid hands, add more for original outfit

|      |          |          |
|------|----------|----------|
| 9"   | $325.00  | $425.00  |
| 13"  | $625.00  | $825.00  |
| 15"  | $700.00  | $950.00  |

**Mold #169,** open mouth, compo bent limb body, wigged

|      |          |          |
|------|----------|----------|
| 23"  | $385.00  | $500.00  |
| 25"  | $425.00  | $575.00  |

**Hanna,** sleep eyes, open/closed mouth, bent leg baby body

|      |            |            |
|------|------------|------------|
| 13"  | $345.00    | $460.00    |
| 15"  | $460.00    | $650.00    |
| 18"  | $600.00    | $800.00    |
| 22"  | $1,000.00  | $1,350.00  |

*Left: 23" bisque Schoenau & Hoffmeister baby, marked 169, $375.00. Right: 11" painted bisque Grace S. Putnam Bye-Lo-Baby, $225.00. Courtesy McMasters Doll Auctions.*

**Toddler**

| | | |
|---|---|---|
| 15" | $600.00 | $800.00 |
| 21" | $1,100.00 | $1,500.00 |

Toddler, brown bisque

| | | |
|---|---|---|
| 7" | $200.00 | $275.00 |
| 9" | $245.00 | $325.00 |

**Princess Elizabeth,** socket head, sleep eyes, smiling open mouth, chubby leg toddler body

| | | |
|---|---|---|
| 16" | $1,450.00 | $1,950.00 |
| 22" | $1,925.00 | $2,550.00 |

**Child**

Dolly face, bisque socket head, open mouth with teeth, sleep eyes, compo ball jointed body

**Mold #1906, 1909, 4000, 4600, 4700, 5500, 5700, 5800**

| | | |
|---|---|---|
| 14" | $225.00 | $300.00 |
| 18" | $325.00 | $425.00 |
| 23" | $425.00 | $575.00 |
| 26" | $600.00 | $800.00 |
| 34" | $1,100.00 | $1,500.00 |
| 42" | $2,400.00 | $3,150.00 |

**Mold #4900, Oriental doll face**

| | | |
|---|---|---|
| 10" | $350.00 | $475.00 |

*30" bisque Schoeau & Hoffmeister girl, $625.00. Courtesy McMasters Doll Auctions.*

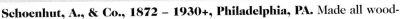

## Schoenhut

**Schoenhut, A., & Co., 1872 – 1930+, Philadelphia, PA.** Made all wooden dolls using spring joints with holes in bottoms of feet to fit into stands. Later made elastic strung with cloth bodies. Carved or painted molded hair or wigged, intaglio or sleep eyes, open or closed mouth. Later made composition dolls.

First price is for dolls in good condition, but with some flaws; second price is for dolls in excellent condition, with original clothes or appropriately re-dressed.

*Marks:*

Paper label:

Pin:Incised:

*SCHOENHUT DOLL PAT. JAN. 17, '11, U.S.A. & FOREIGN COUN-TRIES*

*16" wooden Schoenhut girl, carved hair, #16/101, $2,750.00. Courtesy Sherryl Shirran.*

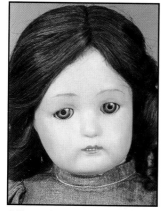

*21" wooden Schoenhut, sleep-eye girl, $275.00. Courtesy McMasters Doll Auctions.*

*13" bride and 15" groom in original outfits, both painted features, $2,500.00+ each. Courtesy Tammye Smith.*

*16" wooden Schoenhut boy, very rare model #16/403, made for only six months, ca. 1911, Graziano period, $3,500.00. Courtesy Sherryl Shirran.*

**Baby**

**Bent leg body, wigged or painted hair**

| | | |
|---|---|---|
| 13" | $400.00 | $525.00 |
| 15" | $525.00 | $700.00 |

**Sleep eyes, open mouth, wigged**

| | | |
|---|---|---|
| 13" | $450.00 | $600.00 |
| 15" | $600.00 | $800.00 |

**Toddler, baby head, fully jointed body, painted eyes, wigged or painted hair**

| | | |
|---|---|---|
| 11" | $500.00 | $650.00 |
| 14" | $575.00 | $750.00 |
| 17" | $650.00 | $850.00 |

**Toddler, baby head, sleep eyes, open mouth**

| | | |
|---|---|---|
| 14" | $675.00 | $900.00+ |
| 17" | $750.00 | $1,000.00+ |

**Child**

**Dolly face,** open/closed mouth, decal eyes, mohair wig, spring jointed body

| | | |
|---|---|---|
| 14" | $450.00 | $600.00 |
| 16" | $525.00 | $700.00 |
| 19" | $575.00 | $765.00 |

**Sleep eyes**

| | | |
|---|---|---|
| 16" | $825.00 | $1,100.00 |
| 19" | $900.00 | $1,200.00 |
| 21" | $975.00 | $1,300.00 |

**Character Face (1911 – 1923), carved hair,** closed mouth or open/closed mouth, intaglio eyes

| | | |
|---|---|---|
| 14" | $1,800.00 | $2,425.00 |
| 19" | $2,250.00 | $3,000.00 |
| 21" | $3,000.00 | $4,000.00 |

**Wedding Party,** Bride and Groom, carved hair, in original specialty outfits

    15 – 16"    $5,000.00+ for pair

*not enough examples in database to give reliable range*

**Girl with molded cap**

    14"    $2,800.00    $3,700.00

**Variations**

**Circus performers**

Ringmaster, bareback riders

    8"    $225.00 – $325.00

Clowns

    8"    $150.00 – $300.00

Animals

        $100.00 – $500.00

*Wooden Schoenhut Bandwagon, $7,000.00, Bandsmen, $14,000.00. Courtesy McMasters Doll Auctions.*

* *some rare animals may be much higher*

Humpty Dumpty Circus Set, with tent, figures, and animals

*may also be much higher for unusual figures*

        $2,600.00+

**Maggie and Jiggs,** from cartoon strip "Bringing up Father"

    7 – 9"    $525.00 each

**Manikin,** carved hair, jointed waist

    19"    $2,250.00    $3,000.00+

**Max and Moritz,** carved figure, painted hair, dowel legs, carved shoes

    8"    $625.00 each

**Roly Poly** figures

    9 – 12"    $350.00    $850.00

**Teddy Roosevelt**

    8"    $1,600.00 – $2,000.00

**Schnickel-Fritz,** 1911 – 1912 infants on child bodies, painted eyes, painted carved hair, grinning open/closed mouth, upper and lower teeth, large ears

    15"    $2,250.00    $3,000.00

*too few examples in database to give reliable range*

**Tootsie Wootsie** only infants on child bodies, open/closed mouth with tongue and two teeth, painted eyes, large ears

    15"    $2,600.00    $3,400.00

*too few examples in database to give reliable range*

**Walkable dolls,** one-piece legs, walker mechanism in body, more for carved hair character or sleep eyes

| | | |
|---|---|---|
| 11" | $375.00 | $500.00 |
| 14" | $525.00 | $700.00 |
| 17" | $675.00 | $900.00 |

# Schoenhut (cont.)

**Composition,** painted molded hair, paper label on torso, with composition jointed body, in factory outfit
      13"      $350.00        $700.00

## Schuetzmeister & Quendt

**1889 – 1930+, Boilstadt, Gotha, Thuringia.** A porcelain factory that made and exported bisque doll heads, all bisque dolls, and Nankeen dolls. Used initials S & Q, mold #301 was sometimes incised Jeannette.

*Marks:*

*15" bisque Schuetzmeister and Quendt with fully jointed toddler body and original clothes, $500.00. Courtesy Matrix.*

**Baby**
    Character face, bisque socket head, sleep eyes, open mouth, bent limb body
    **Mold #201, 204, 300, 301**
        14"      $335.00        $450.00
        19"      $450.00        $600.00
        22"      $550.00        $725.00
    **Mold #252,** character face, black baby
        15"      $575.00
    * *too few examples in database to give reliable range*
**Child**
    **Mold #101,102, dolly face**
        17"      $350.00        $400.00
        22"      $375.00        $500.00
    **Mold #1376,** character face
        19"      $550.00
    * *too few examples in database to give reliable range*

## S.F.B.J.

**Societe Francaise de Fabrication de Bebes & Jouets, 1899 – 1930+, Paris and Montreuil-sous-Bois.** Competition with German manufacturers forced many French companies to join together including Bouchet, Fleischmann & Blodel, Gaultier, Rabery & Delphieu, Bru, Jumeau, Pintel & Godchaux, Remignard, and Wertheimer. This alliance lasted until the 1950s. Fleischman owned controlling interest.

Mark:

**23**

**S.F.B.✓**
**236**

**PARIS**

**4**

First price indicates dolls in good condition, but may have flaws; second price indicates dolls in excellent condition appropriately dressed.

**Baby, Character Face**
Bisque head, wigged or molded, sleep eyes, composition body
**Mold #236**

| 13" | $550,00 | $750.00 |

**Mold #242,** nursing baby

| 15" | $2,250.00 | $3,000.00 |

*too few examples in database to give reliable range*

**Mold #247**

| 6" – 7" | $550.00 | $750.00 |

**Mold #252**

| 10" | $1,950.00 | $2,600.00 |
| 15" | $4,250.00 | $5,575.00 |

**Child**
Bisque head, glass eyes, open mouth, pierced ears, wig, composition jointed French body

Bluette, 1905 – 60, a bisque head doll with various markings, made for a weekly children's periodical, *La Semaine De Suzette* (the week of Suzette), that also had a pattern for her. Bluette was first given as a premium with a year's subscription. She usually had blue set glass eyes, open mouth, four teeth, wig, pierced ears, and a jointed composition body, 10½" tall. Made many variations of Bluette over the years, including mold #60 and 301 and a later variation marked "71 Unis/France 149//301//1 1/2." After 1919, sleeping eyes were added. Some later tagged dolls were 12" and 14" tall. Her clothing reflected the changing fads and fashions.

**Bluette, Mold #60, 301, and 71 Unis/France 149//301**

| 10½" | $635.00 | $850.00 |
| 12" | $725.00 | $975.00 |
| 14" | $850.00 | $1,125.00 |

**Jumeau type,** no mold number
Open mouth

| 13" | $675.00 | $900.00 |
| 20" | $1,200.00 | $1,600.00 |
| 24" | $1,500.00 | $2,050.00 |
| 28" | $1,875.00 | $2,500.00 |

*21" bisque S.F.B.J. child, marked "301," $600.00.Courtesy McMasters Doll Auctions.*

*8" bisque S.F.B.J. toddler, marked "247," $1,400.00. Courtesy McMasters Doll Auctions.*

*18" bisque S.F.B.J., mold #252, $6,250.00. Courtesy Waneta Jost.*

*12½" bisque S.F.BJ. toddler, marked "236," $750.00. Courtesy McMasters Doll Auctions.*

**Mold #60**

| | | |
|---|---|---|
| 16" | $500.00 | $675.00 |
| 22" | $650.00 | $875.00 |
| 25" | $875.00 | $1,250.00 |

**Mold #301**

| | | |
|---|---|---|
| 15" | $600.00 | $800.00 |
| 19" | $675.00 | $900.00 |
| 23" | $825.00 | $1,100.00 |
| 26" | $1,200.00 | $1,600.00 |
| 35" | $2,150.00 | $2,900.00 |

Kiss Thrower
| | | |
|---|---|---|
| 24" | $1,650.00 * at auction | |

Lady body
| | | |
|---|---|---|
| 22" | $1,350.00 | $1,800.00 |

**Child, Character Face**

Set or sleep eyes, molded hair or wig, mold numbers 227, 235, 237, and 266, may have flocked hair, jointed composition body

**Mold #226,** solid dome bisque socket head, brush-stroked hair, glass eyes, closed mouth
| | | |
|---|---|---|
| 20" | $1,800.00 | $2,400.00 |

**Mold #227,** solid dome socket head, open mouth with teeth, glass eyes, painted hair, French compo body
| | | |
|---|---|---|
| 14" | $1,100.00 | $1,450.00 |

**Mold #230,** bisque socket head, glass eyes, open mouth with teeth, pierced ears
| | | |
|---|---|---|
| 22" | $1,125.00 | $1,500.00 |

**Mold #233,** solid dome socket head, glass eyes, molded hair, open/closed crying mouth, French body
| | | |
|---|---|---|
| 13" | $1,500.00 | $2,000.00 |
| 16" | $2,400.00 | $3,200.00 |

**Mold #234**
| | | |
|---|---|---|
| 18" | $2,400.00 | $3,250.00 |

**Mold #235,** solid dome bisque socket head, molded hair, glass eyes, open closed mouth, French body
| | | |
|---|---|---|
| 18" | $1,350.00 | $1,800.00 |

**Mold #237,** solid dome bisque socket head, glass eyes, open mouth with teeth, flocked hair, French body
| | | |
|---|---|---|
| 15" | $3,000.00 | $4,000.00 |

**Mold #238,** socket head, wig, open mouth with teeth, French body
Lady
| | | |
|---|---|---|
| 18" | $1,950.00 | $2,600.00 |

Walker
| | | |
|---|---|---|
| 18" | $2,850.00 | $3,800.00 |

**Mold #239**
>    12"         $3,800.00         $5,100.00
> * *too few examples in database to give reliable range*

**Mold #246,** solid dome socket head, open mouth with molded tongue and teeth, sleep eyes, composition body
>    15"         $1,875.00         $2,500.00
> * *too few examples in database to give reliable range*

**Mold #247,** socket head, glass sleep eyes, closed mouth, two teeth, composition body
>    28"         $2,100.00         $2,800.00

**Mold #248,** socket head, glass eyes, closed mouth
>    12"         $5,600.00         $7,500.00
> * *too few examples in database for reliable range*

**Mold #250,** socket head, sleep eyes, open mouth with teeth, mohair wig,
> with original trousseau box
>    12"         $3,300.00 * at auction
>    13"         $1,500.00         $2,000.00
> * *too few examples in database to give reliable range*

## Simon & Halbig

**1869 – 1930+, Hildburghausen and Grafenhain, Germany.** Porcelain factory that made heads for Jumeau (200 series) bathing dolls (300 series), porcelain figures (400 series), perhaps dollhouse or small dolls (500 – 600 series), bisque head dolls (700 series), bathing and small dolls (800 series), more bisque head dolls (900 – 1000 series). Model beginning types had the last digit of their model number ending with 8, socket heads ended with 9, shoulder heads ended with 0, and models using a shoulder plate for swivel heads ended in 1.

*Marks:*

1079
HALBIG
S&H
Germany

Germany
S H 13 - 1010 DEP.

S&H. 1249
DEP
Germany
SANTA

First price indicates dolls in good condition, with flaws; second price is dolls in excellent condition, appropriately dressed.

**Baby, Character Face 1910+**
    Molded hair or wig, painted or glass eyes, open or closed mouth, bent limb baby body, add more for flirty eyes

**Mold #1294,** bisque socket head, glass eyes, open mouth, wig, bent limb baby body
>    16"         $500.00         $675.00
>    19"         $625.00         $850.00

Mold #1294, Clockwork mechanism allows eyes to move side to side
>    26"         $1,575.00 * at auction

*21" bisque baby, mold #1310, made for Franz Schmidt & Co., flirty eyes, bent limb baby body, $1,050.00. Courtesy Angie Gonzales.*

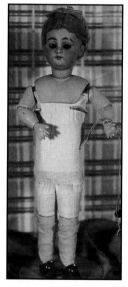

*13¼" bisque Simon & Halbig with cloth and composition pull-string "mama," crier body, $600.00. Courtesy Sue Kinkade.*

**Mold #1428,** bisque socket head, glass eyes, closed mouth, wig, bent limb baby body

| | | |
|---|---|---|
| 10" | $975.00 | $1,300.00 |

Toddler

| | | |
|---|---|---|
| 12" | $975.00 | $1,300.00 |

**Mold #1489, Baby Erika,** socket head, glass eyes, open mouth, tongue, wig, bent limb body

| | |
|---|---|
| 20" | $4,200.00 * at auction |

**Child, shoulder head,** 1870s, molded hair, marked S&H, no mold number

| | | |
|---|---|---|
| 19" | $1,275.00 | $1,700.00 |

*\* too few in database to give reliable range*

**Child, Dolly Face, 1890+**

Open mouth, glass eyes

**Mold #530, 540, 550, 570, Baby Blanche**

| | | |
|---|---|---|
| 19" | $500.00 | $685.00 |
| 22" | $550.00 | $750.00 |

oily bisque

| | |
|---|---|
| 22" | $1,100.00 * auction |

**Mold #719,** socket head, sleep eyes, open mouth, pierced ears, compo and wooden jointed body, add more for closed mouth and square cut teeth

| | | |
|---|---|---|
| 13" | $975.00 | $1,300.00 |
| 20" | $1,725.00 | $2,300.00 |
| 22" | $1,800.00 | $2,400.00 |

**Mold #739,** open or closed mouth, glass eyes, pierced ears, compo and wooden jointed body, add more for closed mouth

| | | |
|---|---|---|
| 14" | $500.00 | $650.00 |
| 22" | $1,875.00 | $2,500.00 |

**Mold #758, 759, 769, 979**

| | | |
|---|---|---|
| 13" | $925.00 | $1,250.00 |
| 20" | $1,575.00 | $2,100.00 |
| 28" | $2, 025.00 | $2,700.00 |

**Mold #1009,** bisque socket head, sleep eyes, open mouth with teeth, pierced ears, wig, add more for closed mouth

Kid body

| | | |
|---|---|---|
| 19" | $300.00 | $400.00 |
| 21" | $500.00 | $650.00 |
| 28" | $600.00 | $800.00 |

Jointed body

| | | |
|---|---|---|
| 13" | $400.00 | $525.00 |
| 15" | $550.00 | $725.00 |
| 27" | $1,050.00 | $1,400.00 |

**Mold #1010** (shoulder head), **1029, 1040** (shoulder head), **1080** (shoulder head), **1170** (shoulder head)

| | | |
|---|---|---|
| 13" | $285.00 | $375.00 |
| 16" | $385.00 | $525.00 |
| 23" | $525.00 | $700.00 |
| 27" | $650.00 | $850.00 |
| 30" | $825.00 | $1,075.00 |

**Mold #1039, 1049, 1059, 1069, 1078, 1079, 1099 (Oriental),** bisque socket or swivel head with bisque shoulder plate, pierced ears, open mouth, glass eyes, less for shoulder plate with kid or cloth body

Compo and wooden or papier mache body

| | | |
|---|---|---|
| 9" | $375.00 | $500.00 |
| 13" | $475.00 | $625.00 |
| 17" | $550.00 | $725.00 |
| 23" | $675.00 | $900.00 |
| 29 | $900.00 | $1,200.00 |
| 34" | $1,725.00 | $2,300.00 |
| 40" | $2,400.00 | $3,200.00+ |

Pull string eyes

| | |
|---|---|
| 18" | $1,000.00+ |

Mold #1079, Asian child, yellow tinted bisque

| | |
|---|---|
| 8" | $1,900.00 * at auction |

Mold #1079, Ondine, swimming doll

| | |
|---|---|
| 16" | $1,600.00 * at auction |

**Mold #1109**

| | | |
|---|---|---|
| 16" | $575.00 | $775.00 |
| 23" | $750.00 | $1,000.00 |

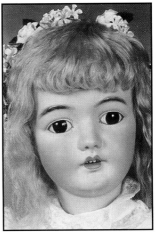

*29" bisque Simon & Halbig child, marked 1079, $750.00. Courtesy McMasters Doll Auctions.*

**Mold #1248, 1249 "Santa"**

| | | |
|---|---|---|
| 10½" | $525.00 | $700.00 |
| 18" | $900.00 | $1,200.00 |
| 21" | $950.00 | $1,275.00 |
| 30" | $2,100.00 | $2,800.00 |

**Mold #1250, 1260,** shoulder head, kid body

| | | |
|---|---|---|
| 15" | $750.00 | $1,000.00 |
| 18" | $900.00 | $1,200.00 |
| 23" | $1,050.00 | $1,400.00 |
| 25" | $1,250.00 | $1,650.00 |
| 31" | $1,725.00 | $2,325.00 |
| 35" | $2,200.00 | $2,900.00 |

**Mold #1269, 1279,** bisque socket head, sleep eyes, open mouth with teeth, pierced ears, wig, jointed composition body

| | | |
|---|---|---|
| 10" | $935.00 | $1,250.00 |
| 14" | $1,050.00 | $1,400.00 |
| 16" | $2,700.00 | $3,600.00 |
| 25" | $2,550.00 | $3,400.00 |
| 32" | $3,300.00 | $4,400.00 |
| 36" | $3,750.00 | $5,000.00+ |

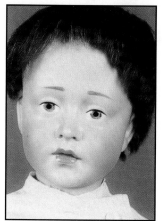

*16½" Simon & Halbig, mold #150, $12,000.00. Courtesy McMasters Doll Auctions.*

**Child, Character Face, 1910+**

**Mold #150,** intaglio eyes, closed mouth

| | | |
|---|---|---|
| 16" | $10,500.00 | $13,850.00 |
| 21" | $13,000.00 | $17,500.00+ |

\* *too few examples in database to give reliable range*

**Mold #151,** painted eyes, closed laughing mouth with molded teeth

| | | |
|---|---|---|
| 15" | $3,750.00 | $5,000.00 |
| 20" | $5,350.00 | $7,100.00 |

\* *too few examples in database to give reliable range*

**Mold #153,** molded hair, painted eyes, closed mouth

| | | |
|---|---|---|
| 15" | $19,500.00 | $26,000.00 |

\* *too few examples in database to give reliable range*

**Mold #600,** sleep eyes, open mouth

| | | |
|---|---|---|
| 16" | $450.00 | $625.00 |

**Mold #601,** glass eyes, open mouth with teeth

| | |
|---|---|
| 31" | $10,000.00 |

\* *too few examples in database to give reliable range*

**Mold #720,** solid dome shoulder head, glass eyes, closed mouth, wig, bisque lower arms, kid body

| | | |
|---|---|---|
| 16" | $1,025.00 | $2,450.00 |

**Mold #729,** laughing face, glass eyes, open/closed mouth with teeth

| | | |
|---|---|---|
| 16" | $1,900.00 | $2,550.00 |

**Mold #740,** solid dome shoulder head, glass eyes, closed mouth, cloth or kid body

| | | |
|---|---|---|
| 13" | $500.00 | $650.00 |
| 16" | $1,050.00 | $1,400.00 |
| 18" | $1,200.00 | $1,600.00 |

**Mold #749,** socket head, glass eyes, pierced ears, compo and wooden jointed body

Closed mouth

| | | |
|---|---|---|
| 21" | $2,325.00 | $3,100.00 |

Open mouth

| | | |
|---|---|---|
| 9" | $700.00 | $950.00 |
| 14" | $1,175.00 | $1,500.00 |

**Mold #905, 908,** socket or swivel head, open or closed mouth, glass eyes

Closed mouth

| | | |
|---|---|---|
| 16" | $2,200.00 | $2,950.00 |
| 20" | $2,650.00 | $3,500.00 |

Open mouth

| | | |
|---|---|---|
| 14" | $1,150.00 | $1,550.00 |
| 18" | $1,350.00 | $1,800.00 |
| 22" | $1,025.00 | $2,200.00 |

**Mold #919**, glass eyes, closed mouth
Closed mouth

| | | |
|---|---|---|
| 15" | $5,700.00 | $7,600.00 |
| 19" | $6,400.00 | $8,550.00 |

* *too few examples in database to give reliable range*

**Mold #929,** glass eyes, open/closed or closed mouth

| | | |
|---|---|---|
| 14" | $1,725.00 | $2,300.00 |
| 25" | $4,950.00 | $6,600.00 |

**Mold #939,** bisque socket head, pierced ears, glass eyes
Open mouth

| | | |
|---|---|---|
| 11" | $700.00 | $925.00 |
| 16" | $1,300.00 | $1,800.00 |
| 26" | $2,000.00 | $2,700.00 |

Closed mouth

| | | |
|---|---|---|
| 15" | $1,750.00 | $2,350.00 |
| 18" | $2,000.00 | $2,650.00 |
| 21" | $2,500.00 | $3,300.00 |
| 25" | $2,100.00 | $2,800.00 |
| 27" | $3,900.00 | $5,000.00 |

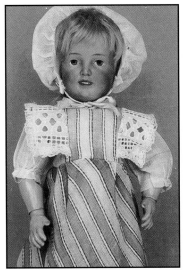

*14" bisque Simon & Halbig child, marked "151 S&H," old clothes not original, $4,500.00. Courtesy Sherryl Shirran.*

**Mold #940, 950,** socket or shoulder head, open or closed mouth, glass eyes
Kid body

| | | |
|---|---|---|
| 14" | $485.00 | $650.00 |
| 18" | $1,200.00 | $1,575.00 |
| 21" | $1,300.00 | $1,700.00 |

Jointed body

| | | |
|---|---|---|
| 13" | $585.00 | $785.00 |
| 15" | $985.00 | $1,300.00 |
| 21" | $1,700.00 | $2,300.00 |

**Mold #949,** glass eyes, open or closed mouth
Closed mouth

| | | |
|---|---|---|
| 16" | $1,750.00 | $2,350.00 |
| 21" | $2,000.00 | $2,700.00 |
| 25" | $2,400.00 | $3,200.00 |
| 31" | $3,200.00 | $4,250.00 |

Open mouth

| | | |
|---|---|---|
| 15" | $1,000.00 | $1,325.00 |
| 19" | $1,300.00 | $1,700.00 |
| 24" | $1,650.00 | $2,200.00 |

*28" Simon & Halbig mold #950, $3,000.00. Courtesy McMasters Doll Auctions.*

**Mold #969,** glass eyes, open smiling mouth

| | | |
|---|---|---|
| 15" | $2,900.00 | $3,850.00 |
| 19" | $5,700.00 | $7,600.00 |
| 23" | $7,500.00 | $10,000.00 |

* *too few examples in database to give reliable range*

*13" bisque Simon & Halbig lady, mold 1159, $800.00.Courtesy McMasters Doll Auctions.*

**Mold #1019,** laughing open mouth
14"      $4,275.00   $5,700.00
* too few examples in database to give reliable range

**Mold #1148,** open/closed smiling mouth with teeth, dimples, glass eyes
15"      $4,350.00   $5,800.00
18"      $5,500.00   $7,300.00
* too few examples in database to give reliable range

**Mold #1246,** bisque socket head, sleep eyes, open mouth with four teeth, compo and wooden jointed body
18"      $2,400.00 * at auction

**Mold #1299,** marked **"FS & Co"** or **"S&H"** for Franz Schmidt & Co.
13"      $1,200.00   $1,600.00

**Mold #1304,** glass eyes, closed mouth
14"      $4,500.00   $6,000.00
*too few examples in database to give reliable range

**Mold #1448,** bisque socket head, sleep eyes, closed mouth, pierced ears, compo, wooden ball jointed body in elaborate original provincial costume
14"      $15,000.00 * at auction

**Mold #1478,** glass eyes, closed mouth
15"      $6,750.00      $9,000.00
* too few examples in database to give reliable range

**Mold #1488,** bisque socket head, glass eyes, wig, open/closed or open mouth
20"      $3,375.00      $4,500.00
24"      $4,500.00      $6,000.00

**Adults**

**Mold #1303,** lady face, glass eyes, closed mouth, adult body
16"      $5,400.00      $7,250.00
* too few examples in database to give reliable range

**Mold #1305,** old woman, glass eyes, long nose, open/closed laughing mouth
16"      $12,700.00      $17,000.00
*too few examples in database to give reliable range

**Mold #1308,** glass eyes, closed mouth, old man with molded mustache or dirty face, may be solid dome
18"      $4,200.00      $5,600.00
*too few examples in database to give reliable range

**Mold #1388,** socket head, glass eyes, closed smiling mouth with molded teeth, wig
20"      $24,000.00 * at auction

**Mold #1469,** flapper, bisque socket head, slender face, glass eyes, closed mouth, pierced ears, wig, composition wooden ball jointed body

    15"   $2,625.00   $3,500.00   *at auction

**Mechanicals**

**Walker, Mold #1039,** bisque socket head, glass eyes, open mouth, wig, composition walking body

    13"   $,1500.00

**Walker, Mold #1078,** bisque socket head, glass eyes, open mouth, pierced ears, clockwork mechanism in torso

    13"   $1,125.00   $1,500.00
    23"   $2,200.00   $2,900.00

**Small Dolls**

Dolls under 9" tall

**Mold #749,** bisque socket head, glass sleep eyes, open mouth with teeth, pierced ears, wig, compo/wooden jointed body

    9"   $700.00   $950.00

*21" Simon & Halbig #1249, bisque socket head, heavy brows, open mouth, upper teeth, human hair wig, jointed composition body with straight wrists, $1,300.00. Courtesy Ruth Brown.*

**Mold #852,** all bisque, Oriental, yellow tinted bisque swivel head, glass eyes, closed mouth, wig, painted shoes and socks

    5½"   $825.00   $1,100.00

**Mold #886,** all bisque swivel head, glass eyes, open mouth, square cut teeth, wig, peg jointed, painted shoes and socks

    9"   $1,125.00   $1,500.00

**Mold #950,** bisque shoulder head, glass eyes, wig, closed mouth, cloth body, bisque forearms

    8"   $375.00   $500.00

**Mold #1078,** bisque socket head, glass eyes, open mouth, teeth, mohair wig, five piece body, painted shoes and socks

    8"   $400.00   $550.00

Mold #1078, pair marquis and marquise, original costume

    8½"   $650.00 each  * at auction

*17" bisque Simon & Halbig, mold #1329, composition, jointed body, $2,000.00. Courtesy Sherryl Shirran.*

Mold #1078, flapper body

    9"   $375.00   $500.00

**Mold #1079,** yellow tinted bisque socket head, glass eyes, open mouth with teeth, five-piece papier mache body

 8"  $1,900.00 * at auction

**Mold #1160, Little Women** doll, bisque shoulder head, glass eyes, closed mouth, wig, cloth body

 7"  $265.00  $350.00

## Snow Babies

*Left: 2¾" bisque Snow Baby on polar bear, marked "Germany," on base, $225.00. Right: 3" Snow Baby, back of head opens like a vase, $200.00. Courtesy McMasters Doll Auctions.*

**1901 – 30+.** All bisque dolls covered with ground porcelain slip to resemble snow, made by Bahr & Proschild, Hertwig, C.F. Kling, Kley & Hahn, and others in Germany. Mostly unjointed, some jointed at shoulders and hips. The Eskimos named Peary's daughter Marie, born in 1893, "Snow Baby" and her mother published a book in which she called her daughter "Snow Baby" and showed a picture of a little girl in white snowsuit. These little figures have painted features and various poses.

First price indicates figures in good condition, but with flaws or lessor quality; second price is for figures in excellent condition.

**Single Snow Baby**

|  |  |  |
|---|---|---|
| 1½" | $40.00 | $55.00 |
| 3" | $130.00 | $175.00 |
| On bear | | |
|  | $225.00 | $300.00 |
| On sled | | |
| 2" | $150.00 | $200.00 |
| On sled pulled by dogs | | |
| 3" | $275.00 | $375.00 |

On sled with reindeer
| 2½" | $225.00 | $300.00 |

**Seated**
Jointed hips, shoulders
| 4" | $215.00 | $290.00 |
| 5" | $275.00 | $375.00 |

With broom
| 4½" | $400.00 | $550.00 |

**Two Snow Babies,** molded together
| 1½" | $100.00 | $125.00 |
| 3" | $185.00 | $250.00 |

On sled
| 2½" | $200.00 | $275.00 |

**Three Snow Babies,** molded together
| 1½" | $185.00 | $250.00 |
| 3" | $190.00 | $350.00 |

On sled
| 2½" | $190.00 | $350.00 |

**New Snowbabies:** Today's commercial reproductions are by Dept. 56 and are larger and the coloring is more like cream. Individual craftsmen are also making and painting reproductions that look more like the old ones.

Reproduction snowbabies, set of ten in various poses
| 1 – 1½" | $25.00 |

## Sonneberg Taufling

**(Motchmann-type) 1851 – 1900+, Sonneberg, Germany.** Various companies made an infant doll with special separated body with bellows and voice mechanism. Motchmann is erroneously credited with the body style; but he did patent the voice mechanism. Some bodies stamped Motchmann refer to the voice mechanism. The Sonneberg Taufling is a wax over papier mache head with wooden body and twill cloth covered bellows, "floating" twill covered upper joints with lower joints of wood or china. They have glass eyes, closed mouth, painted or wigged hair. Other variations include papier mache or wax over composition. The body may be stamped.

*Marks:*

*21" wax over papier mache shoulder head, pupiless glass eyes, composition torso with cloth midsection, squeaker cloth upper arms and legs, wooden lower arms and legs, compo hands and feet, $400.00. Courtesy McMasters Doll Auctions.*

# Sonneberg Taufling (cont.)

**Papier Mache,** brown swivel head, flock – painted hair, black glass eyes, closed mouth, papier mache shoulderplate, muslin body, working squeak crier, original outfit

      5½"    $2,600.00 * at auction

# Steiff, Margarete

*17" felt Steiff fireman, Steiff metal buttons, jointed felt body, large oversize feet, $1,000.00. Courtesy McMasters Doll Auctions.*

*17" felt Steiff man with pipe, Steiff button in ear, jointed felt body, oversize feet and large hands, $1,300.00. Courtesy McMasters Doll Auctions.*

**1877 – 1930 on, Giengen, Wurttembur, Germany.** Known today for their plush stuffed animals, Steiff made clothes for children, dolls with mask heads in 1889, clown dolls by 1898. Most Steiff dolls of felt, velvet, or plush have a seam down the center of the face, but not all. Registered trademark was a button in the ear in 1905. Button type eyes, painted features, sewn on ears, big feet/shoes enabling them to stand alone, all in excellent condition.

*Mark:*

**Button in ear**

First price is for dolls in good condition, but with some flaws; second price is for dolls in excellent condition. For soiled, ragged or worn dolls use 25% or less of second price.

**Adults**

| | | |
|---|---|---|
| 18" | $1,875.00 | $2,500.00 |
| 22" | $2,225.00 | $3,000.00 |

**Characters**

Man with pipe

| | |
|---|---|
| 17" | $1,300.00 * at auction |

**Children**

| | | |
|---|---|---|
| 14" | $900.00 | $1,200.00 |

**Military**
Men in uniform and conductors, firemen, policemen, etc.
|       |            |            |
|-------|------------|------------|
| 14"   | $2,500.00  | $3,300.00  |
| 18"   | $3,200.00  | $4,275.00  |

**Made in U.S., Germany, glass eyes**
|       |          |          |
|-------|----------|----------|
| 12"   | $575.00  | $750.00  |

## Steiner, Hermann

**1909 – 1930+, near Coburg, Germany.** Porcelain and doll factory that first made plush animals, then made bisque, composition, and celluloid head dolls. Patented the Steiner eye with mo⁻ing pupils.

*Marks:*

Germany
S'H 13-1010 DEP.

H. 401 0½ S
made in Germany

**Baby**
   **Mold #240,** newborn, solid dome, cloth or composition body
|       |          |          |
|-------|----------|----------|
| 16"   | $450.00  | $600.00  |
| 19"   | $625.00  | $825.00  |

   **Mold #246,** solid dome, glass eyes, laughing open/closed mouth, baby teeth, cloth or composition body
|       |          |          |
|-------|----------|----------|
| 15"   | $475.00  | $625.00  |
| 17"   | $525.00  | $725.00  |

*too few examples in database to give reliable range*

**Child**
   **Mold #128,** character bisque socket head, sleep eyes, open mouth with teeth, wig, compo/wooden jointed body
|      |                        |
|------|------------------------|
| 9"   | $700.00 * at auction   |

*too few examples in database to give reliable range*

*11" Herm Steiner 245 baby with closed mouth and five-piece baby body, $450.00. Courtesy Matrix.*

   **Mold #401,** shoulder head, solid dome, painted eyes, laughing open/closed mouth with teeth and molded tongue
|       |          |          |
|-------|----------|----------|
| 15"   | $350.00  | $475.00  |

## Steiner, Jules

**1855 – 91+, Paris.** Made dolls with pressed heads, wigs, glass eyes, pierced ears on jointed composition bodies. Advertised talking, mechanical jointed dolls and bebes. Some sleep eyes were operated by a wire behind the ear, marked J. Steiner. May also carry the Bourgoin mark.

*Marks:*

FIGURE A n·12
J· STEINER Bᴛᴇ S.G.D.G
P A R I S

Sᵀᴱ A O
J. Steiner...

First price is for dolls in good condition, but with flaw; second price is for dolls in excellent condition, appropriately dressed. Add more for original clothes, rare mold numbers.

**Bebe with Taufling (Motchmann) type body**
Solid dome bisque head, shoulders, hips, lower arms, and legs, with twill body in-between, closed mouth, glass eyes, wig

| | | |
|---|---|---|
| 14" | $3,600.00 | $4,800.00 |
| 17" | $5,175.00 | $6,900.00 |

**Gigoteur, "Kicker"**
Crying bebe, key wound mechanism, solid dome head, glass eyes, open mouth with two rows tiny teeth, pierced ears, mohair wig, papier mache torso

| | | |
|---|---|---|
| 21" | $1,725.00 | $2,300.00 |

**Early unmarked Bebe**
**Round face,** ca. 1870s, pale bisque socket head, rounded face, pierced ears, bulgy paperweight eyes, open mouth with two rows teeth, pierced ears, wig, compo/wooden jointed body

| | | |
|---|---|---|
| 18" | $4,000.00 | $5,500.00 |

**Bebe with Series marks, ca. 1880s**
Bourgoin red ink, Caduceus stamp on body, pressed bisque socket head, cardboard pate, wig, pierced ears, closed mouth, glass paperweight eyes, wig, French compo/wooden jointed body with straight wrists. Series C and A more common. Marked with series *Mark:* Series and letter and number; rare numbers may be valued much higher.

| | | |
|---|---|---|
| 10½" | $7,500.00* at auction | |
| 16" | $3,750.00 | $5,000.00 |
| 18" | $4,800.00 | $6,400.00 |
| 23" | $5,625.00 | $7,500.00 |
| 29" | $8,000.00 | $9,000.00 |
| 33" | $9,000.00 | $12,000.00 |

Series G

| | |
|---|---|
| 28" | $31,900.00 * at auction |

*20" bisque Jules Steiner Series C, $4,300.00. Courtesy McMasters Doll Auctions.*

*25" bisque marked "Figure B, Steiner," paperweight eyes, open mouth, ten upper and lower teeth, jointed composition Steiner body, $7,500.00. Courtesy McMasters Doll Auctions.*

*10½" Figure A bisque child by Jules Steiner, five-piece composition body, all original, $3,000.00+. Courtesy Rosalie Whyel Museum of Doll Art, Bellevue, WA., photo by Charles Backus.*

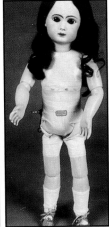

*24" bisque marked "A-15,Paris," on head, "Le Parisien," stamped in red, jointed composition body, kid covering lower torso and upper legs, key wind walking mechanism, voice box, $2,000.00. Courtesy McMasters Doll Auctions.*

## Bebe with Figure marks, ca. 1887+

Bisque socket head, pierced ears, closed mouth, glass eyes, wig, compo/wooden jointed French body. May use body marked *"Le Petit Parisien."* Marked Figure, letter — usually A or C — and number.

Closed mouth

| | | |
|---|---|---|
| 10" | $2,200.00 | $2,950.00 |
| 13" | $2,625.00 | $3,500.00 |
| 16" | $3,600.00 | $4,800.00 |
| 22" | $4,500.00 | $6,000.00 |
| 26" | $5,250.00 | $7,000.00 |
| 32" | $15,400.00 * at auction | |

Open mouth

| | | |
|---|---|---|
| 21" | $2,025.00 | $2,700.00 |

## Bebe le Parisien, ca. 1895+

Bisque socket head, cardboard pate, wig, paperweight eyes, closed or open mouth, pierced ears, wig, compo jointed body. Head marked with letter, number, and Paris; body stamped in red, *"Le Parisien."*

| | | |
|---|---|---|
| 8" | $2,000.00 | $2,750.00 |
| 10 – 12" | $2,400.00 | $3,200.00 |
| 15" | $2,700.00 | $3,600.00 |
| 21" | $3,075.00 | $4,100.00 |
| 27" | $4,000.00 | $5,250.00 |
| 30" | $5,250.00 | $7,000.00+ |

in wardrobe box, with extra outfits

| | |
|---|---|
| 8" | $3,200.00 * at auction |

# Swaine & Co.

**1910 – 1927, Huttensteinach, Thuringia, Germany**. Made porcelain doll heads. Probably S & Co. in green stamp on bisque head dolls stands for this company.

*Marks:*

## Baby

**Baby Lori,** solid dome, molded painted hair, sleep eyes, open/closed mouth, bent limb baby body

| | | |
|---|---|---|
| 18" | $1,200.00 | $1,600.00 |
| 23" | $1,870.00 | $2,500.00 |

**Mold #232,** variation of Lori, solid dome, glass eyes, open mouth

| | | |
|---|---|---|
| 12" | $750.00 | $1,000.00 |
| 21" | $1,300.00 | $1,750.00 |

**DI,** solid dome socket head, intaglio eyes, molded hair, closed mouth

| | | |
|---|---|---|
| 11" | $575.00 | $775.00 |
| 15" | $1,125.00 | $1,400.00 |

*14½" bisque Swaine & Co. child, marked "DIP," $1,600.00. Courtesy McMasters Doll Auctions.*

**DV,** solid dome bisque socket head, painted hair, sleep eyes, closed mouth

| | | |
|---|---|---|
| 12" | $975.00 | $1,300.00 |
| 15" | $1,125.00 | $1,500.00 |

## Child

**DIP, S & C,** bisque socket head, sleep eyes, closed mouth, wig

| | | |
|---|---|---|
| 15" | $1,425.00 | $1,900.00 * at auction |

# Thuiller, A.

**1875 – 93, Paris.** Made bisque head dolls with composition, kid, or wooden bodies. Some of the heads were reported from Francoise Gaultier. Bisque socket head, glass eyes, pierced ears, cork pate, wig, nicely dressed, in good condition.

*Marks:*

## Child

$A . 14 . T$

Closed mouth, more for kid body

| | | |
|---|---|---|
| 13" | $23,250.00 | $31,000.00 |
| 16" | $29,250.00 | $39,000.00 |
| 24" | $33,000.00 | $44,000.00 |

Open mouth

| | | |
|---|---|---|
| 15" | $9,200.00 | $12,200.00 |
| 18" | $11,000.00 | $14,700.00 |

* *too few in database to give reliable range*

*21" bisque head, marked "A 10 T" by Andre Thuiller, ca. 1880s, ball-jointed composition body, $50,000.00+. Private collection.*

# Unis

**1916 – 30+.** Mark used by S.F.B.J. (Societe Francaise de Fabrication de Bebes & Jouets) is Union Nationale Inter – Syndicale.

*Marks:*

E ⟨UNIS FRANCE⟩ T

71 ⟨UNIS FRANCE⟩ 149

**301**

E. ® T.

*Left: 17" bisque S.F.B.J. girl, mold 60, in regional costume, $325.00. Right: 15½" bisque Unis France girl, mold 301, $275.00. Courtesy McMasters Doll Auctions.*

## Child

**Mold #60, 301,** bisque head, jointed compo/wooden body, wig, sleep eyes, open mouth

| | | |
|---|---|---|
| 11" | $350.00 | $475.00 |
| 15" | $425.00 | $575.00 |
| 18" | $475.00 | $650.00 |
| 21" | $575.00 | $750.00 |

**Bluette, see also S.F.B.J.**

| | | |
|---|---|---|
| 10½" | $635.00 | $850.00 |

Composition head and body

| | | |
|---|---|---|
| 12" | $115.00 | $150.00 |
| 18" | $225.00 | $300.00 |

**Mold #251, toddler body**

| | | |
|---|---|---|
| 15" | $1,050.00 | $1,400.00 |
| 27" | $1,650.00 | $2,200.00 |
| 33" | $2,640.00 * at auction | |

*16" Unis France 301, $225.00. Courtesy McMasters Doll Auctions.*

## Wagner & Zetzche

**1875 – 1930+, Ilmenau, Thuringia.** Made dolls, doll parts, and doll clothes and shoes; used heads by Gebruder Heubach, Armand Marseille, and Simon & Halbig.

# Wagner & Zetzche (cont.)

*Marks:*

### CHILD
Bisque head, kid body, bisque lower arms, cloth lower legs

Closed mouth

| | | |
|---|---|---|
| 16" | $500.00 | $665.00 |
| 21" | $675.00 | $900.00 |

Open mouth

| | | |
|---|---|---|
| 14" | $265.00 | $350.00 |
| 21" | $375.00 | $500.00 |

*\* too few examples in database to give reliable range.*

# Wax

**Ca. 1700 – 1930.** Made by English, German, French, and other firms, reaching heights of popularity about 1875. Seldom marked, wax dolls were poured, some were reinforced with plaster, or wax over papier mache or composition, which was more durable and less expensive. English makers included Montanari, Pierotti, and Peck. German makers included Heinrich Stier.

First price indicates dolls in good condition, but with flaws; second price is for dolls in excellent condition, original clothes, or appropriately dressed.

### BABY
Poured wax shoulder head, painted facial features, glass eyes, closed mouth, cloth body, wig made of hair inserted into wax

| | | |
|---|---|---|
| 17" | $1,125.00 | $1500.00 |
| 25" | $1,700.00 | $2,250.00 |

Infant nurser, poured wax, slightly turned shoulder head, set glass eyes, open mouth, inserted hair wig, cloth body, wax limbs, nicely dressed

| | |
|---|---|
| 26" | $1,320.00 * at auction |

### CHILD
Poured wax shoulder head, inserted hair, glass eyes, wax limbs, cloth body

| | | |
|---|---|---|
| 13" | $825.00 | $1,100.00 |
| 24" | $1950.00 | $2,600.00 |

Reinforced wax with composition, shoulder head, open crown pate, glass eyes, wig, cloth body

| | | |
|---|---|---|
| 12" | $185.00 | $250.00 |
| 15" | $250.00 | $350.00 |
| 20" | $400.00 | $525.00 |

### LADY

| | | |
|---|---|---|
| 8" | $575.00 | $770.00 |
| 15" | $825.00 | $1,100.00 |
| 15" | $1,250.00 | $1,650.00 |

Bride, rose wax shoulder head, blue glass eyes, closed mouth, wig, kid jointed fashion body

| | |
|---|---|
| 15" | $1,650.00 * at auction |

*23" poured wax baby, $225.00. Courtesy McMasters Doll Auctions.*

*26" Lucy Peck Wax Baby, $2,250.00 Courtesy McMasters Doll Auctions.*

*21" poured wax baby, $1,300.00. Courtesy McMasters Doll Auctions.*

*19" wax over composition girl, $120.00 holding 8½" poured wax votive doll, $125.00. Courtesy McMasters Doll Auctions.*

## WAX OVER COMPOSITION OR PAPIER MACHE

**Child,** wax shoulder head, wig, glass eyes, open or closed mouth, cloth body

| | | |
|---|---|---|
| 11" | $150.00 | $200.00 |
| 17" | $225.00 | $300.00 |
| 23" | $400.00 | $550.00 |

**Molded hair**, wax over composition shoulder head, glass eyes, cloth body, wooden limbs, molded shoes

| | | |
|---|---|---|
| 15" | $225.00 | $300.00 |
| 23" | $350.00 | $475.00 |

Alice in Wonderland style with molded headband

| | | |
|---|---|---|
| 16" | $400.00 | $525.00 |
| 19" | $475.00 | $625.00 |

**Slit-head Wax,** English, ca. 1830 – 1860s, wax over composition shoulder head, glass eyes, some close with wire

| | | |
|---|---|---|
| 16" | $625.00 | $850.00 |
| 18" | $1,100.00 | $1,400.00 |
| 25" | $1,900.00 | $2,500.00 |

\* too few examples in database to give reliable range

**Mechanical Baby,** solid dome over papier mache head, glass eyes, painted hair, open mouth, papier mache torso with bellows mechanism

| | |
|---|---|
| 18" | $2,000.00 \* at auction |

# Wax (cont.)

**Two-faced doll,** ca. 1880 – 90s, one laughing, one crying, body stamped "Bartenstein"

| | | |
|---|---|---|
| 15" | $675.00 | $900.00 |

**BONNETHEAD**

1860 – 1880, with cap

**Child** with cap

| | | |
|---|---|---|
| 16" | $250.00 | $325.00 |

**Lady** with poke bonnet

| | |
|---|---|
| 25" | $3,000.00 |

\* *too few in database to give reliable range*

**Man,** turned shoulder head, molded top hat, set eyes, cloth body, wooden arms

17"    $1,000.00 \* at auction

## Wislizenus

**Wislizenus, Adolf, 1850 – 1930+, Walterhausen, Thuringia, Germany.** Doll and toy factory, they specialized in ball-jointed bodies and used Bahr & Proschild, Simon and Halbig, and Ernst Heubach bisque heads for dolls they made.

*Marks:*

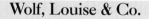

Heubach-Köppelsdorf
A.W.
W
Germany
9

**Child**

Bisque socket head, sleep eyes, open mouth, wig, compo/wooden jointed body

**AW Special, 101 My Sweetheart**

| | | |
|---|---|---|
| 22 – 23" | $375.00 | $500.00 |

## Wolf, Louise & Co.

**1870 – 1930+, Sonneberg, Germany, Boston, and New York City.** They made and distributed dolls, also distributed dolls made for them by other companies such as Hertel & Schwab and Armand Marseille. They made composition as well as bisque dolls and specialized in baby and Red Cross Nurses before World War I. May be marked "L.W. & C."

| | | |
|---|---|---|
| 12" | $360.00 | $475.00 |
| 16" | $450.00 | $600.00 |
| 20" | $545.00 | $725.00 |
| 22" | $700.00 | $950.00 |

*11" Louise Wolf & Co. German bisque A.M. shoulder head doll with incised markings, $475.00+. Courtesy Matrix.*

# Wooden

**1700s – on, England, Germany, Switzerland, Russia, U.S.A. and other countries.**

## English
### William & Mary Period, 1690s – 1700
Carved wooden head, tiny multi-stroke eyebrow and eyelashes, colored cheeks, human hair or flax wig, wooden body, fork-like carved wooden hands, jointed wooden legs, cloth upper arms, medium to fair condition

| | |
|---|---|
| 16" | $53,000.00+ |

*too few in database to give reliable range*

### Queen Anne Period, early 1700s
Dotted eyebrows, eyelashes, painted or glass eyes, no pupils, carved oval-shaped head, flat wooden back and hips, nicely dressed, good condition

*14" glass-eye wooden Queen Anne, $9,000.00. Courtesy McMasters Doll Auctions.*

| | | |
|---|---|---|
| 14" | $7,500.00 | $10,000.00 |
| 18" | $11,000.00 | $14,900.00 |
| 24" | $18,000.00 | $24,000.00 |

*too few in database to give reliable range*

### Georgian Period, 1750s – 1800
Round wooden head, gesso coated, inset glass eyes, dotted eyelashes and eyebrows, human hair or flax wig, jointed wooden body pointed torso, medium to fair condition

| | | |
|---|---|---|
| 13" | $2,300.00 | $3,000.00 |
| 15" | $3,100.00 | $4,100.00 |
| 18" | $3,550.00 | $4,700.00 |
| 24" | $4,500.00 | $6,000.00 |

### 1800 – 1840
Gesso coated wooden head, painted eyes, human hair or flax wig, original clothing comes down below wooden legs

| | | |
|---|---|---|
| 12 – 13" | $900.00 | $1,200.00 |
| 15" | $1,400.00 | $1,875.00 |
| 20" | $2,100.00 | $2,800.00 |

## German
### 1810 – 1850s
Delicately carved painted hairstyle; spit curls, some with hair decorations, all wooden head and body, pegged or ball-jointed limbs

| | | |
|---|---|---|
| 7" | $475.00 | $650.00 |
| 12 – 13" | $1,050.00 | $1,400.00 |
| 16 – 17" | $1,275.00 | $1,700.00 |

### 1850s – 1900
All wood with painted plain hairstyle; some may have spitcurls

| | | |
|---|---|---|
| 5" | $95.00 | $125.00 |
| 8" | $150.00 | $200.00 |
| 14" | $300.00 | $400.00 |

*Unusual 20" German wooden, Empire period, ca. 1800, not marked, excellent condition, $15,000.00+. Courtesy Rosalie Whyel Museum of Doll Art, Bellevue, WA. Photo by Charles Backus.*

*13" Joel Ellis wooden child, $775.00. Courtesy McMasters Doll Auctions.*

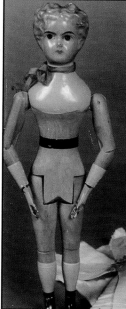

*12" Springfield wooden child, $1,200.00. Courtesy McMasters Doll Auctions.*

Wooden shoulder head, fancy carved hairstyle, wood limbs, cloth body

| | | |
|---|---|---|
| 12" | $375.00 | $500.00 |
| 16" | $450.00 | $600.00 |
| 23" | $650.00 | $875.00 |

**1900+**

Turned wooden head, carved nose, painted hair, lower legs with black shoes, peg jointed

| | | |
|---|---|---|
| 11" | $60.00 | $80.00 |

Child, all wooden, fully jointed body, glass eyes, open mouth

| | | |
|---|---|---|
| 15" | $335.00 | $450.00 |
| 18" | $450.00 | $625.00 |
| 23" | $600.00 | $825.00 |

**Matryoskia, Russian Nesting, 1900+**

Set of wooden canisters that separate in the middle, brightly painted with a glossy finish, represent adults, children, storybook or fairytale characters and animals. These come in sets usually of five or more related characters, the larger doll opening to reveal a smaller doll nesting inside, and so on.

Set pre-1930s

| | | |
|---|---|---|
| 4" | $70.00 | $95.00 |
| 7" | $110.00 | $145.00 |
| 9" | $170.00 | $225.00 |

Set new
| | |
|---|---|
| 5" | $15.00 |
| 7" | $25.00 |

Political set, Gorbachev, Yeltsin
| | |
|---|---|
| 5" | $30.00 |
| 7" | $55.00 |

## SWISS, 1900+

Carved wooden dolls with dowel jointed bodies, joined at elbow, hips, knees, some with elaborate hair

| | | |
|---|---|---|
| 8" | $315.00 | $425.00 |
| 12" | $475.00 | $635.00 |

## ELLIS, JOEL

**Cooperative Manufacturing Co., 1873 – 74. Springfield, VT.** Manufactured wooden dolls patented by Joel Ellis. The head was cut into a cube, steamed until it softened, then compressed in hydraulic press to form features. Metal hands and feet painted black or blue, painted molded hair sometimes blonde. Similar type Springville Wooden dolls were made by Joint Doll Co. and D. M. Smith & Co. have cut out hip joints.

| | | |
|---|---|---|
| 12" | $700.00 | $950.00 |
| 15" | $975.00 | $1,300.00 |

## FORTUNE TELLERS

Wooden half or full doll with folded papers with fortunes printed on them making up the skirt

| | | |
|---|---|---|
| 18" | $2,600.00 | $3,500.00 |

*too few in database to give reliable range*

**Hitty: see Artist Dolls.**

**Schoenhut: see that section.**

# Modern Dolls

◀

*18" Madame Alexander early cloth baby, all original, tagged dress, painted features and cloth body, $500.00+. Courtesy Matrix.*

▲ *18", ca. 1949 Howdy Dowdy with composition head, hands, and feet, cloth body, ventriloquist mouth formed, but not movable, all original, $250.00. Courtesy Sherryl Shirran.*

◀

*19" vinyl Ideal Miss Revlon, boxed, $250.00. Courtesy McMasters Doll Auctions.*

# Madame Alexander

In 1912, Beatrice and Rose Alexander, known for doll costumes, began the Alexander Doll Co. They began using the "Madame Alexander" trademark in 1928. Beatrice A. Behrman became a legend in the doll world with her long reign as head of the Alexander Doll Company. Alexander made cloth, composition, wooden dolls, and eventually hard plastic and vinyl dolls.

First price is for dolls in good condition with flaws, may have soiled or worn clothing; second price is for dolls in mint condition with original clothes, tag, labels, etc.

*16" cloth David Copperfield, tagged clothes, molded mask face of flocked fabric, ca. 1923 – 30, $750.00. Courtesy McMasters Doll Auctions.*

## ALEXANDER-KINS 1953+

7½" – 8", hard plastic, jointed body, synthetic wig, sleep eyes, closed mouth

**1953 – 1954,** straight-leg non-walker

| | | |
|---|---|---|
| Party dress | $95.00 | $475.00 |
| Ballgown | $135.00 | $850.00 |
| Nude | $50.00 | $225.00 |

**1955,** straight-leg walker

| | | |
|---|---|---|
| Party dress | $65.00 | $450.00 |
| Ballgown | $125.00 | $925.00 |
| Basic sleeveless dress | | |
| | $40.00 | $225.00 |
| Nude | $30.00 | $125.00 |

**1956 – 1965,** bent-knee walker

| | | |
|---|---|---|
| Party dress | $60.00 | $365.00 |
| Ballgown | $125.00 | $650.00 |
| Nude: | $45.00 | $225.00 |
| Basic sleeveless dress | | |
| | $60.00 | $375.00 |
| Internationals | $45.00 | $225.00 |

**1965 – 1972,** bent-knee non-walker

| | | |
|---|---|---|
| Party dress | $45.00 | $250.00 |
| Internationals | $20.00 | $50.00 |
| Nude | $20.00 | $80.00 |

**1973 – 1976** (Rosies), straight-leg non-walker

Rosy cheeks, marked "ALEX"

| | | |
|---|---|---|
| | $15.00 | $55.00 |
| Ballerina or Bride, bent-knee walker | | |
| | $35.00 | $140.00+ |
| Bent-knee only | $30.00 | $120.00 |
| Straight-leg | $15.00 | $50.00 |
| Internationals | $10.00 | $45.00 |
| Storybook | $15.00 | $60.00 |

**1977 – 1981,** straight-leg non-walker, marked "Alexander"

| | | |
|---|---|---|
| Ballerina or Bride | $10.00 | $45.00 |

# Madame Alexander (cont.)

| | | |
|---|---|---|
| Internationals | $10.00 | $45.00 |
| Storybook | $10.00 | $50.00 |

**1982 – 1987**, straight-leg non-walker, indentation above upper lip makes doll look like it has a mustache

| | | |
|---|---|---|
| Ballerina or Bride | $12.00 | $45.00 |
| International | $10.00 | $35.00 |
| Storybook | $12.00 | $40.00 |

**1988 – 1989**, straight-leg, non-walker, new face, marked "Alexander"

| | | |
|---|---|---|
| Ballerina or Bride | $12.00 | $35.00 |
| International | $13.00 | $40.00 |
| Storybook | $15.00 | $45.00 |

## BABIES

**Baby Brother or Sister,** 1977 – 1982

| | | | |
|---|---|---|---|
| | 14" | $20.00 | $85.00 |
| | 20" | $20.00 | $90.00 |

**Baby Ellen,** 1965 – 1972, all vinyl

| | | | |
|---|---|---|---|
| | 14" | $30.00 | $130.00 |

**Baby Lynn,** 1973 – 1976 vinyl head, cloth body, sleep eyes, synthetic hair

**Baby McGuffey**, composition

| | | | |
|---|---|---|---|
| | 2" | $50.00 | $200.00 |

**Baby Precious,** 1975

| | | | |
|---|---|---|---|
| | 4" | $20.00 | $85.00 |

**Bonnie,** 1954 – 1955, vinyl

| | | | |
|---|---|---|---|
| | 9" | $25.00 | $95.00 |

**Happy,** 1970, vinyl

| | | | |
|---|---|---|---|
| | 20" | $60.00 | $250.00 |

**Hello Baby,** 1962

| | | | |
|---|---|---|---|
| | 22" | $40.00 | $175.00 |

**Honeybun,** 1951, vinyl

| | | | |
|---|---|---|---|
| | 19" | $40.00 | $175.00 |

**Huggums,** 1963 – 1979

| | | | |
|---|---|---|---|
| | 25" | $20.00 | $95.00 |

**Huggums, Lively**, 1963

| | | | |
|---|---|---|---|
| | 25" | $35.00 | $150.00 |

**Kathy,** vinyl

| | | | |
|---|---|---|---|
| | 18" | $30.00 | $130.00 |
| | 26" | $40.00 | $155.00 |

**Little Bitsey,** 1967 – 68, all vinyl

| | | | |
|---|---|---|---|
| | 9" | $25.00 | $125.00 |

**Little Genius**, composition

| | | | |
|---|---|---|---|
| | 18" | $40.00 | $150.00 |

Little Genius, vinyl, may have flirty eyes

| | | | |
|---|---|---|---|
| | 8" | $50.00 | $250.00 |
| | 21" | $40.00 | $155.00 |

**Littlest Kitten**, vinyl

| | | | |
|---|---|---|---|
| | 8" | $30.00 | $155.00 |

*23" composition McGuffey*
*Ana, $2,100.00. Courtesy*
*McMasters Doll Auctions.*

*17" composition Scarlett*
*O'Hara, $1,600.00. Courtesy*
*McMasters Doll Auctions.*

**Mary Cassatt,** 1969 – 1970
| | | |
|---|---|---|
| 14" | $40.00 | $170.00 |
| 20" | $60.00 | $245.00 |

**Mary Mine**
| | | |
|---|---|---|
| 14" | $20.00 | $80.00 |

**Pinky,** composition
| | | |
|---|---|---|
| 23" | $60.00 | $230.00 |

**Princess Alexandria,** composition
| | | |
|---|---|---|
| 24" | $55.00 | $225.00 |

**Pussy Cat,** vinyl
| | | |
|---|---|---|
| 14" | $20.00 | $90.00 |

Pussy Cat, black
| | | |
|---|---|---|
| 14" | $35.00 | $110.00 |

**Rusty,** vinyl
| | | |
|---|---|---|
| 20" | $80.00 | $330.00 |

**Slumbermate,** composition
| | | |
|---|---|---|
| 21" | $125.00 | $500.00 |

**Sweet Tears**
| | | |
|---|---|---|
| 9" | $15.00 | $70.00 |

With layette
| | | |
|---|---|---|
| | $45.00 | $165.00 |

Sweet Tears, black, 1973 – 1975
| | | |
|---|---|---|
| 20" | $30.00 | $130.00 |

**Victoria**
| | | |
|---|---|---|
| 20" | $20.00 | $85.00 |

# Madame Alexander (cont.)

## CISETTE, 1957 – 63

10" – 11," hard plastic head, synthetic wig, pierced ears, closed mouth, jointed elbows and knees, high-heel feet, mold later used for other dolls.
*Marks:* None on body, clothes tagged "Cissette."

| | | |
|---|---|---|
| Street dress | $65.00 | $270.00 |
| Ballgown | $100.00 | $380.00 |
| Ballerina | $100.00 | $360.00+ |
| Gibson Girl | $150.00 | $700.00 |
| Jacqueline | $145.00 | $650.00+ |
| Margot | $125.00 | $430.00+ |
| Portrette | $125.00 | $450.00 |
| Queen | $90.00 | $360.00 |
| Wigged in case | $215.00 | $825.00+ |

## CISSY, 1955 – 59

20 – 21," hard plastic, vinyl arms, jointed elbows and knees, high heel feet, clothes are tagged "Cissy"

| | | | |
|---|---|---|---|
| Ballgown | | $215.00 | $825.00 |
| Bride | | $125.00 | $500.00 |
| Flora McFlimsey, vinyl head, inset eyes | | | |
| | 15" | $150.00 | $600.00 |
| Queen | | $225.00 | $875.00 |
| Pant suit | | $80.00 | $250.00 |
| Portrait "Godey" | | | |
| | 21" | $250.00 | $1,050.00+ |
| Scarlett | | $325.00 | $1,350.00 |
| Street dress | | $70.00 | $350.00 |

## CLOTH, CA. 1933 – 50+

All cloth head and body, mohair wig, flat or molded mask face, painted, side-glancing eyes

| | | | |
|---|---|---|---|
| **Alice in Wonderland** | | | |
| Flat face | | $200.00 | $800.00 |
| Mask face | 16" | $200.00 | $650.00 |
| **Animals** | | $70.00 | $275.00 |
| Dogs | | $75.00 | $290.00 |
| **Baby** | | | |
| | 13" | $75.00 | $300.00 |
| | 17" | $125.00 | $475.00 |
| **Bunny Belle** | | | |
| | 13" | $175.00 | $700.00 |
| **Dionne Quintuplets** | | | |
| | 15" | $250.00 | $850.00 |
| | 24" | $450.00 | $1,200.00 |
| **Clarabel, the Clown** | | | |
| | 19" | $100.00 | $350.00 |
| **David Copperfield, or other boys** | | | |
| | | $200.00 | $750.00 |
| **Funny** | | | |
| | | $10.00 | $65.00 |

**Little Shaver,** 1942, yarn hair
| | | |
|---|---|---|
| 10" | $90.00 | $350.00 |
| 20" | $140.00 | $550.00 |

**Little Women**
| | | |
|---|---|---|
| 16" | $125.00 | $650.00 |

**Kamkins-type,** hard felt mask face
| | | |
|---|---|---|
| 20" | $250.00 | $650.00 |

**Muffin**
| | | |
|---|---|---|
| 14" | $25.00 | $95.00 |

**So Lite Baby or Toddler**
| | | |
|---|---|---|
| 20" | $100.00 | $425.00 |

**Suzie Q**
| | | |
|---|---|---|
| | $175.00 | $650.00 |

**Teeny Twinkle,** disc floating eyes
| | | |
|---|---|---|
| | $100.00 | $450.00 |

**Tiny Tim**
| | | |
|---|---|---|
| | $230.00 | $725.00 |

# COMPOSITION, CA. 1930 – 50

**Alice in Wonderland**
| | | |
|---|---|---|
| 9" | $85.00 | $325.00 |
| 14" | $100.00 | $435.00 |
| 21" | $250.00 | $900.00 |

**Babs Skater, 1948**
| | | |
|---|---|---|
| 18" | $165.00 | $675.00 |

**Baby Jane**
| | | |
|---|---|---|
| 16" | $300.00 | $300.00 |

**Bride and Bridesmaids**
| | | |
|---|---|---|
| 7" | $60.00 | $265.00 |
| 9" | $75.00 | $300.00 |
| 15" | $80.00 | $335.00 |
| 21" | $150.00 | $535.00 |

**Dionne Quintuplets,** ca. 1935 – 1945

All composition, swivel head, jointed toddler or baby body, painted molded hair or wigged, sleep or painted eyes. Outfit colors: Annette, yellow; Cecile, green; Emelie, lavender; Marie, blue; Yvonne, pink.
| | | |
|---|---|---|
| 8" | $50.00 | $185.00 |
| 11" | $100.00 | $300.00 |

Set of five
| | | |
|---|---|---|
| 8" | $300.00 | $1,200.00 |
| 11" | $500.00 | $2,000.00 |

Dr. Defoe
| | | |
|---|---|---|
| 14" | $500.00 | $1,400.00 |

Nurse
| | | |
|---|---|---|
| 13" | $250.00 | $800.00 |
| Pins | $90.00 | $100.00 |

**Fairy Princess,** 1939
| | | |
|---|---|---|
| 15" | $150.00 | $675.00 |

*8" hard plastic Alexander-Kins Prince Charles, in box, $525.00. Courtesy McMasters Doll Auctions.*

*18" composition Sonja Henie, all original, button reads "Junior Olympic Club//Sonja Henie." $975.00. Courtesy Sherryl Shirran.*

| | | |
|---|---|---|
| 21" | $275.00 | $985.00+ |

**Flora McFlimsey,** freckles, marked "Princess Elizabeth"

| | | |
|---|---|---|
| 15" | $135.00 | $550.00 |
| 21" | $250.00 | $985.00 |

**Flower Girl,** 1939 – 47, marked "Princess Elizabeth"

| | | |
|---|---|---|
| 16" | $135.00 | $535.00 |
| 20" | $160.00 | $635.00 |
| 24" | $195.00 | $775.00 |

**International/Storybook**

| | | |
|---|---|---|
| 7" | $75.00 | $285.00 |
| 9" | $80.00 | $325.00 |

**Jane Withers**

| | | |
|---|---|---|
| 13" | $350.00 | $1,050.00 |
| 18" | $450.00 | $1,350.00 |

**Kate Greenaway,** yellow wig, marked "Princess Elizabeth"

| | | |
|---|---|---|
| 14" | $145.00 | $675.00 |
| 18" | $200.00 | $800.00 |

**Little Betty,** 1939 – 43, painted, side-glancing eyes

| | | |
|---|---|---|
| 9" | $75.00 | $295.00 |

**Little Colonel**

| | | |
|---|---|---|
| 9"(rare size) | $150.00 | $625.00 |
| 13" | $155.00 | $600.00 |
| 23" | $225.00 | $900.00 |

**Madelaine DuBain,** 1937 – 1944

| | | |
|---|---|---|
| 14" | $150.00 | $475.00 |
| 17" | $200.00 | $575.00 |

**Margaret O'Brien,** 1946 – 1948

| | | |
|---|---|---|
| 15" | $185.00 | $735.00 |
| 18" | $200.00 | $825.00 |
| 21" | $250.00 | $1,000.00 |

**Marionettes by Tony Sarg**

| | | |
|---|---|---|
| 12" | $95.00 | $325.00 |

Disney characters

| | |
|---|---|
| $100.00 | $375.00 |

Others

| | |
|---|---|
| $95.00 | $275.00 |

**McGuffey Ana,** 1935 – 1937, marked "Princess Elizabeth"

| | | |
|---|---|---|
| 13" | $165.00 | $675.00 |
| 20" | $225.00 | $850.00 |

**Military,** ca. 1943 – 44

W.A.A.C. (Army)

| | | |
|---|---|---|
| 14" | $250.00 | $750.00+ |

W.A.A.F. (Air Force)

| | | |
|---|---|---|
| 14" | $250.00 | $750.00+ |

W.A.V.E. (Navy)

| | | |
|---|---|---|
| 14" | $250.00 | $750.00+ |

**Portrait dolls,** 1939 – 41, 1946

| | | |
|---|---|---|
| 21" | $500.00 | $2,000.00+ |

**Princess Elizabeth,** ca. 1937 – 1941
Closed mouth
| | | |
|---|---|---|
| 13" | $175.00 | $575.00 |

Open mouth
| | | |
|---|---|---|
| 18" | $250.00 | $700.00 |
| 24" | $300.00 | $850.00 |

**Scarlett,** ca. 1937 – 1938
Little Betty
| | | |
|---|---|---|
| 9" | $165.00 | $550.00 |
| 14" | $200.00 | $775.00 |
| 18" | $350.00 | $1,250.00 |
| 21" | $450.00 | $1,650.00 |

**Snow White,** 1939 – 1942, marked "Princess Elizabeth"
| | | |
|---|---|---|
| 13" | $125.00 | $475.00 |
| 18" | $165.00 | $625.00 |

**Sonja Henie,** 1939 – 1942
| | | |
|---|---|---|
| 17" | $350.00 | $950.00 |
| 20" | $275.00 | $1,100.00 |

With jointed waist
| | | |
|---|---|---|
| 14" | $200.00 | $760.00 |

**Tiny Betty,** 1934 – 1943, painted side-glancing eyes
| | | |
|---|---|---|
| 7" | $75.00 | $325.00 |

**Wendy Ann,** 1935 – 1948
| | | |
|---|---|---|
| 11" | $120.00 | $475.00 |
| 15" | $150.00 | $600.00 |
| 18" | $200.00 | $785.00 |

## HARD PLASTIC, VINYL, 1948+

Jointed body, synthetic wig, sleep eyes, closed mouth. Later body may be vinyl.

**Alice in Wonderland,** 1949 – 1952, Margaret and/or Maggie
| | | |
|---|---|---|
| 14" | $200.00 | $615.00 |
| 17" | $250.00 | $675.00 |
| 23" | $325.00 | $860.00 |

**Annabelle,** 1951 – 1952, Maggie
| | | |
|---|---|---|
| 15" | $175.00 | $575.00 |
| 18" | $200.00 | $675.00 |
| 23" | $275.00 | $825.00 |

**Anne Bellows,** 1987
| | | |
|---|---|---|
| 14" | $20.00 | $75.00 |

**Babs,** 1949, Maggie
| | | |
|---|---|---|
| 20" | $250.00 | $725.00 |

**Babs Skater,** 1948 – 1950, Margaret
| | | |
|---|---|---|
| 18" | $200.00 | $725.00 |
| 21" | $275.00 | $775.00 |

**Ballerina**
| | | |
|---|---|---|
| 14" | $175.00 | $400.00 |

**Brenda Starr,** 12," 1964
| | | |
|---|---|---|
| Street dress | $50.00 | $225.00 |

| | | |
|---|---|---|
| Ballgown | $75.00 | $375.00 |
| Bride | $75.00 | $350.00 |

**Binnie Walker,** 1954 – 55, Cissy

| | | |
|---|---|---|
| 15" | $40.00 | $175.00 |
| 25" | $165.00 | $500.00 |

**Bonnie Blue,** 1989

| | | |
|---|---|---|
| 14" | $20.00 | $85.00 |

**Cinderella,** 1950, Margaret, 14"

| | | |
|---|---|---|
| Ballgown | $200.00 | $800.00 |
| Poor Cinderella | $185.00 | $650.00 |

**Cinderella,** 1966, 12", Lissy

| | | |
|---|---|---|
| Poor outfit | $165.00 | $650.00 |

**Cinderella,** 1970 – 86, 14", vinyl body
Ballgown, pink, blue

| | | |
|---|---|---|
| | $20.00 | $75.00 |

**Cynthia,** black doll

| | | |
|---|---|---|
| 15" | $300.00 | $815.00 |
| 18" | $400.00 | $965.00 |
| 23" | $500.00 | $1,225.00 |

**Edith, The Lonely Doll,** 1958 – 1969, vinyl body

| | | |
|---|---|---|
| 16" | $60.00 | $245.00 |
| 22" | $80.00 | $325.00 |
| 8" | $110.00 | $525.00 |

**Elise,** 1957 – 1964
16½", hard plastic, vinyl arms, jointed ankles and knees

| | | |
|---|---|---|
| Ballerina | $100.00 | $350.00 |
| Ballgown | $200.00 | $675.00+ |
| Bride | | |
| 16" | $165.00 | $365.00 |
| Street dress | $90.00 | $335.00 |

1963
18", hard plastic, vinyl arms, jointed ankles and knees

| | | |
|---|---|---|
| Riding habit | $90.00 | $300.00 |

1961 – 62, 1966+
17", hard plastic, vinyl arms, jointed ankles and knees

| | | |
|---|---|---|
| Street dress | $50.00 | $200.00 |
| Trousseau/Trunk | $175.00 | $750.00 |
| Formal | $40.00 | $175.00 |
| Bride, 1966 – 77 | $40.00 | $175.00 |
| Ballerina, 1966 – 91 | $20.00 | $85.00 |

In Discontinued Costume, 1966 – 1989

| | | |
|---|---|---|
| | $40.00 | $150.00 |

**Fairy Queen,** 1948 – 1950, Margaret

| | | |
|---|---|---|
| 14½" | $160.00 | $715.00 |

1949 – 1950, Margaret

| | | |
|---|---|---|
| 18" | $225.00 | $875.00 |

**First Ladies,** 1976 – 1990

| | | |
|---|---|---|
| Set 1, 1976 – 78 | $100.00 ea. | $750.00 set |

| | | | |
|---|---|---|---|
| Set 2, 1979 – 81 | $90.00 ea. | $500.00 set | |
| Set 3, 1982 – 84 | $90.00 ea. | $550.00 set | |
| Set 4, 1985 – 87 | $80.00 ea. | $500.00 set | |
| Set 5, 1988 | $70.00 ea. | $425.00 set | |
| Set 6, 1989 – 1990 | $100.00 ea. | $500.00 set | |

**Godey Bride,** Margaret
| | | | |
|---|---|---|---|
| 1950 | 14" | $225.00 | $900.00 |
| 1950 – 151 | 18" | $240.00 | $950.00 |

**Godey Groom,** Margaret
| | | | |
|---|---|---|---|
| 1950 | 14" | $250.00 | $950.00 |
| 1950 – 51 | 18" | $375.00 | $1,500.00 |

**Godey Lady,** Margaret
| | | | |
|---|---|---|---|
| 1950 | 14" | $250.00 | $950.00 |
| 1950 – 51 | 18" | $375.00 | $1,500.00 |

**Grandma Jane,** 1970 – 72, #1420, Mary Ann, vinyl body
| | | |
|---|---|---|
| 14" | $80.00 | $225.00 |

**Groom,** 1949 – 1951, Margaret
| | | |
|---|---|---|
| 14" – 18" | $200.00 | $800.00 |

**Groom,** 1953, Wendy Ann
| | | |
|---|---|---|
| 7½" – 8" | $100.00 | $425.00+ |

**Jacqueline,** 1961 – 62, 21" vinyl arms
| | | |
|---|---|---|
| Ballgown | $350.00 | $800.00+ |
| Riding habit | $225.00 | $650.00 |
| Suit, pillbox hat | $250.00 | $650.00 |

**Joanie,** 1960 – 61, 36" vinyl body, add more for flirty eyes
| | | |
|---|---|---|
| | $185.00 | $450.00 |

**Kathy,** 1949 – 1951, Maggie
| | | |
|---|---|---|
| Braids | 15 – 18" | $150.00 | $200.00 |
| | | $575.00 | $775.00 |

**Leslie,** black doll, 1965 – 71, vinyl
| | | |
|---|---|---|
| Ballgown | $350.00 | $800. 00 |
| Riding habit | $225.00 | $650.00 |
| Street dress | $165.00 | $375.00 |

**Lissy,** 1956 – 1958, 12", jointed knees and elbows
| | | |
|---|---|---|
| Ballerina | $90.00 | $350.00 |
| Bride | $75.00 | $300.00 |
| Bridesmaid | $100.00 | $400.00 |
| Formal | $125.00 | $500.00 |
| Street dress | $65.00 | $285.00 |

One piece arms/legs in wardrobe box, 1959 – 1966
| | |
|---|---|
| | $1,000.00 |

**Little Shaver,** 1963 – 1965, painted eyes, vinyl body
| | | |
|---|---|---|
| 12" | $75.00 | $300.00 |

**Little Women,** Meg, Jo, Amy, Beth
1955, plus Marme, Wendy Ann, straight-leg, straight-leg walker
| | | |
|---|---|---|
| 8" | $75.00 | $285.00 |
| Set | $300.00 | $1,500.00 |

1956 – 59, Wendy Ann, bent knee
    8"        $35.00      $155.00
    Set of five        $700.00
1974 – 92, straight-leg
    8"        $15.00      $60.00
    Set        $100.00     $325.00
1959 – 68, Lissy
    12", one piece leg    $55.00     $265.00
    Set        $1,400.00
1957 – 58
    12", jointed limbs    $75.00     $300.00
    Set        $1,600.00
1947 – 1956, plus Marme, Margaret & Maggie
    14 – 15"    $125.00    $450.00
    Set of five     $1,825.00
Bent knee, Margaret & Maggie
    14 – 15"    $1,125.00   $500.00
    Set of five     $2,200.00
**Madeline,** 1950 – 53, jointed elbows, knees
    18"      $300.00    $900.00
**Maggie**
1948 – 1956
    15"      $175.00    $565.00
1949 – 1953
    17"      $225.00    $665.00
1948 – 1952
    23"      $300.00    $785.00
**Maggie Mixup,** 1960 – 1961, freckles
    8"        $150.00    $65.00+
    16½"    $145.00    $415.00
    8" Angel   $175.00    $685.00
**Margaret O'Brien,** 1949 – 1951
    14½"    $400.00    $875.00
    18"      $450.00   $1,000.00
    21"      $550.00   $1,150.00
**Marybel, "The Doll That Gets Well,"** 1959 – 1965, rigid vinyl
    16"      $40.00     $165.00
    In case    $175.00    $350.00+
**Mary Ellen,** 31", rigid vinyl
1954, walker    $200.00    $500.00+
1955, non-walker, jointed elbows
              $125.00    $450.00+
**Mary Martin,** 1948 – 1952, ball gown, sailor outfit
    14"      $425.00    $825.00
    17"      $450.00   $1,000.00
**Melinda,** 1962 – 1970
10" blue gown   $85.00     $350.00
14" cotton dress  $55.00     $300.00
16" party dress   $140.00    $550.00

**McGuffey Ana,** 1948 – 1950, Margaret
   21"        $325.00     $875.00
**Nancy Drew,** 1967, vinyl body
   12"        $25.00      $90.00
**Peter Pan,** 1953 – 1954, Margaret
   15"        $325.00     $725.00
Peter Pan, 1969, 14", Michael, Wendy, Tinker Bell
   Set of four    $1,000.00
**Polly,** 1965
   Ballgown    $80.00     $325.00
**Polly Pigtails,** 1949 – 1951, Maggie
   14½ "    $175.00     $525.00
   17"        $200.00     $650.00
**Prince Charming,** 1948 – 1950, Margaret
   14"        $275.00     $725.00
   18"        $300.00     $835.00
**Queen,** 1953 – 1954
   18"        $325.00     $725.00
**Renoir Girl,** 1967 – 68, vinyl body
Portrait Children Series
             $50.00     $200.00
**Scarlett,** 1950s
Bent-knee walker
   8"         $250.00     $900.00
   14 – 16"  $450.00   $1,300.00
   20"        $500.00   $1,500.00
**Shari Lewis,** 1958 – 1959
   14"        $165.00     $500.00
   21"        $250.00     $825.00
**Sleeping Beauty**
   16½"     $150.00     $625.00
   21"        $425.00     $975.00
**Smarty** 1962 – 63, vinyl body
   12"        $70.00     $275.00
**Sound of Music,** 1965 – 70, large; 1971 – 73, small, vinyl
   10" Brigitta   $95.00    $225.00
   14" Brigitta   $95.00    $225.00
   8" Friedrich   $95.00    $225.00
   10" Friedrich  $100.00   $175.00
   8" Gretl      $95.00    $225.00
   11" Gretl    $100.00   $200.00
   10" Liesl     $95.00    $225.00
   14" Liesl     $95.00    $200.00
   10" Louisa   $125.00   $265.00
   14" Louisa   $75.00    $300.00
   12" Maria    $95.00    $225.00
   17" Maria    $160.00   $375.00
   8" Marta     $75.00    $225.00
   11" Marta    $145.00   $200.00
   Set/seven large $850.00  $1700.00+
   Set/seven small $700.00  $1,400.00+

*14" John Powers Model, wrist tag, black hat box with comb and curlers, $1,650.00+. Courtesy Sherryl Shirran.*

## Madame Alexander (cont.)

**Wendy Ann,** 1948 – 1950

| | | |
|---|---|---|
| 17" | $400.00 | $875.00 |
| 22" | $425.00 | $975.00 |

**Winnie Walker,** 1953, Cissy

| | | |
|---|---|---|
| 15" | $60.00 | $260.00 |
| 18" | $80.00 | $375.00 |
| 23" | $100.00 | $450.00 |

**Portraits, 1960+**

Marked "1961, Jacqueline, 21," early dolls have jointed elbows, later one piece

Prices for portraits show a range for different outfits – all prices are for mint condition dolls.

| | |
|---|---|
| **Agatha,** 1967 – 1980 | $265.00 – $625.00 |
| **Bride,** 1965 | $825.00 – $1,000.00+ |
| **Coco,** 1966 | |
| Portrait Ballgown | $2,000.00 |
| Street dress | $2,200.00 |
| Ballgown, other | $2,400.00 |
| **Cornelia,** 1972 – 1978 | $300.00 – $475.00 |
| **Gainsborough,** 1968 – 78 | $375.00 – $675.00 |
| **Godey,** 1965 – 1967 – 77 | $375.00 – $625.00 |
| **Jenny Lind,** 1969 | $1,400.00 – $1,500.00 |
| **Lady Hamilton,** 1968 | $475.00 |
| **Mme Pompadour,** 1970 | $1,300.00+ |
| **Magnolia,** 1977;1988 | $300.00 – $525.00 |
| **Manet,** 1982 – 1983 | $225.00 |
| **Melanie,** 1967 – 1989 | $300.00 – $600.00 |
| **Mimi,** 1971 | $525.00 |
| **Monet,** 1984 | $285.00 |
| **Morisot,** 1985 – 1986 | $250.00+ |
| **Queen,** 1965 | $800.00+ |
| **Renoir,** 1965 – 1973 | $525.00 – $850.00 |
| **Scarlett,** 1965 – 1989 | $325.00 – $1,050.00+ |
| **Toulouse-Lautrec,** 1986 – 87 | $250.00 |

**Souvenir, UFDC, Limited Editions**

**Little Emperor,** 1992, limit 400

| | |
|---|---|
| 8" | $550.00 |

**Miss Unity,** 1991, limit 310

| | |
|---|---|
| 10" | $325.00 |

**Sailor Boy,** 1990 limit 260

| | |
|---|---|
| 8" | $625.00 |

**Turn of Century Bathing Beauty,** 1992, R9 Conference limit 300

| | |
|---|---|
| 10" | $300.00 |

**Columbia 1893 Sailor,** 1993

| | |
|---|---|
| 12" | $325.00 |

**American Character Doll Co., 1919+, New York City.** In 1923, they began using *Petite* as a trade name for mama and character dolls. The company began by making composition dolls, but later made cloth, hard plastic and vinyl dolls.

First price is for dolls in good condition, but with some flaws; second price is for dolls in excellent condition, in original clothes. All vinyl and hard plastic dolls should have original tagged clothes, wrist tags, etc.

*Sweet Sue, Sunday Best, $375.00. Courtesy Sally McVey.*

**A. C. or Petite** marked baby or mama dolls
Baby, composition head and limbs, cloth bodies

| | | |
|---|---|---|
| 14" | $45.00 | $175.00 |
| 22" | $70.00 | $275.00 |

Mama, composition head and limbs, sleep eyes, mohair or human hair wig, cloth body with crier, swing legs

| | | |
|---|---|---|
| 16" | $75.00 | $265.00 |
| 24" | $100.00 | $375.00 |

**Bottletot,** 1926, composition head, bent limbs, cloth body with crier, sleep eyes, painted hair, open mouth, composition arm formed to hold bottle, painted hair

| | | |
|---|---|---|
| 18" | $125.00 | $325.00 |

1936 – 38, drink and wet rubber doll with bottle and diaper

| | | |
|---|---|---|
| 11" | $35.00 | $75.00 |
| 15" | $40.00 | $95.00 |

**Betsy McCall,** 1957
8", hard plastic, jointed knees

| | | |
|---|---|---|
| Ballerina | $65.00 | $200.00 |
| Ballgown | $90.00 | $200.00 |
| Bathing suit | $40.00 | $100.00 |
| Riding habit | $80.00 | $200.00 |

*Mark:* "*McCall 1958*"
Vinyl, rooted hair, medium high heels, round sleep eyes

| | | |
|---|---|---|
| 14" | $95.00 | $265.00 |

*Mark:* "*McCall 1961*"
Extra joints at ankles, knees, waist and wrists

| | | |
|---|---|---|
| 29" | $140.00 | $400.00 |

All vinyl, rooted hair.

| | | |
|---|---|---|
| 36" | $250.00 | $550.00 |

**Campbell Kids,** 1928, all composition, jointed neck, shoulders, hips, curl in middle of forehead
*Mark:* "*A Petite Doll*"
Allow more for original dress with label reading "*Campbell Kid.*"

| | | |
|---|---|---|
| 12" | $75.00 | $335.00 |

*19" vinyl Bessie, the Bashful Bride, $95.00. Courtesy Amanda Hash.*

**Carol Ann Beery,** 1935, all composition Patsy-type, sleep eyes, closed mouth, braided cornet

Celebrity doll, named for daughter of Hollywood actor, Wallace Beery. Originally came with two outfits such as a playsuit and matching dress.

*Marks: "Petite Sally," or "Petite"*

| | | |
|---|---|---|
| 13" | $100.00 | $400.00 |
| 16½" | $150.00 | $600.00 |
| 19½" | $200.00 | $775.00 |

**Cartwrights, Ben, Hoss, Little Joe,** ca. 1966 from the television show, *Bonanza.*

| | | |
|---|---|---|
| 8" | $35.00 | $140.00 |

**Cricket,** 1964

| | | |
|---|---|---|
| 9" | $15.00 | $35.00 |
| Growing hair | $12.00 | $45.00 |

*14" composition Petite girl, eyeshadow, original pink nylon dress, box, $400.00. Courtesy McMasters Doll Auctions.*

**Eloise,** ca. 1950s, cloth character with orange yarn hair, crooked smile,

| | | |
|---|---|---|
| 15" | $75.00 | $250.00 |
| Christmas dress | $90.00 | $350.00 |
| 21" | $100.00 | $400.00 |
| Christmas dress | $125.00 | $500.00 |

**Freckles,** 1966, face changes

| | | |
|---|---|---|
| 13" | $10.00 | $40.00 |

**Hadda-Get-Betta,** 1960

| | | |
|---|---|---|
| 21" | $35.00 | $110.00 |

**Little Miss Echo,** 1964, talker

| | | |
|---|---|---|
| 30" | $75.00 | $300.00 |

**Puggy,** 1928, all composition, jointed neck, shoulders, hip, pug nose, scowling expression, painted side-glancing eyes, painted molded hair. Original costumes include Boy Scout, cowboy, baseball player and newsboy.

*Marks: "A //Petite// Doll;"* Tag on clothing: **"Puggy// A Petite Doll"**

| | | |
|---|---|---|
| 12" | $120.00 | $475.00 |
| 14" | $135.00 | $550.00 |

**Ricky, Jr.,** 1955 – 1956, vinyl, baby boy from *I Love Lucy* television show, starring Lucille Ball and Desi Arnez

| | | |
|---|---|---|
| 13" | $15.00 | $50.00 |
| 20" | $25.00 | $100.00 |
| Hand puppet | $25.00 | |

**Sally,** 1930, a Patsy-look-alike, composition head, arms, and legs, cloth or composition body, crier, painted or sleep eyes

*Marks:* **"Sally//A Petite Doll"**

| | | |
|---|---|---|
| 12½ " | $50.00 | $200.00 |
| 16" | $75.00 | $275.00 |
| 19" | $85.00 | $325.00 |

**Sally,** 1934, Shirley Temple look-alike, with ringlet curls and bangs, composition shoulder plate, cloth body, sleep eyes, open mouth. Some dressed in ST type costumes.

| | | |
|---|---|---|
| 24" | $95.00 | $365.00 |

**Sally Joy,** 1934, composition shoulder plate, cloth body, sleep eyes, open mouth , curly wig.

*Marks:* **"Petite; Amer Char. Doll Co."**

| | | |
|---|---|---|
| 24" | $100.00 | $375.00 |

**Sally Says,** 1965, plastic and vinyl, talker

| | | |
|---|---|---|
| 19" | $20.00 | $70.00 |

**Sweet Sue,** 1953, hard plastic, some walkers, some with extra joints at knees, elbows, and/or ankles, some hard plastic and vinyl, excellent condition, good cheek color

*Marks:* **"A.C. Amer. Char. Doll." or "American Character" in circle**

| | | |
|---|---|---|
| 15" | $65.00 | $250.00 |
| 18" | $75.00 | $300.00 |
| 22" | $85.00 | $325.00 |
| 25" | $100.00 | $375.00 |

**Sweet Sue Sophisticate,** vinyl head

| | | |
|---|---|---|
| 20" | $65.00 | $250.00 |

**Talking Marie,** 1963, record player in body, battery operated, vinyl and plastic

| | | |
|---|---|---|
| 18" | $25.00 | $90.00 |

**Tiny Tears,** 1955 – 1962, hard plastic and vinyl

| | | |
|---|---|---|
| 8" | $15.00 | $50.00 |
| 13" | $40.00 | $150.00 |
| 17" | $50.00 | $200.00 |

1963, all vinyl

| | | |
|---|---|---|
| 9" | $10.00 | $40.00 |
| 12" | $12.00 | $45.00 |
| 16" | $15.00 | $55.00 |

Mint in box

| | |
|---|---|
| 13" | $300.00+ |

**Toni,** vinyl head

| | | |
|---|---|---|
| 10½ | $45.00 | $165.00 |
| 14" | $50.00 | $600.00+ |
| 20" | $75.00 | $650.00+ |

**Toodles,** 1956 – 60, all vinyl, rooted saran hair, sleep eyes, closed mouth

Baby

| | | |
|---|---|---|
| 14" | $35.00 | $125.00 |
| 18" | $60.00 | $225.00 |

Tiny
| | 10½" | $40.00 | $155.00 |
|---|---|---|---|

**Toddler** with "follow me" eyes
| | 22" | $65.00 | $260.00 |
|---|---|---|---|
| | 24" | $70.00 | $275.00 |
| | 28" | $85.00 | $325.00 |
| | 30" | $90.00 | $350.00 |

Mint in box
| | 28 – 30" | | $400.00+ |
|---|---|---|---|

**Toodle-Loo,** 1961, rooted blonde hair, painted eyes, closed mouth, fully jointed, "Magic Foam" plastic body
| | 18" | $50.00 | $190.00 |
|---|---|---|---|

**Tressy,** 1963 – 66+
| Grow hair, 1963 – 65 | $12.00 | $45.00 |
|---|---|---|

Mary/Magic Makeup, 1965 – 66, pale face, no lashes, bent knees
| | $10.00 | $40.00 |
|---|---|---|
| Miss America, 1963 | $15.00 | $50.00+ |

Preteen Tressy, 1963, child, grow hair.
*Mark: "AM Char. 63"*
| | 14" | $15.00 | $55.00 |
|---|---|---|---|

**Whimette/Little People,** ca. 1963, Pixie, Swinger, Granny, Jump'n, Go-Go
| | 7½" | $6.00 | $30.00 |
|---|---|---|---|

**Whimsie,** 1960, stuffed vinyl, painted on features, tag reads: "Whimsey," with name of doll, Bessie Bride, Dixie, Fanny (angel), Lena the Cleaner, Miss Take, Monk, Polly the Lolly, Raggie, Simon, Strongman, Suzie, Tillie, Wheeler the Dealer, Zack, and Zero (a football player)
| | 19" | $40.00 | $95.00 |
|---|---|---|---|
| Hilda the Hillbilly, or Devil | | $125.00 |

## Annalee

**Annalee Mobiltree Doll Co. Inc.,1934+, Meredith NH.** This company made decorative cloth dolls. Early labels were white with woven red lettering; then white rayon tags with red embroidered lettering. In about 1969, white satin tags with red lettering was used, after about 1976, gauze-type cloth was used. Until 1963, the dolls had yarn hair, ca. 1960 – 63, it was orange or yellow chicken feathers, after 1963, hair was synthetic fur. Collector's Club started in 1983.

**Adults,** 1950s
| | 10" | $500.00 | $2,500.00 |
|---|---|---|---|

1970s
| | 10" | $200.00 | $800.00 |
|---|---|---|---|

**Baby Angels,** 1960s
| | 7 – 8" | $65.00 | $325.00 |
|---|---|---|---|

1970s
| | 7" | $75.00 | $275.00 |
|---|---|---|---|

1980s
| | 7" | $50.00 | $200.00 |
|---|---|---|---|

**Child,** 1950s
| | | |
|---|---|---|
| 10" | $275.00 | $1,000.00+ |

1960s
| | | |
|---|---|---|
| 10" | $165.00 | $650.00+ |

1970s
| | | |
|---|---|---|
| 10" | $75.00 | $300.00+ |

1980s
| | | |
|---|---|---|
| 10" | $50.00 | $175.00+ |

**Clowns,** 1970s
| | | |
|---|---|---|
| 10" | $35.00 | $125.00 |
| 18" | $125.00 | $450.00 |
| 42" | $175.00 | $700.00 |

**Elf/Gnomes,** 1970s
| | | |
|---|---|---|
| 7" | $60.00 | $225.00 |
| 12" | $75.00 | $300.00 |

1980s
| | | |
|---|---|---|
| 7" | $25.00 | $85.00 |
| 12" | $35.00 | $135.00 |
| 16" | $45.00 | $185.00 |
| 22" | $60.00 | $225.00 |

**Indians,** 1970s
| | | |
|---|---|---|
| 7" | $60.00 | $225.00 |

1980s
| | | |
|---|---|---|
| 8" | $45.00 | $175.00 |
| 18" | $65.00 | $250.00+ |

**Monks,** 1970s
| | | |
|---|---|---|
| 8" | $25.00 | $85.00+ |

**Santa/Mrs. Claus,** 1970s
| | | |
|---|---|---|
| 7" | $20.00 | $75.00 |
| 26" | $50.00 | $200.00 |

1980s
| | | |
|---|---|---|
| 7" | $15.00 | $45.00 |
| 30" | $125.00 | $450.00 |

**Skiers,** 1960s
| | | |
|---|---|---|
| 7" | $150.00 | $600.00+ |

1970s
| | | |
|---|---|---|
| 7" | $75.00 | $300.00 |

1980s
| | | |
|---|---|---|
| 7" | $25.00 | $95.00 |

**Bears,** 1970s
| | | |
|---|---|---|
| 7" | $40.00 | $150.00 |
| 10" | $50.00 | $185.00+ |
| 18" | $75.00 | $275.00+ |

1980s
| | | |
|---|---|---|
| 7" | $20.00 | $80.00 |
| 10" | $40.00 | $150.00+ |
| 18" | $50.00 | $175.00 |

**Mice,** 1970s
| | | |
|---|---|---|
| Fireman | $80.00 | $350.00 |
| Groom | $50.00 | $200.00 |

*1995 Annalee Collectors' Club doll, $40.00.*

1991
Desert Storm     $25.00       $90.00

## Arranbee

*18" composition Arranbee Nancy, rosy cheeks and eye-shadow over eyes, $350.00. Courtesy Sally McVey.*

*17" composition R&B doll, Debu'teen, boxed, $350.00. Courtesy McMasters Doll Auctions.*

**Arranbee Doll Co. 1922 – 1958, New York.** Some of their bisque dolls were made by Armand Marseille and Simon & Halbig. They made composition baby, child, and mama dolls. Early dolls have an eight-sided tag. The company sold to Vogue Doll Co., who used molds until 1961.

First price is for soiled, faded, or without complete costume dolls; second price is for perfect dolls, with good color, complete costume.

*Marks:* **"ARRANBEE//DOLL CO.,"** or **"R & B"**

**Babies,** 1930s – 40s, composition, cloth body, original clothes or appropriately dressed

| | | |
|---|---|---|
| 16" | $50.00 | $125.00 |
| 22" | $60.00 | $150.00 |

**Debu-Teen,** 1940, composition girl, some with composition shoulder plate and cloth body, mohair or human hair wig, closed mouth, original costume

| | | |
|---|---|---|
| 12" | $45.00 | $155.00 |
| 14" | $50.00 | $185.00 |
| 18" | $70.00 | $275.00 |
| 21" | $75.00 | $350.00 |

**Kewty,** 1934 – 36, Patsy-type, composition with molded hair, original clothes.

*Marks:* **"R& B"**

| | | |
|---|---|---|
| 10" | $40.00 | $155.00 |
| 16" | $60.00 | $225.00 |

**Lil' Imp,** 1960, hard plastic , red hair and freckles

| | | |
|---|---|---|
| 10" | $20.00 | $75.00 |

**Littlest Angel,** 1956+, all hard plastic

| | | |
|---|---|---|
| 10" | $15.00 | $55.00 |

Vinyl head

| | | |
|---|---|---|
| 10" | $10.00 | $35.00 |

Red hair/freckles, 1960

| | | |
|---|---|---|
| 10" | $20.00 | $70.00 |

**Miss Coty,** 1958, vinyl, marked "P" in a circle (same marked dolls also dressed and marketed by Belle Doll Co.)

| | | |
|---|---|---|
| 10" | $25.00 | $100.00 |

**My Angel,** 1961, hard plastic and vinyl

| | | |
|---|---|---|
| 17" | $10.00 | $45.00 |
| 22" | $20.00 | $70.00 |
| 36" | $45.00 | $165.00 |

Walker, 1957 – 59

| | | |
|---|---|---|
| 30" | $40.00 | $150.00 |

1959, vinyl head, oilcloth body

| | | |
|---|---|---|
| 22" | $15.00 | $60.00 |

**My Dream Baby,** 1925, bisque solid dome heads made by Armand Marseille, painted hair, sleep eyes, open or closed mouth, cloth body, composition hands. See Marseille, Armand for prices.

*Marks:* **"A.M. 341," or "351," or "ARRANBEE"**

1927+, composition head, cloth body

| | | |
|---|---|---|
| 14" | $65.00 | $250.00 |
| 16" | $75.00 | $300.00+ |
| 19" | $125.00 | $475.00+ |

**Nancy,** 1930, a Patsy look-alike, composition, molded hair or wig, sleep eyes, open mouth

*Marks:* **"ARRANBEE" or "NANCY"**

| | | |
|---|---|---|
| 12" | $85.00 | $200.00 |
| 17" | $125.00 | $300.00 |
| 19" | $140.00 | $375.00 |

1951 – 52, vinyl head, arms, hard plastic torso, wigged

| | | |
|---|---|---|
| 14" | $40.00 | $150.00 |
| 18" | $50.00 | $190.00 |

Walker

| | | |
|---|---|---|
| 24" | $75.00 | $285.00 |

**Nancy Lee,** 1939+, composition, sleep eyes, mohair or human hair wig, original clothes

| | | |
|---|---|---|
| 12" | $50.00 | $195.00 |
| 14" | $70.00 | $265.00 |
| 17" | $75.00 | $300.00 |

# Arranbee (cont.)

1950 – 59, hard plastic

| | | |
|---|---|---|
| 14" | $75.00 | $285.00 |
| 20" | $115.00 | $450.00 |

Baby, 1952, painted eyes, crying look

| | | |
|---|---|---|
| 15" | $70.00 | $145.00 |

**Nannette,** 1949 – 59, hard plastic, synthetic wig, sleep eyes, closed mouth, original clothes

| | | |
|---|---|---|
| 14" | $80.00 | $250.00 |
| 17" | $95.00 | $275.00 |
| 21" | $125.00 | $350.00+ |

Walker, 1957 – 59, hard plastic

| | | |
|---|---|---|
| 18" | $125.00 | $300.00 |
| 25" | $200.00 | $400.00 |

Mint in box

| | |
|---|---|
| 17" | $450.00+ |

**Sonja Skater,** 1945, composition (some with Debu-Teen tag)

| | | |
|---|---|---|
| 10 – 12" | $55.00 | $195.00 |
| 14" | $70.00 | $275.00 |
| 17" | $75.00 | $285.00 |
| 21" | $105.00 | $415.00 |

**Storybook Dolls,** 1930 – 36, all composition, molded hair, painted eyes

| | | |
|---|---|---|
| 9 – 10" | $50.00 | $190.00 |
| Mint in box | | $290.00+ |

Taffy, 1956, looks like Alexander's "Cissy"

| | | |
|---|---|---|
| 23" | $45.00 | $165.00 |

## Artist Dolls

*6" Hitty, hand-carved wooden character from Rachel Field's book Hitty, Her First Hundred Years, $300.00. Courtesy NIADA artist, Patti Hale.*

Original, one of a kind, limited edition, or limited production dolls, of any medium (cloth, porcelain, wax, wood, vinyl, or other material), made for sale to the public.

**Himstedt, Annette, 1986+**

Distributed by Mattel, Inc. Swivel rigid-vinyl head with shoulder plate, cloth body, vinyl limbs, inset eyes, real lashes, molded eyelids, holes in nostrils, human hair wig, bare feet, original in box.

**American Heartline,** 1987, 20"

| | | |
|---|---|---|
| Timi | $115.00 | $450.00 |
| Toni | $115.00 | $450.00 |

**Barefoot Children,** 1986, 26"

| | | |
|---|---|---|
| Bastian | $165.00 | $650.00 |
| Ellen | $200.00 | $800.00 |
| Fatou | $250.00 | $1,000.00 |
| Kathe | $200.00 | $800.00 |
| Paula | $175.00 | $700.00 |

*14" artist doll of resin and cloth, 1995, Chocolate Delight, $920.00. Courtesy June Goodnow.*

*33" porcelain Atlantis, extensive hand beading, 1993, $7,000.00. Courtesy Susan Dunham.*

**Reflections of Youth,** 1989 – 90, 26"

| | | |
|---|---|---|
| Adrienne | $185.00 | $750.00 |
| Ayoka | $250.00 | $1,000.00 |
| Janka | $165.00 | $650.00 |
| Kai | $215.00 | $850.00 |

**World Child Collection,** 1988, 31"

| | | |
|---|---|---|
| Frederike | $275.00 | $1,100.00 |
| Kasimir | $375.00 | $1,500.00 |
| Makimura | $215.00 | $850.00 |
| Malin | $325.00 | $1,300.00 |
| Michiko | $250.00 | $1,000.00 |

**Cloth**

**Barrie, Mirren,** historical children     $95.00

**Heiser, Dorthy,** cloth sculpture
Early dolls     $400.00 – $500.00
Queens     $1,100.00 – $1,500.00

**Wright, John**

| | | |
|---|---|---|
| Elfin girl | 7½" | $800.00 |
| Adult characters | | $1,500.00 |
| Children | $900.00 – $1,300.00 | |

Christopher Robin with Winnie the Pooh
          $1,600.00 – $2,500.00
Winnie the Pooh, 1987
          14"     $500.00 – $550.00
          18"     $950.00

**Other Mediums**

**Blackeley, Halle,** high-fired clay lady dolls
          $550.00     $750.00
**Florian, Gertrude,** ceramic composition dressed ladies
          $300.00

*20" Gretchen by Linda Lee Sutton for Ellenbrook, 1996 DOTY nominee, $190.00, artist proof $240.00. Courtesy Linda Lee Sutton.*

*13" wooden dolls with cloth bodies made by Jill Sanders and Nancy Elliot, $300.00. Courtesy Angie Gonzales.*

**Parker, Ann**, historical character
$150.00 – $200.00
**Goodnow, June**
Chocolate Delight, resin, cloth
14"     $920.00
Indian, Singer Drummer, one-of-a-kind, cernit
14"     $3,000.00
The Quilter, resin, cloth
18"     $500.00

**Porcelain and China**
**Armstrong-Hand, Martha,** porcelain babies, children   $1,200.00+
**Brandon, Elizabeth,** porcelain children   ·   $300.00 – $500.00
**Campbell, Astry,** porcelain
Ricky & Becky, pair                $850.00
**Clear, Emma,** porcelain, china, bisque shoulder head dolls
$350.00 – $500.00
**Dunham, Susan,** porcelain babies, children, and adults
$75.00 –  $1,000.00+
**Hoskins, Dorothy**
Lilabeth Rose one-of-a-kind porcelain     $6,000.00+
**Kane, Maggie Head,** porcelain       $400.00 – $450.00
**Oldenburg, Mary Ann,** porcelain children   $200.00 – $250.00
**Redmond, Kathy,** porcelain ladies     $400.00 – $450.00
**Roche, Lynn & Michael,** porcelain
Children     17"             $1,100.00 – $1,500.00

**Thompson, Martha,** porcelain
Betsy $900.00
Little Women, ea.        $800.00 – $900.00
Queen Anne              $2,300.00
Princess Caroline, Prince Charles, Princess
Ann, ea.                $900.00
Princess Margaret, Princess Grace, ea.
                        $1,500.00 – $2,000.00
Young Victoria          $2,300.00
**Thorpe, Ellery,** porcelain children
                        $300.00 – $500.00
**Tuttle, Eunice,** miniature porcelain children
                        $700.00 – $800.00
Angel Baby              $400.00 – $425.00
**Walters, Beverly,** porcelain miniature fashions                $500.00+
**Wick, Faith,** porcelain, other materials
                        $2,500.00+
**Wyffels, Berdine,** porcelain
  6" girl, glass eyes    $195.00
**Zeller, Fawn,** porcelain
One-of-a-kind            $2,000.00+
Angela                  $800.00 – $900.00
Polly Piedmont, 1965    $800.00 – $900.00
Holly, U.S. Historical Society
                        $500.00 – $600.00
Polly II, U.S. Historical Society
                        $200.00 – $225.00

*18" Patrick by John R. Wright, $775.00. Courtesy McMasters Doll Auctions.*

**Wax**
**Park, Irma,** wax-over-porcelain miniatures    $125.00+
**Sorensen, Lewis** wax
Father Christmas        $1,200.00
Toymaker                $800.00
**Wood**
**Beckett, Bob and June,** carved wooden children
                        $300.00 – $450.00
**Bringloe, Frances,** carved wood
American Pioneer Children       $600.00
**Bullard, Helen,** carved wood
Holly                   $125.00
American Family series (16 dolls)    $250.00 ea.
  **Hale, Patti,** NIADA 1978, hand carved character dolls, wooden head, stuffed wired cloth bodies can pose; some all wood jointed dolls
                        $200.00 up
**Sandreuter, Regina,** carved wood        $550.00 – $650.00
**Smith, Sherman,** carved wood
    5 – 6"                $235.00

# Artist Dolls (cont.)

**Hitty,** 6" carved wood character from 1929 book *Hitty, Her First 100 Years*, by Rachel Field

| | |
|---|---|
| **Judy Brown** | $195.00 |
| **Hellen Bullard** | $350.00 |
| **David Green** | $310.00 |
| **Patti Hale** | $300.00 |
| **Lonnie Lindsay** | $205.00 |
| **Jeff Scott** | $167.50 |
| **Larry Tycksen,** son-in-law of Sherman Smith | $53.00 |
| **Michelle Simpson/Fred Hahn** | $185.00 |
| **Mary Lee Sundstrom/Sandy Reinke** | |
| Hitty, limited edition with jointed legs | $500.00+ |
| Frozen Hitty, 1996 | $395.00 |

## Baby Berry

*19" Captain Kangaroo and Dancing Bear, Child Guidance Toys by Baby Berry, $85.00. Courtesy Cathie Clark.*

*19" cloth Captain Kangaroo, $80.00. Courtesy Cathie Clark.*

**Vinyl**

| | | |
|---|---|---|
| **Alfred E. Newman** | | |
| 20" | $50.00 | $200.00 |
| **Captain Kangaroo** | | |
| 19" | $40.00 | $145.00 |
| 24" | $64.00 | $245.00 |
| **Christopher Robin** | | |
| 18" | $60.00 | $175.00 |
| **Daisy Mae** | | |
| 14" | $55.00 | $190.00 |
| **Emmet Kelly (Willie the Clown)** | | |
| 15" | $45.00 | $185.00 |
| 24" | $85.00 | $275.00 |
| **Lil Abner** | | |
| 14" | $50.00 | $200.00 |
| 21" | $70.00 | $265.00 |
| **Mammy Yokum, 1957** | | |
| Molded hair | | |
| 14" | $45.00 | $175.00 |
| 21" | $70.00 | $275.00 |
| Yarn hair | | |
| 14" | $50.00 | $200.00 |
| 21" | $75.00 | $300.00 |

Nose lights up
| | | |
|---|---|---|
| 23" | $85.00 | $325.00 |

**Pappy Yokum, 1957**
| | | |
|---|---|---|
| 14" | $35.00 | $135.00 |
| 21" | $65.00 | $260.00 |

Nose lights up
| | | |
|---|---|---|
| 23" | $85.00 | $325.00 |

# Barbie®

**Mattel, Inc.,1959, Hawthorne, CA**

*Marks:*

1959 – 62: "BARBIE TM/PATS. PEND.//© MCMLVIII//by//Mattel, Inc."

1963 – 68: "Midge TM© 1962//BARBIE ®/ ©1958//BY//Mattel, Inc."

1964 – 66: "©1958//Mattel, Inc. //U.S. Patented//U.S. Pat. Pend."

1966 – 69: "©1966//Mattel, Inc.//U.S. Patented//U.S. Pat. Pend//Made in Japan"

First price indicates less than perfect doll lacking a box, but still must be in very good condition; second price (or one price alone) is for mint in box doll. Even though Barbie is almost 40 years old, she is still considered a newer doll by seasoned collectors. In pricing newer dolls, the doll has to be perfect with mint color, condition, rare pristine outfit, complete with all accessories, retaining all tags, labels, and boxes to command the highest prices. This is not a complete listing of every Barbie, her friends, or accessories, but some of the more popular items.

**Number One Barbie, 1959**

11½", heavy vinyl solid body, faded white skin color, white irises, pointed eyebrows, soft ponytail, brunette or blonde only, black and white striped bathing suit, holes with metal cylinders in balls of feet to fit round – pronged stand, gold hoop earrings

| | | |
|---|---|---|
| #1 Blonde Ponytail Barbie | $1,050.00 | $5,000.00+ |
| #1 Brunette Ponytail Barbie | $1,150.00 | $6,000.00+ |
| #1 Barbie stand | $350.00 | |
| #1 Barbie shoes | $20.00 | |
| #1 Barbie earrings | $65.00 | |

*An unusual variant blonde #1 Barbie with braid was reported sold for $9,000.00

**Number Two Barbie, 1959 – 1960**

11½", heavy vinyl solid body, faded white skin color, white irises, pointed eyebrows, no holes in feet some with pearl earrings, soft ponytail, brunette or blonde only

| | | |
|---|---|---|
| #2 Blonde Ponytail Barbie | $1,000.00 | $4,000.00 |
| #2 Brunette Ponytail Barbie | $1,150.00 | $4,550.00 |

**Number Three Barbie, 1960**

11½" heavy vinyl solid body, some fading in skin color, blue irises, curved eyebrows, no holes in feet, soft ponytail, brunette or blonde only

| | | |
|---|---|---|
| #3 Blonde Ponytail Barbie | $300.00 | $800.00 |
| #3 Brunette Ponytail Barbie | $350.00 | $800.00 |

*11½" vinyl #1 ponytail Barbie doll, $4,100.00. Courtesy McMasters Doll Auctions.*

*11½" vinyl #1 Barbie, reported to be a prototype, ca. 1958, hand-painted face, very rare, $20,000.00. Private Collection.*

*#1 Barbie pedestal stand sold for $125.00. Courtesy McMasters Doll Auctions.*

*11½" vinyl Color Magic Barbie, boxed, $4,300.00. Courtesy McMasters Doll Auctions.*

**Number Four Barbie, 1960**

11½", same as #3, but solid body of skin-toned vinyl, soft ponytail, brunette or blonde only

| | | |
|---|---|---|
| #4 Blonde Ponytail Barbie $250.00 | | $500.00 |
| #4 Brunette Ponytail Barbie | $275.00 | $550.00 |

**Number Five Barbie, 1961**

11½", vinyl head, now less heavy, has hard plastic hollow body, firmer texture Saran ponytail, and now can be redhead, has arm-tag

| | | |
|---|---|---|
| #5 Blonde (pale) Ponytail Barbie | $175.00 | $450.00 |
| #5 Blonde Ponytail Barbie | $165.00 | $420.00 |
| #5 Brunette Ponytail Barbie | $195.00 | $450.00 |
| #5 Redhead Ponytail Barbie | $220.00 | $475.00 |

## More Barbie Dolls

Listed alphabetically, year of issue and value: First price indicates dolls in very good condition, no box; second price indicates mint in box dolls

| | | | |
|---|---|---|---|
| **Air Force** | 1991 | $15.00 | $50.00 |
| **American Girl,** bendable leg | 1965 | $200.00 | $800.00 |
| Bendable leg, side part | 1965 | $850.00 | $3,300.00 |
| Side part | 1965 | $2,000.00 | $4,200.00 |
| Long hair, high color | 1966 | $975.00 | $1,950.00 |
| Blonde | 1965 | $450.00 | $950.00 |
| **Angel Face** | 1983 | $15.00 | $30.00 |
| **Army** | 1989 | $12.00 | $35.00 |
| **Army Desert Storm** | 1993 | $12.00 | $25.00 |
| **Astronaut** | 1986 | $25.00 | $95.00 |
| **Barbie & Ken Thunderbirds** | 1993 | $10.00 | $25.00 |
| **Beautiful Bride,** 18" | 1978 | $50.00 | $200.00 |
| **Beauty Secrets** | 1980 | $15.00 | $45.00 |
| **Benefit Performance,** | 1992 | $65.00 | $200.00 |
| **Bubble cut,** brunette | 1961 | $75.00 | $250.00 |
| Brownett | 1961 | $500.00 | $900.00 |
| **Busy Barbie** | 1972 | $75.00 | $200.00 |
| **Color Magic,** midnight | 1965 | $475.00 | $1,850.00 |
| Blonde | 1965 | $450.00 | $1,100.00 |
| **Crystal** | 1984 | $10.00 | $35.00 |
| **Day to Night** | 1985 | $10.00 | $35.00 |
| **Dream Date** | 1983 | $12.00 | $45.00 |
| **Dream Glow** | 1986 | $12.00 | $35.00 |
| **Fashion Queen,** no wigs | 1963 | $75.00 | $100.00 |
| With wigs | 1963 | $100.00 | $300.00 |
| **Japanese** | 1985 | $75.00 | $150.00 |
| **Jewel Secrets** | 1985 | $25.00 | $50.00 |
| **Kissing,** with bangs | 1980 | $15.00 | $50.00 |
| **Live Action** on Stage | 1971 | $60.00 | $175.00 |
| **Living** | 1970 | $45.00 | $100.00 |
| **Loving You** | 1984 | $25.00 | $75.00 |
| **Magic Curl** | 1982 | $20.00 | $75.00 |
| **Malibu** | 1971 | $10.00 | $100.00 |
| **Miss Barbie,** sleep eyes | 1964 | $200.00 | $600.00 |
| **My First Barbie** | 1981 | $5.00 | $20.00 |
| **Navy** | 1991 | $15.00 | $45.00 |
| **Newport** | 1974 | $20.00 | $100.00 |
| **Oriental** | 1981 | $75.00 | $150.00 |
| **Parisian** | 1981 | $75.00 | $155.00 |
| **Peaches & Cream** | 1985 | $7.00 | $25.00 |
| **Pink & Pretty Modeling** | 1982 | $25.00 | $60.00 |
| **Plus Three** | 1976 | $20.00 | $40.00 |

| | | | |
|---|---|---|---|
| **Pretty Changes** | | 1980 | $20.00 | $35.00 |
| **Quick Curl** | | 1972 | $20.00 | $75.00 |
| With extra outfit | | 1973 | $20.00 | $100.00 |
| **Red Silver Sensations** | | 1984 | $50.00 | $150.00 |
| **Rocker Barbie** | | 1986 | $20.00 | $40.00 |
| **Roller Skating** | | 1981 | $15.00 | $35.00 |
| **Swirl Ponytail**, blonde | | 1964 | $100.00 | $300.00 |
| Brunette | | 1964 | $100.00 | $325.00 |
| **Talking Busy** | | 1971 | $40.00 | $100.00 |
| **Twist & Turn** | | 1966 | $50.00 | $250.00 |
| **Wedding Fantasy** | | 1990 | $25.00 | $40.00 |
| **Western** | | 1981 | $20.00 | $35.00 |
| **Western Fun** | | 1990 | $20.00 | $30.00 |

**Gift Sets**

Mint in box prices

| | | | |
|---|---|---|---|
| **Color Magic Gift Set** | Sears | 1966 | $1,000.00 |
| **Fashion Queen & Friends** | | 1963 | $2,000.00 |
| **Fashion Queen & Ken Trousseau** | | 1963 | $2,300.00 |
| **Hostess** | | 1965 | $2,300.00 |
| **Little Theatre** | | 1964 | $3,500.00 |
| **Mix 'n Match**, redhead | | 1963 | $1,100.00 |
| **On Parade** | | 1964 | $1,400.00 |
| **Party Set** | | 1960 | $1,600.00 |
| **Pep Rally** | | 1964 | $700.00 |
| **Pink Silhouette** | | | $800.00 |
| **Round the Clock** | | 1964 | $900.00 |
| **Sparkling Pink** | | 1963 | $1,000.00 |
| **Tennis** | | 1962 | $1,100.00 |
| **Trousseau Set** | | 1960 | $2,100.00 |
| **Wedding Fantasy** | | 1993 | $65.00 |
| **Wedding Party** | | 1964 | $2,000.00 |

**Store Specials**

Listing includes type of special, store, year, and value; it does not include all issues. These special editions and store exclusives remain some of the best bets for steady increase in value, because generally a smaller number of these dolls were produced.

Price is for complete mint in box doll.

| | | | |
|---|---|---|---|
| **25th Anniversary** | Montgomery Ward | 1972 | $600.00 |
| **Action Accents** | Sears | 1969 | $700.00 |
| **All American** | Wholesale clubs | 1991 | $20.00 |
| **Anniversary Star** | Wal-Mart | 1992 | $40.00 |
| **Ballerina on Tour** | Department store | 1976 | $100.00 |
| **Ballroom Beauty** | Wal-Mart | 1991 | $30.00 |
| **Barbie for President** | Toys 'R Us | 1991 | $75.00 |
| **Barbie Style** | Applause | 1990 | $45.00 |
| **Beautiful Bride** | Department store | 1976 | $125.00 |
| **Beauty Belle** | Applause | 1991 | $45.00 |
| **Blossom Beauty** | Shopco/Venture | 1991 | $45.00 |

| Blue Elegance | Hills | 1992 | $45.00 |
|---|---|---|---|
| Blue Rhapsody | Service Merchandise | 1991 | $275.00 |
| City Sophisticate | Service Merchandise | 1994 | $95.00 |
| Cute & Cool | Target | 1991 | $25.00 |
| Disney Special | Children's Palace | 1991 | $50.00 |
| Dream Princess | Sears | 1992 | $45.00 |
| Enchanted Evening | J. C. Penney | 1991 | $95.00 |
| Evening Sparkle | Hills | 1990 | $45.00 |
| Fantastica | Sam's Club | 1992 | $55.00 |
| Festiva | Sam's Club | 1993 | $45.00 |
| Fire Fighter | Toys 'R Us | 1995 | $25.00 |
| Frills & Fantasy | Wal-Mart | 1988 | $40.00 |
| Golden Elegance | Target | 1991 | $35.00 |
| Golden Greetings | F.A.O. Schwarz | 1989 | $275.00 |
| Holiday Hostess | Supermarket | 1992 | $35.00 |
| Jewel Jubilee | Sam's Club | 1991 | $85.00 |
| Jeweled Splendor | F.A.O. Schwarz | 1995 | $400.00 |
| Lavender Looks | Wal-Mart | 1989 | $45.00 |
| Little Debbie | Little Debbie Snack Cake | 1994 | $75.00 |
| Live Action | Montgomery Wards | 1971 | $150.00 |
| Madison Avenue | F. A. O. Schwarz | 1991 | $275.00 |
| Moonlight Rose | Hills | 1991 | $50.00 |
| Night Sensation | F.A.O. Schwarz | 1991 | $195.00 |
| Party in Pink | Ames | 1991 | $35.00 |
| Party Sensation | Sam's Club | 1990 | $85.00 |
| Pepsi Spirit | Toys 'R Us | 1990 | $100.00 |
| Pink Sensation | Winn Dixie | 1990 | $25.00 |
| Plantation Belle | Disney | 1992 | $500.00 |
| Regal Reflections | Spiegel | 1992 | $300.00 |
| Rockette | F.A.O. Schwarz | 1992 | $275.00 |
| School Fun | Toys 'R Us | 1991 | $25.00 |
| Special Expressions | Woolworth | 1990 | $15.00 |
| Sweet Roses | Toys 'R Us | 1990 | $25.00 |
| Theatre Elegance | Spiegel | 1994 | $225.00 |
| Very Violet | Price Club | 1992 | $75.00 |
| Winter Fantasy | F.A.O. Schwarz | 1990 | $295.00 |

### Custom, Exclusive Barbies

Often the most sought after are the first edition of a series or "exclusive" Barbie dolls such as those produced for Disney, F.A.O. Schwarz, Wal-Mart, Target, and others. These types of Barbie dolls usually increase in price because the number made is less than others, so they are not as easily found. Prices indicate mint in box.

#### Bob Mackie Barbie dolls

| | | | |
|---|---|---|---|
| Gold | | 1990 | $900.00 |
| Platinum | | 1991 | $800.00 |
| Starlight Splendor | | 1991 | $800.00 |
| Empress Bride | | 1992 | $1,200.00 |
| Neptune Fantasy | | 1992 | $1,200.00 |

# Barbie (cont.)

| | | |
|---|---|---|
| Masquerade Ball | 1993 | $600.00 |
| Queen of Hearts | 1994 | $250.00 |
| **Happy Holidays Barbie** | | |
| Red dress, blonde | 1988 | $750.00 |
| | 1989 | $255.00 |
| | 1990 | $200.00 |
| | 1991 | $200.00 |
| | 1992 | $150.00 |
| | 1993 | $150.00 |
| | 1994 | $150.00 |
| | 1995 | $65.00 |
| **Other Designers** | | |
| Benefit Ball, Carol Spenser | 1992 | $200.00 |
| City Style, Janet Goldblatt | 1993 | $115.00 |
| Opening Night, Janet Goldblatt | 1993 | $95.00 |

**Related Dolls, Friends, Family**

First price indicates dolls in good condition, no box; second price indicates mint in box.

| | | | |
|---|---|---|---|
| **Allan**, 1964 – 67 | | | |
| Bendable legs | | $150.00 | $300.00 |
| Straight legs | | $25.00 | $100.00 |
| **Bild Lilli,** German doll made prior to Barbie, clear plastic cylinder case | | | |
| | | $500.00 | $600.00 |
| **Casey, Twist & Turn** | 1967 | $55.00 | $250.00 |
| **Chris**, brunette | 1967 – 70 | $40.00 | $75.00 |
| **Francie** | | | |
| 1st black, hair oxidized to red | 1967 | $225.00 | $900.00 |
| Bendable leg | 1966 | $65.00 | $250.00 |
| Malibu | | $15.00 | $35.00 |
| Straight leg | 1966 | $75.00 | $300.00 |
| Twist & Turn | 1967 | $85.00 | $325.00 |
| Twist and Turn, black | 1967 | $100.00 | $985.00 |
| **Julia,** Talking | 1969 | $45.00 | $150.00 |
| **Quick Curl Kelly** | 1973 | $20.00 | $80.00 |
| Yellowstone Kelly | 1974 | $50.00 | $150.00 |
| **#1 Ken,** straight leg, blue eyes hard plastic hollow body, flocked hair | | | |
| *Marks:* **"Ken®MCMLX//by//Mattel//Inc."** | | | |
| 12" | 1961 | $40.00 | $135.00 |
| Straight leg, molded hair | 1962 | $40.00 | $125.00 |
| Bendable legs | 1965 | $75.00 | $300.00 |
| **Midge,** straight leg | 1963 | $50.00 | $175.00 |
| Bendable legs | | $100.00 | $400.00 |
| No freckles | 1963 | $100.00 | $400.00 |
| **P.J. Live Action** on Stage | 1971 | $60.00 | $150.00 |
| Twist and Turn | 1970 | $40.00 | $175.00 |
| **Ricky,** redhead | 1965 | $40.00 | $150.00 |

| | | | |
|---|---|---|---|
| **Skipper,** straight leg blonde | 1964 | $35.00 | $125.00 |
| Bendable leg | 1965 | $50.00 | $200.00 |
| **Skooter,** straight leg | 1965 | $35.00 | $150.00 |
| Bendable leg | 1966 | $50.00 | $250.00 |
| **Stacy,** talking | 1968 | $65.00 | $200.00 |
| Twist & Turn, Titian | 1968 | $75.00 | $225.00 |
| **Todd** | 1966 | $40.00 | $100.00 |
| **Twiggy** | 1967 | $90.00 | $350.00 |
| **Whitney,** Jewel Secrets | 1987 | $35.00 | $95.00 |

**Barbie Accessories**

**Animals**

| | | |
|---|---|---|
| Blinking Beauty, horse | 1980 | $45.00 |
| Dallas, horse | 1981 | $30.00 |
| Dancer, horse | 1971 | $50.00 |
| Dream Horse Prancer | 1984 | $30.00 |
| Mitzi Meow Cat | 1994 | $10.00 |
| Prince, French poodle | | $20.00 |
| Sachi, dog | 1991 | $18.00 |
| Snowball, dog | 1990 | $20.00 |
| Tag a Long Wags | 1992 | $15.00 |

**Cases**

| | | |
|---|---|---|
| Barbie & Midge, red, European | | $150.00 |
| Black, 4-doll | 1961 | $35.00 |
| Fashion Queen | | $75.00 |
| Goes Travelin' | | $75.00 |
| Miss Barbie | | |
| black patent leather | 1963 | $100.00 |
| Miss Barbie Carrying Case | | $75.00 |

**Clothing**

Price indicates mint in package.

| | | |
|---|---|---|
| After 5 | 1962 | $175.00 |
| American Airlines Stewardess | 1961 | $200.00 |
| Baby Sits | 1962 | $175.00 |
| Baby Sits with layette | 1964 | $150.00 |
| Ballerina | 1961 | $125.00 |
| Barbie in Japan | 1964 | $375.00 |
| Barbie Q outfit | 1959 | $150.00 |
| Beau Time | 1966 | $200.00 |
| Bride's Dream | 1963 | $200.00 |
| Campus Sweetheart | 1964 | $800.00 |
| Career Girl | 1963 | $250.00 |
| Cinderella | 1964 | $300.00 |
| Club Meeting | 1966 | $250.00 |
| Country Club Dance | 1965 | $300.00 |
| Debutante Ball | 1966 | $875.00 |
| Disco Date | 1965 | $225.00 |
| Dream Team | 1971 | $35.00 |
| Drum Majorette | 1964 | $150.00 |

| | | |
|---|---|---|
| Easter Parade | 1959 | $2,600.00 |
| Evening Enchantment | 1967 | $175.00 |
| Fabulous Fashion | 1966 | $500.00 |
| Fancy that Purple | 1972 | $35.00 |
| Fashion Luncheon | 1966 | $950.00 |
| Festival Fashion | 1971 | $190.00 |
| Floral Printed Dress | 1976 | $35.00 |
| Flying Colors | 1972 | $165.00 |
| Fraternity Dance | 1965 | $450.00 |
| Garden Tea Party | 1964 | $125.00 |
| Garden Wedding | 1966 | $375.00 |
| Gay Parisienne | 1959 | $2,250.00 |
| Glowin' Out | 1971 | $60.00 |
| Gold 'n Glamour | 1965 | $800.00 |
| Graduation | 1963 | $60.00 |
| Guinevere | 1964 | $225.00 |
| Here Comes the Bride | 1966 | $950.00 |
| Holiday Dance | 1965 | $400.00 |
| Hot Togs | 1972 | $455.00 |
| In Stitches | 1971 | $100.00 |
| Invitation to Tea | 1965 | $375.00 |
| Jump into Lace | 1968 | $80.00 |
| Junior Prom | 1965 | $425.00 |
| Knit Ensemble | 1976 | $35.00 |
| Let's Dance | 1960 | $125.00 |
| London Tour | 1966 | $295.00 |
| Lovely 'n Lavender | 1972 | $35.00 |
| Lunch Date | 1964 | $100.00 |
| Lunch on the Terrace | 1966 | $250.00 |
| Made for Each Other | 1969 | $125.00 |
| Magnificence | 1965 | $450.00 |
| Majestic Blue | 1972 | $495.00 |
| Miss America, red gown | 1972 | $50.00 |
| Miss Astronaut | 1965 | $775.00 |
| Movie Date | 1962 | $100.00 |
| Movie Groovie | 1969 | $65.00 |
| Nighty Negligee | 1959 | $125.00 |
| Now Wow | 1969 | $95.00 |
| Olympic Warm-ups | 1975 | $40.00 |
| On the Avenue | 1965 | $400.00 |
| Outdoor Art Show | 1966 | $375.00 |
| Pajama Party | 1964 | $100.00 |
| Pan American Stewardess | 1966 | $2,500.00 |
| Peasant Pleasant | 1972 | $120.00 |
| Picnic Set | 1979 | $300.00 |
| Pink Sparkle | 1967 | $140.00 |
| Poodle Doodles | 1972 | $550.00 |

| | | |
|---|---|---|
| Pretty as a Picture | 1966 | $350.00 |
| Princess Aurora | 1976 | $40.00 |
| Rainbo Wraps | 1970 | $180.00 |
| Reception Line | 1966 | $400.00 |
| Red Fantastic | 1967 | $575.00 |
| Red Riding Hood & Wolf | 1964 | $400.00 |
| Registered Nurse | 1961 | $150.00 |
| Roman Holiday separates | 1959 | $3,200.00 |
| Saturday Matinee | 1965 | $725.00 |
| Scuba Do's | 1970 | $35.00 |
| Shimmering Magic | 1966 | $1,600.00 |
| Show Stopper | 1984 | $45.00 |
| Skater's Waltz | 1965 | $300.00 |
| Ski Queen | 1963 | $125.00 |
| Skiing | 1974 | $36.00 |
| Solo in the Spotlight | 1960 | $275.00 |
| Stardust | 1965 | $85.00 |
| Sugar Plum Fairy | 1976 | $40.00 |
| Sunday Visit | 1966 | $350.00 |
| Suburban Shopper | 1959 | $200.00 |
| Sweet Dreams | 1964 | $200.00 |
| Sweet Dreams | 1965 | $35.00 |
| Tennis Anyone | 1962 | $75.00 |
| Theatre Date | 1963 | $125.00 |
| Trail Blazer | 1968 | $110.00 |
| Tunic 'n Tights | 1969 | $175.00 |
| United Airline Stewardess | 1973 | $75.00 |
| Weekenders | 1967 | $900.00 |
| White Magic | 1964 | $220.00 |
| Winter Holiday | 1959 | $175.00 |
| Zokko | 1968 | $110.00 |

**Furniture**

| | | |
|---|---|---|
| Piano & Bench, Music Box | 1964 | $300.00 |
| Suzy Goose Vanity & Bench | ca. 1960 | $100.00 |
| Suzy Goose Bed | ca. 1960 | $100.00 |
| Suzy Goose Wardrobe | ca. 1960 | $100.00 |
| 57 Chevy | 1989 | $100.00 |
| Country Camper | 1971 | $35.00 |

**Vehicles**

| | | |
|---|---|---|
| Dune Buggy | 1970 | $200.00 |
| Hot Rod | 1963 | $200.00 |
| Sports Car, orange Austin Healy | 1962 | $175.00 |
| Sport Plane | 1964 | $2,300.00 |
| Friend Ship | 1973 | $100.00 |

*20" vinyl, Betsy McCall $300.00. Courtesy Shirley Grime.*

*14" vinyl Betsy McCall by Ideal, boxed, $225.00. Courtesy McMasters Doll Auctions.*

First price is for dolls in good condition, but with flaws; second price is for dolls in excellent condition with original outfit.

**American Character**

**1957,** 8", hard plastic, jointed knees

| | | |
|---|---|---|
| Ballerina | $50.00 | $190.00 |
| Ballgown | $60.00 | $230.00 |
| Bathing Suit/romper | $40.00 | $150.00 |
| Cowgirl | $50.00 | $200.00 |
| Riding Habit | $50.00 | $190.00 |
| Street Dress | $45.00 | $175.00 |
| Original shoes & socks | $25.00 | |

**1961,** vinyl, rooted hair, medium high heels, round sleep eyes
*Marked "McCall 1958"*

| | | |
|---|---|---|
| 14" | $50.00 | $290.00 |
| In School Days outfit | $75.00 | $300.00 |

Vinyl, rooted hair, slender limbs, more for flirty eyes

| | | |
|---|---|---|
| 20" | $75.00 | $290.00 |

All vinyl, rooted hair

| | | |
|---|---|---|
| 29 – 30" | $125.00 | $475.00 |
| 36" | $175.00 | $625.00 |

*Marked "McCall 1959"*

**Sandy McCall,** boy

| | | |
|---|---|---|
| 38" | $200.00 | $725.00 |

Extra joints, ankles, knees, waist, wrists
*Marked "McCall, 1961"*

| | | |
|---|---|---|
| 29" | $140.00 | $400.00 |

**Horsman**

1975, vinyl

*Marked "Horsman Dolls, Inc. 1967"*

| | | |
|---|---|---|
| 13" | $25.00 | $85.00 |

**1971, marked "B.M.C. Horsman, 1971"**

| | | |
|---|---|---|
| 29" | $50.00 | $190.00 |

**Ideal Doll Co., 1952 – 1953**

Designed by Bernard Lipfert, from *McCall's* magazine's paper doll, vinyl head, hard plastic, Toni body, saran wig

*Marked "McCall Corp. ®" on head, "IDEAL DOLL//P 90" on back*

| | | |
|---|---|---|
| 14" | $90.00 | $250.00 |

Vinyl/plastic with extra joints

| | | |
|---|---|---|
| 22" | $100.00 | $275.00 |

cas

| | | |
|---|---|---|
| 36" | $225.00 | $550.00 |

**Sandy McCall, 39"**
*Marked "McCall 1959"*

| | | |
|---|---|---|
| | $300.00 | $650.00 |

**Uneeda**

Ca. 1964, vinyl and hard plastic, brown or blue sleep eyes, reddish rooted hair, no marks

| | | |
|---|---|---|
| 11½" | $35.00 | $125.00 |

## Bucherer

**1921 – 30+, Armiswil, Switzerland.** Made metal body dolls with compo head, hands, and feet. Some dolls had changeable heads. Charlie Chaplin, Mutt and Jeff, regional costumes, and others.

6½" – 7½"

| | | |
|---|---|---|
| Regional | $100.00 | $285.00 |
| Mutt and Jeff, ea. | $175.00 | $600.00+ |

## Buddy Lee

**Ca. 1920 – 63.** Trademark doll of H.D. Lee Co., Inc. It was first made of composition, then about 1948, it was made in hard plastic, unmarked. The engineer had a Lee label on the hat and overalls; the cowboy's hatband was printed with, "Ride 'Em in Lee Rider Overalls."

First price for played with, incomplete outfit; second price for mint doll.

**Coca-Cola uniform**

| | | |
|---|---|---|
| White with green stripe | $125.00 | $625.00 |
| Tan with green stripe | $135.00 | $650.00 |
| **Cowboy** | $90.00 | $350.00 |
| **Engineer** | $85.00 | $325.00 |
| **Gas station attendant** | $65.00 | $285.00+ |
| **Hard plastic** | $200.00 | $375.00 |

## 1978+, Babyland General Hospital, Cleveland, GA.

| | | |
|---|---|---|
| "A" blue edition | 1978 | $1,500.00+ |
| "B" red edition | 1978 | $1,200.00+ |
| "C" burgundy edition | 1979 | $900.00+ |
| "D" purple edition | 1979 | $800.00+ |
| "X" Christmas edition | 1979 | $1,200.00+ |
| "E" bronze edition | 1979 | $1,200.00+ |
| Preemie edition | 1980 | $650.00+ |
| Celebrity edition | 1980 | $600.00+ |
| Christmas edition | 1980 | $600.00+ |
| Grand edition | 1980 | $750.00+ |
| New Ears edition | 1981 | $125.00+ |
| Ears edition | 1982 | $150.00+ |
| Green edition | 1983 | $400.00+ |
| "KP," dark green edition | 1983 | $550.00+ |
| "KPR," red edition | 1983 | $550.00+ |
| "KPB," burgundy edition | 1983 | $200.00 |
| Oriental edition | 1983 | $850.00 |
| Indian edition | 1983 | $850.00 |
| Hispanic edition | 1983 | $750.00 |
| "KPZ" edition | 1983 – 84 | $175.00 |
| Champagne edition | 1983 – 84 | $900.00 |
| "KPP," purple edition | 1984 | $250.00 |
| Sweetheart edition | 1984 | $250.00 |
| Bavarian edition | 1984 | $250.00 |
| World Class edition | 1984 | $175.00 |
| "KPF," "KPG," "KPH," "KPI," "KPJ" editions | | |
| | 1984 – 85 | $100.00 – 150.00+ |
| Emerald edition | 1985 | $100.00+ |

## Coleco

**1983,** Have powder scent and black signature stamp

| | |
|---|---|
| Boys and Girls | $95.00 |
| Bald babies | $100.00 |
| With pacifiers | $50.00 – $75.00 |
| With freckles | $100.00 |
| Black boys or girls with freckles | $175.00 |
| Without freckles | $75.00 |
| Red hair boys, fuzzy hair | $175.00 |

**1984 – 85,** green signature stamp in 1984; blue signature stamp in 1985. Most dolls are only worth retail price, exceptions are:

| | |
|---|---|
| Single tooth, brunette with ponytail | $165.00+ |
| Popcorn hairdos, rare | $200.00 |
| Gray-eyed girls | $165.00 |
| Freckled girl, gold hair | $95.00 |

## Other Coleco Cabbage Patch Dolls

Baldies, popcorn curl with pacifier, red popcorn curls, single tooth, freckled girls, and gold braided hair are valued at retail to $65.00. Still easily obtainable for collectors are a host of other Cabbage Patch including ringmaster, clown, baseball player, astronaut, travelers, twins, babies, talking Preemie, Splash Kid, Cornsilk Kid, valued at $30.00 – $50.00.

# Cameo Doll Company

**1922 – 30+, New York City, Port Allegheny, PA.** Joseph L. Kallus's company made composition dolls, some had wooden segmented bodies and cloth bodies.

First price for played with dolls; second price for mint dolls.

**Annie Rooney, 1926**
Jack Collins, designer, all composition, yarn wig, legs painted black, molded shoes

|     |         |          |
|-----|---------|----------|
| 12" | $125.00 | $475.00+ |
| 17" | $175.00 | $700.00+ |

**Baby Blossom, 1927**
Composition and cloth

|     |         |           |
|-----|---------|-----------|
| 19" | $300.00 | $1,100.00 |

**Baby Bo Kaye**
**1925**
Bisque head, made in Germany, molded hair, open mouth, glass eyes, cloth body, composition limbs, good condition
Marks: *"J.L. Kallus: Copr. Germany// 1394/30"*

|     |           |           |
|-----|-----------|-----------|
| 17" | $1,875.00 | $2,500.00 |
| 20" | $2,100.00 | $2,800.00 |

**All Bisque,** molded hair, glass sleep eyes, open mouth, two teeth, swivel neck, joint arms and legs, molded pink or blue shoes, socks, unmarked, some may retain original round sticker on body

|    |         |           |
|----|---------|-----------|
| 5" | $700.00 | $1,500.00 |
| 6" | $900.00 | $1,800.00 |

Celluloid head, made in Germany, molded hair, open mouth, glass eyes, cloth body

|     |         |         |
|-----|---------|---------|
| 12" | $200.00 | $400.00 |
| 15" | $350.00 | $750.00 |

Composition head, molded hair, open mouth, glass eyes, light crazing

|     |         |         |
|-----|---------|---------|
| 14" | $350.00 | $675.00 |

**Baby Mine, 1962 – 64**
Vinyl and cloth, sleep eyes

|     |        |         |
|-----|--------|---------|
| 16" | $25.00 | $100.00 |
| 19" | $35.00 | $125.00 |

On Miss Peep hinged body

|     |        |         |
|-----|--------|---------|
| 16" | $35.00 | $135.00 |

**Betty Boop, 1932**
Composition character head, wooden segmented body, molded hair, painted features, label on torso

|       |         |         |
|-------|---------|---------|
| 11"   | $200.00 | $650.00 |
| 13½"  | $200.00 | $950.00 |

**Champ, 1942**
Composition with freckles

|     |         |         |
|-----|---------|---------|
| 16" | $175.00 | $585.00 |

**Giggles, 1946**
Composition with molded loop for ribbon

|     |         |         |
|-----|---------|---------|
| 12" | $90.00  | $350.00 |
| 14" | $150.00 | $600.00 |

*11" composition cameo Betty Boop, $475.00. Courtesy McMasters Doll Auctions.*

*19" Baby Blossom, composition upper torso, arms, and head, cloth lower body and legs, molded hair, green tin sleep eyes, open mouth with teeth, all original, marked "DES & copyright//by J.L. Kallus// Made in U.S. A," $1,000.00. Courtesy Janet Hill.*

### Ho-Ho, 1940
Plaster

| | | |
|---|---|---|
| 5½" | $20.00 | $75.00 |

Vinyl

| | | |
|---|---|---|
| 7" | $4.00 | $15.00 |

### Joy, 1932
Composition character head, wooden segmented body, molded hair, painted features, label on torso

| | | |
|---|---|---|
| 10" | $75.00 | $300.00 |
| 15" | $125.00 | $475.00 |

### Margie, 1929
Composition character head, wooden segmented body, molded hair, painted features, label on torso

| | | |
|---|---|---|
| 10" | $75.00 | $285.00 |

Composition, 1935

| | | |
|---|---|---|
| 6" | $50.00 | $190.00 |
| 10" | $75.00 | $285.00 |

### Miss Peep, 1957 – 1970s+
Pin jointed shoulders and hips, vinyl

| | | |
|---|---|---|
| 15" | $10.00 | $45.00 |
| 18" | $15.00 | $60.00 |

Black

| | | |
|---|---|---|
| 18" | $28.00 | $75.00 |

1970s+, ball jointed shoulders and hips

| | | |
|---|---|---|
| 17" | $12.50 | $50.00 |
| 21" | $25.00 | $70.00 |

**Newborn,** 1962, vinyl head and rigid plastic body

| | | |
|---|---|---|
| 18" | $10.00 | $40.00 |

### Pete, the Pup, 1930 – 35
Composition character head, wooden segmented body, molded hair, painted features, label on torso

| | | |
|---|---|---|
| 9" | $70.00 | $265.00 |

## Pinkie, 1930 – 35

Composition character head, wooden segmented body, molded hair, painted features, label on torso

| | | |
|---|---|---|
| 10" | $100.00 | $375.00 |

Composition body

| | | |
|---|---|---|
| 10" | $75.00 | $285.00 |

Vinyl and plastic, 1950s

| | | |
|---|---|---|
| 10 – 11" | $75.00 | $150.00 |

## Pop-Eye, 1935

Composition character head, wooden segmented body, molded hair, painted features, label on torso

| | |
|---|---|
| $75.00 | $300.00 |

## Pretty Bettsie

Composition head, molded hair, painted side-glancing eyes, open/closed mouth, composition one-piece body and limbs, wooden neck joint, molded and painted dress with ruffles, shoes and socks. Triangular red tag on chest marked *"Pretty Bettsie//Copyright J. Kallus."*

| | | |
|---|---|---|
| 18" | $125.00 | $500.00 |

## Scootles, 1925+

Rose O'Neill design, all composition, no marks, painted side-glancing eyes, paper wrist tag

| | | |
|---|---|---|
| 8" | $100.00 | $365.00 |
| 13" | $125.00 | $475.00 |
| 15" | $160.00 | $625.00 |
| 20" | $185.00 | $725.00 |

Composition, sleep eyes

| | | |
|---|---|---|
| 15" | $175.00 | $700.00 |

Black composition

| | | |
|---|---|---|
| 15" | $200.00 | $725.00 |

Vinyl, 1964

| | | |
|---|---|---|
| 14" | $50.00 | $195.00 |
| 19" | $90.00 | $350.00 |
| 27" | $135.00 | $535.00 |

## "The Selling Fool," 1926

Wooden segmented body, hat represents radio tube, composition advertising doll for RCA Radiotrons

| | | |
|---|---|---|
| 16" | $200.00 | $800.00 |

*8" all original composition Scootles, molded hair, painted eyes, hang tag, $365.00. Courtesy Sue Kinkade.*

# Composition

American, unknown or little known manufacturer.

First price is for poorer quality, worn dolls; second price is for mint quality dolls, all original, wonderful color.

*12" composition unmarked baby, original outfit, $350.00. Courtesy McMasters Doll Auctions.*

*16" American composition baby, unmarked, molded hair, tin sleep eyes, cloth body with compo lower limbs, all original, $300.00. Courtesy Matrix.*

## American
### Baby, 1910+
Wigged or molded hair, painted or sleep eyes, composition or cloth body with bent legs

| | | |
|---|---|---|
| 12" | $65.00 | $225.00 |
| 18" | $75.00 | $300.00 |
| 24" | $110.00 | $425.00 |

Dionne-types

Ca. 1934+, all composition, jointed five-piece baby or toddler body, molded hair or wig, with painted or sleep eyes, closed or open mouth

| | | |
|---|---|---|
| 7" | $35.00 | $140.00 |
| 13" | $65.00 | $250.00 |
| 18" | $90.00 | $350.00 |

### Costumed in Ethnic or Theme Outfit
All composition, sleep or painted eyes, mohair wig, closed mouth, original costume

9 – 11"

| | | |
|---|---|---|
| lesser quality | $15.00 | $75.00 |
| better quality | $45.00 | $175.00 |

### Early Child, ca. 1910 – 1920
Unmarked, cork stuffed cloth body, painted features, may have molded hair

| | | |
|---|---|---|
| 12" | $35.00 | $140.00 |
| 18" | $50.00 | $200.00 |

Character face, ca. 1910 – 1920

| | | |
|---|---|---|
| 12" | $50.00 | $200.00 |
| 18" | $75.00 | $300.00 |
| 24" | $115.00 | $450.00 |

### MaMa Doll, ca. 1922+

Wigged or painted hair, sleep or painted eyes, cloth body with crier and swing legs, lower composition legs and arms

| | | |
|---|---|---|
| 16" | $70.00 | $250.00 |
| 20" | $90.00 | $350.00 |
| 24" | $115.00 | $450.00 |

### Patsy-type Girl, 1928+

Painted, molded, bobbed hair, sleep or painted eyes, closed pouty mouth, composition or hard stuffed cloth body

| | | |
|---|---|---|
| 10" | $45.00 | $175.00 |
| 14" | $70.00 | $250.00 |
| 19" | $80.00 | $300.00 |

With molded hair loop

| | | |
|---|---|---|
| 15" | $50.00 | $200.00 |

### Shirley Temple-type Girl, 1934+

All composition, five-piece jointed body, blonde curly wig, sleep eyes, open mouth, teeth, dimples

| | | |
|---|---|---|
| 16" | $100.00 | $400.00 |
| 19" | $125.00 | $450.00 |

*10" composition Little Orphan Annie, boxed, $175.00. Courtesy McMasters Doll Auctions.*

### Others

Animal head doll, ca. 1930s, all composition on Patsy-type five-piece body, could be wolf, rabbit, cat, monkey

| | | |
|---|---|---|
| 9½" | $50.00 | $200.00 |

Jackie Robinson

| | | |
|---|---|---|
| 13" in box | $300.00 | $1,000.00 |

Kewty, 1930, made by Domec of Canada, all composition Patsy-type, molded bobbed hair, closed mouth, sleep eyes, bent left arm

| | | |
|---|---|---|
| 13½" | $80.00 | $350.00 |

Miss Curity, composition

| | | |
|---|---|---|
| 18" | $150.00 | $500.00 |

Monica, 1941 – 51

| | | |
|---|---|---|
| 18" | $185.00 | $550.00 |

Puzzy, 1948, H of P

| | | |
|---|---|---|
| 15" | $100.00 | $400.00 |

Royal, Spirit of America

| | | |
|---|---|---|
| 15" | $75.00 | $350.00 |

Santa Claus, composition molded head

| | | |
|---|---|---|
| 19" | $150.00 | $500.00 |

Sizzy, 1948, H of P

| | | |
|---|---|---|
| 4" | $75.00 | $300.00 |

### German

Composition head, composition or cloth body, wig or painted molded hair, closed or open mouth with teeth, dressed

# Composition (cont.)

*21" composition child by Dora Petzold, ca. 1920, Berlin, Germany, with cloth body, replaced clothes, $500.00. Courtesy Sherryl Shirran.*

*8" composition-type Thumb's Up doll, tagged: "The Manufacturers of this official Thumbs Up Doll is participating in the Buy To Aid Britain Campaign by donating a portion of his profit on this sale to Ambulances to Britain," $175.00. Courtesy Bev Mitchell.*

*8" composition German black Puz baby, original white shirt, box, $225.00. Courtesy McMasters Doll Auctions.*

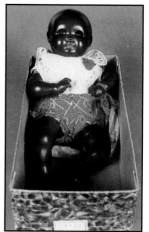

**Character Baby**
Cloth body

| | | |
|---|---|---|
| 18" | $95.00 | $350.00 |

Composition baby body, bent limbs

| | | |
|---|---|---|
| 16" | $125.00 | $425.00 |

**Character child,** composition body

| | | |
|---|---|---|
| 19" | $175.00 | $550.00 |

Child, all composition body

| | | |
|---|---|---|
| 13" | $75.00 | $275.00 |
| 19" | $125.00 | $425.00 |
| 21" | $175.00 | $500.00 |

# Cosmopolitan

**Ginger,** hard plastic, bent knee

| | | |
|---|---|---|
| 7½" | $15.00 | $50.00 |

Straight leg

| | | |
|---|---|---|
| 7½" | $23.00 | $90.00 |

Large round sleep eyes

| | | |
|---|---|---|
| 8" | $50.00 | $175.00 |

**Little Miss Ginger,** vinyl, rooted hair, sleep eyes, closed mouth, tagged clothes

| | | |
|---|---|---|
| 10½" | $50.00 | $190.00 |

**Pam,** hard plastic, sleep eyes, synthetic wig, closed mouth

| | | |
|---|---|---|
| 8" | $20.00 | $65.00 |

*10½" vinyl Miss Ginger and 8" Ginger, $190.00. Courtesy Cathie Clark.*

# Dee & Cee

**Ca. 1967+, Canada.** Rigid vinyl, rooted hair, sleep eyes
**Marylee**

| | | |
|---|---|---|
| 17" | $75.00 | $300.00 |

# Deluxe Reading

**Deluxe Topper, Deluxe Premium,** also used names Topper Toys and Topper Corp. Made mechanical and battery operated dolls ca. 1960 – 1970s. These dolls are collectible because so few survived intact after being well played with.

First price is for played with dolls, second price is for complete dolls, in excellent to mint condition.

**Baby Boo,** 1965, battery operated

| | | |
|---|---|---|
| 21" | $12.00 | $45.00 |

**Baby Catch A Ball,** 1969, battery operated

| | | |
|---|---|---|
| 18" | $15.00 | $55.00 |

**Baby Magic,** 1966, blue sleep eyes, rooted saran hair, magic wand has magnet that opens or closes eyes

| | | |
|---|---|---|
| 18" | $15.00 | $50.00 |

**Baby Peek 'N Play,** 1969, battery operated

| | | |
|---|---|---|
| 18" | $12.00 | $45.00 |

**Baby Tickle Tears**

| | | |
|---|---|---|
| 14" | $9.00 | $35.00 |

**Betty Bride,** 1957, also called, Sweet Rosemary, one-piece vinyl body and limbs

| | | |
|---|---|---|
| 30" | $25.00 | $90.00 |

**Candy Fashion,** 1958, made by Deluxe Premium, a division of Deluxe Reading, sold in grocery stores, came with three dress forms, extra outfit

| | | |
|---|---|---|
| 21" | $23.00 | $85.00 |

**Dawn,** in box

| | | |
|---|---|---|
| 6" | $7.50 | $30.00 |

**Dawn Model Agency**

| | | |
|---|---|---|
| In box | $18.00 | $45.00 |

**Dawn Series, boys**

| | | |
|---|---|---|
| In box | $35.00 | $45.00 |

**Little Miss Fussy,** battery operated

    18"    $6.00    $35.00

**Party Time,** 1967, battery operated

    18"    $10.00    $45.00

**Penny Brite,** child

    8"    $5.00    $17.50

**Private Ida,** 1965, one of the Go Go's

    6"    $6.00    $45.00

**Smarty Pants,** and other mechanicals, 1971, battery operated

*8" vinyl Penny Brite with extra outfits, ca. 1964, $30.00. Courtesy Cathie Clark.*

    19"    $6.00    $35.00

**Suzy Cute,** move arm and face changes expressions

    7"    $7.00    $28.00

**Suzy Homemaker,** 1964, hard plastic and vinyl, jointed knees

*Marks:"Deluxe Reading Co."*

    21"    $12.00    $45.00

**Tom Boy,** 1965, one of the Go Go's

    6"    $12.00    $45.00

## Duchess Doll Corporation

**Ca. 1948 – 1950s.** They made small hard plastic adult dolls with mohair wigs, painted or sleep eyes, jointed arms, stiff or jointed neck, painted molded shoes, about 7 – 7½" tall, with costumes stapled to body.

    7"    $2.50    $7.50

*A nun doll in hard plastic by Duchess Doll Mfg., $7.50. Courtesy Cathie Clark.*

## Eegee

**1917+, Brooklyn, NY.** E.G. Goldberger made composition and cloth dolls, imported bisque heads from Armand Marseille, made character head composition, mama dolls, babies, carnival dolls, and later the company made hard plastic and vinyl dolls.

First price for played with dolls, second price for complete, original, excellent condition dolls.

*Marks:* Trademark, *"EEGEE,"* or circle with the words, *"TRADEMARK//EEGEE//DOLLS//MADE IN USA,"* later changed to just initials **"E.G."**

**Andy,** 1963, vinyl, teen type, painted molded hair, painted eyes, closed mouth

| | | |
|---|---|---|
| 12" | $9.00 | $35.00 |

**Annette,** 1963, vinyl, teen-type fashion doll, rooted hair, painted eyes

| | | |
|---|---|---|
| 11½" | $15.00 | $55.00 |

Child, 1966, marked *"20/25 M/13"*

| | | |
|---|---|---|
| 19" | $10.00 | $50.00 |

Child, walker, all vinyl, long rooted blonde hair or short curly wig, blue sleep eyes, closed mouth

| | | |
|---|---|---|
| 25" | $15.00 | $50.00 |
| 28" | $20.00 | $65.00 |
| 36" | $25.00 | $85.00 |

**Babette,** 1970, vinyl head, stuffed limbs, cloth body, painted or sleep eyes, rooted hair

| | | |
|---|---|---|
| 15" | $10.00 | $40.00 |
| 25" | $18.00 | $65.00 |

**Baby Care,** 1969, vinyl, molded or rooted hair, sleep or set glassine eyes, drink and wet doll, complete nursery set

| | | |
|---|---|---|
| 18" | $12.00 | $45.00 |

**Baby Carrie,** 1970, rooted or molded hair, sleep or set glassine eyes
With plastic carriage or carry seat

| | | |
|---|---|---|
| 14" | $10.00 | $40.00 |
| 18" | $10.00 | $45.00 |
| 24" | $15.00 | $60.00 |

**Baby Luv,** 1973, vinyl head, rooted hair, painted eyes, open/closed mouth, marked *"B.T. Eegee,"* cloth body, pants are part of body

| | | |
|---|---|---|
| 14" | $10.00 | $35.00 |

**Baby Susan,** 1958, marked *"Baby Susan,"* on head

| | | |
|---|---|---|
| 8½" | $4.00 | $20.00 |

**Baby Tandy Talks,** 1963, pull string activates talking mechanism, vinyl head, rooted hair, sleep eyes, cotton and foam stuffed body and limbs

| | | |
|---|---|---|
| 14" | $10.00 | $35.00 |
| 20" | $20.00 | $65.00 |

**Ballerina,** 1964, vinyl head and hard plastic body

| | | |
|---|---|---|
| 31" | $25.00 | $100.00 |

1967, vinyl head, foam filled body

| | | |
|---|---|---|
| 18" | $8.00 | $30.00 |

**Barbara Cartland,** painted features, adult

| | | |
|---|---|---|
| 15" | $15.00 | $52.00 |

**Boys,** vinyl, molded hair

| | | |
|---|---|---|
| 13" | $9.00 | $35.00 |
| 21" | $15.00 | $55.00 |

**Composition Baby,** cloth body, bent limbs

| | | |
|---|---|---|
| 16" | $25.00 | $100.00 |

**Composition Child,** open mouth, sleep eyes

| | | |
|---|---|---|
| 14" | $40.00 | $160.00 |
| 18" | $55.00 | $210.00 |

*Clampett family in the Beverly Hillbillies car from 1960s TV sitcom, $350.00. Courtesy Cathie Clark.*

*Celebrity vinyl ventriloquist doll by Juron, a division of Goldberger Doll Mfg. Co. Eegee Co., ca. 1980, stuffed cloth body, $200.00. Courtesy Cathie Clark.*

**Composition MaMa Doll,** ca. 1920s – 30s, composition head, sleep or painted eyes, wigged or molded hair, cloth body with crier, swing legs, compo lower arms and legs

| | | |
|---|---|---|
| 16" | $75.00 | $250.00 |
| 20" | $100.00 | $350.00 |

**Flowerkins,** 1963, hard plastic and vinyl, marked "F-2," on head, seven dolls in series

| boxed | 16" | $15.00 | $60.00 |
|---|---|---|---|

**Gemmette,** 1963, rooted hair, sleep eyes, jointed vinyl, dressed in gem colored dress, includes child's jeweled ring, Misses Amethyst, Diamond, Emerald, Ruby, Sapphire, and Topaz

| 15½" | $15.00 | $50.00 |
|---|---|---|

**Georgie and Georgette,** 1971, vinyl head, cloth bodied redheaded twins

| 22" | $12.00 | $50.00 |
|---|---|---|

**Gigi Perreau,** 1951, early vinyl head, hard plastic body, open/closed smiling mouth

| 17" | $175.00 | $700.00 |
|---|---|---|

**Granny,** from TV sitcom, *The Beverly Hillbillies*, gray rooted hair

| 14" | $20.00 | $65.00 |
|---|---|---|

**Karena Ballerina,** 1958, vinyl head, rooted hair, sleep eyes, closed mouth, hard plastic body, jointed knees, ankles, neck, shoulders, and hips, head turns when walks

| 21" | $12.00 | $45.00 |
|---|---|---|

**Little Debutantes,** 1958, vinyl head, rooted hair, sleep eyes, closed mouth, hard plastic body, swivel waists, high-heeled feet

| 18" | $15.00 | $50.00 |
|---|---|---|
| 20" | $20.00 | $75.00 |

**Miss Charming,** 1936, all composition, Shirley Temple look-alike

| 19" | $125.00 | $450.00 |
|---|---|---|
| Pin back button | $50.00 | |

**My Fair Lady,** 1958, all vinyl, fashion type, swivel waist, fully jointed

| | | |
|---|---|---|
| 20" | $15.00 | $75.00 |

**Parton, Dolly,** 1980

| | | |
|---|---|---|
| 12" | $5.00 | $20.00 |
| 18" | $12.00 | $45.00 |

**Posi Playmate,** 1969, vinyl head, foam filled vinyl body, bendable arms and legs, painted or rooted hair, sleep or painted eyes

| | | |
|---|---|---|
| 12" | $5.00 | $20.00 |

**Puppetrina,** 1963+, vinyl head, cloth body, rooted hair, sleep eyes, pocket in back for child to insert hand to manipulate doll's head and arms

| | | |
|---|---|---|
| 22" | $8.00 | $35.00 |

**Shelly,** 1964, Tammy-type, grow hair

| | | |
|---|---|---|
| 12" | $5.00 | $18.00 |

**Sniffles,** 1963, vinyl head, rooted hair, sleep eyes, open/closed mouth
*Mark:"13/14 AA – EEGEE"*

| | | |
|---|---|---|
| 12" | $5.00 | $20.00 |

**Susan Stroller,** ca. 1955, vinyl head and hard plastic walker body, rooted hair, closed mouth

| | | |
|---|---|---|
| 20" | $12.00 | $45.00 |
| 23" | $15.00 | $60.00 |
| 26" | $20.00 | $80.00 |

**Tandy Talks,** 1961, vinyl head, hard plastic body, freckles, pull string talker

| | | |
|---|---|---|
| 20" | $15.00 | $50.00 |

## Effanbee

**Effanbee Doll Company, 1910+, New York, NY.** Bernard E. Fleischaker and Hugo Baum founders, trademark **"EFFANBEE DOLLS//THEY WALK//THEY TALK//THEY SLEEP"** registered in 1918. Made dolls in composition and later hard plastic and vinyl. Currently, the company is owned by Stanley and Irene Wahlberg, who are reintroducing limited edition collectible dolls, such as Patsy Joan, Skippy, Wee Patsy, and others.

First price indicates played with dolls in good condition, but with flaws; second price indicates dolls in excellent condition with original clothes.

*Marks:*
*NRA label, ca. 1934 – 36*
*Gold paper hangtag*

16" composition Mary Lee
with a Patsy body with
Lovums head, $300.00.
Courtesy Vickie Applegate.

21" composition
American Chil-
dren, sleep eyes,
closed mouth,
human hair wig,
original dress,
$750.00. Cour-
tesy Vickie
Applegate.

## COMPOSITION

### American Children, 1936 – 39

All composition, designed by Dewees Cochran, open mouth, separated fingers can wear gloves, unmarked

**Barbara Joan**

| | | |
|---|---|---|
| 15" | $325.00 | $650.00 |

**Barbara Ann**

| | | |
|---|---|---|
| 17" | $375.00 | $750.00 |

**Barbara Lou**

| | | |
|---|---|---|
| 21" | $425.00 | $850.00 |

Closed mouth, marked *"Effanbee//American //Children"* on head "Effanbee//Anne Shirley" on body, sleep or painted eyes.

Boy

| | | |
|---|---|---|
| 17" | $400.00 | $1,600.00 |

Girl

| | | |
|---|---|---|
| 20½" | $350.00 | $1,500.00 |

### Anne Shirley, 1936 – 1940

All composition, marked **"EFFANBEE//ANNE SHIRLEY"** on back of head, more grown up body style, some costumed in fancy formals

| | | |
|---|---|---|
| 14" | $75.00 | $275.00 |
| 18" | $95.00 | $300.00 |
| 21" | $125.00 | $400.00 |
| 27" | $150.00 | $500.00 |

### Movie Anne Shirley, 1935 – 1940

All composition, marked *"Patsy"* or other Effanbee doll, red braids, wearing Anne Shirley movie costume and gold paper hang tag stating "I am Anne Shirley." The costume changes the identity of these dolls

Mary Lee/Anne Shirley, open mouth, head marked "©*Mary Lee*," on marked Patsy Joan body

| | | |
|---|---|---|
| 16" | $250.00 | $500.00 |

Patsyette/Anne Shirley, body marked "*Effanbee//Patsyette// Doll*"

| | | |
|---|---|---|
| 9½" | $150.00 | $325.00 |

Patricia/Anne Shirley, body marked "*Patricia*"

| | | |
|---|---|---|
| 15" | $200.00 | $450.00 |

Patricia-kin/Anne Shirley, head marked "*Patricia-kin,*" body marked "*Effanbee//Patsy Jr.,*" hang tag reads "*Anne Shirley.*"

| | | |
|---|---|---|
| 11½" | $175.00 | $375.00 |

**Baby Dainty, 1912+**

Name given to a variety of dolls, with composition heads, cloth bodies, some toddler types, some mama types with crier. Some marked on shoulder plate, "*Effanbee//Baby Dainty*" or "*Effanbee//Dolls// Walk. Talk. Sleep*" in oval.

| | | |
|---|---|---|
| 12 – 14" | $80.00 | $245.00 |
| 16" | $100.00 | $285.00 |

Vinyl

| | | |
|---|---|---|
| 10" | $10.00 | $40.00 |

**Baby Effanbee, ca. 1925**

Composition head, cloth body

| | | |
|---|---|---|
| 12 – 13" | $45.00 | $165.00 |

**Baby Evelyn, ca. 1925**

Composition head, cloth body

| | | |
|---|---|---|
| 17" | $75.00 | $275.00 |

**Brother or Sister, 1943**

Composition head and hands, cloth body and legs, yarn hair, painted eyes

Brother

| | | |
|---|---|---|
| 16" | $60.00 | $235.00 |

Sister

| | | |
|---|---|---|
| 12" | $45.00 | $175.00 |

**Bubbles, ca. 1924+**

Composition shoulder head, open/closed mouth, painted teeth, painted molded hair, sleep eyes, cloth body, cloth bent legs, some with compo toddler legs, compo arms, finger of left hand fits into mouth, wore heart necklace

*Marks : "Effanbee//Bubbles//Copr. 1924//Made in U.S.A."*

| | | |
|---|---|---|
| 16" | $100.00 | $350.00 |
| 22" | $125.00 | $500.00 |
| 24" | $135.00 | $525.00 |

**Butin-nose, see Patsy family and vinyl**

**Candy Kid, 1946+**

All composition, sleep eyes, toddler body, painted molded hair, closed mouth

| | | |
|---|---|---|
| 13½" | $75.00 | $300.00 |

Black

| | | |
|---|---|---|
| 13½" | $150.00 | $600.00 |

*14" composition Anne Shirley character from Anne of Green Gables movie, ca. 1935+, uses Patricia mold, $600.00. Courtesy McMasters Doll Auctions.*

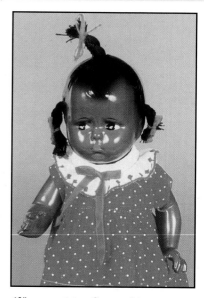

*12" composition Grumpykins, $375.00. Courtesy McMasters Doll Auctions.*

## Charlie McCarthy, 1937

Composition head, hands, feet, painted features, mouth opens, cloth body and legs, marked *"Edgar Bergen's Charlie McCarthy//An Effanbee Product"*

| | | |
|---|---|---|
| 15" | $125.00 | $535.00 |
| 17 – 19" | $175.00 | $750.00 |
| With box , button, mint | | $900.00 |

## Early Composition Characters, 1912+

Composition, heavily molded hair, painted eyes, pin jointed cloth body, compo arms, cloth or compo legs, some marked *"Deco."*

### Baby Bud, 1918+

All composition, painted features, molded hair, open/closed mouth, jointed arms, legs molded to body, one finger goes into mouth

| | | |
|---|---|---|
| 6" | $50.00 | $195.00 |
| Black | $65.00 | $225.00 |

### Baby Grumpy, 1915+

Composition, heavily painted molded hair, frowning eyebrows, painted intaglio eyes, pin jointed limbs, cork stuffed cloth body, gauntlet arms, pouty mouth

Mold #172, 174, 176

| | | |
|---|---|---|
| 11½" | $75.00 | $300.00 |
| 14½" | $85.00 | $350.00 |

Baby Grumpy Gladys, 1923, composition shoulderhead, cloth body. Marked in oval, *"Effanbee//Baby Grumpy// copr. 1923."*

| | | |
|---|---|---|
| 15" | $85.00 | $350.00 |

Grumpy Aunt Dinah

| | | |
|---|---|---|
| 14½" | $100.00 | $400.00 |

Grumpykins, 1927, composition head, cloth body, compo arm, some with cloth legs, others with compo legs

| | | |
|---|---|---|
| 12" | $75.00 | $300.00 |
| Black | $85.00 | $375.00 |

Grumpykins, Pennsylvania Dutch Dolls, ca. 1936, dressed by Marie Pollack in Mennonite, River Brethren, and Amish costumes

| | | |
|---|---|---|
| 12" | $80.00 | $275.00 |

**Coquette, Naughty Marietta,** ca. 1915+

Composition girl, molded bow in hair, side-glancing eyes, cloth body

| | | |
|---|---|---|
| 12" | $85.00 | $325.00 |

**Harmonica Joe,** 1923

Cloth body with rubber ball provides air to open mouth with harmonica

| | | |
|---|---|---|
| 15" | $85.00 | $325.00 |

**Irish Mail Kid, Or Dixie Flyer,** 1915

Compo head, cloth body, arms sewn to steering handle of wooden wagon

| | | |
|---|---|---|
| 10" | $125.00 | $350.00 |

*18" Honey, composition, human hair wig, in original negligee and undies, $325.00. Courtesy Angie Gonzales.*

**Johnny Tu-face,** 1912

Composition head with face on front and back, painted features, open/closed crying mouth, closed smiling mouth, painted molded hair, cloth body, red striped legs, cloth feet, dressed in knitted romper and hat

| | | |
|---|---|---|
| 16" | $150.00 | $325.00 |

**Pouting Bess,** 1915

Composition head with heavily molded curls, painted eyes, closed mouth, cork stuffed cloth body, pin jointed, marked "166" on back of head.

| | | |
|---|---|---|
| 15" | $85.00 | $325.00 |

**Whistling Jim, 1916**

Compo head, with heavily molded hair, painted intaglio eyes, perforated mouth, cork stuffed cloth body, black sewn on cloth shoes, wears red striped shirt, blue overalls with label, reading: **"Effanbee//Whistling Jim//Trade Mark"**

*14" composition 1625 historical with painted eyes, original outfit depicting 1625 style, one of a series of 30 dolls each displaying the fashion of a different era, $500.00. Courtesy Bev Mitchell.*

| | | |
|---|---|---|
| 15" | $85.00 | $325.00 |

**Historical Dolls, 1939+**

All composition, jointed body, human hair wigs, painted eyes, made only three sets of 30 dolls depicting history of apparel, 1492 – 1939, very fancy original costumes, metal heart bracelet. Head marked *"Effanbee//American//children,"* on body, *"Effanbee//Anne Shirley"*

| | | |
|---|---|---|
| 21" | $650.00 | $1,500.00 |

# Effanbee (cont.)

### Historical Replicas, 1939+
All composition, jointed body, copies of sets above, but smaller, human hair wigs, painted eyes, original costumes

| | | |
|---|---|---|
| 14" | $250.00 | $600.00 |

## Honey, ca. 1947 – 1948
All composition jointed body, human hair wig, sleep eyes, closed mouth

| | | |
|---|---|---|
| 18" | $80.00 | $275.00 |

Honey, all hard plastic, ca. 1949 – 55, see Vinyl and Hard Plastic later in this category

## Howdy-Doody, 1949+
Composition swivel head, hands, cloth body, painted molded red hair, brown tin sleep eyes, blushed cheeks, freckles, painted open mouth with teeth and tongue, red and white gingham shirt, navy pants, gray felt cowboy hat, blue bandana, gold letters

| | | |
|---|---|---|
| 19" | $45.00 | $250.00, pull string opens mouth |

### Puppet on string
Composition head and limbs

| | | |
|---|---|---|
| 20" | $50.00 | $225.00 |

### Howdy-Doody, 1947 – 49
Composition head, brown sleep eyes, open/closed mouth, painted molded teeth, cloth body, plaid shirt, personalized neck scarf, "HOWDY DOODY," jeans and boots, cowboy hat, Effanbee gold heart paper hang tag reads "I AM AN//EFFANBEE//DURABLE DOLL//THE DOLL//SATIN – SMOOTH//SKIN"

| | | |
|---|---|---|
| 20" | $65.00 | $275.00 |
| 23" | $75.00 | $300.00 |

### Howdy-Doody, 1950s, hard plastic head, cloth body

| | | |
|---|---|---|
| 18" | $50.00 | $200.00 |

## Ice Queen, 1937+
Composition, open mouth, skater outfit

| | | |
|---|---|---|
| 17" | $200.00 | $850.00 |

## Lamkins, ca. 1930+
Composition molded head, sleep eyes, open mouth, cloth body with crier, chubby compo legs with feet turned in, fingers curled, molded gold ring on middle finger

| | | |
|---|---|---|
| 16" | $150.00 | $475.00 |

## Little Lady, 1939+
All composition, wigged, sleep eyes, more grown up body, separated fingers, gold paper hang tag, many in formals, as brides, or fancy gowns with matching parasol

| | | |
|---|---|---|
| 14" | $75.00 | $275.00 |
| 18" | $95.00 | $300.00 |
| 21" | $125.00 | $400.00 |
| 27" | $150.00 | $600.00 |

## Lovums, ca. 1928
Composition swivel head, shoulder plate, and limbs, cloth body, sleep eyes, painted molded hair or wigged, can have bent baby legs or toddler legs

| | | |
|---|---|---|
| 16" | $100.00 | $400.00 |
| 20" | $125.00 | $450.00 |

## Mae Starr, ca. 1928

Talking doll, composition shoulder head, cloth body, open mouth, four teeth, with cylinder records, marked: *"Mae//Starr// Doll"*

| | | |
|---|---|---|
| 29" | $200.00 | $750.00 |

## MaMa Dolls, ca. 1921+

Composition shoulder head, painted or sleep eyes, molded hair or wigged, cloth body, swing legs, crier, compo arms and lower legs

| | | |
|---|---|---|
| 18" | $75.00 | $350.00 |
| 24" | $125.00 | $400.00 |

## Marionettes, 1937+

Designed by Virginia Austin, composition, painted eyes

Clippo

| | | |
|---|---|---|
| 15" | $50.00 | $185.00 |

Emily Ann

| | | |
|---|---|---|
| 14" | $40.00 | $160.00 |

Lucifer

| | | |
|---|---|---|
| 15" | $75.00 | $300.00 |

*27" Little Lady with gold heart hang tag, all original in velveteen dress and bolero, human hair wig, blue sleep eyes, $500.00+. Courtesy Vickie Applegate.*

## Mary Jane, ca. 1920

Some with bisque heads, others all composition; bisque head, manufactured by Lenox Potteries, NJ, for Effanbee, sleep eyes, compo body, wooden arms and legs, wears Bluebird pin

| | | |
|---|---|---|
| 20" | $75.00 | $300.00 |

## Merrilee, ca. 1924

Mama doll with compo shoulder head, sleep eyes, open mouth, cloth body, crier, swing legs, marked on shoulder plate, *"Effanbee// Merrilee// Copyr.// Doll"* in oval

| | | |
|---|---|---|
| 24" | $150.00 | $550.00 |
| 27" | $175.00 | $600.00 |

## Pat-o-pat, 1925+

Composition head, painted eyes, cloth body with a mechanism, that when pressed causes hands to clap

| | | |
|---|---|---|
| 13" | $50.00 | $150.00 |
| 15" | $80.00 | $200.00 |

*18" composition Lovums, all original with tagged dress, slip, and bonnet, $425.00.*

## Patsy Family

Composition through 1947, later issued in vinyl and porcelain. Many had gold paper hang tag, and metal bracelet, that read, "Effanbee Durable Dolls." More for black, or special editions.

*7" composition Patsy Tinyette, original pink organdy dress and bonnet, gold paper heart tag, $300.00. Courtesy McMasters Doll Auctions.*

## Babies

Patsy Baby, 1931, painted or sleep eyes, wigged or molded hair, composition baby body, advertised as Babykin, marked on head: *"Effanbee//Patsy Baby,"* on body, *"Effanbee //Patsy// Baby,"* came also with cloth body, in pair, layettes, trunks.

| | | |
|---|---|---|
| 10 – 11" | $125.00 | $325.00 |

Patsy Babyette, 1932, sleep eyes, marked on head *"Effanbee"* on body, *"Effanbee//Patsy //Babyette"*

| | | |
|---|---|---|
| 9" | $100.00 | $300.00 |

Patsy Baby Tinyette, 1934, painted eyes, bent leg composition body, marked on head, *"Effanbee"* on body, *"Effanbee//Baby//Tinyette"*

| | | |
|---|---|---|
| 6½" | $90.00 | $300.00 |

Quints, 1935, set of five Patsy Baby Tinyettes, in original box from F.A.O. Schwarz, with organdy christening gowns and milk glass bottles, all in excellent condition

Set of five

| | | |
|---|---|---|
| 6½" | $450.00 | $1,750.00 |

## Children

Patsy, ca. 1924, cloth body, open mouth, upper teeth, sleep eyes, painted or human hair wig, compo legs to hips, marked in half oval on back shoulder plate, *"Effanbee//Patsy."*

| | | |
|---|---|---|
| 15" | $100.00 | $300.00 |

Patsy, ca. 1926, mama doll, open mouth, upper teeth, sleep eyes, human hair wig, cloth body with crier and swing legs, compo arms and lower legs. Marked on shoulder plate in oval: *"Effanbee//Patsy//Copr.// Doll"*

| | | |
|---|---|---|
| 22" | $100.00 | $400.00 |
| 29" | $150.00 | $550.00 |

Patsy, 1928, all composition jointed body, painted or sleep eyes, molded headband on red molded bobbed hair, or wigged, bent right arm, gold paper hang tag, metal heart bracelet marked on body: *"Effanbee//Patsy //Pat.Pend.//Doll."*

| | | |
|---|---|---|
| 14" | $175.00 | $500.00 |

Patsy, with Oriental black painted hair, painted eyes, in fancy silk pajamas, and matching shoes

| | | |
|---|---|---|
| 14" | $350.00 | $750.00 |

Patsy, 1946, all composition jointed body, bright facial coloring, painted or sleep eyes, wears pink or blue checked pinafore

| | | |
|---|---|---|
| 14" | $125.00 | $400.00 |

Patsy Alice, ca. 1933, advertised in Effanbee's "Patsytown News" for two years, no doll with this name has been positively identified

| | | |
|---|---|---|
| 24" | $400.00 | $1,200.00 |

\* *too few examples in database to give reliable range*

*13½" composition Patsy, ca. 1946, $400.00. Courtesy McMasters Doll Auctions.*

*19" composition Patsy Ann, $1,025,00. Courtesy McMasters Doll Auctions.*

**Patsy Ann**, 1929, all composition, closed mouth, sleep eyes, molded hair or wigged, marked on body: *"Effanbee//Patsy – Ann//©//Pat. #1283558*

 19" $250.00 $550.00

**Patsy Ann,** 1959, all vinyl, fully jointed, rooted saran hair, sleep eyes, freckles across nose, head marked *"Effanbee// Patsy Ann// © 1959,"* body marked *"Effanbee"*

Official Girl Scout

 15" $65.00 $200.00

**Patsy Ann,** 1959, limited edition, vinyl, sleep eyes, marked *"Effanbee//Patsy Ann// © 1959//,"* on head, *"Effanbee"* on body, white organdy dress, pink hair ribbon

 15" $100.00 $285.00

Patsyette, 1931

 9½" $125.00 $400.00

 Black, Dutch, Hawaiian

 $175.00 $500.00+

Patsy Fluff, 1932, all cloth, painted features

 16" $500.00 $1,000.00

 \* *too few examples in database to give a reliable range.*

Patsy Joan, 1931

 16" $200.00 $500.00

Patsy Joan, 1946, marked, *"Effanbee"* on body, with extra "d" added

 17" $175.00 $450.00

Patsy Jr., all composition, advertised as Patsykins, marked on body: *"Effanbee//Patsy Jr.//Doll"*

 11½" $150.00 $400.00

22" composition Patsy Lou, tagged dress, hat, and box, $575.00. Courtesy McMasters Doll Auctions.

Left: 16" composition Patsy Joan, tagged dress, box, $500.00. Right: 11" Suzette, original, $200.00. Courtesy McMasters Doll Auctions.

Patsy Lou, 1930, all composition, molded red hair or wigged, marked: "Effanbee//Patsy Lou" on body

|       |          |          |
|-------|----------|----------|
| 22"   | $250.00  | $575.00  |

Patsy Mae, 1934, shoulder head, sleep eyes, cloth body, crier, swing legs, marked: "Effanbee//Patsy Mae" on head, "Effanbee//Lovums//©//Pat. No. 1283558" on shoulder plate.

|       |          |            |
|-------|----------|------------|
| 29"   | $650.00  | $1,300.00  |

Patsy Ruth, 1934, shoulder head, sleep eyes, cloth body, crier, swing legs, marked: "Effanbee//Patsy Ruth," on head, "Effanbee//Lovums/©(//Pat. No. 1283558" on shoulder plate.

|       |          |            |
|-------|----------|------------|
| 26"   | $550.00  | $1,100.00  |

Patsy Tinyette Toddler, ca. 1935, painted eyes, marked: "Effanbee" on head, "Effanbee//Baby//Tinyette" on body.

|       |          |            |
|-------|----------|------------|
| 7¾"   | $100.00  | $300.00+   |

Wee Patsy, 1935, head molded to body, painted molded shoes and socks, jointed arms and hips, marked on body "Effanbee//Wee Patsy," advertised only as "Fairy Princess"

|                   |          |            |
|-------------------|----------|------------|
| 5¾"               | $150.00  | $375.00    |
| In trousseau box  | $250.00  | $650.00+   |

**Related Items**

Metal Heart Bracelet, reads "Effanbee Durable Dolls," $25.00
(original bracelets can still be ordered from Shirley's Doll House)
Metal Personalized Name Bracelet for Patsy family, $65.00
Patsy Ann, Her Happy Times, ©1935, book by Mona Reed King, $65.00
Patsy For Keeps, © 1932, by Ester Marian Ames, $125.00

## Patricia Series, 1935

All composition, slimmer bodies, sleep eyes, wigged. WWII era Patricias had yarn hair and cloth bodies

*too few examples in database to give reliable range*

**Patricia,** wigged, sleep eyes, marked: *"Effanbee//Patricia"* on body

15"      $225.00      $500.00

**Patricia Ann,** wigged, possibly marked: *"Effanbee Patsy Ann"* on body

19"      $375.00      $750.00

**Patricia Joan,** wigged, possibly marked: *"Effanbee//Patsy Joan"* on body

16"      $325.00      $650.00

**Patricia-Kin,** wigged, marked: *"Patricia-Kin"* on head, *"Effanbee //Patsy Jr."* on body

11½"      $275.00      $450.00

*6" composition Fairy Princess (Wee Patsy), boxed, $600.00. Courtesy Pat Schuda.*

**Patricia Lou,** wigged, possibly marked: *"Effanbee//Patsy Lou"* on body

22"      $300.00      $600.00

**Patricia Ruth,** marked on head: *"Effanbee//Patsy Ruth,"* no marks on composition body

27"      $600.00      $1,200.00

## Patsy Related Dolls, variants

**Betty Bee,** tousel head, 1932, all composition, short tousel wig, sleep eyes, marked on body: *"Effanbee//Patsy Lou"*

22"      $250.00      $400.00

**Betty Bounce,** tousel head, 1932+, all composition, sleep eyes, uses Lovums head on body marked: *"Effanbee// 'Patsy Ann'//©//Pat. #1283558"*

19"      $200.00      $350.00

**Betty Brite,** 1932, all composition, short tousel wig, sleep eyes, some marked: *"Effanbee//Betty Brite"* on body and others marked on head: *"© Mary-Lee"* on body, *"Effanbee Patsy Joan,"* gold hang tag reads, "This is Betty Brite, The lovable Imp with tiltable head and movable limb, an Effanbee doll"

16"      $175.00      $300.00

**Butin-nose,** ca. 1936+, all composition, molded painted hair, features, distinct feature is small nose, usually has regional or special costume

8"      $85.00      $250.00

Cowboy outfit

8"      $95.00      $300.00

Dutch pair, with gold paper hang tags 'reading: "Kit and Kat"

8"      $250.00      $500.00+

*Two 14" composition dolls. Left: Suzanne as atten-*
*dant in pink dress, $225.00. Right: Suzanne as*
*bride, $250.00. Courtesy Dorothy Vaughn.*

*14" composition Skippy in*
*military uniform with gold*
*heart hang tag, magnet in*
*hands holds binoculars,*
*flag, bugle, and other acces-*
*sories, in box, $750.00.*
*Courtesy Sharon Kolibaba.*

Oriental, with layette

| | | |
|---|---|---|
| 8" | $250.00 | $500.00 |

**Mary Ann, 1932,** composition, sleep eyes, wigged, open mouth, marked: *"Mary Ann"* on head, *"Effanbee//Patsy Ann'//©//Pat. #1283558"* on body

| | | |
|---|---|---|
| 19" | $200.00 | $350.00 |

**Mary Lee, 1932,** composition, sleep eyes, wigged, open mouth, marked *"©//Mary Lee"* on head, *"Effanbee//Patsy Joan'"* on body

| | | |
|---|---|---|
| 16½" | $200.00 | $300.00 |

**MiMi, 1927,** all composition, blue painted eyes, prototype of 1928 Patsy, name change indicates a very short production run, marked on body: *"Effanbee//MiMi//Pat.Pend//Doll"*

| | | |
|---|---|---|
| 14" | $250.00 | $600.00 |

**Patsy/Patricia, 1940,** incorporated a Patsy head on a Patricia body, all composition, painted eyes, molded hair, may have magnets in hands to hold accessories, marked on body: *"Effanbee//Patricia'"*

| | | |
|---|---|---|
| 15" | $300.00 | $600.00 |

**Skippy, 1929,** advertised as Patsy's boy friend, composition, painted eyes, blonde painted molded hair, compo or cloth body, with compo molded shoes and legs, marked on head *"Effanbee//Skippy//©//P. L. Crosby,"* on body, *"Effanbee//Patsy//Pat. Pend// Doll"*

| | | |
|---|---|---|
| 14" | $275.00 | $550.00 |

With magnet hands, mint in box  $900.00

**Skippy, 1979**, limited edition, vinyl, wine coat and hat, painted features, marked: "*Effanbee//Limited Edition//( Skippy 1979// Skippy Inc.// © 1979*" and "*Effanbee//Limited Edition//( Skippy 1979//Skippy Inc.// © 1979*"

|      |        |          |
|------|--------|----------|
| 14"  | $75.00 | $225.00  |

**Portrait Dolls, ca. 1940**
All composition, Bo Peep, Ballerina, Bride, Groom, Gibson Girl, Colonial

|      |        |          |
|------|--------|----------|
| 12"  | $65.00 | $250.00  |

**Rosemary, 1926**
Marked: "*EFFANBEE//ROSEMARY//WALK//TALK//SLEEP*" in oval, "*MADE IN US*" below

|      |         |          |
|------|---------|----------|
| 18"  | $100.00 | $300.00  |
| 24"  | $150.00 | $395.00  |

**Suzanne, ca. 1939**
All composition, jointed body, sleep eyes, wigged, closed mouth, may have magnets in hands to hold accessories

|      |        |          |
|------|--------|----------|
| 14"  | $95.00 | $275.00  |

**Suzette, ca. 1940**
All composition, fully jointed, painted side – glancing eyes, closed mouth, wigged

|      |        |          |
|------|--------|----------|
| 11"  | $75.00 | $255.00  |

**Sweetie Pie, 1939+**
Also called Baby Bright Eyes, Tommy Tucker, and Mickey, composition bent limbs, sleep eyes, caracul wig, cloth body, crier. Issued again in 1952+ in hard plastic, cloth body, vinyl limbs, painted hair or synthetic wigs. Wore same pink rayon taffeta dress with black and white trim as Noma doll.

|      |         |          |
|------|---------|----------|
| 16"  | $75.00  | $300.00  |
| 19"  | $85.00  | $350.00  |
| 22"  | $100.00 | $400.00  |

## Rubber

**Dy-Dee, 1934+**
Hard rubber head, sleep eyes, jointed bent leg rubber body, drink/wet mechanism, painted molded hair. Early dolls had molded ears, after 1940 had applied rubber ears, nostrils, and tear ducts. Marked: "*Effanbee//Dy-Dee Baby*" with four patent numbers. Later made in hard plastic and vinyl

**Dy-Dee Wee**

|      |         |          |
|------|---------|----------|
| 9"   | $75.00  | $300.00  |

**Dy-Dee-ette, Dy-Dee Ellen**

|      |         |          |
|------|---------|----------|
| 11"  | $50.00  | $200.00  |

**Dy-Dee Kin**

|      |         |          |
|------|---------|----------|
| 13"  | $65.00  | $225.00  |

**Dy-Dee Baby, Dy-Dee Jane**

|      |         |          |
|------|---------|----------|
| 15"  | $75.00  | $275.00  |

**Dy-Dee Lou, Dy-Dee Louise**

|      |         |          |
|------|---------|----------|
| 20"  | $125.00 | $450.00  |

**Dy-Dee** in layette trunk with accessories

|      |         |          |
|------|---------|----------|
| 15"  | $150.00 | $475.00  |

**Dy-Dee Accessories**

| | | |
|---|---|---|
| Dy-Dee marked bottle | $7.50 | $15.00 |
| Dy-Dee pattern pajamas: | $8.00 | $25.00 |

Dy-Dee book, *Dy-Dee Doll's Days*, © 1937, by Peggy Vandegriff, with black and white pictures

| | | |
|---|---|---|
| 5½" by 6¾" | $25.00 | $55.00 |

**VINYL, HARD PLASTIC**

**Alyssa, ca. 1960 – 61,** vinyl head, jointed hard plastic body, including elbows, walker, rooted saran hair, sleep eyes

| | | |
|---|---|---|
| 23" | $90.00 | $225.00 |

**Armstrong, Louis, 1984 – 1985,** vinyl.

| | | |
|---|---|---|
| 15½" | $25.00 | $85.00 |

**Baby Lisa, 1980,** vinyl, designed by Astry Campbell to represent a 3-month-old baby, in wicker basket with accessories

| | | |
|---|---|---|
| 11" | $50.00 | $150.00 |

**Baby Lisa Grows Up, 1983,** vinyl, toddler body, in trunk with wardrobe

| | | |
|---|---|---|
| | $50.00 | $150.00 |

**Button nose, ca. 1968,** vinyl head, cloth body

| | | |
|---|---|---|
| 18" | $9.00 | $35.00 |

**Champagne Lady, 1959,** vinyl head and arms, rooted hair, blue sleep eyes, lashes, hard plastic body, from Lawrence Welk's TV show, Miss Revlon-type.

| | | |
|---|---|---|
| 21" | $75.00 | $275.00 |
| 23" | $85.00 | $300.00 |

**Churchill, Sir Winston, 1984,** vinyl

| | |
|---|---|
| $20.00 | $75.00 |

**Currier & Ives,** vinyl and hard plastic

| | | |
|---|---|---|
| 12" | $12.00 | $45.00 |

**Disney dolls, 1977 – 78**

Snow White, Cinderella, Alice in Wonderland, and Sleeping Beauty

| | | |
|---|---|---|
| 14" | $45.00 | $185.00 |
| 16½" | $85.00 | $325.00 |

**Fields, W. C., 1929+,** composition shoulder head, painted features, hinged mouth, painted teeth, marked: *"W.C. Fields//An Effanbee Product."* In 1980 made in vinyl as Legend Series.

| | | |
|---|---|---|
| 17½" | $250.00 | $950.00 |
| 1980 | | |
| 22" | $85.00 | $250.00 |

**Fluffy, 1954+,** all vinyl

| | | |
|---|---|---|
| 10" | $10.00 | $35.00 |

**Black**

| | | |
|---|---|---|
| 10" | $12.00 | $45.00 |

**Girl Scout**

| | | |
|---|---|---|
| 10" | $15.00 | $50.00 |

**Katie, 1957,** molded hair

| | | |
|---|---|---|
| 8½" | $15.00 | $50.00 |

**Gumdrop, 1962+,** vinyl, jointed toddler, sleep eyes, rooted hair.

| | | |
|---|---|---|
| 16" | $9.00 | $35.00 |

**Hagara, Jan,** designer, all vinyl, jointed, rooted hair, painted eyes.

    **Christina,** 1984

        15"      $50.00       $200.00

    **Larry,** 1985

        15"      $25.00       $95.00

    **Laurel,** 1984

        15"      $40.00       $150.00

    **Lesley,** 1985

        15"      $20.00       $85.00

**Half Pint, 1966 – 1983,** all vinyl, rooted hair, sleep eyes, lashes

        11"      $8.00       $30.00

**Happy Boy, 1960,** vinyl, molded teeth and freckles, painted eyes, molded hair

        11"      $10.00       $45.00

**Hibel, Edna,** designer, 1984, all vinyl

    **Flower Girl**

        11"      $40.00       $165.00

    **Contessa**

        11"      $50.00      $185.00

**Honey, 1949 – 1958,** hard plastic, saran wig, sleep eyes, closed mouth, marked on head and back, "Effanbee," had gold paper hang tag that read: *"I am// Honey//An//Effanbee//Sweet//Child."*

    Honey, ca. 1949 – 55, all hard plastic, closed mouth, sleep eyes

        14"      $65.00      $250.00

        18"      $90.00      $350.00

        21"     $115.00      $450.00

        27"     $150.00      $600.00

**Honey Walker, 1952+,** all hard plastic with walking mechanism; **Honey Walker Junior Miss, 1956 – 57,** hard plastic, extra joints at knees and ankles permit her to wear flat or high heel shoes. Add $50.00 for jointed knees and ankles.

        15"      $65.00      $260.00

        18"      $75.00      $300.00

      20 – 21"    $85.00      $350.00

        25"     $100.00      $400.00

**Humpty Dumpty, 1985**

                  $25.00      $75.00

**Legend Series**

    **1980, W.C. Fields**      $70.00      $265.00

    **1981, John Wayne,** soldier    $50.00      $300.00

    **1982, John Wayne,** cowboy   $50.00      $350.00

*27" hard plastic Sweetie Pie, boxed, $115.00. Courtesy McMasters Doll Auctions.*

*14" hard plastic Tintair, $400.00. Courtesy McMasters Doll Auctions.*

| | | |
|---|---|---|
| **1982, Mae West** | $25.00 | $100.00 |
| **1983, Groucho Marx** | $20.00 | $95.00 |
| **1984, Judy Garland, Dorothy** | $20.00 | $90.00 |
| **1985, Lucile Ball** | $17.50 | $85.00 |
| **1986, Liberace** | $17.50 | $95.00 |
| **1987, James Cagney** | $15.00 | $70.00 |

**Lil Sweetie, 1967,** nurser with no lashes or brow

| | | |
|---|---|---|
| 16" | $25.00 | $45.00 |

**Limited Edition Club**

| | | |
|---|---|---|
| **1975, Precious Baby** | $115.00 | $350.00 |
| **1976, Patsy Ann** | $85.00 | $300.00 |
| **1977, Dewees Cochran** | $40.00 | $135.00 |
| **1978, Crowning Glory** | $35.00 | $105.00 |
| **1979, Skippy** | $75.00 | $265.00 |
| **1980, Susan B. Anthony** | $35.00 | $100.00 |
| **1981, Girl with Watering Can** | $25.00 | $90.00 |
| **1982, Princess Diana** | $25.00 | $100.00 |
| **1983, Sherlock Holmes** | $40.00 | $150.00 |
| **1984, Bubbles** | $25.00 | $100.00 |
| **1985, Red Boy** | $25.00 | $85.00 |
| **1986, China head** | $17.50 | $60.00 |
| **1987/88 Porcelain Grumpy** | (2,500) | $125.00 |
| Vinyl Grumpy | | $50.00 |

**Martha and George Washington, 1976 – 1977**, all vinyl, fully jointed, rooted hair, blue eyes, molded lashes

| | | |
|---|---|---|
| 11" pair | $40.00 | $155.00 |

**Mickey, 1956 – 1972,** all vinyl, fully jointed, some with molded hat, painted eyes

| | | |
|---|---|---|
| 10" | $20.00 | $75.00 |

**Miss Chips, 1966 – 1981**, all vinyl, fully jointed, side-glancing sleep eyes, rooted hair

| | | |
|---|---|---|
| 17" | $9.00 | $35.00 |

    **Black**

| | | |
|---|---|---|
| 17" | $12.00 | $45.00 |

**Noma, The Electronic Doll**, ca. 1950, hard plastic, cloth body, vinyl limbs, battery-operated talking doll, pink rayon taffeta dress with black and white check trim

| | | |
|---|---|---|
| 28" | $125.00 | $375.00 |

**Polka Dottie, 1954,** vinyl head, molded pigtails, fabric body, or hard plastic body

| | | |
|---|---|---|
| 21" | $60.00 | $165.00 |

    **Polka Dottie,** vinyl head, latex body

| | | |
|---|---|---|
| 11" | $30.00 | $120.00 |

**Presidents, 1984+**

    **Lincoln**

| | | |
|---|---|---|
| 18" | $15.00 | $75.00 |

    **Washington**

| | | |
|---|---|---|
| 16" | $15.00 | $65.00 |

**Teddy Roosevelt**
      17"       $17.50      $75.00

**F. D. Roosevelt,** 1985
             $15.00      $75.00

**Prince Charming or Cinderella,** Honey, all hard plastic
      16"      $165.00    $425.00

**Pun'kin, 1966 – 1983,** all vinyl, fully jointed toddler, sleep eyes, rooted hair
      11"      $15.00      $30.00

**Rootie Kazootie, 1954,** vinyl head, cloth or hard plastic body, smaller size has latex body
      21"      $60.00     $165.00
      11"      $30.00     $120.00

**Roosevelt, Eleanor, 1985**
      14½"     $15.00      $70.00

**Santa Claus, 1982+,** designed by Faith Wick, "Old Fashioned Nast Santa," No. 7201, vinyl head and hands, stuffed cloth body, painted molded features, marked *"Effanbee//7201 ©//Faith Wick"*
      18"      $25.00      $75.00

**Suzie Sunshine, 1961 – 79,** designed by Eugenia Dukas, all vinyl, fully jointed, rooted hair, sleep eyes, lashes, freckles on nose
      18"      $15.00      $50.00

    **Black**
      18"      $20.00      $70.00

**Sweetie Pie,** 1952, hard plastic
      27"      $65.00     $275.00

**Twain, Mark,** 1984, all vinyl, molded features
      16"      $20.00      $70.00

**Wicket Witch,** 1981 – 1982, designed by Faith Wick, No. 7110, vinyl head, blonde rooted hair, painted features, cloth stuffed body, dressed in black, with apple and basket, head marked: *"Effanbee//Faith Wick//7110 19©c81"*
      18"      $25.00      $75.00

# Ethnic

*10½" ethnic Soviet Union rayon stockinette doll in regional costume, $125.00. Courtesy Amanda Hash.*

*6" small Skookums Indian child with plastic feet, cloth body, wrapped with blanket, side-glancing eyes, $45.00.*

*Three 13" composition dolls — Colleen of Ireland, Sophie of Poland, and Katrika of Holland, $195.00 each. Courtesy Patsy Corrigan.*

This category describes dolls costumed in regional dress to show different nationalities, facial characteristics, or cultural background. An example are dolls in regional costumes that are commonly sold as souvenirs to tourists.

Cloth
| | | |
|---|---|---|
| 7" | $15.00 | $45.00 |
| 13" | $35.00 | $125.00 |

Composition
| | | |
|---|---|---|
| 9" | $25.00 | $100.00 |

Hard Plastic
| | | |
|---|---|---|
| 7" | $4.00 | $15.00 |
| 12" | $7.50 | $30.00 |

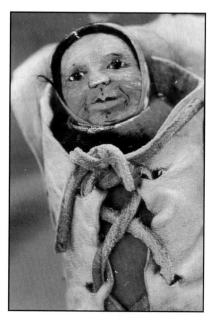

*4½" papoose with plaster-type head, covered with crepe paper, painted and molded features, body wrapped like Skookums in blanket, set in leather cradle, mohair wig, scarf, made ca. 1920s by Mary Frances Wood, $200.00. Courtesy Jean Thompson.*

# Freundlich

**Ralph A. Freundlich, 1923+, New York City.** Formerly Jeanette Doll Co, then Ralph Freundlich, Inc. Made composition dolls, some with molded caps in military uniforms.

*11" Three Little Pigs, all jointed composition, original outfits, painted eyes, $650.00. Courtesy Sherryl Shirran.*

**Baby Sandy, ca. 1939 – 42,** all composition, jointed toddler body, molded hair, painted or sleep eyes, smiling mouth

| | | |
|---|---|---|
| 8" | $50.00 | $200.00 |
| 12" | $75.00 | $300.00 |
| 15" | $100.00 | $400.00 |

**Dummy Dan,** ventriloquist doll, Charlie McCarthy look-alike

| | | |
|---|---|---|
| 15" | $40.00 | $150.00 |
| 21" | $90.00 | $350.00 |

**General Douglas MacArthur,** ca. 1942, all composition, jointed body, bent arm salutes, painted features, molded hat, jointed, in khaki uniform, with paper tag

| | | |
|---|---|---|
| 18" | $85.00 | $350.00 |

**Military dolls, ca. 1942+,** all composition, molded hats, painted features, original clothes, with paper tag.

Soldier, Sailor, WAAC, or WAVE

| | | |
|---|---|---|
| 15" | $65.00 | $250.00 |

**Orphan Annie and her dog, Sandy**

| | | |
|---|---|---|
| 12" | $85.00 | $325.00 |

**Pinocchio,** compo and cloth, with molded hair, painted features, brightly colored cheeks, large eyes, open/closed mouth, tagged, *"Original as portrayed by C. Collodi"*

| | | |
|---|---|---|
| 16" | $125.00 | $500.00 |

**Red Riding Hood, Wolf, Grandma,** set of three, in schoolhouse box, original clothes

| | | |
|---|---|---|
| 9½" | $250.00 | $750.00 |

# Gabriel

*10" long all vinyl Lassie and 8½" all vinyl boy, plus collie pup and basket for Lassie to carry, ca. 1976, $125.00. Courtesy Cathie Clark.*

**The Lone Ranger Series,** vinyl action figures with horses, separate accessory sets available

**Dan Reed on Banjo,** blonde hair, figure on palomino horse
9"    $15.00    $50.00

**Butch Cavendish on Smoke,** black hair, mustache, on black horse
9"    $20.00    $80.00

**Lone Ranger on Silver,** masked figure on white horse
9"    $25.00    $100.00

**Little Bear,** Indian boy
6"    $25.00    $100.00

**Red Sleeves,** vinyl Indian figure, black hair, wears shirt with red sleeves
9"    $25.00    $100.00

**Tonto on Scout,** Indian on brown and white horse
9"    $20.00    $80.00

## Gerber Baby

Advertising doll, tie in with Gerber Baby food.

**1936,** all printed cloth, holds can of baby food and toy dog
8"    $100.00    $375.00

**1954,** rubber doll, made by Sun Rubber Co., mint in box
12"    $65.00    $225.00

**1966,** soft vinyl doll, made by Arrow Industries, lopsided smile
14"    $20.00    $75.00

**1972,** plastic/vinyl doll made by Uneeda Doll Co
10"    $15.00    $45.00

## Gibbs, Ruth

**Flemington, NJ.** Made dolls of china and porcelain heads and limbs, pink cloth bodies. Marked: *"RG"* on back shoulderplate. Box labeled: "Godey Little Lady Dolls." Dolls designed by Herbert Johnson.

Boxed
7"    $47.50    $210.00

Boxed
10½"    $75.00    $255.00

Wigged
10"    $45.00    $175.00

Hard plastic, mint in box, with identification
11"    $200.00

# Gilbert Toys

**The Man From U.N.C.L.E.** characters from TV show of the 1960s. Other outfits available

**Illya Kuryakin** (David McCallum)
    11"    $25.00    $100.00
**Napoleon Solo** (Robert Vaughn)
    11"    $25.00    $100.00
**James Bond, Secret Agent 007,** character from James Bond movies
    11"    $20.00    $75.00

# Girl Scout

**1920+, listed chronologically**
First price for played-with dolls missing accessories; second price is for mint in box.

**1920s Girl Scout doll in Camp Uniform,** ca. 1920s, pictured in Girls Scout 1920 handbook, all cloth, mask face, painted features, wigged, gray green uniform
    13"    $250.00    $600.00+
*too few in database to give reliable range*

**Grace Cory, 1929,** composition shoulder head, cloth body with crier, molded hair, painted features, original uniform, mark on shoulder plate: "*by Grace Cory,*" body stamped "*Madame Hendren Doll//Made in USA*"

*Two 15" cloth Georgene Novelties, Inc., Girl Scout and Brownie, $400.00 each. Courtesy Diane Miller.*

    13"    $350.00    $700.00+
*too few in database to give reliable range*

**Averill Mfg. Co,** ca. **1936,** believed to be designed by Maud Tousey Fangel, all cloth, printed and painted features
    16"    $100.00    $400.00+
*too few in database to give reliable range*

**Georgene Novelties, ca. 1940,** all cloth, flat faced painted features, yellow yarn curls, wears original silver green uniform with red triangle tie., hang tag reads: "*Genuine Georgene Doll//A product of Georgene Novelties, Inc., NY//Made in U.S.A.*"
    15"    $100.00    $400.00

**Georgene Novelties, ca. 1949 – 1954,** all cloth, mask face, painted features and string hair
    13½"    $45.00    $250.00
1954 – 58, same as above, but now has a plastic mask face
    13½"    $35.00    $100.00

**Terrie Lee, 1949 – 1958,** hard plastic, Brownie and Intermediate Scout had felt hats and oilcloth saddle shoes
    16"    $125.00    $450.00

*16" Terri Lee Girl Scout, Brownie, and Blue Bird, hard
plastic, painted eyes, ca. 1946, $350.00 each. Courtesy
Angie Gonzales.*

Tiny Terri Lee, 1956 – 1958, hard plastic, walker, sleep eyes, wig, plastic shoes

   10"   $65.00   $225.00

Ginger, hard plastic, straight leg walker, synthetic wig, made by Cosmopolitan for Terri Lee

   8"   $100.00   $200.00

**Vogue, 1956 – 57+,** Ginny, hard plastic, straight legged walker with sleep eyes and painted eyelashes, in 1957 had bending leg and felt hat.

**Uneeda, 1959 – 61,** Ginny lookalike, vinyl head, hard plastic body, straight leg walker, marked "U" on head. Dynel wig

   8"   $50.00   $150.00

**Effanbee, Patsy Ann, 1959+,** all vinyl, jointed body, saran hair, sleep eyes, freckles on nose, Brownie or Girl Scout

   15"   $95.00   $350.00

**Effanbee Suzette, ca. 1960,** jointed vinyl body, sleep eyes, Saran hair, thin body, long legs

   15"   $95.00   $350.00

**Effanbee Fluffy, 1964 – 72,** vinyl dolls, sleep eyes, curly rooted hair, Brownie had blonde wig, Junior was brunette, box had clear acetate lid, printed with Girl Scout trademark, and catalog number

   8"   $65.00   $175.00

**Effanbee Fluffy Cadette, 1965**

   11"   $75.00   $300.00

**Effanbee Pun'kin Jr., 1974 – 79+,** all vinyl, sleep eyes, long straight rooted hair, Brownie and Junior uniforms

11.5"    $25.00    $75.00

**Hallmark, 1979,** all cloth, Juliette Low, from 1916 handbook, wearing printed 1923 uniform

6.5"    $25.00    $65.00

**Jesco, ca. 1985,** Katie, all vinyl, sleep eyes, long straight rooted hair, look-alike Girl Scout, dressed as Brownie, and Junior

9"    $25.00    $75.00

**Madame Alexander, 1992,** vinyl, unofficial Girl Scout, sleep eyes

8"    $15.00    $60.00

## Hard Plastic

*All hard plastic walker, 1953, unknown maker, saran wig, camera around neck; this is a celebrity doll named after Roxanne, who appeared on the TV game show, Beat the Clock, $350.00. Courtesy Cathie Clark.*

*14" hard plastic, marked "U.S.A.," all original with tagged coat and hat, $250.00. Courtesy Matrix.*

Numerous companies made hard plastic dolls, ca. 1948 through the 1950s; doll have all hard plastic jointed body, sleep eyes, lashes, synthetic wig, open or closed mouth. *Marks:* none, letters, little known, or other unidentified companies.

14"    $65.00    $250.00
18"    $75.00    $300.00
24"    $85.00    $325.00

**Miss Curity,** ca. 1953, by Kendall Company, hard plastic, jointed only at shoulders, blonde wigs, blue sleep eyes, molded on shoes, painted stockings, uniform sheet vinyl, Miss Curity marked in blue on hat

7½"    $20.00    $75.00

## Hartland Industries

**1950s+,** made action figures and horses, many figures from Warner Brothers television productions.

James Arness, 1955 – 75, as Matt Dillon on *Gunsmoke*

# Hartland Industries (cont.)

James Garner, as Bret Maverick on *Maverick*
John Lupton, 1956 – 1960, as John Jeffords on *Broken Arrow*
Gail Davis, 1953 – 1956, as Annie Oakley on *Annie Oakley*
Hugh O'Brien, 1955 – 1961, as Wyatt Earp on *Life & Legend of Wyatt Earp*
Dale Robertson, 1957 – 1962, as Jim Hardie on *Tales of Wells Fargo*
Pat Conway, 1957 – 59, as Clay Hollister on *Tombstone Territory*
Wayde Preston, 1957 – 1960, as Captain Chris Colt on *Colt 45*
Richard Boone, 1957 – 1963, as Paladin on *Have Gun, Will Travel*
John Payne, 1957 – 1959, as Clint Bonner on *The Restless Gun*
Clint Walker, 1955 – 1963, as Cheyenne Bodie on *Cheyenne*
Ward Bond, as Major Seth Adams on *Wagon Train*
**Other figures:**
Brave Eagle and his horse, White Cloud
Buffalo Bill and horse
Chief Thunderbird and his horse Northwind
Cochise with pinto horse
Dale Evans with her horse, Buttermilk
General George Custer and his horse, Bugler
General George Washington and his horse, Ajax
Jim Bowie with his horse, Blaze
Lone Ranger with his horse, Silver
Robert E. Lee with his horse, Traveler
Sgt. Preston of the Yukon with his horse
Tonto with his horse, Scout
Figure and horse in box, with accessories

|  | | |
|---|---|---|
|  | $125.00 | $500.00 |
| Figure alone: | $35.00 | $125.00 |
| Horse alone | $45.00 | $175.00 |

**Baseball Figures**
Ed Mathews
Hank Aaron
George "Babe" Ruth
Mickey Mantle
Stan Musial
Ted Williams

| | | |
|---|---|---|
| Figure alone | $85.00 | $325.00 |

# Hasbro

**Ca. 1960s+,** Hassenfeld Bros. toy manufacturer, also makes plastic or plastic and vinyl dolls and action figures.

First price for dolls in played with condition, or missing some accessories; second price for mint dolls.

**Adam, 1971,** boy for "World of Love" Series, all vinyl, painted molded brown hair, painted blue eyes, *Mark: "Hasbro//U.S. Pat Pend//Made in//Hong Kong,"* red knit shirt, blue denim jeans

| | | |
|---|---|---|
| 9" | $5.00 | $18.00 |

**Aimee, 1972,** rooted hair, amber sleep eyes, jointed vinyl body, long dress, sandals, earrings

| | | |
|---|---|---|
| 16" | $12.50 | $50.00 |

**Charlie's Angels, 1977,** Jill, Kelly, or Sabrina, each
       8½"      $5.00      $20.00

**Defender, 1974,** one piece arms and legs
       11½"    $25.00      $85.00

**Dolly Darling, 1965**
       4½"      $3.00      $10.00

**Flying Nun, 1965,** plastic and vinyl
       5"      $9.00      $35.00

**G.I. Joe, see G.I. Joe section, following in this category**
**Jem, see Jem section, following in this category**
**Leggie, 1972**
       10"     $7.50      $30.00
  Black
       $10.00      $40.00

**Little Miss No Name, 1965**
       15"    $25.00      $95.00

**Mamas and Papas, 1967**
             $12.00      $45.00

Show Biz Babies, 1967
             $12.00      $50.00

Mama Cass
             $15.00      $50.00

**Monkees,** set of four
       4"    $28.00    $110.00

**Storybook, 1967, 3"**
  Goldilocks       $12.50      $50.00
  Prince Charming   $15.00      $60.00
  Rumplestilkin     $15.00      $55.00
  Sleeping Beauty    $12.50      $50.00
  Snow White and Dwarfs
             $20.00      $75.00

**Sweet Cookie, 1972**
       18"      $8.00      $35.00

**That Kid, 1967**
       21"    $22.50      $95.00

**World of Love Dolls, 1971**
  White
       9"      $5.00      $18.00
  Black
       9"      $5.00      $20.00

## G.I. JOE ACTION FIGURES
## 1964 – 1966

**1964,** marked on right lower back: "*G.I. Joe ™//Copyright 1964// By Hasbro ®//Patent Pending//Made in U.S.A.*" **1965,** slight change in marking: "*G.I. Joe ®//Copyright 1964//By Hasbro ®//Patent Pending//Made in U.S.A.*" This mark appears on all four armed service branches, excluding the black action figures. Hard plastic head with facial scar, painted hair and no beard.

*G.I. Joe, action soldier, $150.00.*
*Courtesy Cathie Clark.*

First price indicates complete dolls, no package; second price indicates mint dolls package. Add more for pristine package.

**G.I. Joe Action Soldier,** flocked hair
$120.00     $450.00

**G.I. Joe Action Soldier,** painted hair, fatigues, brown jump boots, green plastic cap, training manual, metal dog tag, two sheets of stickers
$100.00     $150.00

**G.I. Joe Action Soldier,** painted black hair
$325.00   $1,300.00

**G.I. Joe Action Soldier, Green Beret,** teal green fatigue jacket with four pockets, pants, Green Beret cap w/red unit flashing, M-16 rifle, 45 automatic pistol with holster, tall brown boots, four grenades, camouflage scarf, field communication set
$275.00          $1,500.00

**G.I. Joe Action Marine,** camouflage shirt, pants, brown boots, green plastic cap, metal dog tag, insignia stickers, and training manual
$80.00          $275.00

**G.I. Joe Action Sailor,** blue chambray work shirt, blue denim work pants, black boots, white plastic sailor cap, dog tag, rank insignia stickers
$75.00          $250.00

**G.I. Joe Action Pilot,** orange flight suit, black boots, dog tag, stickers, blue cap, training manual
$125.00          $300.00
Dolls only          $50.00          $95.00

**G.I. Joe Action Soldier of the World,** 1966, figures in this set may have any hair and eye color combination, no scar on face, hard plastic heads, same marks as 1965

Australian Jungle Fighter, boxed
$255.00          $1,050.00
British Commando, boxed
$300.00          $1,150.00
French Resistance Fighter, boxed
$280.00          $1,200.00
German Storm Trooper, boxed
$400.00          $1,200.00
Japanese Imperial Soldier, boxed
$500.00          $1,400.00
Russian Infantryman, boxed
$350.00          $1,100.00
Doll only          $50.00          $200.00

**Talking G.I. Joe, 1967 – 69,** *Marks: "G.I. Joe ®//Copyright 1964//By Hasbro®// Pat. No. 3,277,602//Made in U.S.A.,"* talking mechanism added, excluding black figure, semi-hard vinyl head

**Talking G.I. Joe Action Soldier**, green fatigues, dog tag, brown boots, insignia, stripes, green plastic fatigue cap, comic book, insert with examples of figures speech

$150.00 $300.00

**Talking G.I. Joe Action Sailor**, denim pants, chambray sailor shirt, dog tag, black boots, white sailor cap, insignia stickers, Navy training manual, illustrated talking comic book, insert examples of figures speech

$200.00 $1,000.00

**Talking G.I. Joe Action Marine**, camouflage fatigues, metal dog tag, Marine training manual, insignia sheets, brown boots, green plastic cap, comic, and insert

$60.00 $800.00

**Talking G.I. Joe Action Pilot**, blue flight suit, black boots, dog tag, Air Force insignia, blue cap, training manual, comic book, insert

$150.00 $1,000.00

**G.I. Joe Action Nurse, 1967**, vinyl head, blonde rooted hair, jointed hard plastic body, nurse's uniform, cap, red cross armband, white shoes, medical bag, stethoscope, plasma bottle, two crutches, bandages, splints, *Marks: "Patent Pending ®//1967 Hasbro//Made in Hong Kong"*

| | | |
|---|---|---|
| Boxed | $1,200.00 | $1,850.00 |
| Dressed | $200.00 | $800.00 |
| Nude | $40.00 | $150.00 |

**G.I. Joe, Man of Action**, 1970 – 75, marks: *"G.I. Joe ®//Copyright 1964//By Hasbro®// Pat. No. 3, 277, 602//Made in U.S. A.,"* flocked hair, scar on face, dressed in fatigues with Adventure Team emblem on shirt, plastic cap

| | | |
|---|---|---|
| | $15.00 | $60.00 |
| Talking | $45.00 | $175.00 |

**G.I. Joe, Adventure Team**

*Marks: "®1975 Hasbro®//Pat. Pend. Pawt. R.I.,"* flocked hair and beard, six team members:

**Air Adventurer,** orange flight suit

$75.00 $285.00

**Astronaut,** talking, white flight suit

$115.00 $450.00

**Land Adventurer,** black, tan fatigues, no beard

$90.00 $350.00

**Land Adventurer,** talking, camouflage fatigues,

$115.00 $450.00

**Sea Adventurer,** light blue shirt, navy pants

$70.00 $265.00

**Talking Adventure Team Commander,** flocked hair and beard, green jacket and pants

$115.00 $450.00

**G.I. Joe Land Adventurer,** flocked hair and beard, camouflage shirt, green pants

$70.00 150.00

**G. I. Joe Negro Adventurer,** flocked hair

$110.00 $170.00

# Hasbro (cont.)

| | | |
|---|---|---|
| G. I. Joe, "Mike Powers, Atomic Man" | $25.00 | $55.00 |
| G.I. Joe Eagle Eye Man of Action | $40.00 | $125.00 |
| G.I. Joe Secret Agent, unusual face, mustache | $115.00 | $450.00 |
| Sea Adventurer w/King Fu Grip | $80.00 | $145.00 |
| Bulletman, muscle body, silver arms and hands, silver helmet, red boots | | |
| | $55.00 | $125.00 |

**Accessory Sets, mint, no doll**
**Adventures of G.I. Joe:**

| | |
|---|---|
| The Adventure of the Perilous Rescue | $250.00 |
| The Eight Ropes of Danger Adventure | $200.00 |
| The Fantastic Free Fall Adventure | $275.00 |
| The Hidden Missile Discovery Adventure | $150.00 |
| The Mouth of Doom Adventure | $150.00 |
| The Adventure of the Shark's Surprise | $200.00 |
| The Adventure of the Perilous Rescue | $250.00 |

**Accessory Packs or Boxed Uniforms and accessories**

| | |
|---|---|
| Air Force, Annapolis, West Point Cadet | $200.00 |
| Action Sailor | $350.00 |
| Astronaut | $250.00 |
| Crash Crew Fire Fighter | $275.00 |
| Deep Freeze with Sled | $250.00 |
| Deep Sea Diver | $250.00 |
| Frogman Demolition Set | $375.00 |
| Green Beret | $450.00 |
| Landing Signal Officer | $250.00 |
| Marine Dress Parade | $225.00 |
| Marine Jungle Fighter | $850.00 |
| Marine Mine Detector | $275.00 |
| Military Police | $325.00 |
| Pilot Scramble Set | $275.00 |
| Rescue Diver | $350.00 |
| Secret Agent | $150.00 |
| Shore Patrol | $300.00 |
| Ski Patrol | $350.00 |

**Vehicles, Other Accessories**
**Mint in package**

| | |
|---|---|
| Amphibious Duck, green plastic, by Irwin | $600.00 |
| Armored Car, green plastic, 1 figure | $150.00 |
| Crash Crew Fire Truck, blue, pumps water | $1,400.00 |
| Desert Patrol Attack Jeep, tan, 1 figure | $1,400.00 |
| Footlocker | $55.00 |
| Iron Knight Tank, green plastic | $1,400.00 |
| Jet Aeroplane, dark blue plastic | $550.00 |
| Jet Helicopter, dark green, yellow blades | $350.00 |
| Motorcycle & Side Car, by Irwin | $225.00 |
| Personnel Carrier & Mine Sweeper | $700.00 |
| Sea Sled & Frogman | $300.00 |
| Space Capsule & Suit, gray plastic | $425.00 |
| Staff Car, four figures, green plastic, by Irwin | $900.00 |

*Left: Flash 'n Sizzle Jem wearing Command Performance of the On Stage Fashions, $40.00. Right: Jem/Jerrica (first issue Jem) wearing Only the Beginning of the On Stage Fashions, one of the easiest outfits to find, $20.00. Courtesy Linda Holton.*

*Glitter 'n Gold Jem wearing Star Struck Guitar of the Music is Magic Fashion, $50.00. Courtesy Linda Holton.*

## JEM, 1986 – 1987

Jem dolls were patterned after characters in the animated television series Jem, ca. 1985 – 88, and include a line of 27 dolls. All vinyl, fashion type, with realistic proportioned body, jointed elbows, wrists, and knees, swivel waist, rooted hair, painted eyes, open or closed mouth, and hole in bottom of each foot. *Marks:* On head, *"HASBRO, Inc,"* on back, *"COPY-RIGHT 1985 (or 1986 or 1987) HASBRO, INC,"* followed by either *"CHINA"* or *"MADE IN HONG KONG."* Not all are marked on head. All boxes say "Jem" and "Truly Outrageous!" Most came with cassette tape of music from Jem cartoon, plastic doll stand, poster, and hair pic. All 12½" tall, except Starlight Girls, 11".

First price is for excellent to near mint dolls wearing complete original outfit; anything less is of lower value. Second price is for never removed from box dolls (NRFB) which includes an excellent quality box. For an "Audition Contest" labeled box, add $10.00. A rule of thumb to calculate loose dolls which have been dressed in another outfit is the price of the mint/complete outfit plus the price of mint loose nude doll.

| Jem & Rio | Stock No. | Mint | NRFB |
|---|---|---|---|
| Jem/Jerrica first issue | 4000 | $20.00 | $30.00 |
| Jem/Jerrica, star earrings | 4000 | $25.00 | $35.00 |

# Hasbro (cont.)

| | | | |
|---|---|---|---|
| Glitter 'n Gold Jem | 4001 | $50.00 | $75.00 |
| Rock 'n Curl Jem | 4002 | $15.00 | $25.00 |
| Flash 'n Sizzle Jem | 4003 | $20.00 | $35.00 |
| Rio, first issue | 4015 | $20.00 | $30.00 |
| Glitter 'n Gold Rio | 4016 | $20.00 | $25.00 |
| Glitter 'n Gold Rio, pale vinyl | | | |
| | 4016 | $50.00 | $75.00 |
| **Holograms** | | | |
| Synergy | 4020 | $30.00 | $45.00 |
| Aja | | | |
| first issue | 4201/4005 | $30.00 | $60.00 |
| second issue | 4201/4005 | $75.00 | $100.00 |
| Kimber | | | |
| first issue | 4202/4005 | $20.00 | $45.00 |
| second issue | 4202/4005 | $35.00 | $75.00 |
| Shana | | | |
| first issue | 4203/4005 | $100.00 | $175.00 |
| second issue | 4203/4005 | $150.00 | $250.00 |
| Danse | 4208 | $30.00 | $45.00 |
| Video | 4209 | $20.00 | $30.00 |
| Raya | 4210 | $60.00 | $100.00 |
| **Starlight Girls,** 11", no wrist or elbow joints | | | |
| Ashley | 4211/4025 | $25.00 | $35.00 |
| Krissie | 4212/4025 | $35.00 | $50.00 |
| Banee | 4213/4025 | $20.00 | $25.00 |
| **Misfits** | | | |
| Pizzazz | | | |
| first issue | 4204/4010 | $40.00 | $75.00 |
| second issue | 4204/4010 | $40.00 | $75.00 |
| Stormer | | | |
| first issue | 4205/4010 | $35.00 | $45.00 |
| second issue | 4205/4010 | $35.00 | $45.00 |
| Roxy | | | |
| first issue | 4206/4010 | $35.00 | $45.00 |
| second issue | 4206/4010 | $40.00 | $50.00 |
| Clash | 4207/4010 | $15.00 | $25.00 |
| Jetta | 4214 | $30.00 | $45.00 |

**Jem Fashions**

Prices reflect NRFB, never removed from box or card, with excellent packaging. Damaged boxes or mint and complete prices are approximately 25% less

| On Stage Fashions, first year, "artwork" on card | | |
|---|---|---|
| Award Night | 4216/4040 | $25.00 |
| Music is Magic | 4217/4040 | $25.00 |
| Dancin' the Night Away | 4218/4040 | $20.00 |
| Permanent Wave | 4219/4040 | $20.00 |
| Only the Beginning | 4220/4040 | $20.00 |
| Command Performance | 4221/4040 | $35.00 |

| | | |
|---|---|---|
| Twilight in Paris | 4222/4040 | $30.00 |
| Encore | 4223/4040 | $25.00 |

**On Stage Fashions,** second year, "photo" on card

| | | |
|---|---|---|
| Award Night | 4216/4040 | $30.00 |
| Music is Magic | 4217/4040 | $30.00 |
| Permanent Wave | 4219/4040 | $25.00 |
| Encore | 4223/4040 | $30.00 |
| Friend or Stranger | 4224/4040 | $40.00 |
| Come On In | 4225/4040 | $40.00 |
| There's Melody Playing | 4226/4040 | $75.00 |
| How You Play Game | 4227/4040 | $25.00 |
| Love's Not Easy | 4228/4040 | $50.00 |
| Set Your Sails | 4229/4040 | $25.00 |

**Flip Side Fashions,** first year, "artwork" on box

| | | |
|---|---|---|
| Up & Rockin' | 4232/4045 | $25.00 |
| Rock Country | 4233/4045 | $30.00 |
| Gettin' Down to Business | 4234/4045 | $25.00 |
| Let's Rock this Town | 4235/4045 | $25.00 |
| Music in the Air | 4236/4045 | $25.00 |
| Like a Dream | 4237/4045 | $25.00 |
| Sophisticated Lady | 4238/4045 | $20.00 |
| City Lights | 3129/4045 | $25.00 |

**Flip Side Fashions,** second year, "photo" on box

| | | |
|---|---|---|
| Gettin' Down to Business | 4234/4045 | $30.00 |
| Let's Rock This Town | 4235/4045 | $30.00 |
| Music in the Air | 4236/4045 | $30.00 |
| Sophisticated Lady | 4238/4045 | $25.00 |
| Putting it All Together | 4240/4045 | $50.00 |
| Running Like the Wind | 4241/4045 | $100.00 |
| We Can Change It | 4242/4045 | $75.00 |
| Broadway Magic | 4243/4045 | $60.00 |
| She Makes an Impression | 4244/4045 | $50.00 |
| Lightnin' Strikes | 4245/4045 | $30.00 |

**Smashin' Fashions,** first year, "artwork" on card (includes Rio fashions)

| | | |
|---|---|---|
| Rappin' | 4248/4051 | $30.00 |
| On the Road with Jem | 4249/4051 | $30.00 |
| Truly Outrageous | 4250/4051 | $75.00 |
| Makin' Mischief | 4251/4050 | $25.00 |
| Let the Music Play | 4252/4050 | $25.00 |
| Outta My Way | 4253/4050 | $15.00 |
| Just Misbehavin' | 4254/4050 | $50.00 |
| Winning is Everything | 4255/4050 | $20.00 |

**Smashin' Fashions,** second year, "photo" on card (Misfits fashions only)

| | | |
|---|---|---|
| Let the Music Play | 4252/4050 | $30.00 |
| Just Misbehavin' | 4254/4050 | $60.00 |
| Gimme, Gimme, Gimme | 4256/4050 | $30.00 |

| | | |
|---|---|---|
| You Can't Catch Me | 4257/4050 | $35.00 |
| We're Off & Running | 4258/4050 | $30.00 |
| You Gotta' Be Fast | 4259/4050 | $25.00 |
| There Ain't Nobody Better | 4260/4050 | $40.00 |
| Designing Woman | 4261/4050 | $35.00 |

**Rio Fashion,** second year only, "photo" on card

| | | |
|---|---|---|
| Rappin' | 4248/4051 | $35.00 |
| On the Road with Jem | 4249/4051 | $35.00 |
| Truly Outrageous | 4250/4051 | $75.00 |
| Time is Running Out | 4271/4051 | $20.00 |
| Share a Little Bit | 4272/4051 | $75.00 |
| Congratulations | 4273/4051 | $20.00 |
| Universal Appeal | 4274/4051 | $20.00 |
| It Takes a Lot | 4275/4051 | $20.00 |
| It all Depends on Mood | 4276/4051 | $15.00 |

**Glitter 'n Gold Fashions,** second year only, "photo" on boxes

| | | |
|---|---|---|
| Fire and Ice | 4281/4055 | $45.00 |
| Purple Haze | 4282/4055 | $30.00 |
| Midnight Magic | 4283/4055 | $25.00 |
| Gold Rush | 4284/4055 | $45.00 |
| Moroccan Magic | 4285/4055 | $50.00 |
| Golden Days/Diamond Nights | | |
| | 4286/4055 | $45.00 |

**Music is Magic Fashion,** second year, only, "photo" on boxes

| | | |
|---|---|---|
| Rock'n Roses | 4296/4060 | $35.00 |
| Splashes of Sound | 4297/4060 | $25.00 |
| 24 Carat Sound | 4298/4060 | $25.00 |
| Star Struck Guitar | 4299/4060 | $50.00 |
| Electric Chords | 4300/4060 | $25.00 |
| Rhythm & Flash | 4301/4060 | $30.00 |

## Horsman, E.I.

1865 – 1980+, New York City. Founded by Edward Imeson Horsman, distributed, assembled, and made dolls, merged with Aetna Doll and Toy Co., and in 1909 obtained first copyright for a complete doll with his Billiken. Later made hard plastic and vinyl dolls.
*Marks: "E.I. H. //CO." and "CAN'T BREAK 'EM"*

### COMPOSITION

First price is for played-with dolls, or missing some clothing or accessories; second price is for dolls in excellent condition with original clothing and tags.

**Baby Bumps, 1910 – 17**

Composition head, cloth cork stuffed body, blue and white cloth label on romper, copy of K*R #100 Baby mold

| | | |
|---|---|---|
| 11" | $65.00 | $250.00 |
| Black | $75.00 | $300.00 |

**Baby Butterfly, ca. 1914**

Oriental baby, composition head and hands, painted features

| | | |
|---|---|---|
| 12" | $65.00 | $375.00 |

**Betty**
Composition, see also Hard Plastic and Vinyl
    16"    $65.00    $250.00

**Betty Ann**
All composition, see also Hard Plastic and Vinyl
    19"    $90.00    $365.00

**Betty Jane**
All composition, see also Hard Plastic and Vinyl
    25"    $100.00    $400.00

**Betty Jo**
All composition, see also Hard Plastic and Vinyl
    16"    $70.00    $265.00

**Billiken, 1909**
Composition head, molded hair, slanted eyes, smiling closed mouth, on stuffed mohair or velvet body, cloth label on body, "Billiken," on right foot.
    12"    $100.00    $375.00

*12" each composition Campbell Kids, $450.00. Courtesy McMasters Doll Auctions.*

**Body Twist, 1930**
Horsman acquired Amberg's American branch, including its line of dolls with waist joints. All composition, with jointed waist
    11"    $65.00    $250.00

**Bright Star, 1937 – 46**
All composition, also made in hard plastic
    19"    $75.00    $350.00

**Campbell Kids, 1910+**
By Helen Trowbridge, based on Grace Drayton's drawings, composition head, painted molded hair, side-glancing painted eyes, closed smiling mouth, compo arms, cloth body and feet
    *Mark:* "EIH©1910+," composition head, cloth body, cloth label on sleeve, *"The Campbell Kids// Trademark by //Joseph Campbell// Mfg. by E.I. Horsman Co."*
    14"    $85.00    $325.00+
    1930 – 1940s, all composition
    13"    $100.00    $350.00

**Composition Characters, 1910 – 30+**
Composition head, cloth body, *Marks:* "EIH" "CAN'T BREAK 'EM"
    11 – 13"    $50.00    $200.00

    **Cotton Joe**
    Black
        13"    $100.00    $400.00

# Horsman, E.I. (cont.)

## Gene Carr Kids

1915 – 16, composition head, painted, molded hair, painted eyes, open/closed smiling mouth with teeth, big ears, cloth body, compo hands, original outfit, cloth tag reads: "*MADE GENE CARR KIDS U.S.A.//FROM NEW YORK WORLD'S //LADY BOUNTIFUL COMIC SERIES//By E.I. HORSMAN CO. NY. 13Z\x*"

| | | |
|---|---|---|
| Blink | $90.00 | $360.00 |
| Carnival Kids | $75.00 | $300.00 |
| Lizzie | $90.00 | $360.00 |
| Mike | $90.00 | $360.00 |
| Skinney | $90.00 | $360.00 |
| Snowball, black | $135.00 | $550.00 |

## Dimples, 1927 – 30+

Composition head and arms on cloth body or bent limb baby body, molded dimples, open mouth, sleep or painted eyes, marked "E.I.H."

| | | |
|---|---|---|
| 16" – 18" | $70.00 | $250.00 |
| 20" – 22" | $90.00 | $350.00 |

Laughing Dimples, open/closed mouth, with painted teeth

| | | |
|---|---|---|
| 22" | $185.00 | $425.00 |

Dimples, toddler body

| | | |
|---|---|---|
| 20" | $100.00 | $385.00 |
| 24" | $150.00 | $425.00 |

## Dolly Rosebud, 1926 – 30

Mama doll, composition head and limbs, dimples, sleep eyes

| | | |
|---|---|---|
| | $50.00 | $125.00 |

## Ella Cinders, 1928 – 29

Based on a cartoon character, composition head, black painted hair or wig, round painted eyes, freckles under eyes, open/closed mouth, cloth body, also came as all cloth, *marks: "1925//MNS"*

| | | |
|---|---|---|
| 14" | $100.00 | $400.00 |
| 18" | $175.00 | $650.00 |

## Gold Metal doll, 1930s

Composition head, upper and lower teeth, cloth body, see also Hard Plastic and Vinyl

| | | |
|---|---|---|
| 21" | $50.00 | $265.00 |

## HEBee-SHEbees, 1925 – 27

Based on drawings by Charles Twelvetrees, all bisque or all composition, painted features, molded undershirt and booties or various costumes. *Marks:* on all bisque, "*Germany,*" and paper sticker on tummy: "*COPYRIGHT BY//HEbee SHEbee//TRADEMARK//CHAS. TWELVETREES*"

| | | |
|---|---|---|
| 10½" | $125.00 | $500.00 |

## Jackie Coogan, "The Kid," 1921 – 22

Compo head and hands, molded hair, painted eyes, cloth body, turtleneck sweater, long gray pants, checked cap, button reads:, "*HORSMAN DOLL// JACKIE// COOGAN// KID// PATENTED*"

| | | |
|---|---|---|
| 13½" | $135.00 | $465.00+ |
| 15½" | $160.00 | $550.00+ |

**Jeanne Horsman, 1937**
Composition head and limbs, painted molded brown hair, sleep eyes, cloth body
    14"    $65.00        $250.00

**Jo Jo, 1937**
All composition, blue sleep eyes, wigged, over molded hair, toddler body. *Marks:* "*HORSMAN JO JO//© 1937*"
    13"    $60.00        $250.00

**Mama Dolls**
1920+, composition head, arms, and lower legs, cloth body with crier and stitched hip joints so lower legs will swing, painted or sleep eyes, mohair or molded hair, original clothes
    14 – 15"    $50.00        $185.00
    19 – 21"    $75.00        $285.00

**Naughty Sue, 1937**
Composition head, jointed body
    16"    $100.00        $400.00

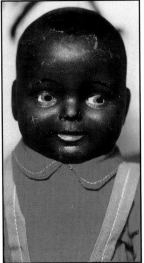

*11" black Horsman early Can't Break 'Em composition character with original clothes, $300.00. Courtesy Matrix.*

**Peterkin, 1914 – 1930+**
Composition head, cloth or composition body, character face, molded hair, painted or sleep eyes, closed smiling mouth, rectangular tag with name "Peterkin"
    11"    $75.00        $300.00
    13½"    $85.00        $350.00

**Roberta, 1937**
All composition
    16"    $65.00        $250.00

**Tynie Baby, ca, 1924 – 1929**
Bisque or composition head, sleep or painted eyes, cloth body, some all bisque, *Marks:* "*©1924//E.I. HORSMAN//CO. INC.,*" or "*E.I.H. Co. 1924*" on composition or "*©1924 by//E I Horsman Co. Inc.//Germany// 37*" incised on bisque head, see also Hard Plastic and Vinyl
    All Bisque
        8"    $450.00        $1800.00
    wardrobe, cradle
        6"    $1,785.00 * at auction
    Bisque
        9" head circumference    $150.00    $600.00
        12" head circumference    $200.00    $800.00
    Composition
        15"    $75.00        $300.00

**HARD PLASTIC, VINYL**
First price is for played with dolls; second price is for complete, mint in box dolls.
**Angelove, 1974**, plastic/vinyl made for Hallmark
    12"    $7.00        $22.50

*20" composition Horsman Bright Star, $250.00. Courtesy McMasters Doll Auctions.*

**Answer Doll, 1966**, button in back moves head

| | | |
|---|---|---|
| 10" | $5.00 | $20.00 |

**Baby First Tooth, 1966**, vinyl head and limbs, cloth body, open/closed mouth with tongue and one tooth, molded tears on cheeks, rooted blonde hair, painted blue eyes, *Marks: "© Horsman Dolls Inc. //1014"*

| | | |
|---|---|---|
| 16" | $8.00 | $27.50 |

**Baby Tweaks, ca. 1967**, vinyl head, cloth body, inset eyes, rooted saran hair, *Marks: "54//HORSMAN DOLLS INC.//Copyright 1967/67191"* on head

| | | |
|---|---|---|
| 20" | $8.00 | $27.50 |

**Ballerina, 1957**, vinyl, one-piece body and legs, jointed elbows

| | | |
|---|---|---|
| 18" | $15.00 | $40.00 |

**Betty, 1951**, all vinyl, one-piece body and limbs

| | | |
|---|---|---|
| 14" | $15.00 | $50.00 |

**Betty,** vinyl head, hard plastic body

| | | |
|---|---|---|
| 16" | $15.00 | $22.50 |

**Betty Ann**, vinyl head, hard plastic body

| | | |
|---|---|---|
| 19" | $15.00 | $80.00 |

**Betty Jane,** vinyl head, hard plastic body

| | | |
|---|---|---|
| 25" | $22.00 | $85.00 |

**Betty Jo,** vinyl head, hard plastic body

| | | |
|---|---|---|
| 16" | $6.00 | $22.50 |

**Bright Star, ca. 1952+,** all hard plastic

| | | |
|---|---|---|
| 15" | $125.00 | $325.00 |

**Bye-Lo Baby, 1972**, reissue, molded vinyl head and limbs, cloth body, white nylon organdy bonnet dress, *Marks: "3 (in square)//HORSMAN DOLLS INC.//©1972"*

| | | |
|---|---|---|
| 14" | $15.00 | $55.00 |

**Bye- Lo Baby, 1980 – 1990s**

| | | |
|---|---|---|
| 14" | $8.00 | $25.00 |

**Celeste,** portrait doll, in frame, eyes painted to side

| | | |
|---|---|---|
| 12" | $10.00 | $35.00 |

**Christopher Robin**

| | | |
|---|---|---|
| 11" | $10.00 | $35.00 |

**Cindy, 1950s**

**All hard plastic,** *marks: "170"*

| | | |
|---|---|---|
| 15" | $50.00 | $190.00 |
| 17" | $65.00 | $235.00 |

**1953,** early vinyl

| | | |
|---|---|---|
| 18" | $20.00 | $75.00 |

**1959,** lady-type with jointed waist

| | | |
|---|---|---|
| 19" | $25.00 | $90.00 |

**Cindy Walker**
| | | |
|---|---|---|
| 16" | $65.00 | $250.00 |

**Cindy Kay, 1950s+**, all vinyl child with long legs
| | | |
|---|---|---|
| 15" | $25.00 | $90.00 |
| 20" | $35.00 | $140.00 |
| 27" | $60.00 | $260.00 |

**Cinderella, 1965,** vinyl head, hard plastic body, painted eyes to side
| | | |
|---|---|---|
| 11 ½" | $8.00 | $30.00 |

**Crawling Baby, 1967**, vinyl, rooted hair
| | | |
|---|---|---|
| 14" | $8.00 | $30.00 |

**Disney Exclusives, 1981**, Cinderella, Snow White, Mary Poppins, Alice in Wonderland
| | | |
|---|---|---|
| 8" | $10.00 | $40.00 |

**Elizabeth Taylor, 1976**
| | | |
|---|---|---|
| 11 ½" | $15.00 | $55.00 |

**Floppy, 1958,** vinyl head, foam body and legs
| | | |
|---|---|---|
| 18" | $8.00 | $25.00 |

**Flying Nun, 1965,** TV character portrayed by Sally Field
| | | |
|---|---|---|
| 12" | $30.00 | $110.00 |

**Gold Metal doll, 1953,** vinyl, molded hair
| | | |
|---|---|---|
| 26" | $50.00 | $200.00 |

1954, vinyl, boy
| | | |
|---|---|---|
| 15" | $22.00 | $85.00 |

**Hansel & Gretel, 1963,** vinyl head, hard plastic body, rooted synthetic hair, closed mouth, sleep eyes
*Mark:* **"MADE IN USA"** on body, on tag, *"HORSMAN, ©Michael Meyerberg, Inc., Reproduction of the famous Kinemins in Michael Myerberg's marvelous Technicolor production of Hansel and Gretel"*
| | | |
|---|---|---|
| 15" | $60.00 | $235.00 |

**Jackie Kennedy, 1961,** vinyl doll, rooted hair, blue sleep eyes, long lashes, closed mouth, high-heel feet, small waist, nicely dressed, designed by Irene Szor who says this doll named "Jackie" was not meant to be Jackie Kennedy. *Marks: "HORSMAN//19©61//BC 18"*
| | | |
|---|---|---|
| 25" | $35.00 | $135.00 |

**Lullabye Baby, 1967 – 68,** vinyl bent leg baby body, rooted hair, inset station blue eyes, drink and wet feature, musical mechanism, 1968 Sears catalog, came on suedette pillow, in terry-cloth p.j.s., *marks: "2580//B144 8 //HORSMAN DOLLS INC//19©67"*
| | | |
|---|---|---|
| 12" | $4.00 | $15.00 |

**Mary Poppins, 1964**, vinyl, nanny character from movie
| | | |
|---|---|---|
| 12" | $9.00 | $35.00 |
| 16" | $20.00 | $70.00 |

1966
| | | |
|---|---|---|
| 26" | $50.00 | $200.00 |
| 36" | $90.00 | $350.00 |

*Black vinyl Horsman Baby Clap Hands, recites Patty Cake poem when you press hands together, battery operated, $75.00. Courtesy Cathie Clark.*

In box with Michael and Wendy
    12" and 8"    $150.00

**Police Woman, ca. 1976,** vinyl, plastic fully articulated body, blonde rooted hair

| | | |
|---|---|---|
| 9" | $10.00 | $35.00 |

**Tynie Baby,** vinyl, ca. 1950s, boxed

| | | |
|---|---|---|
| 15" | $30.00 | $110.00 |

## Mary Hoyer

*1950s hard plastic Mary Hoyer in trunk with extra outfits, $650.00. Courtesy Sally McVey.*

**Mary Hoyer Doll Mfg. Co. Reading, PA, 1925+.** Designed by Bernard Lipfert, all composition, later hard plastic, then vinyl, swivel neck, jointed body, mohair or human hair wig, sleep eyes, closed mouth, original clothes or knitted from Mary Hoyer patterns. *Marks: "The //Mary Hoyer//Doll" or "ORIGINAL//Mary Hoyer Doll"*

Composition

| | | |
|---|---|---|
| 14" | $115.00 | $450.00 |

Hard Plastic

| | | |
|---|---|---|
| 14" | $250.00 | $500.00 |
| 18" | $300.00 | $575.00+ |

Vinyl, 1990s

| | | |
|---|---|---|
| | $65.00 | $275.00 |

## Ideal

**Ideal Novelty and Toy Co. 1906 – 80+, Brooklyn, NY.** Produced their own composition dolls in early years.

*Marks:* Various including *"IDEAL"* (in a diamond) *US of A;" "IDEAL Novelty and Toy Co., Brooklyn, New York"* and others.

### COMPOSITION, RUBBER AND OTHERS

**Betsy Wetsy, 1937 – 38**

Hard rubber head, soft rubber body, sleep or painted eyes, molded hair, open mouth for bottle, drinks, wets, came with bottle, some in layettes. In the 1950s, came with hard plastic head on vinyl body and she had tear ducts. Circa 1959, she was all vinyl; reissued again in vinyl in 1983.

*Marks: "IDEAL,"* (on head), *"IDEAL"* (on body)

| | | |
|---|---|---|
| 11" | $30.00 | $110.00 |
| 15" | $40.00 | $150.00 |
| 19" | $45.00 | $175.00 |

Hard plastic, head, vinyl body

| | | |
|---|---|---|
| 12" | $22.00 | $80.00 |
| 14" | $40.00 | $150.00 |

All vinyl

| | | |
|---|---|---|
| 12" | $10.00 | $35.00 |

**Buster Brown, 1929**
Composition head, hands, legs, cloth body, tin eyes, red outfit
*Marks:* "*IDEAL*" (in a diamond)
    16"    $75.00    $300.00

**Charlie McCarthy, 1938 – 39**
Hand puppet, compo head, felt hands, molded hat, molded features, wire monocle, cloth body, painted tuxedo, *marks: "Edgar Bergin's //©CHARLIE MCCARTHY//MADE IN U.S.A."* (on front of body)
    8"    $15.00    $60.00

**Cinderella, 1938 – 39**
All composition, brown, blonde or red human hair wig, flirty brown sleep eyes, open mouth, 6 teeth, same head mold as Ginger, Snow White, Mary Jane with dimple in chin, some wore formal evening gowns of organdy and taffeta, velvet cape, had rhinestone tiara, silver snap shoes, Sears catalog version has Celanese rayon gown. *Marks:* none on head; "*SHIRLEY TEMPLE//13*" (on body).

*16" Buster Brown, composition head, cloth body, brass buttons read "Buster Brown," $325.00. Courtesy Stephanie Prince.*

| | | |
|---|---|---|
| 13" | $75.00 | $300.00+ |
| 16" | $80.00 | $325.00+ |
| 20" | $85.00 | $350.00+ |
| 25" | $90.00 | $375.00+ |
| 27" | $100.00 | $400.00+ |

**Composition Baby, 1913+**
Composition head, molded hair or wigged, painted or sleep eyes, cloth or composition body, may have Ideal diamond mark or hang tag, original clothes

| | | |
|---|---|---|
| 12" | $40.00 | $150.00 |
| 16" | $50.00 | $200.00 |
| 20" | $65.00 | $275.00+ |
| 24" | $85.00 | $325.00+ |

**Composition Child or Toddler, 1915+**
Composition head, molded hair or wigged, painted or sleep eyes, cloth or composition body, may have Ideal diamond mark or hang tag, original clothes

| | | |
|---|---|---|
| 13" | $40.00 | $150.00 |
| 15" | $40.00 | $200.00 |
| 18" | $50.00 | $300.00 |

**Composition Mama Doll, 1921+**
Composition head and arms, molded hair or wigged, painted or sleep eyes, cloth body with crier and stitched swing leg, lower part composition

| | | |
|---|---|---|
| 16" | $50.00 | $250.00+ |
| 20" | $75.00 | $300.00+ |
| 24" | $85.00 | $350.00+ |

*24" composition Deanna Durbin, tagged dress, $300.00. Courtesy McMasters Doll Auctions.*

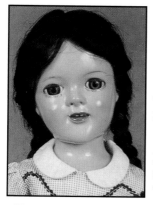

*18" composition Judy Garland, $575.00. Courtesy McMasters Doll Auctions.*

**Cracker Jack Boy, 1917**

Compo head, gauntlet hands, cloth body, molded boots, molded hair, wears blue or white sailor suit, cap, carries package of Cracker Jacks

| | | |
|---|---|---|
| 14" | $100.00 | $375.00 |

**Deanna Durbin, 1938 – 41**

All composition, fully jointed, dark brown human hair wig, brown sleep eyes, open mouth, six teeth, felt tongue, original clothes, pin reads: *"DEANNA DURBIN//A UNIVERSAL STAR."* More for fancy outfits.

*Marks: "DEANNA DURBIN//IDEAL DOLL,"* on head, on body, *"IDEAL DOLL//21"*

| | | |
|---|---|---|
| 15" | $125.00 | $500.00 |
| 18" | $190.00 | $650.00 |
| 21" | $200.00 | $750.00 |
| 24" | $225.00 | $850.00 |
| 27" | $250.00 | $1,000.00 |

**Flexies, 1938 – 42**

Composition head, gauntlet hands, wooden torso and feet, flexible wire tubing for arms and legs, original clothes, paper tag. *Marks: "IDEAL DOLL//Made in U.S.A.,"* or just *"IDEAL DOLL,"* on head.

**Black Flexy,** painted molded hair, painted eyes, closed smiling mouth, tweed patched pants, felt suspenders

| | | |
|---|---|---|
| 13½" | $85.00 | $325.00 |

**Baby Snooks,** based on radio personality Fannie Brice, designed by Kallus, painted molded hair, painted eyes, open/closed mouth with teeth

| | | |
|---|---|---|
| 13½" | $70.00 | $275.00 |

**Clown Flexy,** looks like Mortimer Snerd, painted white as clown

| | | |
|---|---|---|
| 13½" | $60.00 | $225.00 |

**Mortimer Snerd,** Edgar Bergen's radio show dummy, painted molded blonde hair, smiling closed mouth showing two teeth

| | | |
|---|---|---|
| 13½" | $70.00 | $275.00 |

**Soldier,** closed smiling mouth, molded painted features in khaki uniform

| | | |
|---|---|---|
| 13½" | $65.00 | $250.00 |

**Sunny Sam and Sunny Sue,** painted molded hair, girl bobbed hair, pouty mouth, boy has smiling mouth

| | | |
|---|---|---|
| 13½" | $65.00 | $250.00 |

**Flossie Flirt, 1924 – 31**

Composition head and limbs, cloth body, crier, tin flirty eyes, open mouth, upper teeth, original outfit, dress and bonnet, combination, socks and shoes, *marks: "IDEAL"* in diamond with *"U.S. of A."*

| | | |
|---|---|---|
| 14" | $60.00 | $225.00+ |
| 18" | $65.00 | $250.00+ |
| 20" | $70.00 | $275.00+ |
| 22" | $75.00 | $300.00+ |
| 24" | $80.00 | $350.00+ |
| 28" | $100.00 | $400.00+ |

**Jiminy Cricket, 1940**

8½", composition head and wooden segmented body, yellow suit black coat, blue felt trim on hat, felt collar, ribbon necktie, carries a wooden umbrella, *Marks: "JIMINY CRICKET//DEA & BY IDEAL NOVELTY & TOY CO.,"* on foot

| | | |
|---|---|---|
| 9" | $115.00 | $450.00 |

**Judy Garland**

1939 – 1940, as Dorothy from *The Wizard of OZ*, all composition, jointed, wig with braids, brown sleep eyes, open mouth, six teeth, designed by Bernard Lipfert, blue or red checked rayon jumper, white blouse.

*Marks: "IDEAL"* on head plus size number, and *"USA"* on body

| | | |
|---|---|---|
| 13" | $250.00 | $1,000.00+ |
| 15½" | $300.00 | $1,200.00+ |
| 18" | $350.00 | $1,500.00+ |

1940 – 42, teen, all composition, wig, sleep eyes, open mouth, four teeth, original long dress, hang ag reads: *"Judy Garland// A Metro Gold-wyn Mayer//Star//in// 'Little Nellie//Kelly',"* original pin reads *"JUDY GAR-LAND METRO GOLDWYN MAYER STAR,"* marks: *"MADE IN U.S.A.,"* on head, *"IDEAL DOLLS,"* a backwards *"21"* on body

| | | |
|---|---|---|
| 15" | $90.00 | $350.00 |
| 21" | $125.00 | $500.00 |

**Liberty Boy, 1918**

All composition, painted features, molded hair, painted molded brown Army uniform with detachable felt hat, *marks: "Ideal,"* in diamond on back, **"U.S.,"** on front collar.

| | | |
|---|---|---|
| 12" | $150.00 | $325.00 |

**Marama, 1940**

Representing a character in the movie, *Hurricane*, uses the Shirley Temple mold, all composition, black yarn wig, brown complexion, painted side-glancing eyes, painted teeth, *Marks: "13/Shirley Temple,"* on head, *"U.S.A.//13,"* on body. See also Shirley Temple section.

| | | |
|---|---|---|
| 13" | $200.00 | $800.00 |
| 18" | $250.00 | $950.00 |

**Pinocchio, 1939**

Composition head, wooden segmented body, painted features , clothes, yellow felt cap, *marks: "PINOCCHIO//Des. © by Walt Disney//Made by Ideal Novelty & Toy Co.,"* on front, *"©W.D.P.//ideal doll//made in USA"* on back

| | | |
|---|---|---|
| 9" | $75.00 | $300.00 |
| 11" | $115.00 | $450.00 |
| 20" | $125.00 | $550.00 |

*13½" Mortimer Snerd and Fanny Brice as Baby Snooks are Flexies with composition head, arms, and feet, spring type armature for body, $275.00 each. Courtesy Amanda Hash.*

## Princess Beatrix, 1938 – 43

Represents Princess Beatrix of the Netherlands, composition head, arms, legs, cloth body, flirty sleep eyes, fingers molded into fists, original organdy dress and bonnet

| | | |
|---|---|---|
| 14" | $40.00 | $150.00 |
| 16" | $50.00 | $185.00 |
| 22" | $55.00 | $215.00 |
| 26" | $65.00 | $250.00 |

## Strawman, 1939

All cloth, scarecrow character portrayed by Ray Boger in *Wizard of Oz* movie, yarn hair, all original, wearing dark jacket and hat, tan pants, round paper hang tag

| | | |
|---|---|---|
| 17" | $200.00 | $800.00 |
| 21" | $250.00 | $1,000.00 |

## Seven Dwarfs, 1938

Composition head and cloth body, or all cloth, painted mask face, head turns, removable clothes, pick and lantern with each doll, each dwarf has name on cap

Cloth

| | | |
|---|---|---|
| 12" | $50.00 | $175.00 |

Composition

| | | |
|---|---|---|
| 12" | $65.00 | $250.00 |

## Dopey, 1938

One of Seven Dwarfs, a ventriloquist doll, composition head and hands, cloth body, arms, and legs, hinged mouth with drawstring, molded tongue, painted eyes, large ears, long coat, cotton pants, felt shoes sewn to legs, felt cap with name, can stand alone, *marks: "IDEAL DOLL,"* on neck

| | | |
|---|---|---|
| 20" | $200.00 | $800.00 |

## Shirley Temple, see that section

**Snoozie, 1933+**

Composition head, painted hair, hard rubber hands, feet, cloth body, open yawning mouth, molded tongue, sleep eyes, designed by Bernard Lifert, *marks: "©B. Lipfert//Made for Ideal Doll & Toy Corp. 1933,"* or *"©by B. Lipert or IDEAL SNOOZIE//B. LIPFERT,"* on head

| | | |
|---|---|---|
| 14" | $40.00 | $150.00 |
| 18" | $75.00 | $300.00 |
| 20" | $90.00 | $350.00 |

**Snow White, 1938+**

All composition, jointed body, black mohair wig, flirty glass eyes, open mouth, 4 teeth, dimple in chin, used Shirley Temple body, red velvet bodice, rayon taffeta skirt pictures seven Dwarfs, velvet cape, some unmarked, *marks:* **"Shirley Temple/18,"** or other size number on back

| | | |
|---|---|---|
| 11½" | $125.00 | $500.00 |
| 13 – 14" | $135.00 | $550.00 |
| 19" | $150.00 | $600.00 |
| 22" | $165.00 | $650.00 |
| 27" | $175.00 | $700.00 |

**1938 – 39,** as above, but with painted, molded bow and black hair, painted side-glancing eyes, add 50% more for black version, *marks:* IDEAL DOLL (on head).

| | | |
|---|---|---|
| 14½" | $50.00 | $200.00 |
| 17½" | $100.00 | $400.00 |
| 19½" | $150.00 | $600.00 |

**Snow White, 1938,** cloth body, mask face, painted eyes, black human hair wig, variation of red and white dress with small cape, Snow White and Seven Dwarfs printed on it, no other marks

| | | |
|---|---|---|
| 16" | $150.00 | $550.00 |

**Soozie Smiles, 1923**

Two-headed compo doll with smiling face, sleep or painted eyes, and crying face with tears, molded painted hair, cloth body and legs, compo arms, original clothes, tag, also in gingham check romper

| | | |
|---|---|---|
| 15 – 17" | $75.00 | $350.00 |

**Tickletoes, 1928 – 39**

Composition head, rubber arms, legs, cloth body, crier, squeaker in each leg, flirty sleep eyes, open mouth, two painted teeth, original organdy dress, bonnet, paper hang tag, add more for flirty eyes, *Marks: "IDEAL,"* in diamond with *"U.S. of A.,"* on head

| | | |
|---|---|---|
| 14" | $40.00 | $150.00 |
| 17" | $50.00 | $250.00 |
| 20" | $65.00 | $300.00 |

**Uneeda Kid, 1916**

Advertising doll, carries package of Nabisco crackers, some have molded yellow hats, wears yellow raincoat, molded black boots

Painted eyes

| | | |
|---|---|---|
| 11" | $75.00 | $300.00 |

Sleep eyes

| | | |
|---|---|---|
| 16" | $125.00 | $475.00 |

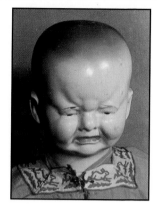

*Soozie Smiles, two faces, one crying, one
with sleep eyes smiling, original dress, tag,
missing hat, $350.00.*

### ZuZu Kid, 1916 – 17

Composition head, molded hair, compo hands and feet, cloth body,
jointed hips and shoulders, girl in yellow with brown star clown costume,
hat, hold small box ZuZu gingersnaps, licensed by National Biscuit Co.

15½"        $115.00              $450.00

### HARD PLASTIC, VINYL

#### April Showers, 1968

Vinyl, battery operated, splashes hands, head turns

14"        $7.00              $25.00

#### Baby Coos, 1948 – 1952

**Also Brother and Sister Coos,** designed by Bernard Lipfert, hard plastic
head, stuffed magic skin body, jointed arms, sleep eyes, molded painted hair,
closed mouth or cloth and vinyl body, many magic skin bodies deteriorated or
turned dark, *marks:* on head, *"16 IDEAL DOLL//MADE IN U.S. A.,"* or
unmarked

| | | |
|---|---|---|
| 14" | $25.00 | $100.00 |
| 16" | $35.00 | $125.00 |
| 18" | $40.00 | $150.00 |
| 20" | $45.00 | $175.00 |
| 22" | $50.00 | $200.00 |
| 27" | $65.00 | $260.00 |
| 30" | $75.00 | $300.00 |

### Baby Crissy, 1973 – 76

All-vinyl, jointed body, legs and arms foam filled, rooted auburn grow
hair, two painted teeth, brown sleep eyes, *marks:* *"©1972//IDEAL TOY
COPR.//2M 5511//B OR GHB-H-225,"* on back

White

24"        $15.00              $75.00

Black

24"        $20.00              $85.00

**Baby Pebbles, 1963 – 64**
Character from the Flintstone cartoons, Hanna Barbera Productions, vinyl head, arms, legs, soft body, side-glancing blue painted eyes, rooted hair with topknot and bone, leopard print nightie and trim on flannel blanket. Also as an all- vinyl toddler, jointed body, outfit with leopard print
Baby
| | 14" | $7.00 | $25.00 |
Toddler
| | 16" | $10.00 | $35.00 |

**Tiny Pebbles, 1964 – 66,** smaller version, came with plastic log cradle in 1965
Toddler
| | 12" | $8.00 | $30.00 |

**Bam-Bam, 1964,** character from Flintstone TV cartoon, Hanna Barbera Productions, all-vinyl, head, jointed body, rooted blonde Saran hair, painted blue side-glancing eyes, leopard skin suit, cap, club
| | 12" | $5.00 | $20.00 |
| | 16" | $7.00 | $25.00 |

**Batman characters**
**Bat Girl**
| | 11½" | $40.00 | $155.00 |

**Batman,** 1966, vinyl and cloth hand puppet, vinyl head, blue mask
| | | $40.00 | $155.00 |
Action figure
| | 12" | $65.00 | $250.00 |

**Belly Button Babies, 1971**
**Me So Glad, Me So Silly, Me So Happy,** vinyl head, rooted hair, painted eyes, press button in belly to move arms, head, and bent legs, both boy and girl versions
White
| | 9½" | $5.00 | $18.00 |
Black
| | 9½" | $9.00 | $25.00 |

**Big Jim Series**
Vinyl action figures, many boxed accessory sets available
**Big Jim,** black hair, muscular torso
| | 9½" | $7.00 | $25.00 |
**Big Josh,** dark hair, beard
| | 9½" | $9.00 | $35.00 |
**Dr. Steele,** bald head, silver tips on right hand.
| | 9½" | $8.00 | $32.00 |

**Bizzie-Lizzie, 1971 – 72**
Vinyl head, jointed body, rooted blonde hair, sleep eyes, plugged into power pack, she irons, vacuums, uses feather duster, 2 D-cell batteries
White
| | 18" | $9.00 | $35.00 |
Black
| | 18" | $12.00 | $45.00 |

# Ideal (cont.)

*13" vinyl Bonnie Braids, boxed, $150.00. Courtesy McMasters Doll Auctions.*

### Bonnie Braids, 1951 – 53

Comic strip character daughter of Dick Tracy and Tess Trueheart, vinyl head, jointed arms, "Magic Skin" rubber one piece body, open mouth, one tooth, painted yellow hair, two yellow saran pigtails, painted blue eyes, coos when squeezed, long white gown, bed jacket, toothbrush, Ipana toothpaste. *Marks: "©1951//Chi. Tribune//IDEAL DOLL//U.S.A.,"* on neck

**Baby**

| | | |
|---|---|---|
| 11½" | $25.00 | $100.00 |
| 13" | $30.00 | $145.00 |

**Toddler,** 1953, vinyl head, jointed hard plastic body, open/closed mouth with 2 painted teeth, walker

| | | |
|---|---|---|
| 11½" | $35.00 | $140.00 |
| 13" | $40.00 | $165.00 |

### Butterick Sew Easy Designing Set, 1953

Plastic mannequin of adult woman, molded blonde hair, came with Butterick patterns and sewing accessories

| | | |
|---|---|---|
| 14" | $15.00 | $60.00 |

### Captain Action® Superhero, 1966 – 68

Caption Action represents a fictional character who changes disguises to become a new identity, vinyl articulated figure, dark hair and eyes.

**Captain Action, 1967 Promo**

| | | | |
|---|---|---|---|
| | 12" | $75.00 | $300.00 |
| Batman disguise | | $65.00 | $250.00 |
| Capt. American disguise only | | | $250.00 |
| Capt. Flash Gordon acces. | | $40.00 | $150.00 |
| Phantom disguise only | | $50.00 | $200.00 |
| Steve Canyon disguise | | $50.00 | $200.00 |
| Superman set w/dog | | $45.00 | $175.00 |
| Lone Ranger outfit only | | $50.00 | $200.00 |
| Spiderman disguise only | | $65.00 | $250.00 |
| Tonto outfit only | | $50.00 | $200.00 |
| Action Boy, 9" | | $65.00 | $250.00 |
| Robin accessories | | $45.00 | $175.00 |
| Special Ed. | | $75.00 | $300.00 |
| Dr. Evel | | $50.00 | $200.00 |
| Dr. Evel's accessories | | $50.00 | $250.00 |
| Super Girl | | $75.00 | $300.00 |

### Chelsea, 1967

Vinyl head, posable body, rooted long straight hair, dressed in mod fashions, earrings, strap shoes

| | | |
|---|---|---|
| 24" | $15.00 | $50.00 |

**Cinnamon, Velvet's Little Sister, 1972 – 1974**
Vinyl head, painted eyes, rooted auburn growing hair, orange polka dotted outfit, additional outfits sold separately, *marks: "©1971//IDEAL TOY CORP.//G-H-12-H18//HONG KONG//IDEAL 1069-4 b,"* head, *"©1972//IDEAL TOY CORP.//U.S. PAT-3-162-976//OTHER PAT. PEND.//HONG KONG,"* on back
 White
   13½"  $12.00  $45.00
 Black
   13½"  $15.00  $60.00

**Clarabelle, 1954**
Clown from Howdy Doody TV show, mask face, cloth body, dressed in satin Clarabelle outfit with noise box and horn
   16"  $20.00  $80.00
   20"  $25.00  $100.00

**Crissy®, Beautiful Crissy, 1969 – 74**
All vinyl, dark brown eyes, long hair, turn knob in back to make hair grow, some with swivel waist (1971), pull string to turn head (1972), pull string to talk (1971), reissued ca. 1982 – 83. First year hair grew to floor length. More for black version.
 1969, white
   17½"  $12.00  $50.00
 1969, black
   17½"  $40.00  $60.00
 Floor length hair, 1968 $75.00  $150.00
 1971, Movin' Groovin' $10.00  $40.00
 Twirly Beads, 1974  $9.00  $35.00

**Daddy's Girl, 1961**
Vinyl head and arm, plastic body, swivel waist, jointed ankles, rooted Saran hair, blue sleep eyes, closed smiling mouth, pre – teen girl, label on dress, reads "Daddy's Girl," *marks: "IDEAL TOY CORP.//g-42-1,"* on head, *"IDEAL TOY CORP.//G-42,"* on body
   38"  $200.00  $800.00
   42"  $250.00  $1,000.00

**Davy Crockett and his horse, 1955 – 56**
All plastic, can be removed from horse, fur cap, buckskin clothes
   4 ½"  $13.00  $50.00

**Dennis, the Menace, 1976**
All cloth, printed doll, comic strip character by Hank Ketcham, blond hair, freckles, wearing overalls and striped shirt
   7"  $5.00  $20.00
   14"  $7.50  $30.00

**Diana Ross, 1969**
Celebrity from the Supremes (singing group), all vinyl black doll, rooted black bouffant hairdo, gold sheath, feathers, gold shoes, or chartreuse mini-dress, print scarf, and black shoes
   17½"  $45.00  $190.00

# Ideal (cont.)

**Dorothy Hamill, 1978**

Olympic skating star, vinyl head, plastic posable body, rooted short brown hair, comes on ice rink stand with skates, also extra outfits available

| | | |
|---|---|---|
| 11½" | $8.00 | $25.00 |

**Evel Knievel 1974 – 77**

All plastic stunt figure, helmet, more with stuntcycle

| | | |
|---|---|---|
| 7" | $7.50 | $25.00 |

**Harriet Hubbard Ayer**

Cosmetic doll, vinyl stuffed head, hard plastic (Toni) body, wigged or rooted hair, came with eight piece H. H. Ayer cosmetic kit, beauty table and booklet, *marks: "MK 16//IDEAL DOLL,"* on head *"IDEAL DOLL//P-91,"* on body

| | | |
|---|---|---|
| 14" | $50.00 | $200.00 |
| 16" | $60.00 | $225.00 |
| 19" | $65.00 | $250.00 |
| 21" | $75.00 | $300.00 |

**Hopalong Cassidy, 1949 – 1950**

Vinyl stuffed head, vinyl hands, painted molded gray hair, painted blue eyes, one-piece body, dressed in black cowboy outfit, leatherette boots, guns, holster, black felt hat, *marked: "Hopalong Cassidy,"* on buckle

| | | |
|---|---|---|
| 18" | $20.00 | $80.00 |
| 21" | $22.50 | $85.00 |
| 23" | $25.00 | $100.00 |
| 25" | $35.00 | $125.00 |
| 27" | $40.00 | $150.00 |

Plastic, with horse, Topper

| | | |
|---|---|---|
| 4½" | $10.00 | $40.00 |

**Howdy Doody, 1950 – 53**

Television puppet personality, hard plastic head, red painted molded hair, freckles, ventriloquist doll, mouth operated by pull string, cloth body and limbs, dressed in cowboy outfit, scarf reads: *"HOWDY DOODY."* *Marks: "IDEAL,"* on head

| | | |
|---|---|---|
| 19" | $25.00 | $100.00 |
| 24" | $40.00 | $150.00 |

**1954,** with vinyl hands, wears boots, jeans

| | | |
|---|---|---|
| 18" | $50.00 | $200.00 |
| 20" | $65.00 | $250.00 |
| 25" | $75.00 | $300.00 |

**Kissy, 1961 – 64**

Vinyl head, rigid vinyl toddler body, rooted Saran hair, sleep eyes, jointed wrists, press hands together and mouth puckers, makes kissing sound, original dress, panties, t-strap sandals, *marks: "©IDEAL CORP.//K-21-L,"* on head, *"IDEAL TOY CORP.//K22//PAT. PEND.,"* on body

White

| | | |
|---|---|---|
| 22½" | $20.00 | $135.00 |

Black

| | | |
|---|---|---|
| 22½" | $35.00 | $165.00 |

**Kissy Baby,** 1963 – 64, all vinyl, bent legs
|  |  |  |
|---|---|---|
| 22" | $15.00 | $55.00 |

**Tiny Kissy,** 1963 – 68, smaller version toddler, red outfit, white pinafore with hearts, *marks: "IDEAL CORP.//K-16-1,"* on head, *"IDEAL TOY CORP./K-16-2,"* on body
White
|  |  |  |
|---|---|---|
| 16" | $12.00 | $45.00 |

Black
|  |  |  |
|---|---|---|
| 16" | $20.00 | $80.00 |

**Loni Anderson, 1981**
    Star of TV sitcom, *WKRP in Cincinnati,* vinyl, posable fashion doll packaged with picture of Loni Anderson. This doll was featured in Ideal's 1981 catalog in a red dress, white high heels, blond wig, unsure how many produced
|  |  |  |
|---|---|---|
| 11½" | $10.00 | $50.00 |

**Lori Martin, 1961**
    Character from *National Velvet* TV show, all vinyl, swivel waist, jointed body, including ankles, blue sleep eyes, rooted dark hair, individual fingers, dressed in shirt, jeans, black vinyl boots, felt hat, *marks: "Metro Goldwyn Mayer Inc.//Mfg. by//IDEAL TOY CORP//38,"* on head, *"©IDEAL TOY CORP.//38,"* on back.
|  |  |  |
|---|---|---|
| 36" | $175.00 | $750.00 |
| 38" | $200.00 | $800.00 |

**Magic Skin Baby, 1940, 1946 – 49**
    Hard plastic head, one-piece molded latex body and legs, jointed arms, sleep eyes, molded painted hair, some with fancy layettes or trunks, latex usually darkened
|  |  |  |
|---|---|---|
| 13 – 14" | $25.00 | $50.00 |
| 15 – 16" | $20.00 | $75.00 |
| 17 – 18" | $25.00 | $100.00 |
| 20" | $35.00 | $125.00 |

**Mary Hartline, 1952**
    From TV personality on *Super Circus* show, hard plastic, fully jointed blonde nylon wig, blue sleep eyes, lashes, black eyeshadow over and under eye, red, white, or green drum majorette costume and baton, red heart paper hang tag, with original box, *marks: "P-91//IDEA"IDEAL//16,"L DOLL//MADE IN U.S.A.,"* on head, *"IDEAL DOLL//P-91,"* or on body
|  |  |  |
|---|---|---|
| 7½" | $35.00 | $125.00 |
| 16" | $100.00 | $400.00 |
| 23" | $150.00 | $600.00 |

**Miss Clairol, Glamour Misty, 1965 – 66**
    Vinyl head and arms, rigid plastic legs and body, rooted platinum blonde Saran hair, side-glancing eyes., teen doll had cosmetics to change her hair, high-heel feet., all original, *marks: "©1965//IDEAL TOY CORP//W-12-3,"* on neck, *"© 1965 IDEAL,"* in oval on lower rear torso
|  |  |  |
|---|---|---|
| 12" | $10.00 | $35.00 |

*Tammy MIB with extra outfit, $85.00. Courtesy Cathie Clark.*

*14" vinyl Miss Curity, boxed, $325.00. Courtesy McMasters Doll Auctions.*

### Miss Curity, 1953

Hard plastic, Saran wig, sleep eyes, black eyeshadow, nurse's outfit, navy cape, white cap, Bauer & Black First Aid kit and book, curlers, uses Toni body, *marks: "P – 90 IDEAL DOLL, MADE IN U.S.A.,"* on head

|        |          |          |
|--------|----------|----------|
| 14½"   | $85.00   | $325.00  |
| 22"    | $125.00  | $475.00  |

### Miss Ideal, 1961

All vinyl, rooted nylon hair, jointed ankles, wrists, waist,. arms, and legs, closed smiling mouth, sleep eyes, original dress, with beauty kit and comb, *marks: "© IDEAL TOY CORP.//SP-30-S,"* on head, *"© IDEAL TOY CORP.//G-30-S,"* on back.

|        |          |          |
|--------|----------|----------|
| 25"    | $100.00  | $375.00  |
| 30"    | $125.00  | $475.00  |

### Miss Revlon, 1956 – 59

Vinyl, hard plastic teenage body, jointed shoulders, waist hips, and knees, high-heel feet, rooted saran hair, sleep eyes, lashes, pierced ears, hang tag, original dress, some came with trunks, *marks: "VT 20//IDEAL DOLL"*

|        |          |          |
|--------|----------|----------|
| 15"    | $40.00   | $175.00  |
| 18"    | $50.00   | $200.00  |
| 20"    | $65.00   | $250.00  |
| 23"    | $70.00   | $275.00  |

1957

|        |          |          |
|--------|----------|----------|
| 26"    | $75.00   | $300.00  |

### Little Miss Revlon, 1958 – 60, vinyl head and strung body, jointed

head, arms, legs, swivel waist, high-heel feet, rooted hair, sleep eyes, pierced ears with earrings, original clothes, with box, many extra boxed outfits available

|        |          |          |
|--------|----------|----------|
| 10½"   | $40.00   | $125.00  |

**Mysterious Yokum, Li'l Honest Abe, 1953**
Son of comic strip character, Li'l Abner, hard plastic head and body, "Magic Skin" arms and legs, painted eyes, molded hair, forelock, wears overalls, one suspender, knit cap and socks.
$15.00          $55.00

**Palooka, Joan,** 1953, daughter of comic strip character, Joe Palooka, vinyl head, "Magic Skin" body, jointed arms and legs, yellow molded hair, topknot of yellow Saran, blue painted eyes, open/closed mouth, smells like baby powder, original pink dress with blue ribbons, came with Johnson's baby powder and soap, *marks: "©1952//HAM FISHER//IDEAL DOLL,"* on head
          14"          $25.00          $95.00

**Patti Play Pal, 1959 – 1962**
All vinyl, jointed wrists, sleep eyes, curly or straight saran hair, bangs, closed mouth, blue or red and white checked dress with pinafore, 3-year-old size. Reissued in 1981 and 82 from old molds, *marks: "IDEAL TOY CORP.//G 35 OR B-19-1,"* on head
          35"          $100.00          $400.00

**Patti Play Pal, 1981 – 82,** all vinyl reissue from 1959 mold
White
          35"          $25.00          $100.00
Black
          35"          $30.00          $125.00

**Pattite, 1960,** all vinyl, rooted saran hair, sleep eyes, red and white checked dress, white pinafore with her name on it, looks like Patti Playpal
          18"          $65.00          $250.00
Walker
          18"          $70.00          $300.00

**Bonnie Play Pal, 1959,** Patti's 3-month-old sister, made only one year, vinyl, rooted blond hair, blue sleep eyes, blue and white checked outfit, white shoes and socks
          24"          $65.00          $250.00

**Penny Play Pal, 1959,** vinyl jointed body, rooted blonde or brown curly hair, blue sleep eyes, wears organdy dress, vinyl shoes, socks, Patti's 2-year-old sister, made only 1 year, *marks: "IDEAL DOLL//32-E-L,"* or *"B-32-B PAT. PEND.,"* on head, *"IDEAL,"* on back
          32"          $75.00          $300.00

**Johnny Play Pal,** 1959, vinyl, blue sleep eyes, molded hair, Patti's 3-month-old brother.
          24"          $65.00          $250.00

**Peter Play Pal, 1960 – 61,** vinyl, gold sleep eyes, freckles, pug nose, rooted blonde, brunette hair, original clothes, black plastic shoes, *marks: "©IDEAL TOY CORP.// BE-35-38,"* on head, *"©IDEAL TOY CORP.//W-38//PAT. PEND.,"* on body
          38"          $225.00          $850.00
Walker
          38"          $225.00          $850.00

315

**Suzy Play Pal, 1959,** vinyl, jointed body, rooted curly short blonde Saran hair, blue sleep eyes, wears purple dotted dress, Patti's 1-year-old sister

| | | |
|---|---|---|
| 28" | $75.00 | $300.00 |

**Peanuts Gang, 1976 – 78**

All cloth, stuffed printed dolls from "Peanuts" cartoon strip by Charles Schultz. Charlie Brown, Lucy, Linus, Peppermint Patty and Snoopy

| | | |
|---|---|---|
| 7" | $5.00 | $20.00 |
| 14" | $8.00 | $25.00 |

**Plassie, 1942**

Hard plastic head, painted molded hair, composition shoulder plate, composition limbs, stuffed pink oilcloth body, blue sleep eyes, original dress, bonnet, *marks: "IDEAL DOLL//MADE IN USA//PAT.NO. 225 2077,"* on head

| | | |
|---|---|---|
| 17" | $25.00 | $200.00 |
| 19" | $35.00 | $250.00 |
| 22" | $40.00 | $300.00 |
| 24" | $45.00 | $350.00 |

**Samantha, 1965 – 66**

From TV show, *Bewitched,* vinyl head and body, rooted saran hair, posable arms and legs, wearing red witch's costume, with broom, painted side-glancing eyes, other costumes included negligee, *marks: "IDEAL DOLL//M-12-E-2,"* on head

| | | |
|---|---|---|
| 12" | $35.00 | $135.00 |

**Tabitha,** 1966, baby from TV show, *Bewitched,* vinyl head, body, rooted platinum hair, painted blue side-glancing eyes, closed mouth, came in pajamas, *marks: "©1965//Screen Gems, Inc.//Ideal Toy Corp.//T.A. 18-6//H-25,"* on head

| | | |
|---|---|---|
| 14" | $20.00 | $75.00 |

**Saucy Walker, 1951 – 55**

All hard plastic, walks, turns head from side to side, flirty blue eyes, crier, open/closed mouth, teeth, holes in body for crier, saran wig, plastic curlers, came as toddler, boy, and "Big Sister"

| | | |
|---|---|---|
| 16" | $35.00 | $125.00 |
| 22" | $50.00 | $200.00 |

Black,

| | | |
|---|---|---|
| 16" | $50.00 | $200.00 |

**Big Sister,** 1954

| | | |
|---|---|---|
| 25" | $40.00 | $150.00 |

**1960 – 61,** all vinyl, rooted saran hair, blue sleep eyes, closed smiling mouth, walker, original print dress, pinafore, box, *marks: "©IDEAL TOY CORP.//T28X-60,"* or "IDEAL TOY CO.//BYE S 285 B," on head, "*IDEAL TOY CORP.//T-28 Pat. Pend.,"* on body

| | | |
|---|---|---|
| 28" | $50.00 | $200.00 |
| 32" | $65.00 | $250.00 |

**Smokey, the Bear, 1953+**

Bakelite vinyl face and paws, rayon plush stuffed body, vinyl forest ranger hat, badge, shovel, symbol of USA National Forest Serves, wears "Smokey" marked belt, twill trousers, came with Junior Forest Ranger kit, issued on 50th anniversary of Ideal's original Teddy Bear.

| | | |
|---|---|---|
| 18" | $15.00 | $50.00 |
| 25" | $20.00 | $75.00 |
| 1957, talking | $25.00 | $100.00 |

**Snoozie, 1949**

1933 doll reissued in vinyl, cloth body with Swiss music box

| | | |
|---|---|---|
| 11" | $20.00 | $75.00 |
| 16" | $25.00 | $100.00 |
| 20" | $40.00 | $150.00 |

**1958 – 65,** all vinyl, rooted Saran hair, blue sleep eyes, open/closed mouth, cry voice, knob makes doll wiggle, closes eyes, cries, in flannel pajamas

| | | |
|---|---|---|
| 14" | $6.00 | $25.00 |

**1964 – 65,** vinyl head, arms, legs, soft body, rooted Saran hair, sleep eyes, turn knob, she squirms, opens and closes eyes, and cries, *marks:* "©1965//IDEAL TOY CORP//YTT-14-E," on head, "IDEAL TOY CORP//U.S. PAT. NO. 3,029,552," on knob on back

| | | |
|---|---|---|
| 20" | $12.00 | $45.00 |

**Tammy and Her Family**

**Tammy, 1962+,** vinyl head and arms, plastic legs and torso, head joined at neck base, *marks:* "©IDEAL TOY CORP.//BS12," on head, "©IDEAL TOY CORP.//BS-12//1," on back

| | | | |
|---|---|---|---|
| | 12" | $15.00 | $50.00 |
| Black | | | |
| | 12" | $40.00 | $80.00 |
| Pos'n | | | |
| | 12" | $25.00 | $50.00 |
| **Dad** | 12" | $20.00 | $50.00 |
| **Mom** | 12" | $20.00 | $50.00 |
| **Ted** | 12" | $30.00 | $50.00 |
| **Pepper** | 9" | $20.00 | $45.00 |
| Clothing on cards | | $8.00 | $20.00 |

**Thumbelina, 1961 – 62**

Vinyl head and limbs, soft cloth body, painted eyes, rooted saran hair, open/closed mouth, wind knob on back moves body, crier in 1962

| | | |
|---|---|---|
| 16" | $9.00 | $35.00 |
| 20" | $12.00 | $45.00 |

**1982 – 83,** all vinyl one-piece body, rooted hair, comes in quilted carrier, also black

| | | |
|---|---|---|
| 7" | $4.00 | $15.00 |

**1982, 85,** reissue from 60s mold, vinyl head, arms and legs, cloth body, painted eyes, crier, open mouth, molded or rooted hair, original with box

| | | |
|---|---|---|
| 18" | $8.00 | $30.00 |

# Ideal (cont.)

*14" hard plastic Toni, $600.00. Courtesy McMasters Doll Auctions.*

**Thumbelina, Ltd. Production Collector's Doll,** 1983 – 85, porcelain, painted eyes, molded painted hair, beige crocheted outfit with pillow booties, limited edition of 1,000

| | | |
|---|---|---|
| 18" | $20.00 | $75.00 |
| 24" | $25.00 | $100.00 |

**Tiny Thumbelina,** 1962 – 68, vinyl head, limbs, cloth body, painted eyes, rooted Saran hair, wind key in back makes body and head move, original tagged clothes. *Marks: "IDEAL TOY CORP.//OTT-14,"* on head, *"U.S. PAT. #3029552,"* on body

| | | |
|---|---|---|
| 14" | $7.50 | $30.00 |

## Tiffany Taylor, 1974 – 76

All vinyl, rooted hair, top of head turns to change color, painted eyes, teenage body, high-heels, extra outfits available.

| | | |
|---|---|---|
| 19" | $12.00 | $45.00 |

Black

| | | |
|---|---|---|
| 19" | $15.00 | $50.00 |

## Toni, 1949

Designed by Bernard Lipfert, all hard plastic, jointed body, Dupont nylon wig, usually blue eyes, rosy cheeks, closed mouth, came with Toni wave set and curlers in original dress, with hang tag, *marks: "IDEAL DOLL//MADE IN U.S.A.,"* on head, *"IDEAL DOLL,"* (and P-series number) on body

P – 90

| | | |
|---|---|---|
| 14" | $135.00 | $550.00 |

P – 91

| | | |
|---|---|---|
| 16" | $150.00 | $600.00 |

Ideal Doll//17

| | | |
|---|---|---|
| | $165.00 | $650.00 |

P – 92

| | | |
|---|---|---|
| 18" | $165.00 | $650.00 |

P – 93

| | | |
|---|---|---|
| 21" | $175.00 | $700.00 |

P – 94

| | | |
|---|---|---|
| 23" | $195.00 | $750.00 |

**Velvet,** 1971 – 73, Crissy's cousin, vinyl head, body, grow hair, talker, pull string, *marks: "©1969//IDEAL TOY CORP.//GH-15-H-157,"* on head, *"©1971//IDEAL TOY CORP.//TV 15//US PAT 3162973//OTHER PATENTS PEND.,"* on back

| | | |
|---|---|---|
| 15" | $12.00 | $45.00 |

**1974,** non talker, other accessories, grow hair

| | | |
|---|---|---|
| 15" | $9.00 | $35.00 |

**Wizard of Oz Series, 1984 – 85**, Tin Man, Lion, Scarecrow, Dorothy and Toto, all vinyl, six-piece posable bodies
    9"    $7.00    $25.00

**Wonder Woman, 1967 – 68**, all vinyl, posable body, rooted hair, painted side-glancing eyes, dressed in costume
    11½"    $35.00    $125.00

## Kenner

First price indicates played with, or missing accessories dolls; second price is for mint condition dolls.

**Baby Bundles**

| | | | |
|---|---|---|---|
| White | 16" | $4.00 | $20.00 |
| Black | 16" | $6.00 | $25.00 |

**Baby Yawnie, 1974**
Vinyl head, cloth body
    15"    $5.00    $20.00

**Blythe, 1972**
Pull string to change color of eyes, "mod" clothes
    11½"    $10.00    $40.00

**Butch Cassidy or Sundance Kid**
    4"    $4.00    $15.00

**Charlie Chaplin, 1973**
All cloth, walking mechanism
    14"    $25.00    $90.00

**Cover Girls, 1978**
Posable elbows and knees, joined hands
**Dana,** black
    12½"    $20.00    $50.00
**Darci,** brunette
    12½"    $15.00    $45.00
Blonde
    12½"    $10.00    $30.00
Redhead
    12½"    $15.00    $45.00
**Erica,** redhead
    12½"    $45.00    $100.00

**Crumpet, 1970**
Vinyl and plastic
    8"    $8.00    $30.00

**Dusty**
    12"    $5.00    $18.00

**Gabbigale,** 1972
White
    18"    $10.00    $35.00
Black
    18"    $12.00    $45.00

**Garden Gals, 1972**
Hand bent to hold watering can
    6½"    $3.00    $10.00

*12" Bionic Woman, $40.00, and Six Million Dollar Man with Mission Control Center set, $50.00. Courtesy Cathie Clark.*

**Hardy Boys, 1978, Shaun Cassidy, Parker Stevenson**
12"    $5.00    $27.50
**International Velvet, 1976, Tatum O'Neill**
11½"   $8.00    $25.00
**Jenny Jones, and baby, 1973,** all vinyl
Jenny, 9", Baby, 2½"
        $4.00    $15.00
Set    $8.00    $25.00

## Six Million Dollar Man figures, 1975 –77
TV show starring Lee Majors
Bionic Man, Big Foot
    12"      $7.00          $25.00
Bionic Man Masketron Robot
    12"      $8.00          $30.00
Bionic Woman Robot
    12"     $10.00         $40.00
Jamie Summers, Bionic Woman
    12"     $10.00         $40.00
Oscar Goldman, 1975 – 77, with exploding briefcase
    13"     $15.00         $50.00
Skye, black doll
    12"      $8.00          $25.00
Steve Austin, The Bionic Man, with equipment and accessories
    13"     $20.00         $50.00
Steve Austin, Bionic Grip, 1977
    13"     $25.00         $95.00

## Star Wars figures, 1974 – 78
Large size action figures prices
First price indicates dolls played with, or missing accessories; second price is for mint-in-box/package dolls. Complete dolls in excellent condition would be somewhere in between. Never removed from box would bring greater prices.
Ben-Obi-Wan Kenobi
    12"     $25.00         $95.00
Boba Fett
    13"     $55.00        $175.00
C-3PO
    12"     $35.00        $135.00
Chewbacca
    12"     $40.00        $145.00
Darth Vader
    12"     $50.00        $200.00
Han Solo
    12"    $125.00        $475.00

| IG-88 | | |
|---|---|---|
| 15" | $150.00 | $600.00 |
| Jawa | | |
| 8½" | $25.00 | $100.00 |
| Leia Organa | | |
| 11½" | $65.00 | $275.00 |
| Luke Skywalker | | |
| 12" | $65.00 | $275.00 |
| R2-D2 | | |
| 7½" | $45.00 | $175.00 |
| Stormtrooper | | |
| 12" | $50.00 | $200.00 |

**Strawberry Shortcake, ca. 1980 – 86**

| | | |
|---|---|---|
| 5" | $6.00 | $25.00 |
| Sleep eyes | $8.00 | $35.00 |
| Purple Pie Man | | |
| 9" | $9.00 | $36.00 |

**Steve Scout, 1974**

White

| 9" | $5.00 | $20.00 |
|---|---|---|

Black

| 9" | $7.00 | $25.00 |
|---|---|---|

**Sweet Cookie, 1972**

| 18" | $8.00 | $30.00 |
|---|---|---|

*13" hard plastic Kewpie in original outfit, $300.00. Courtesy McMasters Doll Auctions.*

# Kewpie

**Bisque Kewpies, see Antique Kewpie section**

**All Cloth**

All cloth made by Kreuger, all one piece, including clothing

| 12" | $50.00 | $185.00 |
|---|---|---|
| 16" | $100.00 | $350.00 |
| 20" | $150.00 | $600.00 |
| 25" | $400.00 | $1,200.00 |

**Kewpie Baby, 1960s,** hinged joints

| 15" | $45.00 | $185.00 |
|---|---|---|
| 18" | $75.00 | $300.00 |

**Kewpie Baby,** one-piece stuffed body and limbs

| 15" | $60.00 | $225.00 |
|---|---|---|
| 18" | $75.00 | $300.00 |

**All Composition**

**Jointed Arms Only**

| 9" | $40.00 | $165.00 |
|---|---|---|
| 12" | $60.00 | $250.00 |
| 14" | $50.00 | $300.00 |

**Jointed neck, shoulders, hips**

| 9" | $60.00 | $225.00 |
|---|---|---|
| 14" | $100.00 | $375.00 |

Black

| 12" | $100.00 | $435.00 |
|---|---|---|

*Set of seven 3" celluloid wedding party Kewpie figures, probably made in England, box label reads: "See you get Barratts Best of all Christmas Cracker, They all Crack," $40.00. Courtesy Sue Kinkade.*

**Composition head,** cloth body

| | | |
|---|---|---|
| 14" | $85.00 | $325.00 |

**Celluloid**

| | | |
|---|---|---|
| 2" | $9.00 | $35.00 |
| 5" | $20.00 | $85.00 |
| 9" | $35.00 | $135.00 |

  Black

| | | |
|---|---|---|
| 5" | $40.00 | $170.00 |

**Hard Plastic, 1950s**

**One-piece body and head**

| | | |
|---|---|---|
| 8" | $60.00 | $120.00 |
| 12" | $95.00 | $185.00 |
| 16" | $140.00 | $265.00 |

**Fully jointed at shoulder neck, hips**

| | | |
|---|---|---|
| 12 – 13" | $220.00 | $435.00 |
| 16" | $270.00 | $535.00 |

**Vinyl**

**Vinyl head, limbs, cloth body**

| | | |
|---|---|---|
| 16" | $50.00 | $185.00 |

**Hinge jointed** (Miss Peep's body)

| | | |
|---|---|---|
| 16" | $55.00 | $225.00 |

**Jointed shoulder only**

| | | |
|---|---|---|
| 9" | $10.00 | $40.00 |
| 12" | $18.00 | $60.00 |
| 14" | $20.00 | $70.00 |

**Jointed neck, shoulder, hips**

| | | |
|---|---|---|
| 9" | $20.00 | $75.00 |
| 12" | $35.00 | $130.00 |
| 14" | $50.00 | $170.00 |
| 27" | $90.00 | $275.00 |

**Molded one piece, no joints**

| | | |
|---|---|---|
| 9" | $7.00 | $25.00 |
| 12" | $12.00 | $40.00 |
| 14" | $15.00 | $55.00 |

**Black**

| | | |
|---|---|---|
| 9" | $17.00 | $50.00 |
| 12" | $20.00 | $70.00 |
| 14" | $40.00 | $115.00 |

**Bean Bag type body, 1970s**

| | | |
|---|---|---|
| 10" | $10.00 | $35.00 |

**Plush, 1960s,** usually red body with vinyl face mask, made by Knickerbocker

| | | |
|---|---|---|
| 6" | $5.00 | $35.00 |
| 10" | $15.00 | $55.00 |

**Ragsy,** 1964, vinyl, one-piece, molded on clothes with heart on chest

| | | |
|---|---|---|
| 8" | $10.00 | $40.00 |

No heart, 1971

| | | |
|---|---|---|
| 8" | $4.00 | $15.00 |

**Thinker,** 1971, one-piece vinyl, sitting down

| | | |
|---|---|---|
| 4" | $5.00 | $20.00 |

Ward's Anniversary, 1972

| | | |
|---|---|---|
| 8" | $15.00 | $55.00 |

# Klumpe

Caricature figures made of felt over wire armature with painted mask faces, produced in Barcelona, Spain, from about 1952 to the mid 1970s. Figures represent professionals, hobbyists, Spanish dancers, historical character and contemporary men and women performing a wide variety of tasks. Of the 200 or more different figures, the most common are Spanish dancers, bull fighters, and doctors. Some Klumpes were imported by Effanbee in the early 1950s. Originally the figures had two sewn-on identifying cardboard tags.

Average figure

| | | |
|---|---|---|
| 10½" | $25.00 | $95.00+ |

Elaborate figure, MIB with accessories  $225.00

*Klumpe felt clown with typical gold/red foil paper label, circa 1960, $95.00. Courtesy Sondra Gast.*

*16" Little Orphan Annie and her dog, Sandy, rayon tag on dress, circa 1977, $50.00. Courtesy Angie Gonzales.*

**Bozo Clown**

| | | |
|---|---|---|
| 14" | $7.00 | $25.00 |
| 24" | $17.00 | $60.00 |

**Cinderella**

Two face, one sad and one with tiara

| | | |
|---|---|---|
| 16" | $5.00 | $20.00 |

**Clown**

Cloth

| | | |
|---|---|---|
| 17" | $5.00 | $25.00 |

**Composition child, 1938+**

| | | |
|---|---|---|
| 15" | $55.00 | $285.00 |

**"Dagwood" comic strip characters**

Composition, painted features, hair

Alexander

| | | |
|---|---|---|
| 9" | $100.00 | $375.00 |

Dagwood

| | | |
|---|---|---|
| 14" | $175.00 | $650.00 |

**Disney characters**

Donald Duck, Mickey Mouse, etc., all cloth

| | |
|---|---|
| $125.00 | $425.00 |

**Jiminy Cricket**

All composition

| | | |
|---|---|---|
| 10" | $125.00 | $495.00 |

**Mickey Mouse, 1930s – 40s**

Composition , cloth body

| | | |
|---|---|---|
| 18" | $300.00 | $1,100.00 |

**Pinocchio**

Cloth and plush

| | | |
|---|---|---|
| 13" | $65.00 | $250.00 |

All composition

| | | |
|---|---|---|
| 13" | $70.00 | $285.00 |

**Seven Dwarfs, 1939+**

Compo

| | | |
|---|---|---|
| 10" | $75.00 | $275.00 |

Cloth

| | | |
|---|---|---|
| 14" | $65.00 | $260.00 |

**Sleeping Beauty, 1939+**

Composition, bent right arm

| | | |
|---|---|---|
| 15" | $100.00 | $425.00 |
| 18" | $130.00 | $495.00 |

**Snow White, 1937+**

All composition, bent right arm, black wig

| | | |
|---|---|---|
| 15" | $110.00 | $435.00 |
| 20" | $125.00 | $475.00 |

Molded hair, and ribbon, *marks: "Walt Disney//1937//Knickerbocker"*

| | | |
|---|---|---|
| 13" | $75.00 | $360.00 |
| All cloth 16" | $95.00 | $365.00 |

**Flintstone Characters**

| | | |
|---|---|---|
| 6" | $3.00 | $10.00 |
| 17" | $9.00 | $43.00 |

**Kewpies, see that section**

**Little House on the Prairie, 1978**

| | | |
|---|---|---|
| 12" | $6.00 | $22.00 |

**Little Orphan Annie comic strip characters, 1982**

**Little Orphan Annie, vinyl**

| | | |
|---|---|---|
| 6" | $5.00 | $17.50 |

**Daddy Warbucks**

| | | |
|---|---|---|
| 7" | $5.00 | $17.50 |

**Punjab**

| | | |
|---|---|---|
| 7" | $4.00 | $18.00 |

**Miss Hannigan**

| | | |
|---|---|---|
| 7" | $4.00 | $18.00 |

**Molly**

| | | |
|---|---|---|
| 5½" | $4.00 | $12.00 |

**Soupy Sales, 1966**

Vinyl and cloth, non-removable clothes

| | | |
|---|---|---|
| 13" | $35.00 | $135.00 |

**Two-faced Dolls, 1960s**

Vinyl face masks, one crying, one smiling

| | | |
|---|---|---|
| 12" | $5.00 | $18.00 |

# Lawton

**Lawton Doll Company, Wendy Lawton, 1979+ Turlock, CA.**

First price indicates complete, mint in box dolls; dolls missing accessories or with flaws would be priced less.

**Alice in Wonderland**, limited edition 100, 1983

| | | |
|---|---|---|
| | 13" | $3,000.00+ |

**She Walks In Beauty**

| | |
|---|---|
| 18" | $500.00 |

**Anne of Green Gables**

| | |
|---|---|
| 14" | $1,600.00+ |

**Ba Ba Black Sheep** (first Guild doll)

| |
|---|
| $750.00 |

| | | |
|---|---|---|
| **Hans Brinker** | 14" | $850.00 |
| **Heidi** | 14" | $850.00 |
| **Highland Mary** | 18" | $500.00+ |

*1989 Disney World's first limited edition, Main Street U.S.A., $450.00. Courtesy Toni Winder.*

# Lawton (cont.)

| | | |
|---|---|---|
| **Marcella & Raggedy Ann** (2,500) | | $795.00 |
| **Laura Ingalls** | | $600.00 |
| **Lil' Princess** | 14" | $850.00 |

**Josephine,** souvenir doll of Modesto, CA, UFDC Region 2 North Conference, extra outfits, book, duck, and suitcase

| | | |
|---|---|---|
| | 12" | $1,200.00+ |
| **Young Charlotte** | 18" | $500.00 |
| **Disney World Specials** | | |
| 1 Main Street | | $450.00 |
| 2 Liberty Square (250) | | $400.00 |
| 3 Tish | | $400.00 |
| 4 Karen (50) | | $800.00 |
| 5 Goofy Kid (100) | | $800.00 |
| 6 Melissa & Her Mickey | | $750.00 |
| 7 Christopher, Robin & Pooh | 12" | $750.00 |
| **Other Specials** | | |
| Britta, Marta, Toy Village, Lansing, MI | | $595.00 |
| Morgan, Toy Village, Lansing MI | | $695.00 |
| Kitty, The Toy Store, Toledo, OH | | $400.00 |
| Little Colonel, Dolly Dears, Birmingham, AL | | $425.00 |
| First WL Convention, Lotta Crabtree | | $1,300.00+ |
| Second WL Convention, Through the Looking Glass | | |
| | 16" | $1,100.00+ |

## Marcie

**1950s+ Hard plastic,** jointed hips and shoulders, some with molded shoes.

Glamour Cowgirl, Laurie Anders, from TV's *Ken Murray Show*, 1950 – 53, western outfit, sleep eyes, closed mouth

| | | |
|---|---|---|
| 7" | $5.00 | $20.00 |

Man, circus ringleader, red and white crocheted outfit, black plastic top hat

| | | |
|---|---|---|
| 7" | $5.00 | $10.00 |

## Marx

### ARCHIE AND FRIENDS

Characters from comics, vinyl, molded hair or wigged, painted eyes, in package

| | | |
|---|---|---|
| **Archie** | $7.00 | $25.00 |
| **Betty** | $7.00 | $25.00 |
| **Jughead** | $7.00 | $25.00 |
| **Veronica** | $5.00 | $20.00 |

### JOHNNY APOLLO ASTRONAUT

Vinyl, jointed, posable

| | | |
|---|---|---|
| 8" | $10.00 | $40.00 |

## JOHNNY WEST FAMILY ACTION FIGURES
### 1965 – 76

**Adventure or Best of the West Series,** rigid vinyl, articulated figures, molded clothes, came in box with vinyl accessories, and extra clothes. Had horses, dogs, and other accessories available.

**Bill Buck,** brown molded on clothing, 13 pieces, coon skin cap

| | | |
|---|---|---|
| 11½" | $30.00 | $120.00 |

**Captain Tom Maddox,** blue molded on clothing, brown hair, 23 pieces

| | | |
|---|---|---|
| 11½" | $25.00 | $85.00 |

**Chief Cherokee,** tan or light color molded on clothing, 37 pieces

| | | |
|---|---|---|
| 11½" | $25.00 | $100.00 |

**Daniel Boone,** tan molded on clothing, coonskin cap

| | | |
|---|---|---|
| 11½" | $25.00 | `$100.00 |

**Fighting Eagle,** tan molded on clothes, with Mohawk hair, 37 pieces

| | | |
|---|---|---|
| 11½" | $35.00 | $125.00 |

**General Custer,** dark blue molded on clothing, yellow hair, 23 pieces

| | | |
|---|---|---|
| 11½" | $20.00 | $80.00 |

**Geronimo,** light color molded clothing

| | | |
|---|---|---|
| 11½" | $25.00 | $90.00 |

**Jamie West,** dark hair, molded on tan clothing, 13 accessories

| | | |
|---|---|---|
| 9" | $10.00 | $40.00 |

**Jane West,** blonde hair, turquoise body, 37 pieces

| | | |
|---|---|---|
| 11½" | $12.00 | $45.00 |
| Orange body | $10.00 | $40.00 |

**Janice West,** dark hair, turquoise molded on clothing, 14 pieces

| | | |
|---|---|---|
| 9" | $10.00 | $40.00 |

**Jay West,** blond hair, tan molded on clothing, 13 accessories, later brighter body colors

| | | |
|---|---|---|
| 9" | $10.00 | $40.00 |

**Jeb Gibson,** ca. 1973, black figure, molded on green clothing

| | | |
|---|---|---|
| 12" | $100.00 | $200.00 |

**Johnny West,** brown hair, molded on brown clothing, 25 pieces

| | | |
|---|---|---|
| 12" | $23.00 | $85.00 |

Johnny West, with quick draw arm, blue clothing

| | | |
|---|---|---|
| 12" | $10.00 | $40.00 |

**Josie West,** blonde, turquoise molded on clothing, later with bright green body

| | | |
|---|---|---|
| 9" | $10.00 | $40.00 |

*12" rigid vinyl Johnny West articulated figure, later issue, the quick draw version with molded blue clothing and lever on back for the quick draw, $20.00 with few accessories.*

*11½" rigid vinyl, articulated figure Princess Wildflower with papoose in vinyl cradle, 22-piece accessory set from Johnny West Best of the West Series, came in either orange or turquoise vinyl, $125.00.*

**Princess Wildflower,** off-white molded on clothing, with papoose in vinyl cradle, 22 pieces of accessories

    11½"    $35.00    $125.00

**Sam Cobra,** outlaw, with 26 accessories

    11½"    $25.00    $100.00

Sam Cobra, quick draw version

           $35.00    $125.00

**Sheriff Pat Garrett** (Sheriff Goode in Canada), molded on blue clothing, 25 pieces of accessories

    11½"    $35.00    $125.00

**Zeb Zachary,** dark hair, blue molded on clothing, 23 pieces

    11½"    $25.00    $100.00

## KNIGHT, VIKING SERIES, CA. 1960s

Action figures with accessories

### Knights

**Gordon, the Gold Knight,** molded on gold clothing, brown hair, beard, mustache

    11½"    $35.00        $125.00

**Sir Stuart, Silver Knight,** molded on silver clothing, black hair, mustache, goatee

    11½"    $35.00        $125.00

### Vikings

**Brave Erik with horse,** ca. 1967, molded on green clothing, blond hair, blue eyes

    11½"    $50.00        $150.00

**Odin, the Viking,** ca. 1967, brown molded on clothing, brown eyes, brown hair, beard

    11½"    $35.00        $100.00

## MISS TODDLER

Also know as Miss Marx, vinyl, molded hair, ribbons, battery operated walker, molded clothing

    18"    $75.00        $150.00

## SOLDIERS, CA. 1960s

Articulated action figures with accessories.

**Buddy Charlie,** Montgomery Wards exclusive, a buddy for GI Joe, molded on military uniform, brown hair

    11½"    $25.00    $100.00

**Stony "Stonewall" Smith,** molded on Army fatigues, blond hair, 36-piece accessories

    11½"    $25.00    $100.00

## Matchbox

**PeeWee Herman,** TV character, vinyl and cloth, ventriloquist doll in gray suit, red bow tie

    26"    $20.00    $65.00

## Mattel

**Baby Beans, 1971 – 75**
Vinyl head, bean bag dolls, terry cloth or tricot bodies filled with plastic and foam

    12"    $5.00    $18.00

    Talking

    12"    $7.00    $22.00

**Baby First Step, 1965 – 67**
Battery operated walker, rooted hair, sleep eyes, pink dress

    18"    $7.00    $22.00

    Talking

    18"    $8.00    $27.00

**Baby Go Bye-Bye and Her Bumpety Buggy, 1970**
Doll sits in car, battery operated, 12 maneuvers

    11"    $4.00    $12.00

**Baby's Hungry, 1967 – 68**
Battery operated, eyes move and lips chew when bottle or spoon put to mouth, wets, plastic bib over polka dot dress

    17½"    $8.00    $22.00

**Baby Love Light**
Battery operated  16"    $5.00    $18.00

**Baby Pattaburp, 1964 – 66**
Vinyl, drinks milk, burps when patted, pink jacket, lace trim

    16"    $7.00    $22.00

**Baby Play-A-Lot, 1972 – 73**
Posable arms, fingers can hold things, comes with 20 toys, moves arm to brush teeth, moves head, no batteries, has pull string and switch

    16"    $5.00    $22.00

**Baby Say 'n See, 1967 – 68**
Eyes and lips move while talking, white dress, pink yoke

    17"    $5.00    $18.00

**Baby Secret, 1966 – 67**
Vinyl face and hands, stuffed body, limbs, red hair, blue eyes, whispers 11 phases, moves lips

    18"    $8.00    $27.00

*6¼" vinyl Buffy from TV sitcom, Family Affair, with her doll, Mrs. Beasley, 1967, $200.00. Courtesy Cathie Clark.*

**Baby Small Talk, 1968 – 69**
Says 8 phrases, infant voice, addition outfits available

| | | |
|---|---|---|
| 10¾" | $4.00 | $12.00 |
| Black | | |
| 10¾" | $7.00 | $22.00 |

**Baby Tender Love, 1970 – 73**
Baby doll, realistic skin, wets, can be bathed
**Newborn**

| | | |
|---|---|---|
| 13" | $4.00 | $12.00 |

**Talking**

| | | |
|---|---|---|
| 16" | $5.00 | $18.00 |

**Living, 1970**

| | | |
|---|---|---|
| 20" | $8.00 | $27.00 |

**Molded hairpiece, 1972**

| | | |
|---|---|---|
| 11½" | $9.00 | $33.00 |

**Brother,** sexed

| | | |
|---|---|---|
| 11½ | $10.00 | $38.00 |

**Baby Teenie Talk, 1965**

| | | |
|---|---|---|
| 17" | $7.00 | $22.00 |

**Baby Walk 'n Play, 1968**

| | | |
|---|---|---|
| 11" | $4.00 | $12.00 |

**Baby Walk 'n See**

| | | |
|---|---|---|
| 18" | $5.00 | $18.00 |

**Barbie: see that section**

**Bozo**

| | | |
|---|---|---|
| 18" | $8.00 | $28.00 |

**Buffy and Mrs. Beasley, 1967 & 74**
Characters from TV sitcom, *Family Affair*
**Buffy,** vinyl, rooted hair, painted features, holds small Mrs. Beasley, vinyl head, on cloth body

| | | |
|---|---|---|
| 6½" | $75.00 | $200.00 |

**Talking Buffy,** vinyl 1969 – 71, holds tiny 6" rag, Mrs. Beasley

| | | |
|---|---|---|
| 10.75" | $45.00 | $165.00 |

**Mrs. Beasley,** 1967 – 74, talking vinyl head, cloth body, square glasses, blue polka-dot dress

| | | |
|---|---|---|
| 22" | $20.00 | $80.00 |

Mrs. Beasley, 1973, non-talker

| | | |
|---|---|---|
| 15½" | $9.00 | $35.00 |

**Captain Kangaroo, 1967**
Sears only, talking character, host for TV kids program

| | | |
|---|---|---|
| 19" | $20.00 | $75.00 |

**Captain Laser, 1967**
Vinyl, painted features, blue uniform, silver accessories, batteries operate laser gun, light-up eyes

| | | |
|---|---|---|
| 12" | $70.00 | $265.00 |

*24" vinyl Charmin' Chatty Travels 'Round the World Set, box, $175.00. Courtesy McMasters Doll Auctions.*

**Casper, the Ghost, ca. 1964**

| | | |
|---|---|---|
| 16" | $7.00 | $28.00 |
| 1971  5" | $3.00 | $10.00 |

*20" Chatty Cathy, circa 1962, pull string talker, all original with box, $250.00. Courtesy Angie Gonzales.*

**Chatty Cathy Series**

**Chatty Cathy, 1960 – 63,** all vinyl, pull string activates voice, pink and white checked dress or blue party dress. 1963 – 65, says 18 new phrases, red velvet and white lace dress, extra outfits available

Blonde
| 20" | $25.00 | $100.00 |
|---|---|---|

Brunette, brown eyes
| 20" | $25.00 | $135.00 |
|---|---|---|

Black, 1961 – 63
| 20" | $100.00 | $400.00 |
|---|---|---|

**Chatty Baby, 1962 – 64,** red pinafore over rompers
| 18" | $15.00 | $55.00 |
|---|---|---|

**Charmin' Chatty, 1963 – 64,** talking doll, soft vinyl head, closed smiling mouth, hard vinyl body, long rooted hair, long legs, five records placed in left side slot, one piece navy skirt, white middy blouse with red sailor collar, red socks and saddle shoes, glasses, five disks, extra outfits and 14 more disks available
| 24" | $50.00 | $175.00 |
|---|---|---|

**Tiny Chatty Baby,** 1963 – 64, smaller version of Chatty Baby, blue rompers, blue, white striped panties, bib with name, talks, other outfits available
| 15½" | $7.00 | $25.00 |
|---|---|---|

Black
| 5½" | $10.00 | $40.00 |
|---|---|---|

**Tiny Chatty Brother,** 1963 – 64, boy version of Tiny Chatty Baby, blue and white suit and cap, hair parted on side
| 15½" | $8.00 | $30.00 |
|---|---|---|

**Cheerful Tearful, 1966 – 67**

Vinyl, blonde hair, face changes from smile to pout as arm is lowered, feed her bottle, wet and cries real tears
| 13" | $5.00 | $18.00 |
|---|---|---|

# Mattel (cont.)

*17" vinyl Dancerella, hard plastic body, circa 1972, she spins when you hold top of head, $100.00. Courtesy Angie Gonzales.*

### Dancerina, 1969 – 71
Battery operated, posable arms and legs, turns, dances with control knob on head, pink ballet outfit

| | | |
|---|---|---|
| 24" | $20.00 | $75.00 |

**Baby Dancerina**, 1970, smaller version, no batteries, turn knob on head, white ballet outfit.

| | | |
|---|---|---|
| 16" | $15.00 | $50.00 |
| Black | | |
| 16" | $20.00 | $60.00 |

**Teeny Dancerina**

| | | |
|---|---|---|
| 12" | $8.00 | $30.00 |

### Debbie Boone, 1978

| | | |
|---|---|---|
| 11½" | $12.00 | $40.00 |

### Dick Van Dyke, 1969
As Mr. Potts in movie, *Chitty Chitty Bang Bang*, all cloth, flat features, talks in actor's voice. *Marks: "©Mattel 1969"* on cloth tag.

| | | |
|---|---|---|
| 24" | $18.00 | $85.00 |

### Drowsey, 1965 – 74
Vinyl, head, stuffed body, sleepers, pull string talker

| | | |
|---|---|---|
| 15½" | $5.00 | $18.00 |

### Dr. Doolittle, 1968,
Character patterned after Rex Harrison in movie version, talker, vinyl with cloth body

| | | |
|---|---|---|
| 24" | $18.00 | $55.00 |
| All vinyl | | |
| 6" | $6.00 | $22.00 |

### Gramma Doll, 1970 – 73
Sears only, cloth, painted face, gray yarn hair, says 10 phrases, talker, foam filled cotton

| | | |
|---|---|---|
| 11" | $4.00 | $15.00 |

### Grizzly Adams, 1971

| | | |
|---|---|---|
| 10" | $10.00 | $40.00 |

### Guardian Goddesses, 1979

| | | |
|---|---|---|
| 11½" | $40.00 | $165.00 |

### Herman Munster, 1965
Cloth doll, talking TV character, *The Adams Family*

| | | |
|---|---|---|
| 21" | $8.00 | $28.00 |

### Julia, 1969
TV character nurse, from *Julia*
One-piece uniform

| | | |
|---|---|---|
| 11½" | $35.00 | $125.00 |
| Two-piece uniform | | |
| 11½ | $45.00 | $175.00 |
| Talking | | |
| 11½" | $40.00 | $135.00 |

## Liddle Kiddles, 1966+

Small dolls of vinyl over wire frame, posable, painted features, rooted hair, and came with bright costumes and accessories, packaged on 8½" x 9½" cards. *Marks: "1965// Mattel Inc.// Japan"* on backs

First price is for complete dolls and accessories, excellent condition; second price (or one price only) is for mint complete dolls and accessories. Add more for mint in package (or card) and never removed from package. Less for worn dolls with missing accessories.

### 1966, First Series

| | | | |
|---|---|---|---|
| 3501 Bunson Bernie | 3" | $40.00 | $50.00 |
| 3502 Howard "Biff" Boodle | 3½" | $45.00 | $60.00 |
| 3503 Liddle Diddle | 2¾" | $40.00 | $50.00 |
| 3505 Babe Biddle | 3½" | $40.00 | $50.00 |
| 3506 Calamity Jiddle | 3" | $40.00 | $50.00 |
| 3507 Florence Niddle | 2¾" | $40.00 | $50.00 |
| 3508 Greta Griddle | 3" | $40.00 | $50.00 |
| 3509 Millie Middle | 2¾" | $50.00 | $65.00 |
| 3510 Beat A Diddle | 3½" | $150.00 | $175.00 |

### 1967, Second Series

| | | | |
|---|---|---|---|
| 3513 Sizzly Friddle | 3" | $50.00 | $60.00 |
| 3514 Windy Fiddle | 2¾" | $50.00 | $60.00 |
| 3515 Trikey Triddle | 2¾" | $40.00 | $55.00 |
| 3516 Freezy Sliddle | 3½" | $40.00 | $50.00 |
| 3517 Surfy Skiddle | 3" | $50.00 | $60.00 |
| 3518 Soapy Siddle | 3½" | $45.00 | $55.00 |
| 3519 Rolly Twiddle | 3½" | $125.00 | $150.00 |
| 3548 Beddy Bye Biddle (with robe) | | $60.00 | $70.00 |

### 1968, Third Series

| | | | |
|---|---|---|---|
| 3549 Pretty Priddle | 3½" | $50.00 | $65.00 |
| 3587 Baby Liddle | 2¾" | $175.00 | $200.00 |
| 3551 Telly Viddle | 3½" | $50.00 | $65.00 |
| 3552 Lemons Stiddle | 3½" | $50.00 | $65.00 |
| 3553 Kampy Kiddle | 3½" | $50.00 | $65.00 |
| 3554 Slipsy Sliddle | 3½" | $50.00 | $60.00 |
| Storybook Kiddles, 1967 – 68 | | $60.00 – $100.00 | |
| Skediddle Kiddles, 1968 – 1970 | 4" | $25.00+ | |
| Playhouse Kiddles, 1970 | 3½" | $95.00 | |
| Kiddles 'N Kars, 1969 – 1970 | 2¾" | $55.00 | |
| Tea Party Kiddles, 1970 – 71 | 3½" | $100.00 | |
| Lucky Locket Kiddles, 1967 – 70 | 2" | $25.00+ | |
| Kiddle Kolognes, 1968 – 1970 | 2" | $25.00+ | |
| Kola Kiddles, 1968 – 69 | 2" | $35.00 | |
| Sweet Treat Kiddles, 1969 – 70 | 2" | $35.00 | |
| Liddle Kiddle Playhouses, 1966 – 68 | | $25.00+ | |

## Osmond Family

### Donny Osmond, 1978

| | | | |
|---|---|---|---|
| | 12" | $12.00 | $35.00 |

**Jimmy Osmond, 1979**
    10"    $15.00    $65.00

**Scooby Doo, 1964**
    Vinyl head, rooted hair, cloth body, talks in Beatnik phrases, blond or black hair, striped dress
    21"    $15.00    $60.00

**Shogun Warrior**
    All plastic, battery operated
    23½"    $65.00    $250.00

**Shrinkin' Violette, 1964 – 65**
    Cloth, yarn hair, pull-string talker, eyes close, mouth moves
    12"    $12.00    $45.00

*Cynthia and fashion accessories pack, $100.00. Courtesy Cathie Clark.*

**Small Talk, Baby 1968 – 69**
Pull-string talker, addition costumes available
White    10¾"    $5.00    $20.00
Black    10¾"    $7.00    $25.00
    **Small Talk, Sister, 1968 – 69,** little girl, will stand alone, talker, mini dress, white boots, addition costumes available
    10¾"    $7.00    $25.00

**Star Spangled dolls**
Uses Sunshine Family adults, marked "1973"
Regina/Richard Stanton    $12.00    $45.00
Southern Bell    $12.00    $45.00
New England Girl    $12.00    $45.00
Pioneer Daughter    $12.00    $45.00

**Sunshine Family, The**
Vinyl, posable, come with idea book, father, mother, baby
Steve    9"    $6.00    $25.00
Stephie    7½"    $6.00    $25.00
Sweets    3½"    $4.00    $15.00

**Tatters, 1965 – 67**
Talking cloth doll, wears rag clothes
    19"    $10.00    $38.00

**Teachy Keen, 1966 – 70**
Sears only, vinyl head, cloth body, ponytail, talker, tells child to use accessories included, buttons, zippers, comb
    16"    $9.00    $32.00

**Tinkerbelle**
    19"    $7.00    $22.00

**Tippee Toes, 1968 – 70**
Battery operated, legs move, rides accessory horse, tricycle; knit sweater, pants
    17"    $5.00    $18.00
Tricycle/horse    $5.00    $18.00

## Welcome Back Kotter, 1973

Characters from TV sitcom

**Freddie, "Boom Boom" Washington**

    9"    $4.00    $15.00

**Arnold Horshack**

    9"    $5.00    $20.00

**Gabe Kotter**

    9"    $8.00    $30.00

**Zython, 1977**

Has glow-in-the- dark head, enemy in "Space 1999" series

    $25.00    $100.00

# Mego

## Action Jackson, 1971 – 72

Vinyl head, plastic body, molded hair, painted black eyes, action figure, many accessory outfits, *marks: "© Mego Corp//Reg. U.S. Pat. Off.//Pat. Pend.//Hong Kong//MCMLXXI"*

    8"    $8.00    $30.00

Black

    8"    $20.00    $75.00

Dinah-mite, black

    $5.00    $20.00

## Batman, 1974

    8"    $4.00    $15.00

Arch enemy

    8"    $4.00    $15.00

## Captain & Tennille

Daryl Dragon and Toni Tennille, 1977, recording and TV personalities, Toni Tennille doll has no molded ears

    12½"    $5.00    $20.00

## Cher, 1976

TV and recording personality, and husband Sonny Bono, all vinyl, fully jointed rooted long black hair, also as grow hair doll

    12"    $12.00    $45.00

Indian outfit

    12"    $17.00    $65.00

**Sonny Bono**

    12"    $12.00    $45.00

## CHiP's, 1977

California Highway Patrol TV show, Jon Baker, Francis "Ponch" Poncherello

    8"    $4.00    $10.00

## Diana Ross, 1977

Recording and movie personality, all vinyl, fully jointed, rooted black hair, long lashes.

    12½"    $45.00    $125.00

*12¼" all vinyl, jointed celebrity Diana Ross, rooted black hair, $125.00. Courtesy Cathie Clark.*

## Farrah Fawcett, 1977

Model, movie and television personality, starred as Jill in *Charlie's Angels*, vinyl head, rooted blonde hair, painted green eyes

| | | |
|---|---|---|
| 12½" | $10.00 | $45.00 |

## Flash Gordon Series, ca. 1977+

Vinyl head, hard plastic articulated body

**Dale Arden**

| | | |
|---|---|---|
| 9" | $25.00 | $100.00 |

**Dr. Zarkov**

| | | |
|---|---|---|
| 9½" | $25.00 | $100.00 |

**Flash Gordon**

| | | |
|---|---|---|
| 9½" | $25.00 | $100.00 |

**Ming, the Merciless**

| | | |
|---|---|---|
| 9½" | $25.00 | $100.00 |

## Happy Days Series, 1976

Characters from *Happy Days* TV sitcom, Henry Winkler starred as Fonzie, Ron Howard as Richie, Anson Williams as Potsie, and Donny Most as Ralph Malph

| | | | |
|---|---|---|---|
| **Fonzie** | 8" | $5.00 | $20.00 |
| **Richie, Potsie, Ralph** | | $4.00 | $15.00 |

## Joe Namath, 1970

Football player, actor, soft vinyl head, rigid vinyl body, painted hair and features

| | | |
|---|---|---|
| 12" | $15.00 | $55.00 |

## KISS, 1978

Rock group, with Gene Simmons, Ace Frehley, Peter Cris, and Paul Stanley, all vinyl, fully jointed, rooted hair, painted features and make-up

| | | |
|---|---|---|
| 12½" | $20.00 | $80.00 |

## Laverne and Shirley, 1977

TV sitcom. Penny Marshall, played, Laverne, Cindy Williams, Shirley. Also from the same show, Squiggy and Lenny, David Lander as Squiggy, and Michael McKean as Lenny, all vinyl, rooted hair, painted eyes

| | | |
|---|---|---|
| 11½" | $6.00 | $25.00 |

## Our Gang, 1975

From *Our Gang* movie shorts, that replayed on TV, included characters, Alfalpha, Buckwheat, Darla, Mickey, Porky and Spanky

| | | |
|---|---|---|
| 6" | $5.00 | $20.00 |

## Planet of the Apes

### Movie Series, ca. 1970s

| | | | |
|---|---|---|---|
| Astronaut | 8" | $30.00 | $120.00 |
| Ape Soldier | 8" | $25.00 | $100.00 |
| Cornelius | 8" | $35.00 | $140.00 |
| Dr. Zaius | 8" | $40.00 | $150.00 |
| Zira | 8" | $35.00 | $140.00 |

### TV Series, ca. 1970s

| | | | |
|---|---|---|---|
| Alan Verdon | 8" | $40.00 | $150.00 |
| Galen | 8" | $25.00 | $100.00 |
| General Urko | 8" | $40.00 | $150.00 |
| General Ursus | 8" | $25.00 | $100.00 |
| Peter Burke | 8" | $40.00 | $150.00 |

## Star Trek
### Series, ca. 1973 – 75

| | | | |
|---|---|---|---|
| Captain Kirk | 8" | $15.00 | $60.00 |
| Dr. McCoy | 8" | $20.00 | $75.00 |
| Klingon | 8" | $20.00 | $75.00 |
| Lt. Uhura | 8" | $15.00 | $60.00 |
| Mr. Scott | 8" | $20.00 | $75.00 |
| Mr. Spock | 8" | $15.00 | $60.00 |

### Movie Series, ca. 1979

| | | | |
|---|---|---|---|
| Acturian | 12½" | $25.00 | $100.00 |
| Captain Kirk | 12½" | $15.00 | $60.00 |
| Ilia | 12½" | $15.00 | $60.00 |
| Mr. Spock | 12½" | $15.00 | $60.00 |

### Aliens, ca. 1975 – 76

| | | | |
|---|---|---|---|
| Andorian | 8" | $80.00 | $325.00 |
| Cheron | 8" | $35.00 | $130.00 |
| Mugato | 8" | $75.00 | $300.00 |
| Talos | 8" | $65.00 | $250.00 |
| The Gorn | 8" | $50.00 | $200.00 |
| The Romulan | 8" | $110.00 | $425.00 |

## Starsky and Hutch, 1976
Police TV series, Paul Michael Glaser as Starsky, David Soul as Hutch, Bernies Hamilton as Captain Dobey, Antonio Fargas as Huggy Bear, also included a villain, Chopper, all vinyl, jointed waists

| | | | |
|---|---|---|---|
| | 7½" | $6.00 | $25.00 |

## Suzanne Somers, 1978
Actress, TV personality, starred as Chrissy in *Three's Company*, all vinyl, fully jointed, rooted blonde hair, painted blue eyes, long lashes

| | | | |
|---|---|---|---|
| | 12½" | $7.00 | $28.00 |

## Waltons, The, 1975
From TV drama series, set of two dolls per package, all vinyl

| | | | |
|---|---|---|---|
| **Johnboy and Ellen** | 8" | $10.00 | $35.00 |
| **Mom and Pop** | | $10.00 | $35.00 |
| **Grandma and Grandpa** | | $10.00 | $35.00 |

## Wonder Woman Series, ca. 1976 – 77
Vinyl head, rooted black hair, painted eyes, plastic body

| | | | |
|---|---|---|---|
| **Lt. Diane Prince** | 12½" | $40.00 | $150.00 |
| **Nubia** | 12½" | $25.00 | $100.00 |
| **Nurse** | 12½" | $10.00 | $40.00 |
| **Queen Hippolyte** | 12½" | $25.00 | $100.00 |
| **Steve Trevor** | 12½" | $25.00 | $100.00 |
| **Wonder Woman** | 12½" | $40.00 | $150.00 |

# Mollye's

**Molly Goldman, 1920+.** International Doll Co. Philadelphia, PA, designed and created clothes for dolls of cloth, composition, hard plastic, and vinyl. Name marked only on vinyls; others may have had paper hang tags. She used dolls made by other companies. Also designed clothes for other manufacturers.

*14" cloth Raggedy Ann & Andy, circa 1935 – 38, multicolored striped legs, printed features, very rare dolls, $900.00 each. Courtesy Sherryl Shirran.*

### Cloth
#### Child
| | | |
|---|---|---|
| 15" | $40.00 | $150.00 |
| 18" | $45.00 | $165.00 |
| 24" | $65.00 | $215.00 |
| 29" | $85.00 | $325.00 |

#### Internationals
| | | |
|---|---|---|
| 13" | $27.00 | $95.00 |
| 15" | $45.00 | $155.00 |
| 27" | $75.00 | $300.00 |

#### Girl/Lady
| | | |
|---|---|---|
| 16" | $50.00 | $195.00 |
| 21" | $75.00 | $300.00 |

### Composition
#### Baby
| | | |
|---|---|---|
| 15" | $40.00 | $175.00 |
| 21" | $60.00 | $250.00 |

#### Cloth body
| | | |
|---|---|---|
| 18" | $25.00 | $100.00 |

#### Toddler
| | | |
|---|---|---|
| 15" | $50.00 | $235.00 |
| 21" | $75.00 | $295.00 |

#### Child
| | | |
|---|---|---|
| 15" | $50.00 | $185.00 |
| 18" | $70.00 | $265.00 |

#### Girl/Lady, add more for ball gown
| | | |
|---|---|---|
| 16" | $90.00 | $365.00 |
| 21" | $130.00 | $525.00 |

## Hard Plastic
### Baby

|       |          |          |
|-------|----------|----------|
| 14"   | $25.00   | $95.00   |
| 20"   | $40.00   | $150.00  |

### Cloth body

|       |          |          |
|-------|----------|----------|
| 17"   | $25.00   | $90.00   |
| 23"   | $35.00   | $140.00  |

### Child

|       |          |          |
|-------|----------|----------|
| 14"   | $50.00   | $200.00+ |
| 18"   | $75.00   | $300.00+ |
| 23"   | $100.00  | $400.00+ |

### Girl/Lady

|       |          |          |
|-------|----------|----------|
| 17"   | $75.00   | $315.00  |
| 20"   | $80.00   | $415.00  |
| 25"   | $110.00  | $465.00  |

## Vinyl
### Baby

|       |          |          |
|-------|----------|----------|
| 8½"   | $6.00    | $22.00   |
| 12"   | $5.00    | $27.00   |
| 15"   | $9.00    | $43.00   |

### Child

|       |          |          |
|-------|----------|----------|
| 8"    | $7.00    | $25.00   |
| 10"   | $9.00    | $35.00   |
| 15"   | $15.00   | $60.00   |

### Girl/Lady
Little Women

|       |          |          |
|-------|----------|----------|
| 9"    | $9.00    | $40.00   |

# Monica Dolls

**Ca. 1941 – 51.** Monica Dolls from Hollywood, designed by Hansi Share, were made of composition and later hard plastic with long face and painted or sleep eyes, eyeshadow. Their unique feature is very durable rooted human hair. Did not have high-heel feet. Unmarked, but wore paper wrist tag reading: "Monica Doll, Hollywood" Composition dolls had pronounced widow's peak in center of forehead

**Composition,** 1941 – 49, painted eyes

|          |          |            |
|----------|----------|------------|
| 11"      | $75.00   | $295.00    |
| 15"      | $150.00  | $525.00    |
| 17"      | $175.00  | $750.00    |
| 20 – 21" | $250.00  | $950.00    |
| 24"      | $300.00  | $1,200.00  |

* *Veronica, Jean, and Rosalind were names of 17" dolls produced in 1942*

**Hard plastic,** 1949 – 51, sleep eyes, Elizabeth, Marion, or Linda

|          |          |            |
|----------|----------|------------|
| 14"      | $150.00  | $600.00    |
| 18"      | $200.00  | $800.00    |

# Naber Kids

**Ca. 1970s – 94.** Harold Naber early in his career carved wooden figures with an Eskimo theme in Alaska. Later jointed dolls were produced dolls in Prescott, AZ, factory. The Arizona finish shows little wood grain, satin surface.

**Early Handcarved Figures**
Marked on head or foot      $900.00+
**1980s Figures**
Marked plus tag      $315.00+
**Specialty Dressed**
Alpine, Baker, Cheerleader, Detective, Doctor, Eskimo, Farmer, Gangster, Golfer, Indian, Nurse, Pilot, Waitress
     Each      $200.00+
**Specials**
Phil Racer      $675.00
Sara & Benni Indians      $725.00 (20 sets made)

**Dated Retirements:**

| Date | Name | Price |
|---|---|---|
| 6-21-87 | Molli | $3,500.00+ |
| 01-16-88 | Jake | $1,200.00+ |
| 05-04-88 | Max | $1,000.00+ |
| 03-04-88 | Ashley | $725.00+ |
| 07-15-89 | Milli | $525.00+ |
| 09-28-90 | Maurice | $675.00+ |
| 03-04-90 | Maxine | $400.00+ |
| 09-28-90 | Sissi | $825.00 (39 made) Arizona finish |
| 11-30-90 | Frieda | $725.00 (28 made) Arizona finish |
| 12-17-90 | Walter | $675.00 (67 made) Arizona finish |
| 05-03-91 | Peter | $575.00 (325 made) Arizona finish |
| 05-03-91 | Pam | $525.00 (289 made) Arizona finish |
| 07-28-91 | Darina | $525.00 (224 made) Arizona finish |
| 03-09-92 | Henry | $650.00+ other variations |
| | as Carpenter | $725.00+ |
| | as Diver | $1,300.00+ (beige, green, or yellow) |
| | as Farmer | $725.00+ |
| | as Pirate | $800.00 |
| 04-13-92 | Sami and Samantha | $350.00 each |
| 04-20-92 | Freddi | $350.00 |
| 06-28-92 | Amy | $325.00 |
| 12-08-92 | Heide | $425.00 |
| | without braces | $635.00 |
| 05-27-93 | Mishi | $275.00 |
| 05-27-93 | Hoey | $275.00 |
| 07-25-93 | Paula | $275.00 |
| 11-07-93 | Willi | $275.00 |
| 11-13-93 | Eric | $285.00 |
| 12-21-93 | Denise | $275.00 |
| 12-31-93 | Elsi | $285.00 |
| 12-31-93 | Benni | $275.00 |
| 12-31-93 | Posi | $235.00 |

12-31-94    Sarah, Joseph, Josi, Tony, Juanita, Christina, Rita Witch, Richie & Filink, Marcie      $275.00 each

**1936+, San Francisco, CA. Started by Rowena Haskin (Nancy Ann Abbott).**
Painted bisque, mohair wig, painted eyes, head molded to torso, jointed limbs, either sticker on outfit or hang tag, in box, later made in hard plastic.

First price for played-with or missing accessories dolls, second price for mint-in-box. Add 30% + more for black dolls. Painted bisque baby prices vary with outfits.

## BABY ONLY , 1936+

Gold foil sticker, pink/blue mottled or sunburst box with gold label, gold foil sticker on clothes "Nancy Ann Dressed Dolls," *marked "87," "88," or "93 Made in Japan"* no brochure.

*3½" Nancy Ann Storybook baby, painted bisque, star hand-organdy dress and bonnet, $150.00. Courtesy Elaine Pardee.*

Baby
3½" – 4½"      $100.00      $400.00

## BABY OR CHILD

### 1937
Child *marked "Made in Japan," "1146," "1148," or "Japan"* sunburst box with gold label, gold foil sticker on clothes reads "Nancy Ann Dressed Dolls," no brochure

Baby
3½ – 4½"      $275.00      $350.00
Child
5"      $250.00      $500.00

### 1938
Marked *"America"* (baby *marked "87," "88," or "93 Made in Japan"*), colored box, sunburst pattern with gold label, gold foil sticker on clothes: "Judy Ann," no brochure

Baby
3½ – 4½"      $200.00      $325.00
Child
5"      $100.00      $400.00

### 1938
Marked *"Judy Ann USA"* and *"Story Book USA"* (baby *marked "Made in US"* and *"88," "89,"* and *"93 Made in Japan"*), colored box, sunburst pattern with gold or silver label, gold foil sticker on clothes, "Storybook Dolls," no brochure

3½ – 4½"      $175.00      $275.00
5"      $150.00      $250.00

### 1939
Child, molded socks and molded bangs (baby has star-shaped hands), colored box with small silver dots, silver label, gold foil sticker on clothes, "Storybook Dolls," no brochure

*Judy Ann, #87 Bridesmaid, Family Series, painted bisque, $250.00. Courtesy Elaine Pardee.*

Baby

3½ – 4½"    $75.00    $150.00

Child

5"        $125.00    $225.00

**1940**

Child has molded socks only, baby has star-shaped bisque hands, colored box with white polka dots, silver label, gold foil sticker on clothes, "Storybook Dolls," has brochure

Baby

3½ – 4½"    $60.00    $135.00

Child

5"        $50.00    $200.00

**1941 – 42**

Child has pudgy tummy or slim tummy, baby has star- shaped hands or fist, white box with colored polka dots, with silver label, gold foil bracelet with name of doll, and brochure

Baby

3½ – 4½"    $65.00    $125.00

Child

5"        $20.00    $75.00

**1943 – 47**

Child has one-piece head body, and legs, baby has fist hands, white box with colored polka dots, silver label, ribbon tie, or pin fastener, gold foil bracelet with name of doll, and brochure

Baby

3½ – 4½"    $60.00        $125.00

Child  5"    $14.00        $50.00

**1947 – 49**

Child has hard plastic body, painted eyes; baby has bisque body, plastic arms and legs, white box with colored polka dots with "Nancy Ann Storybook Dolls" between dots, silver label, brass snap, gold foil bracelet with name of doll, and brochure

Baby

3½ – 4½"    $45.00        $90.00 * more for special outfit

Child

5½" – 7"    $14.00        $50.00

**Ca. 1949**

Hard plastic, both have black sleep eyes, white box with colored polka dots and "Nancy Ann Storybook Dolls" between dots, silver label, brass or painted snaps, gold foil bracelet with name of doll, and brochure

Baby

3½ – 4½"    $40.00        $75.00

5"        $15.00        $50.00

## Ca. 1953

Hard plastic, child has blue sleep eyes, except for 4½" girls, baby has black sleep eyes, white box with colored polka dots, some with clear lids, silver label, gripper snap, gold foil bracelet with name of doll, and brochure.

Baby
    3½ – 4½" $40.00    $75.00
* comes only in christening dress
Child
    5"        $12.00    $35.00

**SPECIAL**
**Audrey Ann,** toddler, *marked:* *"Nancy Ann Storybook 12"*
    6"        $250.00    $975.00

*Two 5" black, hard plastic Nancy Ann Storybook Topsy dolls, $375.00. Courtesy McMasters Doll Auctions.*

**SERIES**
**All Bisque**

| | | |
|---|---|---|
| **Around the World Series** | | |
| Chinese | $200.00 | $750.00 |
| English Flower Girl | $150.00 | $350.00 |
| Portuguese | $175.00 | $450.00 |
| Poland | $175.00 | $450.00 |
| Russia | $175.00 | $450.00 |
| Other Countries | $100.00 | $300.00 |
| **Masquerade Series** | | |
| Ballet Dancer | $200.00 | $700.00 |
| Cowboy | $200.00 | $500.00 |
| Gypsy | $100.00 | $250.00 |
| Pirate | $200.00 | $500.00 |
| **Sports Series** | $200.00 | $600.00 |
| **Flower Series** | | |
| Bisque | $100.00 | $250.00 |
| **Margie Ann Series** | | |
| Margie Ann | $60.00 | $150.00 |
| Margie Ann in other outfits | | |
| | $85.00 | $200.00 |
| **Powder & Crinoline Series** | | |
| | $45.00 | $165.00 |

**Bisque or Plastic**

| | | |
|---|---|---|
| **Operetta Series** | $40.00 | $125.00 |
| **Hit Parade Series** | $40.00 | $125.00 |

**Hard Plastic**

| | | |
|---|---|---|
| **Big and Little Sister Series** | | |
| | $25.00 | $65.00 |
| **Commencement Series** (except baby) | | |
| | $40.00 | $75.00 |

*6½" A Pretty Girl is Like a Melody from the Nancy Ann Storybook All-Time Hit Parade Series, painted eyes, hard plastic, $125.00. Courtesy Elaine Pardee.*

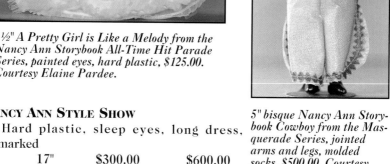

*5" bisque Nancy Ann Storybook Cowboy from the Masquerade Series, jointed arms and legs, molded socks, $500.00. Courtesy Elaine Pardee.*

## NANCY ANN STYLE SHOW

Hard plastic, sleep eyes, long dress, unmarked

|      |          |          |
|------|----------|----------|
| 17"  | $300.00  | $600.00  |

## MUFFIE, 1953 – 56

Hard plastic, wig, sleep eyes

**1953,** straight leg, non-walker, painted lashes

|     |         |          |
|-----|---------|----------|
| 8"  | $50.00  | $190.00  |

**1954,** walker, molded eyelashes, brows

|     |         |          |
|-----|---------|----------|
| 8"  | $40.00  | $160.00  |

**1955 – 56** vinyl head, molded or painted upper lashes, rooted saran wig, walker, or bent knee walker

|     |         |          |
|-----|---------|----------|
| 8"  | $35.00  | $140.00  |

**1968+,** reissued, hard plastic

|     |         |         |
|-----|---------|---------|
| 8"  | $20.00  | $80.00  |

## LORI ANN

Vinyl

|       |         |          |
|-------|---------|----------|
| 17½"  | $45.00  | $165.00  |

## DEBBIE

Hard plastic in school dress, name on wrist-tag/box

|      |         |          |
|------|---------|----------|
| 10"  | $45.00  | $170.00  |

Vinyl head, hard plastic body

|      |         |          |
|------|---------|----------|
| 10"  | $25.00  | $110.00  |

Hard plastic walker

|       |         |          |
|-------|---------|----------|
| 10½"  | $40.00  | $160.00  |

Vinyl head, hard plastic walker

|       |         |         |
|-------|---------|---------|
| 10½"  | $23.00  | $90.00  |

## LITTLE MISS NANCY ANN

|       |         |          |
|-------|---------|----------|
| 8½"   | $35.00  | $125.00  |

*Nancy Ann Storybook Muffie, hard plastic, $190.00. Courtesy Elaine Pardee.*

## MISS NANCY ANN

*Marked "Nancy Ann,"* vinyl head, rooted hair, rigid vinyl body, high-heel feet

| | | |
|---|---|---|
| 10½" | $35.00 | $125.00 |

## BABY SUE SUE

| | | |
|---|---|---|
| Vinyl | $25.00 | $75.00 |

*18" #2902 Forget-Me-Not Nancy Ann Storybook doll from Nancy Ann Style Show, hard plastic walker, $600.00. Courtesy Elaine Pardee.*

## Pleasant Company

**1986+, Pleasant Rowland, Middleton, WI.** Vinyl dolls, sleep eyes, cloth body, vinyl limbs. Each doll has own identity, time era, with many accessories for that time period

**Felicity** and book, 1774
| | | |
|---|---|---|
| 18" | $55.00 | $82.00 |

**Kirsten** and book, 1854
| | | |
|---|---|---|
| 18" | $55.00 | $82.00 |

**Addy** (black) and book, 1864
| | | |
|---|---|---|
| 18" | $65.00 | $82.00 |

**Samatha** and book, 1904
| | | |
|---|---|---|
| 18" | $55.00 | $82.00 |

**Molly** and book, 1944
| | | |
|---|---|---|
| 18" | $55.00 | $82.00 |

## Raggedy Ann & Andy

**1915+.** Designed by Johnny Gruelle in 1915, made by various companies. Ann wears dress with apron, Andy shirt and pants with matching hat.

## P.J. Volland, 1920 – 1934

Early dolls marked: "Patented Sept. 7, 1915." All cloth, tin or wooden button eyes, painted features. Some have sewn knee or arm joints, sparse brown or auburn yarn hair, oversize hands, feet turned outward.

**Raggedy Ann and Andy**
| | | |
|---|---|---|
| 15 – 16" | $350.00 | $1,550.00 |
| 23" | $500.00 | $2,100.00 |

*16" Volland Raggedy Ann, all cloth with shoe button eyes, body stamped "Sept. 7, 1915," all original, $1,550.00. Courtesy Sherryl Shirran.*

*17" Volland Raggedy Andy, $1,250.00. Courtesy McMasters Doll Auctions.*

### Beloved Belindy
| | | |
|---|---|---|
| 13" | $500.00 | $2,000.00 |
| 15" | $600.00 | $2,300.00 |

### Mollye Goldman, 1935 – 38
Marked on chest: "Raggedy Ann and Andy Dolls Manufactured by Mollye's Doll Outfitters." Nose outlined in black, red heart on chest, reddish orange hair, multicolored legs, blue feet, some have oil cloth faces.

| | | |
|---|---|---|
| 14" | $225.00 | $900.00 |
| 18" | $250.00 | $1,000.00 |
| 21" | $275.00 | $1,100.00 |

Did not make Beloved Belindy

### Georgene Novelties, 1938 – 62
Ann has orange hair and a top knot, 6 different mouth styles, early had tin eyes, later plastic, 6 different noses, seams in middle of legs and arms to represent knees and elbows, feet turn forward, red and white striped legs. All have hearts that say: "I love you" printed on chest. Tag sewn to left side seam, several variations, all say "Georgene Novelties, Inc."

#### 1930s
Raggedy Ann or Andy
| | | |
|---|---|---|
| 15" | $90.00 | $350.00 |
| 19" | $165.00 | $625.00 |
| 22" | $175.00 | $750.00 |

Awake/Asleep
| | | |
|---|---|---|
| 13" | $165.00 | $650.00 |

#### 1940s
| | | |
|---|---|---|
| 18" | $85.00 | $325.00 |

#### 1950s
| | | |
|---|---|---|
| 18" | $50.00 | $200.00 |

**1960 – 63**

| | | |
|---|---|---|
| 15" | $25.00 | $110.00 |
| 18" | $35.00 | $150.00 |

**Beloved Belindy**

| | | |
|---|---|---|
| 15" | $125.00 | $750.00 |

**Knickerbocker, 1962 – 82**

Printed features, hair color changes from orange to red; there were 5 mouth and 5 eyelash variations, tags were located on clothing back or pant seam

**1960s**

Raggedy Ann or Andy

| | | |
|---|---|---|
| 12" | $40.00 | $125.00 |
| 16" | $50.00 | $175.00 |
| 24" | $75.00 | $300.00 |
| 30 – 36" | $125.00 | $500.00 |

Beloved Belindy, ca. 1965

| | | |
|---|---|---|
| 15" | $200.00 | $750.00 |

Raggedy Ann
Talking, 1960s

| | |
|---|---|
| $70.00 | $265.00 |

**1970s**

| | | |
|---|---|---|
| 12" | $12.00 | $45.00 |
| 16" | $15.00 | $80.00 |
| 24" | $25.00 | $135.00 |
| 30 – 36" | $50.00 | $300.00 |

Talking, 1974

| | | |
|---|---|---|
| 12" | $12.00 | $48.00 |

**1980s**

| | | |
|---|---|---|
| 16" | $7.00 | $25.00 |
| 24" | $15.00 | $55.00 |
| 30 – 36" | $35.00 | $110.00 |

**Camel with Wrinkled Knees**

| | |
|---|---|
| $45.00 | $175.00 |

**Applause Toy Company, 1981 – 83, Hasbro (Playskool) , 1983+**

| | | |
|---|---|---|
| 8" | $2.00 | $15.00 |
| 12" | $4.00 | $30.00 |
| 17" | $5.00 | $50.00 |
| 25" | $9.00 | $65.00 |
| 36" | $15.00 | $150.00 |
| 48" | $25.00 | $175.00 |

**Nasco/Bobbs-Merrill, 1972**

Cloth head, hard plastic doll body, printed features, apron *marked:* "*Raggedy Ann*"

| | | |
|---|---|---|
| 24" | $45.00 | $150.00 |

**Bobbs- Merill Co., 1974**

Ventriloquist dummies, hard plastic head, hands, foam body, printed face

| | | |
|---|---|---|
| 30" | $50.00 | $175.00 |

# Raleigh

**Jessie McCutcheon Raleigh, 1916 – 20, Chicago, IL.** All composition, painted or sleeping eyes, painted and molded hair or wigged, cloth or composition bodies, some with metal spring joints. Unmarked.

**Baby**

| | | |
|---|---|---|
| 11½" | $100.00 | $400.00 |
| 13½" | $125.00 | $500.00 |

**Child**

| | | |
|---|---|---|
| 11½" | $115.00 | $450.00 |
| 16½" | $165.00 | $650.00 |
| 18½" | $235.00 | $950.00 |

# Ravca, Bernard

**Ca.1924 – 1935+, Paris and New York.** Stitched stockinet characters, label reads "Original Ravca//Fabrication Francaise" or hang tag reads "Original Ravca," some all cloth, or gesso/papier mache.

**Character from books/poems**

| | | |
|---|---|---|
| 7" | $38.00 | $135.00 |
| 9" | $40.00 | $155.00 |
| 12" | $55.00 | $210.00 |
| 15" | $65.00 | $235.00 |
| 17" | $75.00 | $365.00 |

**Gesso/Papier Mache dolls**

| | | |
|---|---|---|
| 12" | $100.00 | $435.00 |
| 15" | $150.00 | $625.00 |
| 17" | $250.00 | $1,000.00 |
| 20" | $375.00 | $1,525.00 |

**Peasants/Old People**

| | | |
|---|---|---|
| 7" | $23.00 | $100.00 |
| 9" | $25.00 | $135.00 |
| 12" | $35.00 | $165.00 |
| 15" | $50.00 | $235.00 |

**Military figures, such as Hitler, Mussolini**

| | | |
|---|---|---|
| 17" | $250.00 | $1,300.00 |
| 20" | $450.00 | $2,600.00 |
| 27" | $1,000.00 | $5,000.00+ |

# Remco Industries

**Ca. 1960 – 74.** One of the first companies to market with television ads. First price is for played with dolls; second price is for mint in box.

**Addams Family**

| | | |
|---|---|---|
| 5½" | $5.00 | $20.00 |

**Baby Crawlalong, 1967**

| | | |
|---|---|---|
| 20" | $5.00 | $20.00 |

**Baby Grow a Tooth, 1968**

Vinyl and hard plastic, rooted hair, blue sleep eyes, open/closed mouth, one tooth, grows her own tooth, battery operated

| | | |
|---|---|---|
| 15" | $7.00 | $25.00 |

Black
  14"       $8.00        $30.00
**Baby Know It All, 1969**
  17"       $4.00        $20.00
**Baby Laugh A Lot, 1970**
  Rooted long hair, painted eyes, open/closed mouth, teeth, vinyl head
and hands, plush body, push button, she laughs, battery operated
  16"       $5.00        $20.00
Black
  16"       $8.00        $30.00
**Baby Glad 'N Sad, 1967**
  Vinyl and hard plastic, rooted blonde hair, painted blue eyes
  14"       $5.00        $20.00
**Baby Stroll A Long, 1966**
  15"       $4.00        $15.00
**Dave Clark 5, 1964**
  Set of five musical group, vinyl heads, rigid plastic bodies
  Set       $50.00
  **Dave Clark**
  5"        $8.00        $15.00
  Other band members have name attached to leg
  3"        $4.00        $10.00
**Heidi and friends, 1967**
  Rooted hair, painted side-glancing eyes, open/closed mouth, all vinyl,
press button dolls wave
  **Heidi**
  5½"       $25.00       $9.00
  **Herby**
  4½"       $3.00        $12.00
  **Jan**, Oriental
  5½"       $4.00        $15.00
  **Spunky**
  5½"       $4.00        $16.00
  **Winking Heidi,** 1968
  $25.00    $13.00
**Jeannie, I Dream of**
  6"        $5.00        $18.00
**Jumpsy, 1970,** vinyl and hard plastic, rooted blonde hair, painted blue
eyes, closed mouth, molded on shoes and socks, jumps rope
  14"       $5.00        $20.00
Black
  14"       $7.00        $25.00
**Laurie Partridge, 1973**
  19"       $22.00       $85.00
**L.B.J., 1964**
  5½"       $9.00        $45.00

*Dr. John, father of the affluent Littlechap family, $95.00. Courtesy Cathie Clark.*

## Littlechap Family, 1963

Vinyl head and arms, jointed hips, shoulders and neck, black painted molded hair, black eyes

| | | |
|---|---|---|
| Set of four | $125.00 | $400.00 |
| **Dr. John Littlechap** | | |
| 14½" | $25.00 | $95.00 |
| **Judy Littlechap** | | |
| 12" | $15.00 | $55.00 |
| **Libby Littlechap** | | |
| 10½" | $15.00 | $50.00 |
| **Lisa Littlechap** | | |
| 13½" | $15.00 | $55.00 |
| **Littlechap Accessories** | | |
| Dr. John's Office | $75.00 | $325.00 |
| Bedroom | $25.00 | $110.00 |
| Family room | $25.00 | $110.00 |

Dr. John Littlechap's outfits
| | |
|---|---|
| Golf outfit | $30.00 |
| Medical | $65.00 |
| Suit | $50.00 |
| Tuxedo | $70.00 |

Lisa's outfits
| | |
|---|---|
| Evening dress | $90.00 |
| Coat, fur trim | $50.00 |

Libby, Judy's outfits
| | |
|---|---|
| Jeans/sweater | $30.00 |
| Dance dress | $45.00 |

## Mimi, 1973

Vinyl and hard plastic, battery operated singer, rooted long blonde hair, painted blue eyes, open/closed mouth, record player in body, sings: "I'd like to teach the world to sing in perfect harmony," song used for Coca-Cola commercial; sings in different languages

| | | | |
|---|---|---|---|
| | 19" | $15.00 | $50.00 |
| Black | | | |
| | 19" | $20.00 | $60.00 |

## Orphan Annie, 1967

| | | | |
|---|---|---|---|
| | 15" | $9.00 | $45.00 |

## Sweet April, 1971

Vinyl

| | | | |
|---|---|---|---|
| | 5½" | $25.00 | $10.00 |
| Black | | | |
| | 5½" | $4.00 | $15.00 |

## Tippy Tumbles, 1968

Vinyl, rooted red hair, stationary blue eyes, does somersaults, batteries in pocketbook

| | | | |
|---|---|---|---|
| | 16" | $5.00 | $20.00 |

**Tumbling Tomboy, 1969**

Rooted blonde braids, closed smiling mouth, vinyl and hard plastic, battery operated

| | | |
|---|---|---|
| 17" | $5.00 | $20.00 |

## Richwood Toys

**Richwood Toys, Inc. Sandra Sue, ca. 1940s, 50s.** Hard plastic walker, head does not turn, slim body, Saran wigs, sleep eyes. Some with high-heel feet, only marks are number under arm or leg. All prices reflect outfits with original socks, shoes, panties, and accessories.

First price is for played with dolls, incomplete costume; second price is for complete mint in box dolls.

*8" Richwood Toys Inc., hard plastic Sandra Sue, strung, MIB with wrist tag and curlers, $175.00. Courtesy Peggy Millhouse.*

**Sandra Sue**

**Flat feet,** in camisole, slip, panties, shoes and socks

| | | |
|---|---|---|
| 8" | $45.00 | $175.00 |

In school dress

| | | |
|---|---|---|
| 8" | $65.00 | $200.00+ |

In party/Sunday dress

| | | |
|---|---|---|
| 8" | $95.00 | $250.00 |

Special coat, hat & dress, limited editions, Brides, Heidi, Little Women Majorette

| | | |
|---|---|---|
| 8" | $85.00+ | $250.00 |

Sport or play clothes

| | | |
|---|---|---|
| 8" | $45.00 | $175.00 |

MIB Twin Sandra Sues

| | |
|---|---|
| 8" | $395.00 |

\* *too few in database to give reliable range*

**High heel,** camisole, slip, panties, shoes and socks

| | | |
|---|---|---|
| 8" | $40.00 | $150.00 |

In school dress

| | | |
|---|---|---|
| 8" | $40.00 | $175.00+ |

In party/Sunday dress

| | | |
|---|---|---|
| 8" | $75.00 | $200.00+ |

Special coat, hat & dress, limited editions, Brides, Heidi, Little Women, Majorette

| | | |
|---|---|---|
| 8" | $75.00 | $200.00+ |

Sport or play clothes

| | | |
|---|---|---|
| 8" | $40.00 | $150.00 |

MIB Twin Sandra Sues

| |
|---|
| $350.00 |

\* *too few in database to give reliable range*

*8" Richwood Sandra Sue, bride, hard plastic, high heel walker, ca. 1955, $200.00+. Courtesy Peggy Millhouse.*

**Sandra Sue Outfits, mint, including all accessories**

| | |
|---|---|
| School dress | $5.00 – $15.00 |
| Party dress | $15.00 – $25.00 |
| Specials | $25.00 – $35.00 |
| Sport sets | $15.00 – $25.00 |

**Cindy Lou**

Hard plastic, jointed dolls were purchased in bulk from NY distributor, fitted with double-stitched wigs by Richwood.

All prices include shoes, socks, panties, slips, and accessories.

**Cindy Lou in camisole, slip, panties, shoes, and socks**

| | | |
|---|---|---|
| 14" | $45.00 | $165.00+ |

In school dress

| | | |
|---|---|---|
| 14" | $75.00 | $175.00+ |

In party dress

| | | |
|---|---|---|
| 14" | $95.00 | $225.00 |

In special outfits

| | | |
|---|---|---|
| 14" | $85.00+ | $250.00 |

In sports outfits

| | | |
|---|---|---|
| 14" | $65.00 | $175.00 |

**Cindy Lou Outfits, mint, including all accessories**

| | |
|---|---|
| School dress | $35.00 |
| Party dress | $45.00 |
| Special outfit | $50.00 |
| Sports clothes | $35.00 |

*8" Richwood Toys Sandra Sue with restored wig, $175.00+. Courtesy Peggy Millhouse.*

# Roddy

**Roddy of England, ca. 1950 – 60s.** Made by D.G. Todd & Co. Ltd., Southport, England. Hard plastic walker, sleep or set eyes.

First price indicates played with dolls; second price for mint in box.
Walking Princess, tagged
9"      $5.00         $20.00

## Roldan

*Trio of felt Roldan Golfers, ca. 1965, fairly common
figures to find, $100.00 each. Courtesy Sondra Gast.*

Roldan Characters are similar to Klumpe figures in many respects. They
were made in Barcelona, Spain, from the early 1960s until the mid 1970s.
They are made of felt over a wire armature with painted mask faces. Like
Klumpe, Roldan figures represent professionals, hobbyists, dancers, historical
characters and contemporary men and women performing a wide variety of
tasks. Some, but not all Roldans, were imported by Rosenfeld Imports and
Leora Dolores of Hollywood. Figures originally came with two sewn on identifying cardboard tags. Roldan characters most commonly found are doctors,
Spanish dancers, and bull fighters. Roldan characters tend to have somewhat
smaller heads, longer necks, and more defined facial features than Klumpe.

Common figures              $30.00      $100.00+
Elaborate figure, MIB with accessories   $225.00

## Ross

**Ross Products Co.,** Tina Cassini, designed by Oleg Cassini, hard plastic, marked on back torso, *"TINA CASSINA,"* clothes tagged, *"Made in
British Crown Colony of Hong Kong."*
12"      $65.00         $250.00

*20" handmade Sasha with different facial types, back row, left: Type B-I and Type B-II. Type B denotes a jointed cloth body. Front row, left: Type CIII and Type BIV. Type C dontes a molded, jointed body of vinyl or plaster, $2,000.00 – $8,000.00. Courtesy Dorisanne Osborn.*

**1965 – 86+.** Sasha dolls were created by Swiss artist, Sasha Morgenthaler, who handcrafted 20" children and 13" babies in Zurich, Switzerland, from the 1940s until her death in 1975. Her handmade studio dolls had cloth or molded bodies, five different head molds, and were hand painted by Sasha Morganthaler. To make her dolls affordable as children's playthings, she licensed Gotz Puppenfabrik (1964 – 1970) in Germany and Frido Trendon Ltd. (1965 – 1986) in England to manufacture 16" Sasha doll in series. The manufactured dolls were made of rigid vinyl with painted features. Gotz Dolls, Inc. was granted a new license in 1994 and is currently producing them in Germany.

Price range reflects rarity, condition, and completeness of dolls outfit, and packaging and varies with geographic location. First price is for dolls without original clothing and/or in less than perfect condition; second price is for mint-in-box (or tube).

**Original Studio Sasha Doll, ca. 1940s – 1974**

Made by Sasha Morganthaler in Switzerland. Some are signed on soles of feet, have wrist tags, or wear labeled clothing.

> 20"        $2,000.00        $5,000.00  – $8,000.00

**Gotz Sasha Dolls, 1964 – 1970, Germany**

Girls or boys, two face molds, *marked "Sasha Series"* in circle on neck and in three circle logo on back. Three different boxes were used. Identified by wrist tag and/or booklet

> 16"        $300.00        $1,500.00

**Frido-Trendon Ltd., 1964 – 1970, England**
Unmarked, wore wrist tags, and current catalogs were packed with doll.
    **Child, 1965 – 1968,** packaged in wide box
        16"      $100.00      $1,000.00
    **Child, 1969 – 1972,** packaged in crayon
tubes
        16"      $100.00      $600.00
    **Sexed Baby,** 1970 – 78, packaged in Styro-
foam cradles or straw box, and box
    White or black    $100.00      $300.00
    **Unsexed Baby,** 1978 – 1986, packaged in Sty-
rofoam wide or narrow cradles or straw basket,
and box
    $100.00      $300.00
    **Child, 1973 – 1975,** packaged in shoe box
style box

*Baby White Bird, Frido-Trendon Ltd., circa late 1970s to 1986, came as sexed girl and unsexed baby, $300.00. Courtesy Dorisanne Osborn.*

        16"      $100.00      $400.00
    **Child, 1975 – 1980,** black, white, packaged
in shoe box style box
        16"      $100.00      $300.00
    **Child, 1980 – 1986,** black, white, packaged
in photo box with flaps
    $100.00      $250.00
    **#1 Sasha Anniversary doll**
        16"      $175.00      $300.00
    **117S, Sasha Sari, 1986,** black hair, *estimated only 400 dolls pro-
duced before English factory closed in January 1986
        16"      $450.00      $700.00
    **130E Sasha Wintersport, 1986,** blond hair*
        16"      $400.00      $600.00
    **330E Gregor Sandy** (hair) **Hiker***
        16"      $450.00      $750.00
**Limited Editions**
    Made by Trendon Sasha Ltd. in England, packaged in box with outer
sleeve picturing individual doll. L.E. Sasha dolls marked on neck with date
and number. Number on certificate matches number on doll's neck.
    **1981 Velvet,** girl, light brown wig, production number planned, 5,000
            $300.00      $450.00
    **1982 Pintucks,** girl, blond wig, production number planned, 6,000
            $300.00      $450.00
    **1983 Kiltie,** girl, red wig, production number planned, 4,000
            $350.00      $500.00
    **1984 Harlequin,** girl, rooted blonde hair, production number planned
4,000.
            $200.00      $350.00
    **1985 Prince Gregor,** boy, light brown wig, production number
planned, 4,000
            $250.00      $400.00

# Sasha (cont.)

**1986 Princess Sasha** girl, blond wig, production number planned, 3,500, but only 350 were made

$1,000.00     $1,500.00

**Gotz Dolls Inc., 1995 +, Germany**

They received the license in September 1994, dolls introduced in 1995.

**Child, 1995 – 96,** marked "Gotz Sasha" on neck and "Sasha Series" in three circle logo on back. About 1,500 of the dolls produced in 1995 did not have mold mark on back. Earliest dolls packaged in generic Gotz box, currently in tube, wear wrist tag, Gotz tag, and have mini-catalog

16½"     $300.00 retail

**Baby, 1996,** unmarked on neck, marked "Sasha Series" in three circle logo on back. First babies were packaged in generic Gotz box or large tube, currently packaged in small "Baby" tube, wears Sasha wrist tag, Gotz booklet and current catalog

12"     $150.00 retail

## Shirley Temple

*12" Ideal vinyl Shirley Temple, boxed, $190.00. Courtesy McMasters Doll Auctions.*

**1934+,** Ideal Novelty Toy Corp. New York, designed by Bernard Lipfert

**1934 – 40s,** composition head, and jointed body, dimples in cheeks, green sleep eyes, open mouth, teeth, mohair wig, tagged original dress, center-snap shoes. Prototype dolls may have paper sticker inside head, and bias trimmed wig.

*Marks: "Shirley Temple//Ideal Nov. & Toy,"* on back of head, and *"Shirley Temple"* on body. Some marked only on head and with a size.

First price is for incomplete or played with dolls. Second price is for doll in excellent to mint condition, all original. Add more for special outfits like Ranger or Wee Willie Winkle.

**Shirley Temple**

| | | |
|---|---|---|
| 11" | $225.00 | $950.00 |
| 13" | $175.00 | $725.00 |
| 16" | $200.00 | $800.00 |
| 17" | $200.00 | $875.00 |
| 18" | $250.00 | $950.00 |
| 20" | $275.00 | $1,100.00 |
| 22" | $325.00 | $1,250.00 |
| 25" | $350.00 | $1,400.00 |
| 27" | $375.00 | $1,500.00 |

**Baby Shirley**

| | | |
|---|---|---|
| 18" | $400.00 | $1,200.00 |

*18" Ideal composition Shirley Temple, mint in box, $2,100.00.Courtesy McMasters Doll Auctions.*

*36" Ideal vinyl Shirley Temple with wrist tag, original outfit, 1957, $1,950.00. Courtesy McMasters Doll Auctions.*

*18" Ideal composition Shirley Temple Little Colonel outfit, $1,800.00. Courtesy Rosemary Dent.*

**Accessories:**

| | |
|---|---|
| Button, 3 types | $125.00 |
| Buggy, wood | $650.00 |
| Buggy, wicker | $500.00 |
| Dress, tagged | $125.00 – $175.00 |
| Trunk | $175.00 – $225.00 |

**Variants**

**Japanese,** unlicensed Shirleys

All bisque

| | | |
|---|---|---|
| 6" | $65.00 | $250.00 |

Celluloid

| | | |
|---|---|---|
| 5" | $45.00 | $185.00 |
| 8" | $65.00 | $245.00 |

Composition, heavily molded brown curls, painted eyes, open/closed mouth with teeth, body stamped "Japan"

| | | |
|---|---|---|
| 7½" | $75.00 | $300.00 |

**Hawaiian, "Marama,"** Ideal used Shirley Temple mold for this doll representing a character from the movie *Hurricane*, black yarn hair, wears grass skirt, Hawaiian costume

| | | |
|---|---|---|
| 18" | $250.00 | $950.00 |

**Shirley at the Organ,** special display stand with composition Shirley Temple at non-functioning organ, music provided by record

$3,500.00+

20" Ideal composition Baby Shirley Temple, $1,500.00+. Courtesy Rosemary Dent.

16" Ideal Marama using a Shirley Temple body with painted eyes, open/closed mouth, yarn hair. Marama was a character in the movie Hurricane, no real connection to Shirley Temple, $850.00. Courtesy Angie Gonzales.

11" Ideal composition Shirley Temple, Texas Rangerette costume, boxed, $1,500.00. Courtesy Iva Mae Jones.

18" Ideal composition Shirley Temple in red and white Stand Up and Cheer dress worn in that movie, mohair wig, pin, eyeshadow over eyes, $950.00. Courtesy Angie Gonzales.

Painted bisque Japanese Shirley Temple lookalike, $225.00. Courtesy Rosemary Dent.

**Dutch Celluloid Shirley Temple, ca. 1937+,** all celluloid, open crown, metal pate, sleep eyes, dimples in cheeks, *marked: "Shirley Temple"* on head, may have additional marks, dressed in Dutch costume

| | | |
|---|---|---|
| 13" | $90.00 | $350.00 |
| 15" | $100.00 | $400.00 |

**1957 Shirley Temple,** all vinyl, sleep eyes, synthetic rooted wig, open/closed mouth, teeth, came in two-piece slip and undies, tagged "Shirley Temple," came with gold plastic script pin reading: "Shirley Temple," marked on back of head: *"ST//12"*

| | | |
|---|---|---|
| 12" | $50.00 | $235.00 |

**1958 – 61 Shirley Temple,** vinyl, marked on back of head: *"S.T.//17,"* or *"S.T.//19,"* some had flirty (twinkle) eyes, add more for flirty eyes

| | | |
|---|---|---|
| 17" | $100.00 | $435.00 |
| 19" | $120.00 | $485.00 |

Jointed wrists

| | | |
|---|---|---|
| 36" | $500.00 | $1,950.00 |

**1972 Shirley Temple,** Montgomery Ward reissue, plain box

| | | |
|---|---|---|
| 17" | $50.00 | $225.00 |

**1973 Shirley Temple,** red dot "Stand Up and Cheer" outfit, box with Shirley pictures, extra outfits available

| | | |
|---|---|---|
| 16" | $45.00 | $165.00 |

**1982 – 83, Shirley Temple,** vinyl

| | | |
|---|---|---|
| 8" | $8.00 | $30.00 |
| 12" | $9.00 | $35.00 |

**1984 Shirley Temple** by Hank Garfinkle, *marked "Doll Dreams & Love"*

| | | |
|---|---|---|
| 36" | $75.00 | $300.00 |

**1987+ Shirley Temple, Danbury Mint,** porcelain

| | | |
|---|---|---|
| 16" | $65.00 | $90.00 |

**1990+ Shirley Temple, Danbury Mint,** porcelain, designed by Elke Hutchens, in costumes from *"The Little Princess, Bright Eyes, Curly Top, Dimples,* and others, marked on neck: *"Shirley Temple//1990"*

| | | |
|---|---|---|
| 20" | $150.00 | $240.00 |

**1994+ Shirley Temple Dress-Up Doll, Danbury Mint,** vinyl, similar to '87 doll, no charge for doll, get two outfits bi-monthly

| | | |
|---|---|---|
| 16" | $30.00 | $60.00 |

## Sun Rubber

**Barberton, OH, ca. 1930+s**
**Betty Bows,** 1953, molded hair with loop for ribbon, drink and wet baby, jointed body

| | | |
|---|---|---|
| 11" | $12.00 | $45.00 |

**Psyllium,** 1937, molded painted hard rubber, moving head, blue pants, white suspenders, black shoes and hat

| | | |
|---|---|---|
| 10" | $3.00 | $15.00 |

**Sun Babe,** ca. 1940s – 1950s, all rubber, painted eyes, drink and wet type

| | | |
|---|---|---|
| 10" | $10.00 | $40.00 |

# Takara

**Japan,** fashion dolls
**Lady Luminous (Duex – L)**
  17"          $45.00          $350.00

## Terri Lee

*16" hard plastic Terri Lee, boxed, $340.00. Courtesy McMasters Doll Auctions.*

**1946 – 1962, Lincoln, NE and Apple Valley, CA.** First dolls composition, then hard plastic and vinyl. Closed pouty mouth, painted eyes, wigged, jointed body, marked on torso: *"TERRI LEE"* and early dolls: *"PAT. PENDING"*

First price indicates played-with dolls or missing accessories; second price is mint-in-box.

**Terri Lee**
Composition, 1946 – 47
  16"     $80.00     $375.00
Painted Hard Plastic, 1947 – 50
  16"     $125.00     $500.00
Hard Plastic, 1951 – 62
  16"     $120.00     $400.00
Vinyl, less if sticky
  16"     $80.00     $250.00
Talking
  16"     $135.00     $400.00
**Benji,** painted plastic, black, 1947 – 1958
  16"     $150.00     $600.00
**Connie Lynn**
  19"     $125.00     $400.00
**Gene Autry,** 1949 – 50, painted plastic
  16"     $450.00     $1,800.00
**Jerry Lee,** hard plastic, caracul wig,
  16"     $125.00     $500.00
**Linda Lee,** 1950 – 51, vinyl
  12"     $20.00     $75.00
**Linda Lee,** 1952 – 58, vinyl baby
  10"     $45.00     $145.00
**Mary Jane,** Terri Lee lookalike, hard plastic walker
  16"     $50.00     $265.00

*16" hard plastic, Terry Lee, box marked "Terri Lee//Established 1947//Manufactured by//I&S Industries//Doll and Toy Division//2134 West Rosecrans//Gardena, CA//non talking/style 1630//Price $15.95," $400.00. Courtesy Sherryl Shirran.*

**Patty Jo, Bonnie Lou,** black
    16"    $150.00        $600.00
**Tiny Terri Lee,** 1955 – 58
    10"    $50.00        $175.00
**Terri Lee Outfits**
Ball gown                $100.00
Brownie uniform        $45.00
Girl Scout uniform      $45.00
Riding habit            $150.00
School dress           $40.00
Skater                 $100.00
**Jerri Lee Outfits**
Two-piece pant suit    $100.00
Short pant suit         $100.00
Western shirt/jeans    $70.00

## Trolls

Trolls portray supernatural beings from Scandinavian folklore. They have been manufactured by various companies including Helena and Martii Kuuslkoski who made Fauni Trolls ca. 1952+, sawdust filled cloth dolls; Thomas Dam, 1960+, and Scandia House, later Norfin®; Uneeda Doll and Toy Wishniks®; Russ Berrie; Ace Novelty, Treasure Trolls™; Applause Toys; Magical Trolls™; and many other companies who made lesser quality vinyl lookalikes, mostly unmarked, to take advantage of the fad. Most are all vinyl or vinyl with stuffed cloth bodies.

**Troll Figures**

| | | |
|---|---|---|
| 2½" | $3.00 | $15.00 |
| 5" | $7.00 | $25.00 |
| 7" | $10.00 | $40.00 |
| 10" | $15.00 | $55.00 |
| 12" | $17.00 | $65.00 |
| 15" | $22.00 | $85.00 |

**Troll Animals**

Cow, unmarked
    6"      $50.00      $125.00
Donkey, Dam, 1964
    9"      $40.00      $150.00
Giraffe, Thomas Dam
    11½"  $35.00      $125.00
Monkey, Thomas Dam
    7"      $75.00      $300.00
Pig, Norfin, Thomas Dam
    6½"  $20.00      $75.00

*10" Sweetums, a drink/wet doll in suitcase box with accessories, $250.00. Courtesy Sharon Kolibaba.*

*Wee Three, set of three vinyl sisters by Uneeda, $200.00. Courtesy Cathie Clark.*

**1917+, New York City.** Made composition head dolls, including Mama dolls, and made the transition to plastics and vinyl.

**Baby Dollikins, 1960**
Vinyl head, hard plastic jointed body, with jointed elbows, wrists, and knees.

| | | |
|---|---|---|
| 21" | $12.00 | $45.00 |

**Baby Trix, 1965**

| | | |
|---|---|---|
| 19" | $8.00 | $30.00 |

**Bareskin Baby, 1968**

| | | |
|---|---|---|
| 12zx" | $5.00 | $20.00 |

**Blabby, 1962+**

| | | |
|---|---|---|
| 14" | $7.00 | $28.00 |

**Coquette, 1963+**

| | | |
|---|---|---|
| 16" | $7.00 | $28.00 |
| Black | | |
| 16" | $9.00 | $36.00 |

**Dollikin, 1960s,** multi-joints

| | | |
|---|---|---|
| 20" | $13.00 | $50.00 |

**Fairy Princess, 1961**

| | | |
|---|---|---|
| 32" | $40.00 | $110.00 |

**Freckles, 1960**

| | | |
|---|---|---|
| 32" | $25.00 | $100.00 |

**Freckles, 1973**
Ventriloquist doll, vinyl head, hands, rooted hair, cotton stuffed cloth body

| | | |
|---|---|---|
| 30" | $17.00 | $70.00 |

**Jennifer, 1973**
Rooted side-parted hair, painted features, teen body, mod clothing

| | | |
|---|---|---|
| 18" | $7.00 | $25.00 |

**Magic Meg, w/Hair That Grows**
Vinyl and plastic, rooted hair, sleep eyes

| | | |
|---|---|---|
| 16" | $7.00 | $25.00 |

**Pir-thilla, 1958**
Blows up balloons, vinyl, rooted hair, sleep eyes

| | | |
|---|---|---|
| 12½" | $4.00 | $12.00 |

**Purty, 1973**
Long rooted hair, vinyl and plastic, painted features

| | | |
|---|---|---|
| 11" | $7.00 | $25.00 |

**Pollyanna, 1960**

| | | |
|---|---|---|
| 11" | $9.00 | $35.00 |
| 17" | $15.00 | $55.00 |
| 31" | $35.00 | $125.00 |
| 35" | $40.00 | $150.00 |

**Rita Hayworth, as Carmen, 1948**

From *The Loves of Carmen* movie, all composition, red mohair wig, unmarked, cardboard tag

14"      $135.00          $565.00

**Seranade, 1962**

Vinyl head, hard plastic body, rooted blonde hair, blue sleep eyes, red and white dress, speaker in tummy, phonograph and records came with doll, used battery.

21"      $15.00          $55.00

**Suzette (Carol Brent)**

12"   $13.00      $65.00

## Vinyl

*13½" all vinyl Baby Face, expressive character faces, rooted hair, jointed elbows, knees, set eyes, by Galoob, marked: "C 1990 LGT 1//#3 China," $55.00. Courtesy Bev Mitchell.*

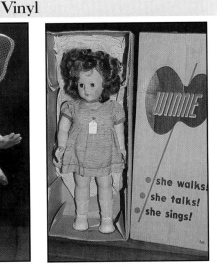

Winnie, vinyl, walks, talks, sings, in box, $75.00. Courtesy Cathie Clark.

**Ca. 1950s+.** By the mid-fifties, vinyl (polyvinylchloride) was being used for dolls. Material that was soft to the touch, and processing that allowed hair to be rooted were positive attractions. Vinyl became a desirable material and the market was soon deluged with dolls manufactured from this product. Many dolls of this period are of a little known manufacturer, unmarked or marked only with a number. With little history behind them, these dolls need to be mint in box and totally complete to warrant top prices.

Last Chance Joe, circa 1953 western character, $35.00. Courtesy Cathie Clark.

363

# Vinyl (cont.)

### Baby
Vinyl head, painted or sleep eyes, molded hair or wig, bent legs, cloth or vinyl body

| | | |
|---|---|---|
| 12" | $25.00 | $10.00 |
| 16" | $3.00 | $12.00 |
| 20" | $5.00 | $20.00 |

### Child
Vinyl head, jointed body, painted or sleep eyes, molded hair or wig, straight legs

| | | |
|---|---|---|
| 14" | $4.00 | $12.00 |
| 22" | $6.00 | $25.00 |

### Adult
Vinyl head, painted or sleep eyes, jointed body, molded hair or wig, smaller waist with male or female modeling for torso

| | | |
|---|---|---|
| 12" | $5.00 | $20.00 |
| 18" | $8.00 | $30.00 |

## Vogue

Hard plastic, #37 Brother, strung Ginny, ca. 1952, $300.00. Courtesy Peggy Millhouse.

**1930s+, Medford, MA.** Jennie Graves started the company and dressed Just Me dolls in early years, also used dolls from Arranbee, had Bernard Lipfert design Ginny. After several changes of ownership, Vogue was recently purchased, in 1995, by the Wendy Lawton Company.

### Ginny Family
#### Toddles
Composition, 1937 – 48, name stamped in ink on bottom of shoe. Some early dolls have been identified by price lists as Toodles which used blank dolls from various companies, painted eyes, mohair wig, jointed body. Some had gold foil labels reading "Vogue."

| | | |
|---|---|---|
| 8" | $100.00 | $400.00 |

#### Ginny, painted hard plastic, 1948 – 50
*Marked "Vogue" on head, "Vogue Doll" on body, painted eyes, molded hair with mohair wig, clothing tagged "Vogue Dolls," or "Vogue Dolls, Inc. Medford Mass."*

| | | |
|---|---|---|
| 8" | $90.00 | $350.00 |

With poodle cut wig

| | | |
|---|---|---|
| 8" | $100.00 | $375.00 |

| | |
|---|---|
| Outfit only | $65.00 – $90.00+ |

#### Ginny, hard plastic, walkers, 1951 – 53
Transitional to walkers, sleep eyes, painted lashes, strung, Dynel wigs, new mark on back torso: "GINNY//VOGUE DOLLS//INC. //PAT PEND.//MADE IN U.S.A."

| | | |
|---|---|---|
| 8" | $90.00 | $325.00 |

*Two 8" hard plastic, painted-eye Ginny Dutch boy and girl, tagged outfits, $400.00. Courtesy McMasters Doll Auctions.*

*12" composition Cynthia, $325.00, and 13" Cynthia, $250.00. Courtesy McMasters Doll Auctions.*

Coronation Queen in elaborate costume with braid, 1953

|   |   |   |
|---|---|---|
| 8" | $250.00 | |

$950.00

Black Ginny, 1953 – 54

| 8" | $150.00 | $600.00 |

**Ginny, hard plastic, 1955 – 56, molded lash**

Sleep eyes, walkers, Dynel or Saran wigs, *marked:* "VOGUE" on head, "GINNY//VOGUE DOLLS//INC.//PAT. NO. 2687594//MADE IN U.S.A." on back of torso

| 8" | $50.00 | $185.00 |
| Outfit only | $40.00+ | |

**Crib Crowd, 1950**

Baby with curved legs, sleep eyes, poodle cut (caracul) wig

| 8" | $175.00 | $650.00+ |

Crib Crowd, Easter Bunny

| 8" | $350.00 | $1,400.00 |

**Ginny, hard plastic, 1957**

Bent knee (jointed) walker, molded lashes, sleep eyes, Dynel or Saran wigs

| 8" | $40.00 | $150.00 |
| Outfit only | $40.00+ | |

**Davy Crockett**, MIB   $850.00

Ginny, 1960, big walker carried 8" dressed just like her

| 36" | $350.00 |

*Hard plastic, painted lash, strung Ginny, ca. 1953, with pink and black box, $325.00. Courtesy Stephanie Prince.*

*Ginny had her own playhouse, $1,500.00.*
*Courtesy Cathie Clark.*

*Hard plastic Jill and Jeff in*
*cowboy outfits, $225.00 each.*
*Courtesy Cathie Clark.*

**Ginny, 1963+**
**Soft vinyl** head, hard plastic walker body, rooted hair
    8"        $13.00        $50.00
**Ginny, 1965**
**All vinyl,** straight legs, non walker
    8"        $10.00        $40.00
**Ginny, 1972**
Painted eyes, made in Hong Kong by Tonka
    8"        $10.00        $40.00
**Ginny, 1977 – 81**
Made in Hong Kong by Lesney, thinner body, painted or sleeping eyes,
vinyl
    8"        $9.00        $35.00
**Sasson Ginny, 1978 – 79**
    8"        $9.00        $35.00
**Ginny, 1984 – 86**
Some porcelain and also vinyl by Meritus, made in Hong Kong
Porcelain
    8"        $15.00        $50.00
**Ginny, 1986+,** vinyl by Dakin
    8"        $5.00        $20.00
**Ginny Baby**
    12"        $10.00        $40.00
    16"        $12.00        $45.00
    18"        $13.00        $50.00
    20"        $15.00        $55.00
**Ginnette, 1955+,** all vinyl baby
    8"        $17.00        $65.00
**Jill, 1957 – 1962**
Hard plastic high heel doll, big sister to Ginny (made in vinyl in 1965)
            10½"        $50.00        $190.00
With fancy evening gown        $75.00        $350.00

**Jan,** 1958 – 62. Jill's girlfriend, soft vinyl head, swivel waist
   10½"    $35.00     $135.00

**Jeff,** 1958 – 62, soft vinyl, painted molded hair
   10¾"    $22.00     $95.00

**Jimmy,** 1958, vinyl, little brother to Ginnette
   8"    $15.00     $60.00

**Miss Ginny, 1972**
   16"    $15.00     $45.00

**Ginny Exclusives**

**Enchanted Doll House**

| | | |
|---|---|---|
| 1988, Ginny | $35.00 | $135.00 |

**Little Friends**

| | | |
|---|---|---|
| 1991, Alaska | $15.00 | $60.00 |

**Meyer's Collectibles**

| | | |
|---|---|---|
| 1985, Gigi's Favorite | $20.00 | $80.00 |
| 1986, Fairy Godmother | $45.00 | $155.00 |
| 1987, Cinderella and Prince Charming | $45.00 | $190.00 |
| 1988, Clown | $20.00 | $90.00 |
| 1989, Cowgirl | $20.00 | $90.00 |
| 1992, Storytime Ginny, limited | $25.00 | $100.00 |
| 1993, Sweet Violet Ginny, limited | $40.00 | $125.00 |
| 1994 Remember Jackie | $30.00 | $110.00 |

**Modern Doll Convention**

| | | |
|---|---|---|
| 1986, Rose Queen | $65.00 | $275.00 |
| 1987, Ginny at Seashore | $22.00 | $100.00 |
| 1988, Ginny's Claim | $20.00 | $90.00 |
| 1989, Ginny in Nashville | $35.00 | $135.00 |
| 1990, Ginny in Orlando | $20.00 | $90.00 |

**Shirley's Doll House**

| | | |
|---|---|---|
| 1985, Ginny Goes Country | $23.00 | $90.00 |
| 1986, Ginny Goes to County Fair | $23.00 | $90.00 |
| 1987, Black Ginny in swimsuit | $25.00 | $95.00 |
| 1988, Santa & Mrs. Claus | $20.00 | $80.00 |
| 1989, Sunday Best, black boy or girl | $15.00 | $60.00 |

**Toy Village, Lansing, MI**

| | | |
|---|---|---|
| Ashley Rose | $15.00 | $70.00 |

**U.F.D.C. (United Federation of Doll Clubs)**

| | | |
|---|---|---|
| 1987 Miss Unity | $45.00 | $155.00 |
| 1988 Ginny Luncheon Souvenir | $35.00 | $140.00 |

**Vogue Doll Club**

| | | |
|---|---|---|
| 1990, Member Special | $25.00 | $95.00 |

**Vogue Review Luncheon**

| | | |
|---|---|---|
| 1989 | $35.00 | $170.00 |
| 1990 | $25.00 | $100.00 |
| 1991 | $18.00 | $85.00 |

**Ginny Accessories**

First price is played with; second price is mint-in-box or package.

Book: *Ginny's First Secret*
    $35.00     $125.00

Furniture: chair, bed, dresser, wardrobe, dress, rocking chair,

| | | |
|---|---|---|
| each | $15.00 | $55.00 |
| Ginny Gym | $115.00 | $450.00 |
| Ginny Name Pin | $12.00 | $50.00 |
| Ginny Pup, Steiff | $45.00 | $165.00+ |
| Luggage Set | $25.00 | $100.00 |
| Parasol | $4.00 | $15.00 |
| School Bag | $20.00 | $75.00 |
| Shoes/Shoe bag | $10.00 | $40.00 |

**Other Vogue Dolls**

**Baby Dear One, 1973**

| | | |
|---|---|---|
| 25" | $40.00 | $175.00 |

Baby Dear Two

| | | |
|---|---|---|
| 27" | $53.00 | $210.00 |

**Baby Dear Musical, 1962**

| | | |
|---|---|---|
| 12" | $10.00 | $40.00 |
| 18" | $20.00 | $75.00 |

**Brikette, 1959**

Swivel waist joint, green flirty eyes in 22" size only, freckles, rooted straight yellow or orange hair, paper hang tag reads "I'm //Brikette//the//red headed//imp."

| | | |
|---|---|---|
| 22" | $18.00 | $65.00 |

1960

| | | |
|---|---|---|
| 16" | $10.00 | $40.00 |

1978, no swivel waist, curly hair

| | | |
|---|---|---|
| 16" | $5.00 | $20.00 |

**Composition Girl**

| | | |
|---|---|---|
| 12" | $70.00 | $265.00 |
| 15" | $75.00 | $365.00 |

**Lil Imp**

| | | |
|---|---|---|
| 10½" | $18.00 | $65.00 |

**Love Me Linda (Pretty as a Picture), 1965 – 68**

| | | |
|---|---|---|
| 15" | $7.00 | $23.00 |

**Star Bright, 1966**

Painted eyes, star- shaped highlights

| | | |
|---|---|---|
| 19" | $25.00 | $90.00 |

Baby Star Bright

| | | |
|---|---|---|
| 18½" | $20.00 | $60.00 |

**Wee Imp, 1960**

Hard plastic body, red wig, green eyes, freckles

| | | |
|---|---|---|
| 8" | $90.00 | $375.00 |

# Robin Woods

**Ca. 1980s+.** Creative designer for various companies, including Le Petit Ami, Robin Woods Company, Madame Alexander (Alice Darling), Horsman, and Playtime Productions.

One price indicates mint complete dolls; anything else would bring a lesser price.

*18" cloth Mollie by Robin Woods, 1985, $1,000.00. Courtesy Toni Winder.*

*14" vinyl Scarlett Christmas, 1989, $250.00+. Courtesy Toni Winder.*

*Vinyl Robin Woods Kyleigh, 1990, $160.00. Courtesy Toni Winder.*

*18" cloth Robin Woods Happy Birthday, ca. 1986, $975.00+. Courtesy Toni Winder.*

*18" cloth Robin Woods Vespers, ca. 1986, $950.00+. Courtesy Toni Winder.*

*14" vinyl Gina – Earthquake Doll, 1989, limited edition for The Doll Place, $250.00. Courtesy Toni Winder.*

**Le Petit Ami**

| | | |
|---|---|---|
| Hard-to-find cloth dolls | | $1,000.00+ |
| **1987** | | |
| Catherine | 14" | $250.00+ |
| Christmas dolls, Nicholas & Noel | | |
| Pair | 14" | $400.00+ |
| **1988** | | |
| Dickens | 14" | $250.00 |
| Kristina Kringle | 14" | $250.00 |
| Merry Carol | 14" | $250.00+ |
| **1989** | | |
| Elizabeth St. John | 14" | $150.00 |
| Heidi, red, white, blue | 14" | $265.00 |
| Heidi, brown outfit | 14" | $150.00 |
| Hope | 14" | $200.00 |
| Lorna Doone | 14" | $150.00 |
| Mary of Secret Garden | 14" | $165.00 |
| Scarlett Christmas | 14" | $250.00+ |
| William Noel | 14" | $150.00 |

**1990**

**Camelot Castle Collection**

| | | |
|---|---|---|
| Bobbi | 16" | $100.00 |
| Kyliegh Christmas | 14" | $160.00 |
| Lady Linet | 14" | $110.00 |
| Lady of the Lake | 14" | $250.00 |
| Marjorie | 14" | $150.00 |
| Meaghan (special) | 14" | $300.00+ |
| Melanie, Phebe | 14" | $150.00 |
| Tessa at the Circus | 14" | $175.00 |
| Tess of the D'urbervilles | 14" | $275.00 |

**1991**

**Shades of Day Collection**

5,000 pieces each, Dawn, Glory, Stormy, Joy, Sunny, Veil, Serenity

| | | |
|---|---|---|
| Each | 14" | $250.00 |

**Others**

| | | |
|---|---|---|
| Alena | 14" | $200.00 |
| Bette Jack | 14" | $200.00 |
| Bouquet, Lily | 14" | $200.00 |
| Delores | 14" | $225.00 |
| Eliza Doolittle | 14" | $150.00 |
| Mistress Mary | 8" | $125.00 |
| Miss Muffet | 14" | $160.00 |
| Pumpkin Eaters | 8" | $100.00 |
| Rose, Violet | 14" | $150.00 |
| Rosemary | 14" | $100.00 |

| | | |
|---|---|---|
| Sleeping Beauty Set | 8" | $275.00 |
| Tennison | 14" | $200.00 |
| Victoria | 14" | $185.00 |

**Limited Editions**

Merri, 1991 Doll Convention Disney World, Christmas Tree doll, doll becomes the tree     14"     $250.00

Mindy, Made for Disney's Robin Wood's Day, Limited to 300
    14"     $200.00

Rainey, 1991 Robin Woods Club
    14"     $200.00+

**J.C. Penney Limited Editions**

Angelina, 1990 Christmas angel
    14"     $250.00

Noelle, Christmas angel
    14"     $250.00

Julianna, 1991, little girl holiday shopper
    14"     $225.00

**Robin Woods Exclusives**

Gina, The Earthquake Doll, The Doll Place, Ann Parsons of Burlingame, CA
    14"     $250.00

No one person can know it all. With the passing of time, as more and more dolls come into the market, more and more collectors are grouping together to share their interests and are specializing in one or more categories. These are clubs or collectors who specialize in one category or type of doll who are willing to network with others. If you specialize in one of the categories listed and want to share your knowledge with other collectors, please send us your specialty and references.

## Collectors' Network

It is recommended that when contacting references below and requesting information that you enclose a SASE (self addressed stamped envelope) if you wish to receive a reply.

### Antique Dolls
Can research your wants
Matrix
PO Box 1410
New York, NY 10023

### Antique and Modern Dolls
Can research your wants
Rosalie Whyel Museum of Doll Art
1116 108th Avenue N.E.
Bellevue, WA 98004
Phone: 206 455-1116
FAX 206 455-4793

### Barbies, Mattel
Jaci Jueden
3096 Williams Hwy
Grants Pass, OR 97527

Steven Pim
3535 17th St.
San Francisco, CA 94110

### Celebrity Dolls
### Celebrity Doll Journal
Loraine Burdick, Editor
413 10th Ave. Ct. NE
Puyallup, WA 98372
Quarterly, $10.00 per year

### Composition and Travel Dolls:
### Effanbee's Patsy Family
### Patsy & Friends Newsletter
P.O. Box 311
Deming, NM 88031
Bi-monthly, $20.00 per year

**Costuming**
**Doll Costumer's Guild**
Helen Boothe, Editor
7112 W. Grovers Ave
Glendale, AZ 85308
$16.00 per year, bimonthly

**French Fashion Gazette**
Adele Leurquin, Editor
1862 Sequoia SE
Port Orchard, WA 98366

**Dionne Quintuplets**
**Quint News**
Jimmy and Fay Rodolfos, Editors
PO Box 2527
Woburn, MA 01888

**Quint Collector**
Connie Lee Martin
4018 East 17th St.
Tucson, AZ, 85711

**Girl Scouts**
**Girl Scout Doll Collectors Patch**
Pidd Miller
PO Box 631092
Houston, TX, 77263

**Girl Scout Dolls**
Diane Miller
13151 Roberta Place
Garden Grove, CA 92643

**Hitty**
**Friends of Hitty Newsletter**
Virginia Ann Heyerdahl, Editor
2704 Bellview Ave
Cheverly, MD 20785
Quarterly, $12.00 per year

**Jem Dolls, Hasbro**
Linda E. Holton
P.O. Box 6753
San Rafael, CA 94903

**Klumpe Dolls**
Sondra Gast
PO Box 252
Spring Valley, CA 91976
FAX 619 444-4215

**Lawton, Wendy**
**Lawton Collectors Guild**
PO Box 969
Turlock, CA 95381

Toni Winder
1484 N. Vagedes
Fresno CA 93728

**Liddle Kiddles**
For a signed copy of her book, *Liddle Kiddles*, $22.95 post pd., write:
Paris Langford
415 Dodge Ave
Jefferson, LA 70127
504-733-0676

**Modern Doll Convention**
Cathie Clark
2018 Kenton St
Springfield, OH 45505
513 322-3780

**Museums**
**Rosalie Whyel Museum of Doll Art**
1116 108th Avenue N.E.
Bellevue, WA 98004
206 455-1116
FAX: 206 455-4793

**Nancy Ann Storybook**
Elaine Pardee
PO Box 6108
Santa Rosa, CA 95406
707 585-3655

**Oriental Dolls**
**Ninsyo Journal**
Japanese American Dolls Enthusiasts
JADE
406 Koser Ave
Iowa City, Iowa 52246

**Roldan Dolls**
Sondra Gast
PO Box 252
Spring Valley, CA 91976
FAX 619 444-4215

**Sandra Sue Dolls, Richwood Toys Inc.**
Peggy Millhouse
510 Green Hill Road
Conestoga, PA 17516

**Sasha Dolls**
**Friends of Sasha (Quarterly Newsletter)**
Dorisanne Osborn, Editor
Box 187
Keuka Park, NY 14478

**Shirley Temple:**
**Shirley Temple Collectors News**
Rita Dubas, Editor
881 Colonial Rd
Brooklyn NY 11209
Quarterly, $20 year

**Lollipop News**
Shirley Temple Collectors By the Sea
PO Box 6203
Oxnard, CA 93031
Membership dues: $14.00 year

**Terri Lee**
**Terri Lee Newsletter**
Betty J. Woten
12 Big Bend Cut Off
Cloudcroft, NM 88317-9411

**Woods, Robin**
Toni Winder
1484 N. Vagedes
Fresno, CA 93728

**Auction Houses:**
Offer absentee bidding for those who cannot attend. Call or write for a
list of upcoming auctions, of if you need information about selling a collection.

**McMasters Doll Auctions**
James and Shari McMasters
PO Box 1755
Cambridge, OH 43725
Phone 1-800-842-35226
Phone: 614-432-4419
FAX 614-432-3191

# Bibliography

Anderton, Johana. *Twentieth Century Dolls*. Trojan Press, 1971.

———. *More Twentieth Century Dolls*. Athena Publishing Co., 1974.

Axe, John. *Effanbee, A Collector's Encyclopedia 1949 thru 1983*. Hobby House Press, 1983.

———. *The Encyclopedia of Celebrity Dolls*. Hobby House Press, 1983.

Borger, Mona. *Chinas, Doll for Study and Admiration*. Borger Publications, 1983.

Casper, Peggy Wiedman. *Fashionable Terri Lee Dolls*. Hobby House Press, 1988.

Cieslik, Jurgen and Marianne. *German Doll Encyclopedia 1800 – 1939*. Hobby House Press, 1985.

Coleman, Dorthy S., Elizabeth Ann and Evelyn Jane. *The Collector's Book of Dolls Clothes*. Crown Publishers, 1975.

———. *The Collectors Encyclopedia of Dolls, Vol. I & II*. Crown Publishers, 1968, 1986.

Corson, Carol. *Schoenhut Dolls, A Collector's Encyclopedia*. Hobby House Press, 1993.

DeWein, Sibyl and Ashabraner, Joan. *The Collectors Encyclopedia of Barbie Dolls and Collectibles*. Collector Books, 1977.

Foulke, Jan, Kestner. *King of Dollmakers*. Hobby House Press, 1982.

Simon & Halbig Dolls. *The Artful Aspect*. Hobby House Press, 1984.

Garrison, Susan Ann. *The Raggedy Ann & Andy Family Album*, Schiffer Publishing, 1989.

Izen, Judith. *A Collector's Guide to Ideal Dolls*. Collector Books, 1994.

Judd, Polly and Pam. *Hard Plastic Dolls*. Hobby House Press, 1987, 1994.

———. *Glamour Dolls of the 1950s & 1960s*. Hobby House Press, 1988.

Langford, Paris. *Liddle Kiddles*. Collector Books, 1996.

Lewis, Kathy and Don. *Chatty Cathy Dolls*. Collector Books, 1994.

Mandeville, A. Glen. *Ginny, An American Toddler Doll*. Hobby House Press, 1994.

McGonagle, Dorothy A. *The Dolls of Jules Nicolas Steiner*. Hobby House Press, 1988.

Niswonger, Jeanne D. *That Doll Ginny*. Cody Publishing, 1978.

Olds, Patrick C. *The Barbie Years*. Collector Books, 1996.

Pardella, Edward R. *Shirley Temple Dolls and Fashions*. Schiffler Publishing, 1992.

Richter, Lydia. *Huebach Character Dolls and Figurines*. Hobby House Press, 1992.

Schoonmaker, Patricia N. *Effanbee Dolls: The Formative Years, 1910 – 1929*. Hobby House Press, 1984.

———. *Patsy Doll Family Encyclopedia*. Hobby House Press, 1992.

Smith, Patricia R. *Madame Alexander Collector Dolls*. Collector Books, 1978.

———. *Doll Values, Antique to Modern, Editions 1 – 12*. Collector Books.

———. *Modern Collector's Dolls, Series 1 – 8*. Collector Books.

Tarnowska, Maree. *Fashion Dolls*. Hobby House Press, 1986.

# Index

# Index

# Index

# Index

# Index

# Index

# Index

383